Romantic Women Writers

Romantic Women Writers

Voices and Countervoices

Edited by

Paula R. Feldman
and
Theresa M. Kelley

University Press of New England / Hanover and London

University Press of New England, Hanover, NH 03755
© 1995 by University Press of New England
All rights reserved
Printed in the United States of America   5   4   3   2   1

Library of Congress Cataloging-in-Publication Data
Romantic women writers: voices and countervoices/edited by Paula R.
Feldman and Theresa M. Kelley.
        p.   cm.
Includes bibliographical references (p.   ) and index.
ISBN 0–87451–711–7 (cl).—ISBN 0–87451–724–9 (pa)
    1. English literature—Women authors—History and criticism.
2. English literature—19th century—History and criticism.
3. English literature—18th century—History and criticism.
4. Women and literature—Great Britain—History. 5. Romanticism—
Great Britain. I. Feldman, Paula R. II. Kelley, Theresa M.
PR457.R4568 1995
820.9'9287'0903—dc20
∞   94-39710

Contents

Contributors

Isobel Armstrong holds the established Chair of English at Birkbeck College, University of London, and has published widely in Victorian literature. Her most recent work includes *Victorian Poetry: Poetry, Poetics and Politics* (1993) and a study of Jane Austen (in press). She is preparing an anthology of women's poetry in the nineteenth century for Oxford University Press.

Stephen C. Behrendt is George Holmes Distinguished Professor of English at the University of Nebraska. His recent books include *Shelley and His Audiences* (1989), *Reading William Blake* (1992), and a collection of poetry, *Instruments of the Bones* (1992). He has edited the MLA volume *Approaches to Teaching Shelley's "Frankenstein"* (1990).

Catherine B. Burroughs is Assistant Professor of English and Chair of the Women's Studies Program at Cornell College. She is co-editor of *Reading the Social Body* (1993) and has published articles on English Romantic drama and theatre. She is also a member of Actor's Equity Association.

Paula R. Feldman, Professor of English at the University of South Carolina, is co-editor of *The Journals of Mary Shelley* (1987), editor of *British Romantic Poetry by Women: 1770–1840* (forthcoming from Johns Hopkins University Press), and author of articles on women writers of the Romantic period.

Moira Ferguson holds the James E. Ryan Chair in English and Women's Literature at the University of Nebraska. Her books include *Mary Wollstonecraft* (1984), *First Feminists: British Women Writers 1578–1799* (1985), and *Subject to Others: British Women Writers and Colonial Slavery 1670–1834* (1991).

Anthony John Harding is Professor of English at the University of Saskatchewan, Canada. Most recently, he co-edited *Milton, the Metaphysicals, and Romanticism* (1994). Other books include *Coleridge and the Idea of Love: Aspects of Relationship in Coleridge's Thought and Writing* (1974), and *Coleridge and the Inspired Word* (1985).

Theresa M. Kelley, Associate Professor of English at The University of Texas at Austin, is author of *Wordsworth's Revisionary Aesthetics* (1988) and essays on aesthetics, the sister arts, rhetoric, William Wordsworth, Keats, J. M. W. Turner, and Robert Browning. She is completing *Reinventing Allegory*, a study of allegory since the Renaissance.

Susan M. Levin is Professor of English and Comparative Literature at the Stevens Institute of Technology, author of *Dorothy Wordsworth and Romanticism* (1987), and performer of *Songs by Women Composers, 1650–1990*.

William McCarthy, Professor of English at Iowa State University, is the author of *Hester Thrale Piozzi* (1985) and co-editor of *The Poems of Anna Letitia Barbauld* (1994). He is at work on a biography of Barbauld.

Jeanne Moskal, Associate Professor of English at the University of North Carolina at Chapel Hill, wrote *Blake, Ethics, and Forgiveness* (1994). Her current projects are a psychoanalytic study of Romantic women travel writers, 1789 to 1815, and an edition of Mary Shelley's travel books.

Mitzi Myers teaches writing and children's and adolescent literature at the University of California, Los Angeles. She has published extensively on historical children's literature and on eighteenth- and nineteenth-century women writers and is currently completing *Romancing the Family: Maria Edgeworth and the Scene of Instruction*.

Judith Pascoe, an Assistant Professor at the University of Iowa, is completing a book that examines the theatricality of British literary culture in the 1790s. She is also editing the collected poems of Mary Robinson.

Judith Pike is an Assistant Professor of English at Salisbury State University and specializes in women's studies and critical theory. She is the co-translator of Hélène Cixous's *Terrible But Unfinished Story of Norodom Sihanouk, King of Cambodia* (1994).

Richard C. Sha, Assistant Professor of Literature at the American University, is currently at work on a book-length study, *The Visual and Verbal Sketch in an Age of British Romanticism*.

Susan Wolfson is Professor of English at Princeton University. She is the author of *The Questioning Presence* (1986) and of numerous essays on Romantic writing. She is completing a book on critical moments in Romanticism's representations of gender, *Figures on the Margin*.

Acknowledgments

The editors gratefully acknowledge the advice and assistance of Dan Albergotti, Susana Castillo, Stuart Curran, Malia Myers, Beth Dethlefson, Sonia Hofkosh, Price McMurray, Dan McCloskey, Claire Miller, Daniel Robinson, Marlon Ross, Denise Sechelski, and Staci Stone. They also wish to thank the Interlibrary Loan Department at Thomas Cooper Library at the University of South Carolina. The Department of English and the University Research Institute at the University of Texas at Austin provided research funds for Theresa Kelley, and the English Department at the University of South Carolina provided Paula Feldman with a research leave.

Theresa M. Kelley and Paula R. Feldman

Introduction

⟨ornament⟩

his collection focuses on a remarkable body of imaginative work that has been virtually ignored during most of this century—writing by British women during the era traditionally called Romantic. Relatively little has been written, even in recent years, about many of these writers, who were a significant part of literary culture in Britain, both profoundly influenced by and influencing what we have come to call Romanticism. As we reimagine a Romanticism that once again includes the voices of women, the insights of thoughtful and sometimes provocative commentators are not only welcome but necessary. To that end, we have gathered new essays by established and by younger scholars, providing a cross-section of the diversity of inquiry that now distinguishes critical and historical discussion of the literary output and careers of Romantic women writers. Renewed interest in these writers and the resulting critical scholarly editions and reprints of their work, either about to be or just recently published, make a collection of critical and historical essays about them and their artistic achievement particularly timely.

Much of the discussion that has taken place has, until now, lain dispersed among journals, conference proceedings, and monographs, its impact diffused and difficult to assess. We have tried to bring together here a critical mass of commentary, not only to demonstrate the range and complexity of women's writing during the Romantic period but to aid in establishing a set of critical terms and directions with which to continue investigating this important body of writing. Several contributors use unpublished archival and cultural materials to situate the works and lives they examine. Some describe the rhetorical strategies women writers used to record or deflect the difficulties of reconciling accepted notions of femininity with the requirements of professional writing and publishing in their time. Others discuss how individual works relate to the conventional canon of Romanticism. A few deal with the better-known women writers of the period—Emily Brontë and Mary Shelley—but most emphasize Romantic women whose work and careers have thus far received less critical attention: Felicia Hemans, Joanna Baillie, Maria Edgeworth, Sydney Owenson (Lady Morgan), Helen Maria Williams, Janet Little, Mary Robinson, Letitia Landon, Amelia Opie, Anna Letitia Barbauld, and Harriett Abrams. Not every literary woman of importance is represented here. Conspicuously absent are Charlotte Smith, Jane Taylor, and Ann Radcliffe, among others. Our goal was not comprehensiveness but *diversity*, and that is here in abundance; the essays treat fiction writers, playwrights, poets, journalists, editors, actors, composers, and writers of children's books, of theoretical essays, and of travel books, and the authors approach their subjects from a variety of critical perspectives. That is precisely our object. Differences between commentators become the basis for fruitful critical exchange; as Stuart Curran and Marilyn Butler have shrewdly observed, without those differences, we risk a myopic view of Romanticism.[1]

The history of the exclusion of women's voices from the ever-changing Romantic canon says more, in some ways, about our own century than about theirs, for contrary to conventional wisdom, the writing of many women Romantics survived through the nineteenth century and into the twentieth. Felicia Hemans is perhaps the most obvious example.[2] How and why have we forgotten that she was one of the most widely read and influential poets of the nineteenth century? Her work, as popular in America as in Britain, was admired by Byron, Shelley, Wordsworth, Matthew Arnold, William Michael Rossetti, George Eliot, Elizabeth Barrett, and countless other writers and literary critics of discerning taste. It continued to be widely anthologized, set to music, quoted, illustrated by artists, ensconced in sumptuous tooled-leather bindings, and made the subject of school recitations well into our own century. Oxford University Press published a volume of her collected works in 1914, and Eyre and Spottiswoode published another in 1920. The change in literary taste brought about by World War I and by the onset of modernist aesthetic values made any Romantic sensibility seem naïve, melodramatic, embarrassingly sentimental. Felicia Hemans became as passé as Percy Bysshe Shelley or William Wordsworth. But when, some decades later, literary critics and the academic world in general began to rediscover and to revive the English Romantics, the male writers seemed to be the only candidates for recanonization; the women authors of the period and their rich artistic legacy were ignored. It was not a conspiracy or a deliberate silencing, for the Romantics had all been silenced for some time. It was, instead, an absence of sufficient curiosity and advocacy—of the zeal necessary to rehabilitate the name of any forgotten writer, whether male or female—an absence of the political power and energy to break the silence already there.

By the 1960s five male poets constituted the Romantic canon. The women of that period were so effectively "not there," except as sisters, wives and mothers, that they were even excluded from consideration as "minor" writers.[3] Occasionally, feminist critics such as Ellen Moers shattered the general complacency with books such as *Literary Women* (1976).[4] But these "women's studies" books tended to be regarded apart, as though the history of women's writing in the early nineteenth century was an issue separate from Romanticism. Even after William Blake broke into the canon in the 1970s and Mary Shelley's *Frankenstein* became a staple in half of all college Romanticism courses offered in the late 1980s, most of the important women Romantics continued to be overlooked. But the combined influence of increasing numbers of women in the profession, the evolving interest in gender studies, deconstruction, New Historicism, the politics of canon formation, and the popularity of various feminisms all conspired to make us reexamine Romanticism. Several books from that decade emerged to paint a markedly different landscape than the accepted one: Jerome McGann's *The Romantic Ideology* (1983) challenged the very notion of Romanticism and its critical construction. James Robert de Jager Jackson's invaluable *Annals of English Verse 1770–1835*, a preliminary survey of the volumes published (1985), documented the many books of poetry authored by women, and Janet Todd's *Dictionary of British and American Women Writers 1660–1800* (1985) embraced the tradition of Matilda Betham's *Biographical Dictionary of . . . Celebrated Women* (1804) and updated it with a focus on literature.[5] Donald H. Reiman, while upholding the hierarchy of the canon, included many women authors in his Garland reprint series of "minor" Romantic works, and Jonathan Wordsworth's Woodstock series, entitled Revolution and Romanticism, reprinted important works such as Mary Robinson's *Lyrical Tales* (1798), Helen Maria Williams's *Letters Written in France in the Summer of 1790*, and Charlotte Smith's *Elegiac Sonnets* (1789). Dale Spender's Mothers of the Novel series at the Pandora Press included reprints of important fiction. Roger Lonsdale's *Eighteenth-Century Women Poets: An Oxford Anthology* (1989) contained not only selected works by intriguing poets such as Ann Batten Cristall and Janet Little but also the circumstances of their authorship and the outlines of their lives. *The Feminist Companion to Literature in English: Women Writers from the Middle Ages to the Present* (1990) by Virginia Blain, Patricia Clements, and Isobel Grundy included many hitherto unacknowledged women authors from the Romantic age, and Donna Landry's *The Muses of Resistance: Laboring Class Women's Poetry in Britain, 1739–1796* (1990) focused attention on this body of writing, together with the social and economic exigencies of class in late-eighteenth-century Britain. In an essay titled "The 'I' Altered," Stuart Curran made a pointed critical issue of the exclusion of women's writing from the Romantic canon. He also joined with other scholars to found the Brown University Women Writers Project, with the aim of disseminating significant texts now become obscure. Works such as *The Contours of Masculine Desire* (1989) by Marlon Ross and *The Bluestocking Circle* (1990) by Sylvia Myers began to explore more fully the implications of gender in Romantic literature.[6]

Much-needed new scholarly texts are now emerging—for example, William McCarthy and Elizabeth Kraft's *The Poems of Anna Letitia Barbauld* (1994), and Stuart Curran's Oxford edition of *The Poems of Charlotte Smith* (1993). At the same time, Harriet Linkin has traced in the pages of *College English* the transformation of the Romantic canon through time and its implications, while Jerome McGann's *New Oxford Book of Romantic Period Verse* (1993) includes selections from twenty-one women poets of the period. Among forthcoming anthologies, Paula Feldman's *British Romantic Poetry by Women, 1770–1840* closely examines the lives and work of almost sixty women poets and includes reprints of hundreds of poetic texts. Andrew Ashfield's *Women Romantic Poets, 1770–1838: An Anthology* provides a good selection of works with a special emphasis on the sublime, and an anthology by Isobel Armstrong and Joseph Bristow will treat women's poetry throughout the nineteenth century. Jennifer Breen's paperback Everyman anthology has, despite its brevity and idiosyncratic choices, the virtue of being inexpensive. Meanwhile, research libraries and archives, the material keepers of the canon, are beginning to reassess their holdings,[7] the annual Conference on Eighteenth- and Nineteenth-Century British Women Writers has attracted more participants each year, and Anne Mellor and Richard Matlak are working on an anthology of work by British romantic writers that will include women.

With the aid of contemporary scholarship, literary histories of the future may record that Walter Scott called Joanna Baillie "the best dramatic writer" in Britain "since the days of Shakespeare and Massinger"; that Wordsworth's "Preface" to the second edition of *Lyrical*

Ballads appropriated without acknowledgment Baillie's call, two years earlier, for the use of natural, spoken language in literary art; that the *Quarterly Review*, the same periodical that later savaged Keats's *Endymion*, praised Mary Tighe's *Psyche*, calling it a poem with "few rivals in delicacy of sentiment, style, or versification," reminiscent of Ariosto and rivaling Spenser's *Fairie Queene*; and that the *Eclectic Review* preferred Tighe to La Fontaine and Apuleius and believed her poetry "scarcely inferior" to Ariosto, Tasso, and Spenser. Future histories may also recall that Tighe's style and choice of subject influenced Keats throughout his poetic career, that Charlotte Smith revolutionized the sonnet in English; and that Coleridge used Smith as his standard when trying to learn the form.

The feminist, materialist, and historicist questions now being asked about Romanticism have, then, as much to do with the present and the future as with the past, as much to do with knowing ourselves as with knowing who the Romantics were, what they wrote, and why they wrote as they did. It is in this sense that the present critical return to Romantic women's writing goes back, as Marjorie Levinson has put it, to the future—to a recognition of how our understanding of Romanticism will change after we reimagine it to include a wider, more densely articulated array of writers and texts.[8] This project demands both the recovery of forgotten or neglected works and some critical reflection on the limitations inherent in all acts of canonization, insofar as canons are synoptic forms—whether ours or someone else's. These limitations are particularly glaring in the reception history that English Romanticism has enjoyed or at least survived. For, as Harriet Linkin has documented so well, the Romantic canon has always been an unstable artifact of its critical reception. Francis Jeffrey's largely favorable 1829 review of Felicia Hemans's poetry remains a chastening example of that instability. As such, it is also a cautionary tale about critical hubris:

We have seen too much of the perishable nature of modern literary fame, to venture to predict to Mrs Hemans that hers will be immortal, or even of very long duration. Since the beginning of our critical career, we have seen a vast deal of beautiful poetry pass into oblivion, in spite of our feeble efforts to recall or retain it in remembrance. The tuneful quartos of Southey are already little better than lumber:—And the rich melodies of Keats and Shelley,—and the fantastical emphasis of Wordsworth,—and the plebeian pathos of Crabbe, are melting fast from the fields of our vision. The novels of Scott have put out his poetry. Even the splendid strains of Moore are fading into distance and dimness, except where they have been married to immortal music; and the blazing star of Byron himself is receding from its place of pride. We need say nothing of Milman, and Croly, and Atherstone, and Hood, and a legion of others. . . . The two who have the longest withstood this rapid withering of the laurel, and with the least marks of decay on their branches, are Rogers and Campbell.[9]

Had his age listened to Jeffrey, this mournful catalog implies, the reputations of several poets might have endured. If we listen to Jeffrey now with something like the sly self-irony of the figures and mental actions Samuel Taylor Coleridge calls "reflections" in "Kubla Khan" and the *Biographia Literaria*, we may be more suspicious of new idealisms and dogmatisms about the Romantic objects (we use this term advisedly) of our critical attention.

For confident late twentieth-century pronouncements about the relative merit of Romantic writers may appear equally bizarre to readers of the future. As we insist that critical discussion needs to widen its focus dramatically to include writers whose work and public careers belong to the cultural mix of Romanticism in ways that were once unimaginable, and as we observe that this entire body of writing—by women more or less well known—needs extensive archival and textual study, we must remember that, despite the seeming liberality of such critical gestures, reopened canons can be dangerous. The logic of canonicity, of course, is exclusion and, more particularly, exclusions that allow critics to remake the canon in their own particular critical image, *whatever* that image may be. Because the essays in this volume approach the terrain of women writers and Romanticism from quite different perspectives and from a diversity of methods, they are the best critical warrant we have to ensure that the Romantic canon is not reopened in one direction only to be closed in another. This diversity, including occasional disagreements, is crucial to the spirit of these essays, whose textual and archival specificity emphasize how particular women wrote, what they wrote, and what makes their writing significant. For this reason, we foreground rather than try to harmonize their antiphony of voices. For it is critical difference, not choral unison, that will cumulatively register the interest of women's writing in the field of inquiry we call Romanticism.

Whatever critical measure we can take of an epoch such as Romanticism requires something more than a convenient short list of writers whose canonical isolation (and canonization) may authorize, in Marilyn Butler's astringent view, the isolation of academic critics.[10] To restrict the Romantic canon to a few writers impoverishes our access, always partial at best, to Romanticism. Yet even readers who assent to calls for a more capacious account of Romantic writers and texts may disagree about how to situate the work of women writers of the period. Contributors to this volume present both sides of this debate. Some argue that writing by Romantic women should be read on its own terms and situated in its own contexts so that its assessment will not be contaminated by critical pre-dispositions derived from the study of the traditional Romantic canon. Others contend rather that the voices of Romantic women writers gain their fullest resonance when read within and against that traditional canon.

Part of the theoretical work performed by contributors to the volume is to suggest how Romantic women writers operated successfully within a patriarchal culture. The women whose work these essays consider often mark their resistance to this culture by reimagining or, to use Mary Robertson's term, "contorting" figures of speech and even genres. Like the incremental measures of resistance Michel de Certeau plots in the practice of everyday life, such contortions are the means individuals use to mark their differences from and with what Pierre Bourdieu calls *habitus*, the set of norms and expectations that defines a culture. Even those Romantic women whose rhetoric does not directly challenge their habitus situate themselves in ways that indicate the stress of their position. In their choices of figure, genre, subject, and even career, other Romantic women offer similar hints or more open declarations of their status as agents who work on the shape of their culture even as it shapes them.[11] Because the terms of engagement between these writers and Romantic culture are often complicated, they are misserved and rarely compassed by ordinary labels. Instead, they offer us the opportunity for rethinking what Romanticism is and who we are as its critics.

Similar questions about agency, innovation, and cultural embeddedness promise to inform archival and critical investigations of Romantic women's writing in the years ahead. Already focusing critical debate across several disciplines, these topics have given theoretical shape to relevant questions: Under what circumstances, under what pressures do these women write in a particular historical moment? What settlements or accommodations do they make or refuse? How do we evaluate textual evidence to take the measure of these writers and their careers?

The essays in this volume vigorously engage these questions, with varying emphases. Essays in part 1, "Reimagining Romantic Canons," present different cases for formulating canons. Isobel Armstrong's analysis of the language of affect in the poetry of Barbauld and other writers contends that its appropriate referent is not the "gush of the feminine" but late-eighteenth-century economic and philosophical hypotheses concerning the senses, representation, and the law. To grant the complexity of Romantic women's poetry, Armstrong declares, we need to read it, at least for now, in isolation from the male Romantic tradition. Susan Wolfson's essay argues instead that, to understand the gendered implications of Romantic arguments about sex and souls, we are well advised to compare what the men and the women writers say, noting when and why some writers change their minds when questions about sex and gender lead them to considerations of soul or essence. Stephen Behrendt uses Shelley's *Frankenstein* to survey the women writers' anxieties about creation and authorship. He assesses textual evidence suggesting that some Romantic women internalized cultural arguments about the monstrosity of women who write and publish or, conversely, chose not to publish their writings because doing so would have meant the loss of a private identity to a monstrous, devouring public persona. Mitzi Myers sees Maria Edgeworth's coming of age as woman and author in a different light, reading Edgeworth's early story "The Bracelets" as an autobiographical fiction about the development of female subjectivity, a subjectivity with little if anything in common with the Wordsworthian model of sublime, Romantic selfhood. Nonetheless, Myers observes, pedagogical theorists continue to promote Wordsworth as the exemplary model of Romantic subjectivity and childhood (male and female), whether or not their theories accurately reflect Wordsworth's poetic subjectivity and despite the fact that they efface Romantic female subjectivity and childhood.

In part 2, "Textual Strategies," three essays track the rhetoric and figures women writers use to specify the role of gender in their writing. William McCarthy considers the degree to which repression and desire are figured in Barbauld's early poems. He identifies a reciprocal relation between the idealization of women in these poems and the poet's "emotionally conflicted" reply to those who would curb her ambition, and he places her firmly within the feminist tradition as it was evolving at the time. Anthony Harding observes that although Hemans records woman's experience without seeming to challenge the cultural paradigms by which it was defined in the early nineteenth century, the experiences thus recorded obliquely register the price of compliance, as female personas and voices are obliterated even as the ordinary women of Herculaneum were smothered by volcanic ash, to cite one of Hemans's most compelling metaphors. Harding concludes by imagining another approach to Hemans and to the poetic excavation of women's voices, one that might find poetic traces of resistance to and subversion of this plot. In a psychoanalytic reading of the resurrection of female corpses in Romantic fiction, Judith Pike observes that characters greet such resurrection with horror because they fear fetishized objects and automatons that threaten to come back to life. Like Emily Brontë's dead Cathy Linton at Lockwood's window, these female corpses work against the early-nineteenth-century cultural desire for a domesticated, private female self who can be more easily contained in life and in death; the fetishized, female object of romantic desire (desired as long as safely dead) keeps erupting, clawing her way back into the public, textual space of narration to embody, in Mary Shelley's admonitory phrase, the "dangerous consequences of movement."

Part 3 "Nationalism, Patriotism, and Authorship," investigates how nationalistic or patriotic convictions allow some women writers to strengthen their claim to authorship when prohibitions regarding a woman writer's class or choice of topic and genre would have otherwise undermined such claims. In her analysis of Lady Morgan's career as novelist and writer of travel books, Jeanne Moskal observes that Morgan deployed her marginal and potentially criminal status as an Irish patriot like her father to protect herself against "the more serious charge" of woman writer. Morgan defends her textual authority in *France*, her first and most popular travel book, with marginalia (extensive notes, two prefaces, and even four appendixes written by Morgan's husband), categorically redefining the uses of marginality as these textual barricades work to protect the female author at the center of the work. Richard Sha discloses another form of rhetorical self-defense in both Morgan's and Helen Maria Williams's use of the term *sketch* to title works whose political and historical analysis of revolutionary France and Ireland go far afield from topics women writers were expected to engage. On these occasions the genre of the female sketch becomes an impervious cover that masks its transgressive expansion of limits assigned to it as a vehicle of polite female accomplishment. Moira Ferguson chronicles the volatile mix of nationalism, class loyalty, deference, erotic attraction, and animosity in Janet Little's poetic assessments of her contemporary, Robert Burns, and her conflicted acknowledgment of the gentry and aristocratic support she received as a working class Scots woman and poet. In tone, subject matter, and figure, Little's *Poems* negotiate a difficult public and private terrain marked by her loyalty to a Scottish working-class experience, her poetic ambition, and a carefully screened sexual wariness.

In part 4, "Performance and the Marketplace," three essays measure the impact of different kinds of performance on individual careers. Catherine Burroughs identifies a fundamental Romantic conflict in Baillie's dramatic theory and practice between a desire for the privacy of closet drama and a recognition that drama, particularly tragedy, requires public performance. In *De Monfort*, Baillie dramatizes this conflict by assigning it to the male protagonist; on the open stage of the drama, he is a heterosexual whose performance of his gender and class is carefully scripted, but the verbal texture of his confrontations with the villain argues a "closeted" homosexual longing. Susan Levin chronicles the career of Harriett Abrams, a singer, theatrical performer, and composer in early Romantic London. The salient feature of Abrams's career is less its apparent success, although it was clearly that, than her transformation of cultural liabilities (to be both Jewish and female) into the distinguishing marks of a respected professional. In her analysis of Mary Robinson's multiform contributions to the *Morning Post*, Judith Pascoe surveys the theatrical and commercial world of Romantic journalism to evaluate Robinson's use of a variety of pseudonyms in writing for the *Post*. If one outcome of this strategy is a fragmented self given over to multiple voices and fictional identities, the gain of such theatrical self-presentation is a degree of public authority as a writer that allows Robinson to put aside the notoriety of her earlier career as an actress, writer, and paramour of the Prince Regent.

On every level, much remains to be done to specify the shape of Romantic women's careers and to situate those careers in something like a general (or particulate) field theory of Romanticism, defined by differences and new instabilities as much as or more than by similarities or by a tightly focused set of attributes. Romantic women's writing thereby makes its own contribution to what A. O. Lovejoy characterized as the problem of discriminating among Romanticisms.[12] This plural is apt. By turns of evidence and argument, the essays included in this volume contribute to our present understanding of Romanticism as a remarkable as well as shifting array of competing particulars.

Part One

Reimagining Romantic Canons

Isobel Armstrong

The Gush of the Feminine

How Can We Read Women's Poetry of the Romantic Period?

Inscription for an Ice-House

Stranger, approach! within this iron door
Thrice locked and bolted, this rude arch beneath
That vaults with ponderous stone the cell; confined
By man, the great magician, who controuls
Fire, earth and air, and genii of the storm,
And bends the most remote and opposite things
To do him service and perform his will,—
A giant sits; stern Winter; here he piles,
While summer glows around, and southern gales
Dissolve the fainting world, his treasured snows
Within the rugged cave.—Stranger, approach!
He will not cramp thy limbs with sudden age,
Nor wither with his touch the coyest flower
That decks thy scented hair. Indignant here,
Like fettered Sampson when his might was spent
In puny feats to glad the festive halls
Of Gaza's wealthy sons; or he who sat
Midst laughing girls submiss, and patient twirled
The slender spindle in his sinewy grasp;
The rugged power, fair Pleasure's minister,
Exerts his art to deck the genial board;
Congeals the melting peach, the nectarine smooth,
Burnished and glowing from the sunny wall:
Darts sudden frost into the crimson veins

Of the moist berry; moulds the sugared hail:
Cools with his icy breath our flowing cups;
Or gives to the fresh dairy's nectared bowls
A quicker zest. Sullen he plies his task,
And on his shaking fingers counts the weeks
Of lingering Summer, mindful of his hour
To rush in whirlwinds forth, and rule the year.

—Anna Letitia Barbauld, 1743–1824

*I*f this extraordinary poem is not quite the first poem written to a refrigerator, it is certainly one of the earliest hymns to technology—though the fusion of celebration, satire, and lyric is enigmatic. Despite the technological feat of bringing contradictions together and making a cave of ice in the sun (the demystifying references to "Kubla Khan" are conscious but by no means hostile), the icehouse, thrice bolted, is like a dungeon or a tomb. It is archaic, gothic, like an ancient monument, yet icehouses were the result of wealth and luxury that could command the resources of sophisticated modern invention and the infrastructure of continental trade—stocks of ice were brought to England from Norway. The icehouse, trapping temperature at freezing point to preserve the products of an estate, is the subterranean double of those more fragile monuments to wealth that trapped light and heat to force growth, the newly fashionable greenhouses.[1] Indeed, the Persephone-like woman appearing almost like some votary or victim, who is addressed as "Stranger" at the beginning of the poem and told that this humanly regulated Winter will not seize her with premature age, is possibly one of those visitors who toured the houses of the rich, a growing practice at this time.

Lest the confidence in technology should seem glib, a trick of syntax makes it fleetingly difficult to decide who the "magician" who "controls" the elements by trapping Winter really is. "Man," universalized but here referring surely to the masculine subject alone, exerts power over natural resources, changing their very nature and bending opposites to his mastery. But the syntax makes it equally possible for the descriptive phrase "great magician" to be the attribute of the "giant" Winter, who is temporarily confined by man. It initiates a power struggle between two great forces, both gendered masculine, both magicians, both commanding the adversarial "genii of the storm." It is unusual to find a personified natural force effectively (if temporarily) denatured and rendered a product of artifice—forced by violence into culture—in a Romantic poem. Barbauld's voluptuously "melting peach" and "nectarine smooth" may be precursors of the diction of Keats's "Ode to Autumn," but Keats's language of the pleasure principle consistently reassimilates the products of labor and culture—the oozings of cider, for instance—back into natural process, and an androgynously personified Autumn roams freely in a world of consumption without violence.

This arresting difference between Barbauld and Keats leads immediately to a fundamental problem, that of addressing the prerequisites for thinking about women's poetry in the Romantic period. We have had two hundred years to discover a discourse of and strategies for reading male poets. They belong to a debate, a dialectic; we know how to think about politics, epistemology, power, and language, in productive ways that, whether it is Matthew Arnold or Paul De Man who writes, make these poets *mean* for us. A hermeneutics has evolved. Not so with the female poets. We are discovering who they are, but there are few ways of talking about them. Mercifully, a canon has not yet been founded, for canons seal poets into hierarchies; but we have not found productive historical ways of thinking about female poets either. Mostly, the female poets are confined to the realm of affect and domesticity and described as W. M. Rossetti described Felicia Hemans; he spoke of the "cloying flow" of her "feminine" poetry.[2] There are enormous differences among women Romantics, but it is important to get away from the gush of the feminine regarded simply as a consent to nonrational and emotional experience. This is often, as in the case of Hemans and Rossetti, a *male* description of women's poetry, and we need to be cautious about it.

As the issue is complex, I will set out the argument that runs through this essay. I contend that what we think of as the gush of the feminine can be misinterpreted. Both now and in the past it can be treated either as a special feminine discourse or censured as nonrational, or both. This is understandable because excess of emotion was censured in the late Enlightenment even by the powerful radical female prose polemicists who wrote on women's rights and education—Catharine Macaulay Graham, Mary Hays, Mary Robinson, Mary Wollstonecraft. However, I believe that many women poets neither consented to the idea of a special feminine discourse nor accepted an account of themselves as belonging to the realm of the nonrational. They engaged with two strategies to deal with the problem of affective discourse. First, they used the customary "feminine" forms and languages, but they turned them to *analytical* account and used them to *think* with. Second, they challenged the male philosophical traditions that led to a demeaning discourse of feminine experience and remade those traditions. They did not take these philosophical traditions—the only traditions they had—as an inert model but reconstructed them through critique. This was a way of thinking through their relationship to knowledge. A subtext of women's poetry is the question of how far the affective *is* knowledge and how far it may just be affect.

There are, of course, different ways of approaching women Romantic poets. Important pioneers such as Anne Mellor, in her collection *Romanticism and Feminism* (Bloomington and Indianapolis: Indiana University Press, 1988), and Marlon B. Ross in *The Contours of Masculine Desire: Romanticism and the Rise of Women's Poetry* (Oxford: Oxford University Press, 1989) have explored the special nature of a women's tradition. Ross, in particular, describes how women poets discovered a feminine space in male culture. Yet another approach is by Jennifer Breen in her anthology *Women Romantic Poets 1785–1832* (London: J. M. Dent and Sons; Rutland, Vermont: Charles E. Tuttle, 1992). She approaches the poetry through questions of class and work. This diversity is welcome, but I would caution against locking women too securely in their feminine space. Women claimed autonomy.

A politics, an epistemology, an account of knowledge, and an understanding of language can be derived from women's questioning of a number of discourses—aesthetic and philosophical, socioeconomic, medical, and legal. To find an interpretative strategy I turn to Barbauld's negotiations with Malthus, Adam Smith, Hume, and Burke in her "Inscription for an Ice-House," a test case for reading a Romantic poem by a woman.

It is important to stress, when turning to the challenge made by women to these powerful and formative male thinkers of the Enlightenment, that the aim of doing so is not to uncover a pristine empirical historical past by returning to an originary moment. The drive to understand these women poets anew has arisen from feminist thought and the reeducation it has accomplished. Effectively, these poets are *new* poets. This is not to abdicate from history but to recognize that history changes history: the category of gender changes our sense of what we know, what we need to know, and how we know it.

It is often hard to place women poets in a network of histories and relationships. Their interests do not follow the same intertextual relations as those of the male poets, nor does the trajectory of their intellectual debates parallel that of male writers. The rhythm of revolution and reaction—French revolution and the subsequent repressive politics pursued in England during the French wars and their aftermath until 1832—

that shapes the work of male writers is different for the women. The war in Spain (1808–1812), for instance, for some reason preoccupied women in a way it did not engage their male contemporaries. Or, as in the case of Mary Wollstonecraft, a politics of republicanism and hatred of despotic government and tyranny is skewed by sexual politics, as in her vehement argument with Rousseau in the footnotes of *A Vindication of the Rights of Woman* (1792). Yet Wollstonecraft's project—to gain access to civic humanism and to belong to the rational male republic of taste from which women were excluded—was not a project with which other women wished to be wholly identified, including Barbauld despite her respect for Wollstonecraft. Nevertheless, Wollstonecraft returns us to Barbauld, and to Keats, through another irascible footnote in *A Vindication.* "After writing these lines, how could Mrs. Barbauld write the following ignoble comparison?" Wollstonecraft's footnote runs.[3] The "ignoble comparison" is between women and flowers ("To a Lady, with Some Painted Flowers"). Like flowers, it is women's function "to please." "So the men tell us" is Wollstonecraft's caustic response. But it is an innocuous poem, forgivable in the context of an oeuvre that was to include poems defending the French revolution, meditations on Coleridge's mystical conservatism, and a critique of the luxury derived from colonial exploitation, *Eighteen Hundred and Eleven* (1812). The violent Tory attack on this last poem would seem enough, in retrospect at least, to align Barbauld with the radical pole of British politics.[4] But one of "the men" who "tell us" that women are like flowers is Burke, whose Tory ideology, apparent in Barbauld's slight poem, would immediately antagonize Wollstonecraft.

This complex set of alignments within British radical and "feminist" thought suggests the necessity of reading at other than the level of content, of what a poem overtly says, if the subtle negotiations with male texts by women poets are to be followed. A formal, structural, and linguistic project is bound up with intellectual debate in women's poetry and asks to be addressed.

Let us begin this structural project with Burke and the deeply gendered aesthetic category of the beautiful. The icehouse poem's dealings with Burke are more subtle than those of the earlier poem. For Burke the beautiful is a property of bodies, not of reason. It belongs to the senses and to the social and sexual drives that make men want to reproduce the species (desire belongs to men, not women). It has nothing to do with proportion, fitness, or utility. It is outside an economy just as it is outside reason. It depends on eroticizing the small, the smooth—smoothness is most beautiful "about the neck and breasts" of women, and one finds among "fine women, smooth skins, and in several sorts of ornamental furniture, smooth and polished surfaces." The attributes of variation, delicacy, melting indistinctness, weakness and imperfection contribute to the lack of power and the *sickness* with which we associate the beautiful: "Women are very sensible of this; for which reason, they learn to lisp, to totter in their walk, to counterfeit weakness and even sickness."[5] No wonder some present-day writers have been more interested in pursuing a female sublime in women's writing than in the category of the beautiful. The sublime is a condition familiar through the enormous body of interpretative writing around it, of individual struggle and self-preservation, of access to reason, of the infinite, of labor and phallic power. Burke speaks of the "swelling" triumph associated with appropriating the power of the sublime object. It speaks of heroic aporia, of recuperated energy in an economy of loss and (re)gain, and might well seem an empowering state.[6] But the icehouse poem does not opt for the sublime any more than it opts for the beautiful.

Winter was traditionally the quintessentially sublime season. James Thomson reaffirmed this in his preface to the second edition of *Winter* (1726), later published as part of *The Seasons* (1730).[7] In Barbauld's poem, however, winter is associated not with transcendence and self-overcoming but with technology and instrumental control. In an apparent reversal of the master/slave power relationship, Winter is "fair Pleasure's minister." Burke had said explicitly that the sublime is superior to pleasure and transcends utility. In "Inscription for an Ice-House," sublime Winter is subordinated to both. The erotic, feminized, and "beautiful" Burkean epithets, "melting" and "smooth," collaborate against Winter. His violence is neutralized, like "fettered Sampson" or like Hercules, who was condemned to dress in women's clothes and spin among women. There is comedy in the sublime expending itself in demasculinized "puny feats" or forced virtually to change gender, cross-dressing in the women's domain. Gross "sinewy" power clumsily handles the small, beautiful object, the "slender" spindle, and the poem makes free use of sexual innuendo. Winter does not understand women's arts, culture, *or* sexuality.

Yet the poem by no means simply affirms the "beautiful" side of the sublime/beautiful antithesis: two separate but unsymmetrical power struggles are going on, that between "Man" and the giant "Winter" and that between the feminine and winter. Delilah gains power through seduction: the "laughing girls"—a wonderfully suggestive crowd of giggling girls is conjured here—gain power through ridicule. Sinisterly, the syntax slides, just as in the master/slave relationship of man and nature. "Midst laughing girls *submiss*" (my emphasis) makes it possible for Winter–Hercules to be "submiss" to the laughing girls and the laughing girls to be "submiss" to Hercules. That is to say, the *structure* of relationships has not really changed with the advent of the technology that can control the climate of the icehouse, despite the seeming reversal of power. Women, locked in the icehouse with Winter, live unequally with him, forced into ruses to control him. The delicate flowers in the scented hair of the apostrophized visitor mark her vulnerability.

What makes women so vulnerable, so little able simply to reverse the place and power of sublime Winter (for the sublime belongs to both man *and* nature here as both become part of culture in contrast to the woman, who falls outside culture except insofar as she can play the role of servant)? It is the open secret, the accepted scandal, of women's fertility, reproductive power, and sexuality. The poem is full of the sensuous and exuberant signs of women's sexuality expressed as both natural growth and domestic economy: summer's dissolution of the "fainting world," the peach, the nectarine, the "moist berry," the "flowing cups" and "nectared bowls" conspire to overdetermine a feminine symbolism that is both subordinated to winter and curiously out of control. The category of the beautiful cannot contain this generative excess, but excess seems to be woman's greatest problem as well as her greatest triumph. We need to turn to Malthus to see why.

Barbauld was well aware of the conservative ecology of Malthus, the writer who much later suggested to Darwin the principles of evolutionary biology. Malthus's *An Essay on the Principle of Population* (1798) is arguably the first major European text after de Sade to foreground sexuality. But in his case, concentrating as he does on the overproduction of children, the scandalous productivity of women's sexuality is the visible marker of excess that is at the heart of his work. Nature, he says, is a Cleopatra (another seducer), squandering production in overpopulation, which results in shortage. His conviction that *dearth* is a universal is as powerful as his understanding that resources will never keep pace with the production of humans. And just as his pessimistic conservative realism sees famine as fate as the feminine, so his unillusioned skepticism makes him possibly the first writer in Europe to suggest that women's oppression was an inevitable and *structural* part of the economy because the capacity to reproduce made women dependent, exploitable, and vulnerable. The poorer the woman, the more oppressed she will be. It is strange that such reactionary deconstruction should be so inestimably important to the sexual politics of the nineteenth century by *exposing* women's oppression as an economic matter, that which is culturally made, even when it insisted that dependence was natural.[8]

In her prose piece "Dialogue in the Shades," Barbauld challenges Malthusian premises. Clio takes advice from Mercury, the "god of expedients," as she calls him, because the expansion of history and the multiplication of modern events and personages will not fit her memorial roll. Something will have to go. This, of course, is a "Malthusian," exponential increase, but the criteria for limiting it when applied to the figures privileged by particular *political* readings of history and to the figures deemed to be important to western European culture very beautifully demonstrate that it is the privileged who survive. The principles that determine their survival are deeply ideological. Clio considers moral criteria for the exclusion of certain groups and figures. The figures and heroes of Greek mythology go, including the battle of Troy, on this criterion. They are also attacked as untruthful and fantastic, fit only for fairy tales, and are swept aside on the additional principle of utility. The piece demonstrates how the principle of utility would wipe out cultural memory through ethical cleansing. The political critique becomes increasingly abrasive. Alexander disappears because his discovery of India is irrelevant to the current colonial exploitation of it: "and the whole peninsula which you scarcely discovered, with sixty millions of inhabitants, is at this moment subject to the dominion of a few merchants in a remote island of the Northern Ocean, the very name of which never reached your ears." So much for the East India Company.

Louis XIV is crisply banished because the French Revolution got rid of the monarchy. But Napoleon, who, Mercury says politely, "has indeed procured you much employment," is a cause of distraction: "Here am I expected to calculate how many hundred thousands of rational beings cut one another's throats at Austerlitz." As the discussion gets closer to the present, the attack on war intensifies. Mercury offers a rationale for war by directly invoking Malthus: "A great philosopher has lately discovered that the world is in imminent danger of being over-peopled, and that if twenty to forty thousand men could not be persuaded every now and then to stand and be shot at, we should be forced to eat one another. The discovery has had a wonderful effect in quieting tender consciences." Clio wonders why these sacrifices should be made to Mars, but Mercury reminds her: "You forget yourself, Clio; Mars is not worshipped now in Christian Europe."[9] If men stand up and shoot one another (again, technological agents of power preoccupy Barbauld), all will be well, even in a Christian country. In the poem, however, the satire on Malthus is nothing like so straightforward. For by bringing together food as product, the literal objects of consumption, that which is both cultivated and *preserved*—peaches, nectarines, dairy produce—and figuring them as the feminine at the same time, the text discloses some problematical possibilities. The affluent household at least can "bend" nature to produce enough and uses nature's own power to preserve produce. The nature/culture antithesis begins to break down as Winter, the power of death, can be forced to create life—"a *quicker* zest." Malthus is refuted as women become the bearers and preservers of life in collaboration with technology.

But it is not so simple. With a voluptuousness and anxiety that prefigures Christina Rossetti's *Goblin Market*, such possibilities emerge only if fruit is inseminated with ice. The melting flesh of the peach must be congealed, the moist berry arrested by "sudden frost." There is destruction and paralysis in the very moment of preservation, as Winter exerts the harshest control over fertility. Such frigidity contrasts strongly with the assurance of the masculinized "genial board," the abundant household table, with its social and bonding function, belonging to the head of the household. "Genial," preserving its origin in the idea of seed, was associated with male procreation at the time Barbauld was writing. Of or pertaining to marriage, generative, jovial, conducive to growth, or pertaining to marriage or to a feast, were some of the meanings of this epithet; it indicated a male power, easy and prodigal. (It may even have an affinity with the "genii" of the storm.) Feminine fertility, on the other hand, is constrained and uneasy, profoundly doubtful about an artificial and death-bringing preservation of its being. The Malthusian fix is not that easy to evade.

The problematical place and function of the feminine are further reinforced. The "genial board," despite the identification of joint interests suggested by "our" flowing cups, is clearly under the economic control of the head of the household and symbolizes the division of labor in the home. But the division of labor is clearly a problem for this poem. To use Adam Smith as an exemplary figure (though clearly, classical economists such as Ricardo and Mill are relevant here too), it is clear that questions of economy are crucial to women writers at this time. In the new principles of interdependence established in the great remapping of the circulation and exchange of labor and produce proposed by *The Wealth of Nations* (1776), it is never clear how Smith thinks about domestic economy in relation to the market. Households perhaps belonged to an archaic, agrarian structure in which a barter economy ruled. Servants were maintained by calculating the exchange value of their

labor in goods. Shortages could be artificially preserved because households produced food for consumption that did not enter the market and
never became part of the circulation of money and goods. And since, in
his distinction between productive and unproductive labor, *services* are
unproductive, the result is to erase the labor of women (in its two senses)
from consideration. Women do not belong to the economy; they do not
circulate in it.[10]

There is just such an uncertainty in Barbauld's poem. It challenges
Smith by wanting the productive and reproductive labor of women to be
acknowledged in all its plenitude and grace but at the same time attacks
the basis on which the division of labor is founded. Whereas "Man"
controls resources and participates in the exchange of "remote and
opposite things" (both geographically remote in colonial space, we assume, and materially different in kind and genus), women are confined to
a narrower range of tasks and objects. Domestic experience in this poem
is broken down into a series of discrete items and, through a quasi-
metonymic use of the definite article, is constructed as a continual repetition of the same structure—"the" spindle, board, peach, nectarine, wall,
berry, hail, dairy. The division of labor, one remembers, takes place as a
series of infinite repetitions of the same discrete task. Broken up into
parts, it refuses, Smith recognized, the integration of both body and
mind.[11] The semantic relation of parts and parturition hovers in the
language of the text. It is as if a grammar of parts has been made the
foundation of women's knowledge and experience—a feminine *cogito*
recognized as fragmenting even when it carries the empowerment of
giving birth. Winter, serving his time in the domestic world, can escape to
ravage the earth. The women belonging to the world of the icehouse do
not escape from him. This is the reverse of the Persephone myth. The
Persephone figure is misled: she will indeed be afflicted with "cramp" as
the "crimson veins" are seized up from within with frost, a sinister figure
for the frozen blockage that prevents movement and circulation in a
universe of parts. Instead, she participates in the ultimate metonymic
substitution of parts, of tomb for womb.

The "male" skills of urbanity, distancing sophistication, and rationality are seized in Barbauld's poem but appropriated so exquisitely for
satirical writing that they cross over to the service of the beautiful. Yet
Barbauld's tight control of affective language is unusual; and unless the
use of affective language can be understood, a new hermeneutics for
women's poetry is unlikely to emerge. I turn to Amelia Opie's "Consumption" (in *Poems*, 1802) and to "Calypso Watching the Ocean" (posthumously printed in 1841), a poem by a rather later poet, Letitia Land-

on, to continue this inquiry into the rhetoric of women's poetry. Nevertheless, it is Barbauld's poem that provides a point of entry into these texts.

"Inscription for an Ice-House" makes a subtle connection between the seizing up of the woman's physical being in "cramp" or paralysis and her exclusion from the public sphere where goods and wealth circulate. To enter the domestic space of the icehouse is to go in fear of seizure and withering through cold. This connection between *physical* paralysis and exile from the free circulation of exchange and commodity and women's ambiguous relation to the new economic models requires more discussion. Apparently belonging to an archaic economy based on the exchange of goods, women's relation to new accounts of value in which a "market" price displaces a "natural" price was bound to be uncertain. Adam Smith contrasted the scarcity value of the beautiful object, such as a jewel, and the cheapness of plentiful natural resources, such as water. Both a creature of artifice and a natural resource for breeding, women held a confused status, her exchange value, as it were, straddling the nature/culture divide. Worse than these contradictions, however, was the negative relation of the feminine to exchange altogether. Smith was quite clear that the world was being transformed by the unprecedented freedom of economic exchange and the circulation of goods and money within and between nations. But women were excluded from this great transformation of the world by commerce: their archaic standing constituted a positive obstruction to it. In Romantic poems by women there is an insistent figuring of illness as paralysis, the obstruction or malfunctioning of the free movement of the body and in particular the inhibition of breathing and the circulation of air. Spasm or paralysis is both a response to and an exacerbation of an obstruction in breathing. This intense physiological figure inscribes the failure of access to circulation as bodily symptom. Yet I believe it figures something more: it suggests the constricting nature of exclusion.

Burke associated the beautiful with imperfection: "[women] learn to lisp, to totter in their walk." Such malfunction and impediment to voice or movement can be connected with the spasm or paralysis of hysteria. Medical taxonomy of that period classified nervous diseases in terms of the obstruction of sense or motion: dyspepsia, epilepsy, gout, and whooping cough are sometimes grouped under the same head in contemporary treatises.[12] But it is less important to understand that the poem is an expression of hysteria than to know what historical moment hysteria itself is an expression *of*. Hysteria comes to mean the seizing up of experience. Illness comes from blocked emotions, a blocked language. In women's poetry from approximately 1790 throughout the nineteenth century there is a powerful figuring of physiological respiration as the breath of life—or love and erotic experience—but this is not the biblical or Mosaic influx of the divine breath of inspiration; these poems figure the *loss* of breath in expiration or sighs. The last line of Amelia Opie's "Consumption" offers the sigh of mourning to the reader: "And, sighing, own the mournful picture just." But the victim of respiratory illness only presents a feverish simulacrum of breathing to the observer in her "cheek's luxuriant red." In an image drawn from the obfuscation of the air, the nurse or carer thinks of herself as a schoolboy who, in "[t]hick gathering clouds," seizes upon any sign of improvement to predict a change of weather. But the healthier the patient seems, the harder it is to breathe, as consumption forces her to bloom "like the nightshade with unwholesome beauty." This disease of the lungs, most like life when it is most deadly, is specifically exempted from the "pledge" of the biblical rainbow. It creates a deceptive "security," as if it has broken its promise to the "Patriarch." Breathing, which is expiration or "expression," is secretly denied because expression is being denied. To make exclusion depend upon exclusion from the circulation of air is illness and deprivation indeed.

The divine promise can be broken in the case of a woman's illness, it seems. It is as if the Mosaic breath of life, continually re-created as the result of a series of agreements between God and men, is withdrawn from women. The promise is made without her. The theological skepticism in Opie's poem is immense, reinforced as it is with the earlier lines that describe the patient's hectic and unexpected beauty in terms of the decking of a victim with flowers in "pagan" ritual before human sacrifice. But Opie makes a double point about women's impeded access to the circulation of the breath of life by ensuring that the theological language is shadowed by a punning economic language. "Pledges," a word used twice in two lines, break down as "[u]pon security Death softly steals." This financial language of classical economics and the circulation of wealth places the woman victim outside its operations. It will not work for her. Fatal illness is not negotiable. The pledge did once work, for a time at least, for Noah, the "Patriarch." But the woman here is *outside* both the theological and economic systems.

The sigh or the sob is an expression of mourning that marks exclusion, disenfranchisement, alienation, and loss of control over experience. The language of emotion, affect, and feeling is so powerfully overdetermined in women's poetry of this time, I suggest, because the sharp intake or loss of breath on which it is founded depends on the inhibition and paralysis at the heart of the category of the beautiful. An expressive language—and breathing out is literally expression—has to be wrested from the choking and constriction dictated by the "imperfection" of the beautiful and the illness and death with which it is associated. It is the language of malfunction, constructed out of the obstruction of circulation (some treatises on nervous disease asserted that hysteria was caused by the arrest of menstruation), or it turns the negative and pathological toward critique. There are innumerable structural puns on breath and air in women's poetry of this time that play simultaneously on the pleasure principle and the death wish, almost invariably raising the question of empowerment and control over experience. A common series, for instance, modulates breath and air to spirit, to song, to the chords sounded in song/air, to the cord vibrating in a musical instrument or in the throat, to the cord plucked or acted on in musical expression, oscillating between active and passive implications as the series evolves: the body is an instrument, sometimes capable of acting, sometimes being acted on. With its expression the sigh or song enters the public world, but they are engendered internally. Art, agency, passion, sexuality—the ambiguities of the figure encompass a range of punning possibilities that are ever-present in women's texts. If we ask for originality, these are banal images, but their point is their banality. They image expressive experience, but they are also *analytical* figures. When we begin to understand that the language of affect is analytical, the question of triteness disappears. The paralysis or spasm of hysteria marks a body out of control, but it is also an attempt to control the body, a gasp for life.

Letitia Landon's poem "Calypso Watching the Ocean" must stand as an exemplary text here.[13] It is a poem about an endless spasm of grief. Empowering because it reads the *Odyssey* through Calypso's experience and not through that of "the hero," Odysseus, and the masculine sublime, the poem nevertheless explores the eternal paralysis that overcomes Calypso when, with the desertion of Odysseus, she is taken out of history. "Years, years have pass'd away" (or *died*), the poem punningly begins. The years can die, but the goddess cannot. The organization of syntax, parallelism, and repetition in the first stanza conspires to negate the central sexual experience, which slips out of the temporality asserted in the first line: we hear only that "years" have "pass'd" since the *Hero* arrived and since *he* departed. "Vex'd with immortality" (st. 4), Calypso is caught in repetition but not in time. The days are "uncounted" (st. 3) because time cannot mean to her—days can be counted only in a Kantian mathematical sublime from which she is excluded. As the refrain describing the "lone and lovely island" reiterates, she inhabits space, but not time: Odysseus can die, but she is forced to weep forever.

> Years, years have pass'd away,
> Since to yonder fated bay
>   Did the Hero come.
> Years, years, have pass'd the while
> Since he left the lovely isle
>   For his Grecian home.
> He is with the dead—but she
> Weepeth on eternally
>   In the lone and lovely island
> Mid the far off southern seas. (St. 1)

Uncannily, her weeping is denied tears (st. 5), so that emotional need is thwarted by physical impossibility. That may be why, without tears, the spasm of grief is arrested. There is a logic to this. Calypso is a goddess who has encountered human sexual experience but cannot *be* human (just as she is "[l]ike" a marble statue but not a statue), and both fully divine and fully human experience are now denied her. Exiled from both, the only category that is common to both is that of being a woman, and it is the only condition she can own. Intolerable incompatibilities—eternity with human grief, duration without death—and the double powerlessness of being nondivine and nonhuman confront her. She is a beautiful *object* only. Logically, the "odours" (st. 6) and "perfume" (st. 7) of the island are redundant and waves suck away its "scented breath" (st. 6) indefinitely, leaving a vacuum on the "lone" island. Forms of expression are stopped up as Calypso neither weaves nor sings, the feminine tasks of her once self-sufficient world (st. 7).

> Far beyond the fragrant pile,
>   Sends it odours through the isle,
>   And the winds that stir
> In the poplars are imbued
> With the cedar's precious wood
>
> . . . .
> Till the azure waves beneath
> Bear away the scented breath . . . (St. 6)

Landon always risks with—almost courts—triteness, but turns it to her use. Her simplicity is rigorous because, though she refuses to write anything that cannot be said simply, the implications of her diction are far from simple; her syntax is condensed, elliptical. If the "heart" asserts its "part," she warns, it invites this punitive fate. This is no simple "moral." The language is exact: The heart claims simply what is due to it; it does not claim in excess of its "part," but, in a world that simply does not know how to deal with the emotions, even this is too much. Landon exacts critique from the essentialist category of woman, which is the only state both goddess and human own, by showing that Calypso's "fate" is man-made, created by the rejection of Odysseus and his assumption that she is other to the institutions to which he belongs—"*his* Grecian home" (st. 1, my emphasis). Calypso sinks into the sadomasochistic structures of the beautiful: no "rosy flower" (st. 2), the mark of the beautiful, which arouses the "social" male desire for procreation (we think of Barbauld's votary), adorns her hair, but her hair is unbound in the seductive "variety" required of the beautiful. Like marble (st. 3)—Burke's "smooth" texture—pallid (st. 4), silent (st. 5), and sick, her "fate" is simply to fulfill the demands of the beautiful.

But there is a positive as well as a negative inflection of hysteria or nervous disease. The body (and the beautiful is entirely of the body) close to illness and death is by the same token close to life and to the experience of *sense*. Such access to sense challenges the Cartesian division between matter and mind and actually inverts the traditional hierarchical relation between mind and sense. Speculations on the nervous system in the early 1820s in the treatises, for instance, of J. C. Prichard and John Cooke considered whether the source of experience was in the senses or the brain. There might be multiple centers of sense perception: the *soul* might be material, existing in fluid or vital spirit circulating in the body, and sense experience might be conducted around the body in the same manner. Or sense experience might be communicated by vibrations carried in fluid or sound waves transmitted from the brain through the body. John Cooke thought that life itself could be isolated in physical sense experience and in what the body takes in through respiration. He hypothesized "a system or combination of gases, communicated to the lungs and heart from the air of the atmosphere, in the act of respiration; and either secerned or separated by the operation of these organs."[14]

Thus, sense is in action in the body. Barbauld's "melting peach" and "moist berry," Amelia Opie's longing for the "lustre" of the eye to confirm the inner evidence of "health's rich glow," and Letitia Landon's fascination with the emanation and movement of fragrance and perfume all, in different ways, register a gendered nearness to sense and become tropes for an access to those multiple centers of sense perception and the vital spirit that contains the soul.

But physiological sense cannot be mediated without mental representation. Like Wordsworth in "Tintern Abbey," women almost invariably adhere to "the language of the sense," and this is not unproblematical.[15] As Amelia Opie's poem suggests, the language of sense can too easily become the language of illness and a *deceptive* language at that. It becomes a false construct, offering a false relation between representation and what is represented. For Burke, sublime language short-circuits the connection between representation and its object: the *less* sublime language is connected to an object, and the more it is connected with associative feeling rather than image, the more sublime it is. By contrast the language of the beautiful must be committed to a tie between the sign and the extralinguistic world. Yet the representation of sensation is elusive, and it is hard to establish this tie. Amelia Opie sees that the empirically exact representation of sensuously recognized physical symptoms can actually be made to seem like the bloom of health. Indeed, an "accurate" sensuous language *would* suggest health rather than sickness. The extreme sexual beauty of the patient owes its "lustre" to unseen "decay," "[a]nd checked forebodings which ill-founded seemed." The "just" "picture" the poem has painted, the final line asserts, must in some sense be false because it has made an accurate representation of the "flattering" hand that "paints the victim's cheek." The poem is a sustained exploration of the gap between representation and its object and the epistemological complexities that arise from this.

Even when a language of the sense does not become a "strange delusion," it tends to be paradoxical, reinforcing connections with the immediate flow and pulse of sensation and yet skeptically questioning the representability of that immediacy. The *evidence* of experience represented in and through the consciousness must be questionable. The warrant for this skeptical epistemology is, of course, David Hume. He, rather than Locke or Hartley or Kant (the philosophical precursor figures of male poets), seems to stand behind women's poetic texts. This is because his work both affirms and questions the nature and evidence of sense. He affirms sense by changing the hierarchical relation of sense to reason, and yet the inferential and retrospective nature of his epistemology makes the meaning of the sensible image and the evidence of the senses highly questionable. But insofar as Hume insisted that ideas are weaker than sense and, so to speak, galvanized by it, his thought is useful to women because it made the beautiful a positive category. Landon's statement in "Petrarch's Dream," "We must feel to think," is Humean in its assertion of the dependence of thought on feeling.

Such language of affect seizes a justification from Hume's arguments on the priority of impressions to ideas. "The constant conjunction of our resembling perceptions," he argues in *A Treatise of Human Nature*, "is a convincing proof, that our impressions are the causes of our ideas, not our ideas of our impressions" (bk. 1, pt. 1, i, 5).[16] Hume was, of course, to sophisticate this relationship of dependence through the introduction of a distinction between simple and complex impressions and ideas, but his initial distinction between impression and ideas emphatically associates impressions with "force and violence." Impressions comprehend "all our sensations, passions and emotions, as they make their first appearance in the soul." Ideas, on the other hand, are "the faint images of these in thinking and reasoning" (bk. 1, pt. 1, i, 1). Even when the interaction of impressions and ideas takes on a relative autonomy, the "first vivacity" (bk. 1, pt. 1, iii, 8) of an impression drives thought and experience—or so it could be argued by those reading Hume to guarantee the language of the sense. It may be strange that a "women's" epistemology should be derived from a philosopher who so clearly presupposes male dominance: whether he is discussing the instrumental nature of women's training in chastity and modesty because it guarantees paternity (bk. 3, pt. 2, xii), the necessity of beauty for sexual arousal (bk. 2, pt. 2, xi), or the transmission of property through the male line (bk. 2, pt. 2, x), Hume writes as an analyst of the patriarchal order. Yet this is evidently his attraction. His skepticism exposes the constructed nature of social and cultural arrangements.

On the other hand, Hume's insistence that our understanding of the necessity of cause and effect is the simple result of recurrence and that there is no inherent necessity or "law" in repetition is destabilizing in its skepticism. When we add to this unstable world Hume's further (and later, in the *Enquiry*) emphasis on the flux and secondariness of sense perception itself, it is clear that the immediacy and plenitude gained in one direction through the language of the sense is lost in another:

[T]he existences which we consider when we say, *this house* and *that tree*, are nothing but perceptions in the mind, and fleeting copies or representations of other existences, which remain uniform and independent. . . . It is acknowledged, that, in fact, many of these perceptions arise not from anything external, as in dreams, madness and other diseases. . . . It is a question of fact, whether the perceptions of the sense be produced by external objects, resembling them: how shall this question be determined? By experience surely; as all other questions of a like nature. But here experience is, and must be entirely silent. The mind has never anything present to it but the perceptions, and cannot possibly reach any experience of their connexion with objects. The supposition of such a connexion is, therefore, without any foundation in reasoning.[17]

This skepticism has repercussions in a range of devices and structures in women's poetry. Landon, for instance, throws the whole weight of speculation on the status of action and perception, making an interpretative problem of events, by using doubled verbs in the past perfect, present perfect, and imperfect: "did come," "have pass'd." The fractional time lag achieved in the doubling of these verbs is enough to create a gap between events and the perception of them as events, a dislocation or hiatus between perception and the representation of perception. The doubling creates the effect of the lisp or stutter that Burke said was characteristic of the feminine beautiful, but the separation of the immediacy of perception and its interpretation creates an afterimage or the sense of "fleeting" copy that makes the verb and the action it portrays problematical.

Verbs are almost invariably, but unobtrusively, problematical in Landon's work. "He is with the dead . . . she weepeth": here the present tense disguises disjunct temporalities; Odysseus *has* died, Calypso weeps in the eternal present. This Humean attention to perception is not an illusionistic experiment with sensation. Verbs are used with intellectual precision in Landon's texts and are part of the woman Romantic poet's analytical project. They foreground Landon's almost "classical" concern with action and the extent to which control over action can be gained. The fractional gap opening up in the doubled verb creates a space for interpretative maneuver. The terrible passivity to which the goddess has been reduced in the eternal present is disclosed: the flickering verb allows a moment of interrogation; *could* things be different for a fully human woman rather than a divine woman? Portraying a moment either just before or just after an event takes place, the scenes of Landon's poems are both static and *tense*.

As with Barbauld's melting fruits, women poets deliberately overdetermine the sensuous, but this is taken up in many ways. In absolute contrast with Landon, Felicia Hemans exploits the evanescent, ambiguous nature of the "fleeting" copy, exploring the psychological flux of consciousness almost to derangement and pushing it toward Hume's "dreams, madness." In the first section of "Arabella Stuart," the poem that begins the long collection *Records of Women* (1828), Hemans presents the consciousness of a woman who is no longer certain that her memories are not dreams or that her dreams are memories; her experience may not have been derived from "external objects." The recognition that experience is unreliable drives her ever further into desperation and insanity, which breeds the very instability she fears. Arabella is in prison, long separated from her husband and without word from him. The language here is mimetic and psychological, representing the experience of unstable "fleeting copies" through dissolving sensation, as everything in the scene quivers and trembles by means of wayward syntax and a diction whose ambiguity foregrounds optical illusion. The first exclamation, "'Twas but a dream!" introduces a multiple perceptual problem. *Was* this simply a dream? Is it a memory that has become dreamlike? Or was the "original" experience simply as unreliable as an illusion, like the "masque" that passes in front of the woman's eyes?

> 'Twas but a dream! I saw the stag leap free,
> Under the boughs where early birds were singing;
> I stood o'ershadowed by the greenwood tree,
> And heard, it seemed, a sudden bugle ringing
> Far through a royal forest. Then a fawn
> Shot, like a gleam of light, from grassy lawn
> To secret covert; and the smooth turf shook,
> And lilies trembled, as, in fleet career,
> A princely band, with horn, and hound, and spear,
> Like a rich masque swept forth. (Pt. 1, ll. 1–10)

Such an epistemological dissolve, in which the identity is at stake, helps to explain, perhaps, why another discourse lurks in women's poetry at this time, the discourse of law. The juxtaposition of the language of the sense and the law may seem unlikely, but when one remembers that at the extreme of the language of the sense is mania and derangement, as Hemans demonstrates, then a concern with what controls and enforces conformity, with what constructs and orders identity, becomes a dialectical inevitability for the woman poet. The transgression and enforcement of norms are bound up with one another. And since, as Mary Wollstonecraft reminded her readers, a married woman's identity was absorbed into that of her husband and only became legally a separate identity if she committed a criminal act, a concern with the law arises because of the material constraints under which women lived.

Barbauld's uncomfortable recognition that the woman has no ownership or property rights in the "genial board," the table that recognizes and ritualizes the social act of eating, despite her labor on it, has already been seen. I will end with a brief look at two poems that demonstrate vividly how the law and its constraints are addressed through the structure and language of the text: Opie's "The Mad Wanderer: A Ballad" (1808) and Hemans's "Casabianca." I understand law both as institutionalized legal customs and taboos and the "law of the fathers." Kate of Grasmere, the mad wanderer of Opie's title, can utter only four words, which always form the last words of each quatrain, though they are never the same four words: "Poor Kate is mad!". . . "My brain is hot" . . "Poor Kate is cold." In brief, terse stanzas that are surely a challenge to

Wordsworth, she is described as a vagrant who will intervene in the social world only at the occasion of a wedding or a funeral, the two religious and legal rituals that certify a woman's being. Weddings send her wild (with sexual fury?), and funerals fill her with horror. But one funeral alters her behavior patterns: she sees the corpse, shrieks, and, deprived even of the four words to which she is reduced, dies. We assume that she has been pushed outside the law and pushed outside language into madness by sexual betrayal. Her entire identity has been formed by this, but the irony is that even *inside* law her identity would have been annihilated.

Opie's fierce, laconic poem is, on the face of it, very different from the almost maternal lament of Hemans's "Casabianca" for the thirteen-year-old boy destroyed by the violence of war because he obeyed the injunctions of a dead father, behaving as if they had legal force. However, this almost too well known poem is savage in its ironies. The boy stood on the "burning" deck, pleading for release against the taboos of the father, who actually lies "unconscious" below deck. A trick of rhythm and syntax allows the epithets to move to a "burning" boy and an "unconscious" boy, suggesting both the sexuality of puberty, which challenges the law of the father, and the boy's unawareness of his unconscious rivalry. The anachronistic reading that invokes the Freudian unconscious is not that far away from the text. The absurdity and cruelty of this patriarchal law becomes evident concurrently with the boy's enforced—and useless—heroism. The boy and the ship are violently destroyed. But so closely have the ship and the boy been identified that the ship comes to stand metonymically for the boy. A stanza break allows, for one horrifying moment, that the "fragments" strewed on the sea are those of the boy's body. They are actually the pieces of the ship—mast, helm—that "well had borne their part." The phallic imagery does indeed disintegrate horribly as the masculine "part" that was acted out in the performance of war is destroyed by its own violence.

The gush of the feminine is a fallacy. Read for its analytical power, the intricacy and self-consciousness of women's poetry become almost self-evident. It will take some time for this work to become fully visible, and this may justify a one-sided study of women's poetry in isolation from male poetry. The next step will be to look at the interaction of the two—but let us postpone this until women's work is known better.

Susan Wolfson

Gendering the Soul

*I do not mean it an injury to women, when I say there is sort of Sex in Souls . . .
the Soul of a man, and that of a Woman, are made very unlike . . . . The virtues have
respectively a masculine and a feminine cast.*—The Tatler, *1710*

*Souls are of no sex, any more than wit, genius, or any other of the intellectual
faculties . . . . the soul may have as fair and ample a chamber in the brain of a woman
as of a man.*—Biographium Fæmineum, *1766*

*I have been led to imagine that the few extraordinary women who have rushed in
eccentric directions out of the orbit prescribed to their sex, were* male *spirits,
confined by mistake in female frames. But [is it] philosophical to think of sex when
the soul is mentioned [?] . . . the love of pleasure may be said to govern [the lives of
most women]; does this prove that there is a sex in souls?*—Wollstonecraft,
A Vindication of the Rights of Woman, *1792*

*Is it true what is so constantly affirmed, that there is no Sex in Souls?—I doubt it—
I doubt it exceedingly.*—Coleridge, Notebooks, *1808–1819*

*I would hazard the impeachment of heresy, rather than abandon my belief that
there is a sex in our* SOULS *as well as in their perishable garments: and he who does
not feel it, never truly loved a Sister—nay, is not capable even of loving a Wife as she
deserves to be loved, if she indeed be worthy of that holy name.*
—Coleridge, Letter [to a Lady], The Friend, *7 December 1809*[1]

I: Sex in Souls and the Gender of the Soul

So repeatedly does *A Vindication of the Rights of Woman* refer to a
notion of soul that is not sex-differentiated that it seems to authorize its
case on this ground alone. "Surely," insists Wollstonecraft, "she has not
an immortal soul who can loiter life away merely employed to adorn her
person, that she may amuse the languid hours" of any man whose

"serious business of life is over" (29). She herself expresses gratitude "to that Being who impressed . . . on my soul" the falsity of giving "a sex to morals" that would authorize different standards of behavior for men and women (36). For "if the dignity of the female soul be as disputable as that of animals," she proposes to any potential antagonist, then women "are surely of all creatures the most miserable" (45; cf. 63). In light of Coleridge's esteem in modern feminist criticism for speculating that "a great mind must be androgynous," it may seem an easy transition from Wollstonecraft's rationalist brief for the moral equality of men's and women's souls to the Romantic-Coleridgean liberalism of a double-sexed genius. Yet Coleridge's textual site reveals that he was thinking only of male minds with feminine qualities; in other texts, we find him rather less sanguine about the invasion of male political and aesthetic territory by actual women.[2] And (as my epigraphs show) unlike Wollstonecraft, he eagerly insisted on the sex of souls.

Sexing of soul for Romantic men was critical in the poetics of inspiration, for the master trope was the analogy of creation with a female muse, and the implicit ideological alliance was with a long-standing "masculinist" tradition of appropriating and subordinating the feminine.[3] Yet the tradition in Romanticism is hardly stable, and this essay will show the consequences—first by reading some (perhaps familiar) soul stories in key male-authored texts and then by investigating the poetics of gender in some (perhaps unfamiliar) soul stories by two women, Maria Jane Jewsbury and Felicia Hemans. The ideological value of telling such a story is evident enough in Wollstonecraft's concern to argue for the rights of woman through reference to, or what amounts to a polemical construction of, the female soul. For all its trascendental reference, the idea of "soul" had substational sociohistorical resonance. Quaint as this term may seem today, it saturated the cultural languages of the Romantic age and was vitally theoretical for its writers. As such, it offers us a historically situated discourse through which to negotiate our present concerns with gender and Romanticism. Moreover, as Wollstonecraft's conversation with tradition demonstrates, its discourse involves the composite text of men's and women's writing; thus, it is the field that most forcefully reveals how the terms of sexual difference matter, both in individual perception and in reflections of cultural values. As we shall see, gendering the soul is vexed on both sides of the divide. Romantic men write stories that contend with uneasy sensations of their souls being or becoming feminine, the difference of gender often naming a decentered power and so bearing important questions about male poetic authority. And Romantic women, as eager as Wollstonecraft was to claim a dignity of soul that the central literary and cultural tradition has reserved for men, do not find easy ways to address this tradition or to imagine enabling alternatives.

I want to return briefly to Coleridge's remarks on the question because some contradictions in his theorizing of sex in souls will alert us to important dilemmas, both in canonical Romantic poetry about the soul and, not coincidentally, in the (not always coherent) critiques emerging in women's texts. Coleridge's idea of sex in souls is involved in a comprehensive theory about what drives creative desire. Noting that "in her homely way the Body tries to interpret all the movements of the Soul" (for example, in the sign of tears or a quickened pulse), he wonders about the strongest of the body's desires, its "yearning to compleat itself by Union." This is what moves him to ask, "Is there not a Sex in Souls?" and to elaborate:

We have all eyes, Cheeks, Lips—but in a lovely woman are not the eyes womanly—yea, every form, every motion, of her whole frame *womanly*? Were there not an Identity in the Substance, man & woman might *join*, but they could never *unify*—were there not throughout, in body & in soul, a corresponding and adapted Difference, there might be addition, but there could be no combination. One *and one* = 2; but one cannot be multiplied into one. $1 \times 1 = 1$—At best, it would be an idle echo, the same thing needlessly repeated—[4]

His conviction is such that he is willing to project the impression of the sexed soul beyond the contours of anatomy into an aura or affect, what may command description as *womanly*, even in features not only common to both sexes but susceptible to androgynous impression—eyes, cheeks, lips.[5] This reading of non-sex-specific features as reflections of a sexed soul is radical in implication. If one tradition of metaphysics opposes soul to body and designates a categorical difference, Coleridge's desire-based theory treats soul as an agent of body, part of the same continuum of identity.

Union of difference is a Coleridgean signature, most famously inscribed in the theory of "poetic Imagination" elaborated in chapter 14 of *Biographia*: this is a "power" that works a "balance or reconciliation of opposite or discordant qualities" (2:16–17). For this generative interaction of difference, the most appropriate metaphor may be the naturally given (and guaranteed) ground of sexual difference.[6] But something else is at work in the text that Coleridge summons to gloss this process. Slightly misquoted from Davies, it gives a story of the soul that is gendered rather than sexed:

> she turns
> Bodies to spirit by sublimation strange,
> As fire converts to fire the things it burns,
> As we our food into our nature change.
>
> From their gross matter she abstracts their forms,
> And draws a kind of quintessence from things;
> Which to her proper nature she transforms
> To bear them light, on her celestial wings.
>
> This does she, when from individual states
> She doth abstract the universal kinds . . . [7]

Measured by the analogy of "Imagination," this is a feminine soul with a difference. The process described in these lines is not a uniting of equal poles, a wedding of "Feminineness" and "Masculineness" at points where they "are one in spirit, a unity in duplicity" (so Coleridge sketches one abstract of sex and souls in his notebooks [3:3308]). Davies's female soul has no such equivalence; it is a subordinate agent of a general metaphysics that, following his subtitle, creates *the Soule of Man*. The she-soul, and implicitly its service to the Coleridgean scheme of "Imagination," is that of a secondary medium.

Coleridge's conscription of this hierarchical gendering is in conflict with his idea of sex in souls. If he proposes sexual difference to explain the creative desire of equal opposites, he tends to deploy the language of gender, as in the lines he quotes from Davies, in tandem with unequal distributions of function and privilege. Even when he is theorizing sex in souls, this contradiction may appear. Recall the image he uses in the letter of 12 March 1811 to set the stage for his theory, "in *her* homely way the Body," which both casts body as categorically feminine and situates it as the lower expression of higher force. The "Impression" of its energy, Coleridge writes, is analogous to all "such embodi[ments] of earthly nature" by which "Divinity . . . declares *his* presence" (3:305; my emphasis). In the verse he quotes from Davies, the feminine graduates to "soul," but (to indulge a Coleridgism) this is a distinction without a difference; for like the she-body of the letter, this she-soul lacks elevation. It remains in a lower-order function, busily sublimating, abstracting, and transforming in behalf of "the Soule of *Man*"—a genitive that, with its female servant, seems more specifically gendered than general.

What Coleridge's texts show us is that sex in souls and gendering the soul are different, often contradictory, matters. This ambivalence—experienced both psychologically and as cultural logic—informs some key but hardly stable or coherent soul-stories in Romantic writing. In male-authored texts, gendering the soul as feminine is endorsed by classical paradigms and the linguistic precedent of the feminine *anima* of Latin. Yet the enactments are tensed in ways that have not received adequate attention in some of the more programmatic arguments about Romanticism and gender.[8] For women writers, moreover, the sexed soul is inherently unstable. Their texts both disclose the contradictions of gendered definitions and reflect the ambivalence of their own desires. Must women regard their intellectual souls as Wollstonecraft is tempted to do, as "*male* spirits, confined by mistake in female frames," and so wrestle with the burden of this contradiction and alienation? Or does alienation offer a position from which to query the very idea of a determining sexual identity in the soul? To get to these questions, we need first to assess the pressures of the feminine registered in, but not always contained by, the soul-stories of Romantic men.

II: Romantic Men and Stories of the Soul

Wordsworth may voice a modern poetics in the "Prospectus" to *The Excursion*; but he proves classical when he writes "the Soul" as a female figure, "an impulse to herself" to be courted for his "spousal verse" (2:37, l. 12).[9] Keats tests a similar arrangement when he conceives a courtship between Cupid and his Psyche true. That both of these works, however, remain scenes of courtship that stop short of the consummation devoutly to be wished suggests that the difference of gender may be generating another script: for a male poet to call his soul feminine or to imagine it embodied in female form, especially at moments of creative crisis, may be to expose his latent apprehension of the fundamental alienation and otherness of his poetic power. The ambiguity of these courtship scenes is intensified for Wordsworth by the critical statements of his autobiography, which represent a self emboldened to claim possession of its soul:

> I was lost as in a cloud,
> Halted without a struggle to break through,
> And now recovering to my Soul I say
> I recognize thy glory. (6.529–32)

> I stand now,
> A sensitive and a creative soul. (11.256–57)

At the close of *The Prelude*, this rhetoric is emphatically gendered: a feminine soul, whether figured as part of the poet's own sensibility or as its nurturer, exists but to influence and serve the masculine creative power. The "Sister of my Soul," the poet gratefully acknowledges, has helped him rise "up to the height of feeling intellect" (13.204–11).[10]

These summary distributions of gender and power are interesting in this story not so much for their orthodoxy as for their entailment by less certain economies. In one stage of revising the passage from book 6 quoted above, for instance, Wordsworth had named the imagination, in its moment of loss and confusion, as unfathered and feminine: "Imagination! . . . Like an unfather'd vapour . . . in the might of her endowments came / Athwart me; I was lost as in a cloud" (C-stage, 602–607). This fleeting inscription of a feminine imagination at a moment of loss casts a revealing light on the struggle Wordsworth recounts in the first half of book 1 to get his poem going. This is a struggle, in many aspects, to claim the soul; and on its success, the epic-minded poet is all too aware, depends proof of his "manhood now mature" (653). Noticeably absent in this phase are the confident soul-genderings of book 13—not only the empowered masculine soul that claims to be the "genuine Counterpart / And Brother of the glorious faculty / Which higher minds bear with them as their own" (88–90) but also the female soul securely subordinate to this fraternal glory. Indeed, in book 1, Wordsworth repeatedly figures his *own* mind and soul as feminine, and more seems at stake in such figures than a potential marriage plot of self-consummating spousal verse. Unable to perform the honorable toil of a major poetic project and so risk default in his claim to manhood, he casts his frustration as an impotent feminine soul—the difference of gender conveying a sense both of otherness in this incapacity and of alienation from its remedy:

> my soul
> Did once more make trial of her strength
> Restored to her afresh; nor did she want
> Eolian visitations; but the harp
> Was soon defrauded. (1.102–6)

This impotence seems to conspire with a mind that cannot find its focus, also feminized.

> if my mind,
> Remembering the sweet promise of the past,
> Would gladly grapple with some noble theme,
> Vain is her wish; where'er she turns she finds
> Impediments from day to day renew'd. (1.138–42)

The thwarting of heroic enterprise—trial, strength, noble grappling, all subverted, fumbled, and betrayed—receives a gender-specific staging: a would-be he-poet caught in toils so inimical to his sense of promise as to compel an alien, feminine gendering.

Wordsworth would later revise the mirror of betrayal, here called "the sweet promise of the past," to "bold promise" (D:1.128)—the new adjective implying a latency tuned to emergence.[11] This revisionary plot opens, in fact, by recasting feminine weakness into legends of masculine distress: "The Poet, gentle creature as he is, / Hath, like the Lover, his unruly times; / His fits" (AB:1.146–48). Yet masculinizing these strange fits does not settle the question of gender, for as this poet elaborates their pathology, the feminized mind returns, its tenacious presence apprehended in instabilities and mysterious urgencies:

> The meditative mind, best pleased, perhaps,
> While she, as duteous as the Mother Dove,
> Sits brooding, lives not always to that end
> But hath less quiet instincts, goadings-on
> That drive her, as in trouble, through the groves.
> With me is now such passion, which I blame
> No otherwise than as it lasts too long.
> When, as becomes a man who would prepare
> For such a glorious work . . . (1.151–59)

At this phase of the report, the brooding of the feminine mind is partly excused by its relative and transient authority in the tale of a man's preparation for glorious work and partly redeemed by its evocation of the figure on whom Milton calls at the start of *Paradise Lost*, the "Heav'nly Muse" that "with mighty wings outspread / Dove-like sat[] brooding on the vast Abyss / And mad[e] it pregnant" (1.6, 20–22).[12]

But only partly. The implicit urgency of such masculine containments becomes explicit at the end of the poem, as Wordsworth draws an image of his mind in lines that simultaneously demote the feminine and transfer the trope of incubation, brooding, to the endeavors of the male "Poetic" soul. The feminine soul itself gets pastoralized and, within this mode, maternalized. Both gestures sentimentalize its claims out of the epic imperative: the "blissful" pair of "the Lamb / And the Lamb's Mother" evokes one kind of love, the poet admits (13:155–60) but not without adding that this love is "human merely." It is to a "higher" or "divine" kind of love—a "love that comes into the heart / With awe and a diffusive sentiment"—that he weds his "brooding," poetic "Soul" (161–65). "This love more intellectual" ("spiritual," by the D text [188]), he explains, needs a "moving soul" of "Imagination," which is a repository of

> absolute strength
> And clearest insight, amplitude of mind,
> And reason in her most exalted mood.
> This faculty hath long been the moving soul
> Of our long labour.(13.166–71)

Yet even as these lines recast the agitations imaged in the anxiously brooding female dove of book 1, they retain a trace of this initial gendering; in the domain of higher love abides a quality of mind cast as the feminine divine—reason in *her* most exalted mood.

How do we read this language? This is partly traditional (Latin) gendering, refreshed for Romanticism by the Enlightenment ideology of *La Raison*, the icon of French Revolutionary philosophy; and for Wordsworth the male possession of this feminine sign is surely informed by the male domain of "Reason" in *Paradise Lost*. In this respect, the she-reason in Wordsworth's summary poetics of the soul seems a sign of the feminine integrated into masculine self-possession. Yet in the larger text of *The Prelude*, this gendering comes to seem the reflexive signature of a sensation of the soul possessed by powers that attenuate masculine self-possession, even, or especially, in its most exalted moods.[13] The question is quite urgent in book 1. Here Wordsworth tries to subsume his feminine-gendered agitation of mind into the "rigorous inquisition" becoming to any man in preparation for glorious work; but it is the language of trouble incorporated as feminine to which inquisition ultimately conducts. The poet finally admits to being "baffled" ("and plagued," adds the D text [257])

> by a mind that every hour
> Turns recreant to her task, takes heart again
> Then feels immediately some hollow thought
> Hang like an interdict upon her hopes. (1.260–63)

In a story dominated by these feminine actors, it seems almost inevitable that the famously desperate interruption—"Was it for this . . . ?" (1.272)—would turn away from the feminine and the present together and discover a retrospective soul-history involving a different organization of gender.

Wordsworth does not cancel this story of frustration; he makes it a pretext. Pivoted on the interruptive question, the turn to the past deposes the conspiracy of feminine soul and mind, the plague of his present-tense agony, with a narrative in which the soul operates as a transcendental, supernatural power, *un*gendered. What *is* gendered is the term of its nurturing. In the story that begins "Fair seed-time had my soul" (1.306), the feminine is effaced from the soul itself and assigned to a lower place and a role of service (albeit at times severe) to the "mind of man" (352): "Nature . . . when she would frame / A favor'd Being" (364–65). This is not to say that the poet's frame of argument contains what is then recollected. It is only, but critically, to observe that his narrative finds direction with a new mapping of gender.[14] Indeed, once the soul is defeminized, it enters the verse supercharged, boosted by a rhetoric that replaces its erstwhile description as wayward with the self-constituting trope of apostrophe—Wordsworth's most confident rhetoric of the soul throughout the poem: "Wisdom and Spirit of the Universe! / Thou Soul that art the Eternity of Thought!" (1.429–30).[15] In a further demotion of the politics of gender in this event, this "Soul" is soon authorized over she-nature: it is not "Nature" per se but the "Souls of lonely places" that minister to the boy (1.493–95) and that, by extension, are credited with engendering the "passions that build up our human Soul" (435). Wordsworth amplifies this confidence in book 2 with a restored language of gender and the soul. He subordinates the feminine, telling us that he "receiv'd" much "[f]rom Nature and her overflowing soul" (2.416), so much that a revision records this debt as due to "Nature overflowing in my soul" (D: 2.397). And this egocentricity stakes out a nascent masculine independence: "by the regular action of the world / My soul was unsubdu'd" (2.380–81).

Yet notwithstanding this claim, the overflow of the feminine thus admitted and seemingly mastered traces another course in book 2, one not secondary but foundational to Wordsworth's psychobiography: the dyad of the infant and the maternal soul. One of the "best conjectures" the autobiographer can pose to "trace / The progress of our being" is that of the "Bless'd . . . infant Babe" whose "soul / Claims manifest kindred with an earthly soul" in the passion of "his Mother's eye!" (2.237–43). If this kindred bond of souls is the cherished point of origin in the poet's history, it also predicts the vexations of the poem's present composition. We are told that the Mother's soul nurtured the infant masculine soul with "most apprehensive habitude" (256), yet the next time the word *soul* appears in book 2, something more than nurture seems to have taken hold. Wordsworth's mother died when he was a boy, but a kindred maternal soul persists in consciousness to feminize his soul. "I was left alone, / Seeking the visible world, nor knowing why" (2.292–93), he recalls, adding that this seeking was answered by sensations of ghostly maternal nurture: "Thence did I drink the visionary power" (2.330), he muses, moving into the present tense to theorize that in such fleeting moods of solitary rapture,

> the soul,
> Remembering how she felt, but what she felt
> Remembering not, retains an obscure sense
> Of possible sublimity, to which,
> With growing faculties she doth aspire,
> With faculties still growing, feeling still
> That, whatsoever point they gain, they still
> Have something to pursue. (2.334–41)

In this pursuit, the very soul is feminine, and this gendering haunts kindred sensations of a self "strengthen'd with a superadded soul, / A virtue not its own" (2.347–48).

In a radical effort to stabilize this decentered psychic economy, Shelley has the poet-hero of *Alastor* spurn the natural and, in this poem, an always feminine-inscribed world, rejecting its macrodomestic sphere to pursue a seemingly antithetical, epipsychic visionary feminine. Yet the larger plot of *Alastor* is to condemn all of these versions of the feminine, using the gender to sum the site of every frustrated desire and every false hope—and every enslavement of masculine independence. True slavery, declares the visionary orator of *The Mask of Anarchy*, is that of the spirit. The politics of this view may be questionable, but its metaphysics— especially in such male-enacted quest romances as *Alastor* and *Epipsychidion*—are emphatic. Shelley's visionary politics can imagine no fate worse than spiritual self-possession:

> to be a slave in soul
> And to hold no strong controul
> Over your own wills, but be
> All that others make of ye. (184–87)[16]

In *Alastor*, this soul slavery is staged as a psychomachia in which the role of "others" is played, variously but with sinister cooperation, by the feminine.

An early symptom is the poet's invocation of a masculine audience— "Earth, ocean, air, beloved brotherhood!" (1)—which abides as his cherished fidelity. Yet when he goes on to say that his soul is bonded to this "beloved brethren" (16) by "our great Mother," the feminine bears uncertain debts into this family romance: is it a secondary agent of brotherly love and communion, or does it name a primary dependency?[17] The issue stirs as a hesitation in the fuller syntax of the opening exhortation:

> *If* our great Mother has imbued my soul
> With aught of natural piety to feel
> Your love, and recompense the boon with mine . . . (2–4, my emphasis)

This *if* is further troubled by its patent echo of the equally tentative syntax of the epigraph Wordsworth had recently affixed to the "Intimations" ode: "And I could wish my days to be / Bound each to each by natural piety"—a text that serves to preface a male soul history in which a feminine-gendered earth, acting "with something of a Mother's mind," weakens the bond of the growing boy to the imperial origin and true "home" of his "Soul."[18]

What Shelley's *if* and the Wordsworthian reference bear into *Alastor* is a tenacious question about what, exactly, gender may signify in the story of the soul. The reflex of this question soon presses the feminine into an image of inaccessible mystery, a natural world that is the enemy of transcendence and poetic power alike:

> Mother of this unfathomable world!
> Favour my solemn song, for I have loved
> Thee ever, and thee only; I have watched
> Thy shadow, and the darkness of thy steps,
> And my heart ever gazes on the depth
> Of thy deep mysteries. (18–23)

Feminist film criticism tells us that the gaze is an erotic bearer of male power.[19] If so, these lines can only expose default. The previously tendered "natural piety," in which a maternal feminine "imbue[s]" the soul of a brotherhood, now mirrors a knowledge withheld. A shadowy mother, associated with "black death" (24), at once possesses and refuses to "render up the tale / Of what we are" (28–29). By gendering this secret as feminine, Shelley signifies both its otherness to masculine consciousness and, by force of its maternal site, its vital necessity. This compound gives the petition an increasing urgency in both tone and terms, with the poet waiting for "breath" to imbue the "strain" that will "modulate with" the beloved brotherhood of nature, poetry ("the tale"), and "the deep heart of man" (44–49). By the end of the petition, the addressee is a neutrally gendered "Great Parent," but the evasion of the feminine debt represses rather than resolves the question of power in gender difference. The status of the poet's ensuing tale of his brother "Poet" extends this indeterminacy, for its rhetorical status is never clear: is it a record of the Mother's answer to him, or is it his reaction to her silence? The poem's language of gender remains entailed in these initial perplexities, first projecting the feminine as the answerer to masculine soul, then avenging frustration by gendering its cause as feminine and emptying it of value.

Indeed, these gestures are not so much sequential as always implicit and implicated. The internal tale begins with an image of its ideal "Poet" removed from the domain of the feminine. At his death, we are told, "no mourning maiden" decked his grave, while in life, such maids were present merely to reflect his surpassing mystery: he takes no heed of the "virgins" who "have pined / And wasted for fond love of his wild eyes" (62–63). Yet contending with this transcendence are Shelley's several figures of this Poet effeminized in the toils of visionary desire. A preliminary symptom is this small embellishment:

> the wild antelope, that starts whene'er
> The dry leaf rustles in the brake [would] suspend
> Her timid steps to gaze upon a form
> More graceful than her own. (103–6)

This scene not only resists but strikingly inverts the empowered scheme of male agency and female objectification in theories of the "gaze." Such inversion is soon repeated in the scene of the enamored Arab maiden's vigil, underscored by its situation in a script seemingly tuned to the Poet's masculine priority: Although this maiden is so utterly devoted to the Poet that she steals from "her father's tent" (130) to supply his comfort—an implicit oedipal victory—such victory is completely revoked in the image of the Poet as the hyperpassive object of a female gaze, whose enamored regard is nothing if not infantilizing:

> [she] watched his nightly sleep,
> Sleepless herself, to gaze upon his lips
> Parted in slumber, when the regular breath
> Of innocent dreams arose. (134–37)

That she gains no power from this gaze—she remains "wildered, and wan, and panting" in unrequited desire (140)—even prefeminizes the Poet in the poem's narrative trajectory, for he too will soon find himself wildered, "wan," and panting (200 ff.).

This feminine-troped plight is the consequence of the pivotal episode of the soul in this tale, the Poet's "vision" of "a veiled maid" (149 ff.), a transsexual embodiment of the soul that appears (as) an epipsychic ideal. Yet the mirroring syntax of the episode's first line, as well as the very event of a dream, also shimmer with narcissism:

> Her voice was like the voice of his own soul
> Heard in the calm of thought; its music long,
> Like woven sounds of streams and breezes, held
> His inmost sense suspended in its web
> Of many-coloured woof and shifting hues. (153–57)

In this intensified reflection, the syntax of two genders, as in Coleridge's sexing of souls, operates as a critical, saving grace. For against the self-reflecting soul music, wherein the maid not only speaks "thoughts most dear to" the Poet but is "herself a poet" (160–61), Shelley deploys a differentiation into male and female as a way of arguing a potentially vain self-reflection into a trope of procreative desire.

This distinction is at best tenuous, and we need only summon the fragment On Love to see why. Here Shelley suggests that the object of love is "the ideal prototype of every thing excellent or lovely that we are capable of conceiving as belonging to the nature of man" (*SPP*, 473–74). This "conceiving" is not sexual but self-reproductive, and the corresponding politics of gender is not one of equals uniting but of masculine desire saving itself from narcissism with an idealizing feminine reflector, "a mirror whose surface reflects only the forms of purity and brightness: a soul within our soul" (ibid.). In *Prince Athanase* (whose spiritual poetics are analogous to *Alastor*'s), Shelley concedes that the visionary's inner vacancy renders him one who, with no other "near to love, // Loves then the shade of his own soul, half seen / In any mirror" (pt. 2, pp. 117–19).[20] It is only a slight Shelleyan shift from the idealism of *On Love* and the pathology of Athanase to the egocentric shades of the proposal, in the fragment *On Life*, that the existence of distinct individual minds might be found to be a "delusion," that the "words, *I, you, they*, are not signs of any actual difference . . . but are merely marks to denote different modifications of the one mind" (*SPP*, 477–78). Erase *one* and what emerges is a radically subjective idealism.

Swerving, and not entirely away, from these signs of no "actual difference," the Poet's dream in *Alastor* summons the necessarily differentiated "sex in souls" that Coleridge hypothesizes ("were there not . . . there might be addition, but there could be no combination"). In the visionary scheme of *Epipsychidion*, Shelley stresses the trope of self and other with a preposition and portentous title: desire is now focused on a "soul *out of* my soul" (238, my emphasis).[21] Yet the question of whether the mirror is self or other, creative difference or sterile narcissism, is the perpetual ambivalence of Shelley's psycho-metaphysics. The ideal of exogamous spiritual union implied by the poem's title competes with the intensified sameness in the poet's designation of soul-spouse as soul-sister. "Spouse! Sister!" he invokes his desire (130), and he later imagines the paradise into which he invites her in a similar conflation: it harbors a pleasure house reared by "[s]ome wise and tender Ocean-King" and "[m]ade sacred" to the woman who is "his sister and his spouse" (489–92).

Yet nothing more reflects Shelley's uncertainty about the work of gender in securing a productive view of visionary desire than the way, in both poems, this scheme is betrayed into vacancy. In *Epipsychidion*, the crucial phrase "this soul out of my soul" does not occur in a syntax of possession but occupies a complaint of absence: "Whither 'twas fled, this soul out of my soul." In *Alastor*, the wanderer's path is one of "[f]ollowing his eager soul" (311), as if his soul were always and irrevocably out of, decentered from, the self—a chimera beyond possession. It is only in idealizing imagination, Shelley concedes in *Epipsychidion*'s thesis of the soul, that two become one, that the soul out of the soul may enter an "antenatal dream" of a "unison" "[w]hich is a soul within the soul" (454–56). He intensifies this vision with a site of delicious enclosure in the very "heart" of which, "like a buried lamp, a Soul no less / Burns" (477–78), anticipating an immortality of soul and epipsyche as "[t]he living soul of this Elysian isle, / Conscious, inseparable, one" (538–40). Yet as his story makes desperately clear, such desire is pressured by an opposite consciousness of wide separation and division, for which the gendering and ultimately the splitting of the soul become an ironically treacherous trope:

> neither prayer nor verse could dissipate
> The night which closed on her; nor uncreate
> That world within this Chaos, mine and me,
> Of which she was the veiled Divinity,
> The world I say of thoughts that worshipped her. (241–45)

Even as the poet would claim a female soul as its epipsyche in a self-created world of "mine and me," the difference attendant on gendering always threatens to shade into duality.

Both here and in *Alastor*, a veiled feminine bears these shades, posing an object of erotic desire inextricable from its impending evanishment—a refiguring in narrative terms of the "chasm of an insufficient void" in the desiring subject that Shelley recognizes as love's very motivation (*On Love, SPP*, 473). In *Epipsychidion*, a sensation of this insufficiency infects poetic capacity itself, a fate voiced in the poet's complaint,

> The winged words on which my soul would pierce
> Into the heights of love's rare Universe,
> Are chains of lead around its flight of fire. (588–90)

To the singular soul betrayed to words of lead, the figure of a female epipsyche operates ultimately to focus and generate a tormenting despair.

It is a short step from this frustration to resentful antagonism, and this is the larger plot of *Alastor*. Its prefiguration is the rhetoric that enwraps the veiled maiden. First, there is the double reference of the similes for her voice: "*like* the voice of his own soul . . . its music long, / *Like* woven sounds of streams and breezes" (153–55; my emphasis). As the Poet apprehends his soul in a feminine form, this doubleness becomes subversive: her voice may be like "his own," but its tones are also like the incommunicable sounds of nature. The alluring likeness of a female voice blends into a "strange symphony" of alien affiliation with the Mother-world of nature's "woven sounds." Even in the moment of epiphany, textual and erotic at once, this alienation prevails. If "the solemn mood /

Of [the maid's] pure mind kindled though all her frame" with such intensity that the blood in the "branching veins" of her "fair hands" seemed "eloquent," the text remains "an ineffable tale" (161–68). Not an access to what the Great Mother withholds, the dream of the female soul repeats a frustration. Another aspect of this female embodiment, moreover, yields an image that is implicitly unmanning: the dream maid's "parted lips" (179), promising the knowledge and truth that the Poet seeks, bears a treacherous genealogy in his story, for it refigures in female form his own "lips / Parted" in the infantine and unresponding slumber upon which the Arab maid gazes.

Of these textual blurrings of the masculine integrity of the Poet's soul, the most visible is Shelley's representation of the Poet's erotic union with his dream-maiden as a motion of her folding "his frame in her dissolving arms" (187): the double grammar makes the participle adjective describing her transience simultaneously a participle verb reporting the effect on the man enamored of her. The "dark flood" that takes possession of the Poet's vacant brain in consequence not only ruptures the promise of feminine nurture that opened the poem but accelerates a progressive confusion of the poem's ideology of gender. Awakening in a newly vacant nature, the Poet cannot hereafter distinguish spiritual yearning from fatal enchantment:

> One darkest glen
> Sends from its woods of musk-rose, twined with jasmine,
> A soul-dissolving odour, to invite
> To some more lovely mystery. Through the dell,
> Silence and Twilight here, twin-sisters, keep
> Their noonday watch. (451–56)

Dissolving and decentering the soul is now nature's work as well, whose sister agents keep what amounts to a death watch over the Poet's desire:

> Obedient to the light
> That shone within his soul, he went, pursuing
> The windings of the dell. (492–94)

The origin of this light—external and illuminating his soul within or internal and mistaken for external?—is the same ambiguity that haunts the metaphysics of the Shelleyan "epipsyche": a revelation of soul out of the soul, or a soul projected by inner lack?

This uncertainty shades the last light, and sight, of the Poet's quest, and the fact that its presider is feminine underscores the scheme against masculine self-knowledge:

> his last sight
> Was the great moon, which o'er the western line
> Of the wide world her mighty horn suspended,
> With whose dun beams inwoven darkness seemed
> To mingle. (645–49)

The she-moon that finally claims dominion over the male poetic soul
tightens the web of pernicious repetitions whereby the masculine gaze is
rendered impotent, a passive witness of its extinction. As this wanderer
"resign[s] his high and holy soul / To images of the majestic past, / That
paused within his passive being" (628–30), the masculine gender becomes the name of defeat: "Ruin calls his brother Death" (618–19).

In this fatal ascendency of the feminine, the moon goddess's inwoven
darkness recalls and darkly embodies the power of the veiled dream
maiden. One of the most telling images of this fatality is the epic simile
that Shelley writes to describe the Poet's restless night wanderings across
a world resonant only with her absence:

> While day-light held
> The sky, the Poet kept mute conference
> With his still soul. At night the passion came,
> Like the fierce fiend of a distempered dream,
> And shook him from his rest, and led him forth
> Into the darkness.—As an eagle grasped
> In folds of the green serpent, feels her breast
> Burn with the poison, and precipitates
> Through night and day, tempest, and calm, and cloud,
> Frantic with dizying anguish, her blind flight
> O'er the wide aëry wilderness: thus driven
> By the bright shadow of that lovely dream,
> Beneath the cold glare of the desolate night,
> Through tangled swamps and deep precipitous dells,
> Startling with careless step the moon-light snake,
> He fled. (222–37)

The epic simile that begins "As an eagle grasped" unfolds a potent
grammar of reversed expectations. Assisted by the line break, its syntax
momentarily poses "eagle" as a subject and "grasped" as its predicate
with an impending direct object: we expect to read of a Poet's passion,
even as it takes control of him, having the heroic stature of a struggling
eagle. Yet in a wicked turn of the line, Shelley reveals that this eagle is not
grasping, but is grasped by a stronger force—a green serpent—that turns
out, in the analogy, to gloss the fierce fiend in possession of the poet's
soul. This syntactic reversal, moreover, involves a crucial reversal of
gender: the helplessly victimized she-eagle is a negative comparison to

what readers would recognize as the famous icon of Napoleonic triumph.[22]

To cast a Poet's possessed soul as a figure of female torment in a ravage of an erstwhile masculine potency is to admit a radical decentering of self and gender, one in which female nature comes to dominate. It is no coincidence that *Alastor*'s final stanza begins not by petitioning the Mother who imbues the poet's soul with natural piety but with a call for Medea's "wondrous alchemy" to revive the dead Poet. Here, for one last time, the feminine is appealed to as a principle of renewed male life. Yet to summon Medea is to overload the case. Shelley's overt allusion is to the account in Ovid's *Metamorphoses* in which her alchemy restores Jason's father, the aged Aeson, to manly vigor. But since Medea is most famous for her unnatural infanticide, the total precedent for the poet of *Alastor*, who has called himself a son of a Mother Nature, is none too reassuring. The deep logic is to herald a poetics of exhaustion in which the tale of the masculine soul, now summed as "some surpassing Spirit" (714) and embodied in the "fled" figure of the Poet, is consummated in a release from the feminine. Indeed, the ultimate business of *Alastor* is to empty anything gendered as feminine of value—or to put this another way, to gender as feminine anything whose value is ultimately to be denied. All that is left in a world "reft at once" of its questing masculine soul is the empty domain of the feminine: "Nature's vast frame, the web of human things, / Birth and the grave, that are not as they were" (719–20).

There is a positive result to this hollowing out, however, and this is to confirm a purely spiritual bonding among men, now a brethren of poets and Poet. If in *Queen Mab*, Shelley links the feminine to ultimate determination—"Spirit of Nature! all-sufficing Power, / Necessity! thou mother of the world!" (6:197–98)—by *Alastor*, this alliance has undergone radical evaluation.[23] The frame poet leaves the brethren with a scene of Mother Nature as a text of spiritual despair and a desire that remains inscribed entirely by and for men: a dyad of a poet and his male "epipsyche," the lost "Poet."[24] *Alastor* closes in this solidarity of masculine spirits with one another and against all powers gendered, in protective anticipation, as feminine.

Keats's soul-stories are alert both to the Shelleyan poetics of evanishment and to the regressive desire that courts such consequence—a desire, as "I stood tip-toe" puts it, to lose "the soul . . . in pleasant smotherings."[25] Yet *Endymion*, despite its neoplatonic "corrective" to the dualism of *Alastor*, repeatedly courts Shelley's scenario of dissolution. Dream-raptured with the moon, the hero reports that "she did soar / So passion-

ately bright, my dazzled soul / Commingling with her argent spheres did
roll" (1.593–95); betrayed to a waking world, he feels its elements
"mission'd to knit / My soul with under-darkness" (701–702). From
beginning to end, his soul is dedicated to the feminine, in the shape of
deities or mortals or of both. To prevent the perpetual repetition of such
surrender, even so pleasurably, Keats intuitively reviews the role of genre
in the genders of soul lost and found. In "Ode to Psyche," the very primer
of the story, he declines the Shelleyan narrative form that underwrites
and potentially solicits trajectories of pursuit and loss and writes in a
genre that risks no more than enthusiastic petition. Its agenda of courtship is deliberately liminal: evoking the Coleridgean idea of sexed souls,
the poet invites a feminine soul into his working brain, wherein it may be
seduced by masculine desire and made creative. The ode begins in deliberate caution, its petition at once expressing desire and parodying it with
affected urbanity:

> O Goddess! hear these tuneless numbers wrung,
>   By sweet enforcement and remembrance dear,
> And pardon that thy secrets should be sung
>   Even into thine own soft-conched ear. (1–4)

The petition soon evokes a displaced mirroring of two, of self and soul. A
"winged boy" (21) whom the poet claims already to know, as if recognizing a figure of his own desire, courts a female counterpart, a "winged
Psyche" (6) on the verge of being recognized, named, and claimed in one
ecstatic moment: "But who wast thou, O happy, happy dove? / His
Psyche true!" (22–23)

Keats's ode is less interested in this epiphany, however, than in speculating about the sort of creativity a female soul will engender. Morris
Dickstein may be right that its "allegorical meaning" is one in which
Psyche signifies more as "mind or soul than as beautiful girl."[26] Yet the
value of the sexual trope is clarified if we recall Keats's earlier, self-
involuted formulations of this process, wherein, for instance, he describes
reading and writing poetry as "the deed / That my own soul has to *itself*
decreed" (*Sleep and Poetry*, 97–98, my emphasis). By dividing and
arranging this self-stimulation as an encounter of different sexes, Keats
can imagine an access of creative and mental power on the analogy of
male erotic success, romancing the feminine in a script of masculine self-
empowerment. If, as Marjorie Levinson notes, Keatsian configurations of
inspiration tend to be *auto*erotic,[27] Keats's heterosexing of the situation
may indicate an alertly anticipatory self-defense. Such motivation seems
patent in the famous letter he wrote a year before this ode to a female
Psyche, with his vocation still uncertain. Here he images the awakening

mind as a liminal feminine space, a "Chamber of Maiden-Thought," that is fated to open into dark passages as it experiences life in the world. Keats conceives of this as a masculine progress, with "Maiden-Thought" regendered as it matures: "the thinking principle," he says, "is father of . . . sharpening one's vision into the heart and nature of Man."[28] "Maiden-Thought," to trope Wordsworth's lineage for the progress of the soul, is father to the "Man."

The gendering of ignorance as a feminine phase of thought in the plot of masculine life configures the last stanza of "Ode to Psyche," where the feminine soul is imaged in a map of impending darker knowledge. The total articulation is one of delicate but profound ambivalence. On the one hand, the stanza drives toward a conclusion of rapturously imagined erotic union: Psyche's chamber in the mind holds "A bright torch, and a casement ope at night, / To let the warm Love in!" (66–67). On the other hand, Keats embeds his scene in a wide "untrodden region of [the] mind" (51), the world beyond the garden and fane into which Psyche is invited. Although cast "[f]ar, far around," this wider figuring is conveyed in terms that seem even vaguely hostile to the well-lit fane of the mind, for its survey is of dark passages, uncertain borders, unknown events,

> Where branched thoughts, new grown with pleasant pain,
>   Instead of pines shall murmur in the wind:
> Far, far around shall those dark-cluster'd trees
>   Fledge the wild-ridged mountains steep by steep. (52–55)

Thoughts grow by pain, and while this is called "pleasant," the echo of "grown" as "groan" makes this less than sure. In the terra incognita mapped by "shadowy thought" (65), moreover, the female psyche is not only a minor (though radiant) presence but is a weird prophet of her own transience. Winged Psyche has a ghostly double in the verb *fledge*, which images new thoughts as a surreal wilderness of disembodied pinions, a less easily contained soul of thought thriving in a world of darkness, density, and sheer space. No wonder that Keats would soon describe his poetry as "the verses of a half-fledged brain" (*LJK*, 2.130). And no wonder, too, that some later poems would attempt aggressive, though futile, containments, such as the desire Lycius expresses to Lamia—"to entangle, trammel up and snare / Your soul in mine, and labyrinth you there / Like the hid scent of an unbudded rose" (*Lamia*, 2.52–54). If this exposes a darker politics of gender in the caginess of Psyche, it is also, by Lycius's undoing, a fragile bravado.

The halt of "Ode to Psyche" before the anticipated union with the feminine soul spells Keats's apprehension about an energy of writing that

remains outside absolute and secure possession.[29] Indeed, Keatsian stories of courtship are either ones of such deferral or they tell of success
with a vengeance, as a feminine power lays devastating claim to the
masculine soul. As his romances of the soul become nervously alert to the
risk of self-loss, the female soul vanishes and is replaced by a femininized
threat to the masculine soul. "Ode on Melancholy" rejects the quiet
retreat of "Ode to Psyche" and urges a "wakeful anguish of the soul"
under the tutelage of the stern goddess "[v]eil'd Melancholy." The feminine here is not the innocent origin of a masculine psychogenesis but a
stern preceptor of its lapses and the ultimate term of its aesthetic self-
realization: "His soul shall taste the sadness of her might, / And be
among her cloudy trophies hung" (29–30). Purged of its aesthetic taste,
this mighty sadness produces Keats's fullest myth of soul and gender, "the
Vale of Soul-making" (*LJK*, 2.102 ff.). In this anti-Platonic, existential
allegory, the ultimate value of life in the world is "to school an Intelligence and make it a soul" by immersion in "a World of Pains." The
"Hornbook" of this school is the heart or, in a transformation into
feminine figuring, "the teat from which the Mind or intelligence sucks its
identity" to become a soul.

The erotic rhapsody of "Ode to Psyche" has vanished, and the feminine has transformed from a sign of innocent soul into a bearer of painful
knowledge. Keats's most desperate poetics of the soul, his late lyrics,
increasingly ally the female soul with pain, frustration, and a collapse of
self-possession in the masculine soul. He suspects that Fanny may not
"prize [his] subdued soul"—the word revised from his initial *heart* ("To
Fanny")—and begs her on another occasion, "O, let me once more rest /
My soul upon that dazzling breast!" ("What can I do . . . ?"). In "I cry
your mercy," the petition to this hyperinfused female object of desire—
"Oh let me have thee whole,—all,—all—be mine!"—plays the term of
plenitude, *whole*, into a muted internal rhyming with *soul* and subjects
this linking to an "all"-or-nothing result: "Yourself—your soul—in pity
give me all, / Withhold no atom's atom or I die." Projected by a sensation
of a radical absence in the man who desires her, the soul of a woman
assumes a vital power, but one that the scheme of gender makes as alien
as it is essential.[30]

III: Romantic Women and the Politics of Gender and Soul

All of these texts show Romantic men formulating a poetics of the soul
that is also a poetics of gender, in designs that are too often a palpable
design against women. So what happens when the writer is a woman?

One answer, which amounts to a sustained display of ideological tensions and contradictions, appears in Maria Jane Jewsbury's "History of an Enthusiast," an account of a young woman's thirst for artistic fame. Rejecting the culturally saturated advice that "the only celebrity that can increase a woman's happiness, is that which results from the esteem excited by her domestic virtues," Julia Osborne is convinced that "Fame . . . would make amends for being a woman—I should not pass away and perish" (25–26). How this involves her soul is spelled out by Jewsbury's epigraph for chapter 5, a verse credited to "Professor Wilson":[31]

> As far as human soul may be let loose
> From impositions of necessity,—
> Forgetting oft, in self-willed fancy's flight,
> All human ties that would enchain her dreams
> Down to a homelier bliss; and loving more
> The dim aerial shadow of this life,
> Even than the substance of the life itself. (p. 43)

In this image of necessity, not only is this errant, "self-willed" soul gendered feminine, but the gendering is reinforced by the fact that its necessary enchainment is to the sentimentalized place that culture has assigned to women, home.

Jewsbury's tale of restless female enthusiasm shifts the professor's traditional wisdom into a new perspective. The chapter headed by the lines above concludes with Julia yearning to be kindled with "boundless, glorious energy" and dedicating herself to artistic "Fame" as the only possible embodiment of such energy (47). Eventually, she writes a satiric poem that frankly names home in all of its guises, "the present, new, and near," as "fetters to our souls" (149). To counter the cultural authority of the professor with another male poet, Jewsbury summons Percy Bysshe Shelley, though a Shelley converted to the uses of female enthusiasm. The texts that Jewsbury interpolates into her female history, that is, are not the ones that gender the soul but ones whose schemes are potentially available to or revisable for female interest.

One such text infuses the voice of Julia's early enthusiasm. When Cecil Percy, a friend from adolescence whom she is convinced she loves, tells her that the books she cherishes "will be productive of more loss than gain," she retorts with Asia's song at the close of act 2 of *Prometheus Unbound* (2.5.72–81, 88–90):

> "My soul is an enchanted boat,
> Which, like a sleeping swan, doth float
> Upon the silver waves of *their* sweet singing.
> And each doth like an angel sit

> Beside the helm conducting it,
> Whilst all the winds with melody are ringing.
> It seems to float, ever, for ever,
> Upon that many-winding river,
> Between mountains, woods, abysses,
> A paradise of wildernesses!
>
> . . . .
> And we sail on, away, afar,
> Without a cloud, without a star,
> But by the instinct of sweet music driven." (*History*, 59)

Julia's emphatic *their* shifts the reference of Asia's *thy*, a voice in the air, to the voices of her books, the feeders of her intellectual soul. Her rewording not only challenges the prescriptions for conduct that Cecil would impose upon her, it also revises Shelley's script for her own ends, namely, a story of female desire that is not subordinate to the urgencies of men in crisis.

We can see the force of this revision by recalling that in Shelley's scene, Asia's soul is tuned to a masculine theomachia; her celebratory song follows her interview of Demogorgon, in the previous scene, about Prometheus's fate.[32] To her urgent metaphysical and theological questions, Demogorgon has replied that "the deep truth is imageless" (2.4.116), and Asia begins to understand that she has to work out answers for herself. As a rhetorical image of this process, Shelley has her final question call on her own "soul" as her standard of trust:

> So much I asked before, and my heart gave
> The response thou hast given; and of such truths
> Each to itself must be the oracle.—
> One more demand . . . and do thou answer me
> As my own soul would answer, did it know
> That which I ask. (2.4.121–26)

In Asia's incipient dialogue of self and soul, Demogorgon's function is analogous to that of art itself, as theorized by Hemans in *The Restoration of the Works of Art to Italy*. The "might of Art," she proposes, is "[t]o bid the soul exultingly possess, / Of all her powers, a heightened consciousness."[33] For both Hemans (here, at least) and Shelley in *Prometheus Unbound*, the female soul is circumscribed by masculine culture and agenda. In Hemans's scene of the soul, "her powers" are indebted to male creation, "Raphael's pure and perfect line," and its male subject, the "heaven-illumined lineament" of "the Saviour's head." And Asia's questions concern Prometheus—"Prometheus shall arise / Henceforth the Sun of this rejoicing world: / When shall the destined hour arrive?" (2.4.126–28).

Jewsbury's history tacitly reconceives Asia's interview as a kind of interval for the female soul in this larger action and makes her song into a hymn of intellectual energy for Julia. It is not long after that Julia's diary records her "enchantment" at the thought of a "communion of spirit" with "a superior being . . . not so much stronger than myself, as wiser, better, gentler, graver; the idea that I may some time or other find such a being . . . seems to give my soul wings" (64). In relocating Asia's song in the history of a female enthusiast, Jewsbury revises what is culturally conservative in Shelley's visionary revolution: its distribution of aspiration and expectation along lines of male privilege. She similarly revises the Shelleyan language that she uses to describe Julia's enjoyment of the energies of her mind: "emparadised in dreams of intellectual beauty" (103). This evocation of "Hymn to Intellectual Beauty" is as important for its contextual revision as for its Shelleyan echo, for it makes the implicit argument (whatever the latent and later ironies for Julia of "emparadised in dreams") that there is a common intellectual soul in men and women and that in women's dreams this soul is drawn to the paradise of intellectual satisfaction denied to them by their material existence in this world.

As a term of intersexual provenance, "intellectual beauty" is particularly resonant, for it accrues value not only from Shelley but also from a female-authored work that he and Jewsbury knew well, Wollstonecraft's *Vindication*. Complaining that the "prevailing opinion of sexual character" does not allow "the soul of woman" to perfect itself "by the exercise of its own reason" (53), Wollstonecraft puts forth the notion of an "intellectual beauty" capable of inspiring in men something "more sublime" than the "sensual homage" paid to physical beauty (47). Beginning her treatise by urging opportunities for women to exercise "ambition and those nobler passions that open and enlarge the soul" (10), Wollstonecraft assumes a sexual equality, a claim for the "soul of woman" (53) that she sets corrosively against that "Mahometan strain" that would "deprive [women] of souls, and insinuate that we were beings only designed . . . to gratify the senses of man when he can no longer soar on the wing of contemplation." If women are allowed by Christian Providence "to have souls," she contends, then they should be "allowed to have sufficient strength of mind to acquire what really deserves the name of virtue" (19). Emphasizing her debt to this text, Jewsbury concludes her *History* with Julia speculating in similar terms about "soul of no sex— versatile powers" (144) and worrying her friends about the likely consequence of touring the Continent alone: "how excessively improper!— well, the reviewers will certainly leave off their compliments about her womanliness" and start regarding her as a "second Mary Wolstonecroft" (*sic*, 143). For inspiration in this adventure, Julia returns to the first feeders of her soul, her books, quoting on the last page "Ode to the West Wind" and, in effect, once again pointedly claiming Shelley's voice as her own: "O lift me as a wave, a leaf, a cloud; / I fall upon the thorns of life—I bleed; / A heavy weight of hours has chained and bowed / One too like thee, tameless, and swift, and proud" (160).

Although this exuberance occupies the last page of Jewsbury's *History*, the ideological restraints with which it contends are apparent enough in the internal economy of Julia's narrative. Before committing herself, not totally joyously, to her final adventure, Julia's life as a London celebrity so pales after five years that she feels the pull of conservative cultural prescriptions: "Ah, what is genius to woman, but a splendid misfortune! What is fame to woman, but a dazzling degradation" (112). This melancholy exacts a price on her soul: she laments the utter absence of any "child-like abandon of the soul to fresh and vigorous impulses" and is gripped by a "sense of present loneliness [that] paralyzes all the finer functions of the soul" (114–15). As if to confirm these sensations in social fate, Jewsbury plots her history to have Julia's enthusiasms alienate the man she secretly loves, Cecil Percy, losing him to a proper English wife. Even so, Jewsbury's ambivalence about this cultural wisdom troubles these conservative correctives in two ways. For one, and despite the regret she gives to Julia, she writes the character of Cecil to suggest that he is not much of a loss, never quite escaping the contour of a dull, conservative twit. A "cold and simple spirit . . . passionless," Julia herself describes him, even as she is excited by a visit from him in the midst of her jaded celebrity (117); he exposes himself as such in his pallid poetics of the soul, exhorting Julia to leave her life of "vanities" and enter "that solemn chamber of the soul wherein conscience sits enthroned as judge" (122). For another, Jewsbury closes Julia's *History* not with her enthusiast exposed and doomed as a figure of emptiness nor recuperated to domesticity but revitalized by a decision to leave England and travel on the Continent. If the female enthusiast's precise future is left untold, what is most evident in the close of her history is that England in the 1830s seems to have no place for such souls.[34]

As a woman of intellect and artistic fame, Hemans figures into Jewsbury's *History* as one of its models—or rather, two. She appears first as the transgressive, unfeminine girl reader of Shakespeare in the apple tree (11–12) and then as the voice of sentimental poetry (58, 86, 116).[35] This double figuration is a shrewd reading of Hemans, for like Jewsbury, her writing, despite its overt commitment to orthodox sentiments, takes on the question of sex in souls, especially to question the cultural norms for women. Hemans's sensitivity to constrictions and contradictions in these norms is compelling in light of her general adoration in Regency and high Victorian cultures as the soul of femininity. The terms are baldly stated in Francis Jeffrey's 1829 review: the natural concerns of women writers epitomized by Hemans, he says, are "tenderness and loftiness of feeling, and an ethereal purity of sentiment, which could only emanate from the soul of a woman."[36] Lest we think this is only gallant male bias, here is a woman's subtly gendered diagnosis of Hemans's soul: "I admire her genius—love her memory—respect her piety & high moral tone," Barrett Browning writes to a mutual friend; "But she always does seem to me a lady rather than a woman, & so, much rather than a poetess—her refinement, like the prisoner's iron . . . enters into her soul."[37]

Much in Hemans's poetry justifies these impressions, and their conservative infusions are strengthened by the religious pieties of Hemans's last poems, which, in the burden of her fatal ill health, seek the traditional consolation of a dualism that anticipates the soul's release:

> Come to the land of peace!
> Come where the tempest hath no longer sway,
> The shadow passes from the soul away,
>   The sounds of weeping cease! ("The Angels' Call")[38]

In this spirit, these poems also produce more than a few meditations on the vanity of fame as nurture to the female soul. "Women and Fame," a poem that the Gall and Inglis edition prints on the same page as "The Angels' Call," concludes in tones that resonate with Julia Osborne's most depressed meditations:

> Fame! Fame! thou canst not be the stay
>   Unto the drooping reed,
> The cool fresh fountain, in the day
>   Of the soul's most feverish need.
> Where must the lone one turn or flee?—
> Not unto thee, oh! not to thee!

Yet even this caution emerges from a rhetoric that constantly has to face the attractions against which it guards: "Thou hast a voice, whose thrilling tone / Can bid each life-pulse beat." In earlier poems, moreover, when Hemans was alive to her prospects in this world, the soul is a much less stable and much more temptable site of desire.

Like Jewsbury, Hemans wonders about the soul of female desire, whose fevers are not allayed—and are often aggravated—by domestic stays. The tensions of her ambivalence unsettle even a poem with so

unpromising a title as "The Domestic Affections," the summary piece in
The Domestic Affections and Other Poems (1812).[39] If its opening verses
seem a hornbook of Jeffrey's "Mrs. Hemans," the poem as a whole
compels attention for the way its very effort to formulate such terms
hints at a terribly corrupt economy for a woman's soul. It begins with
standard polarities—material and spiritual life, worldly and domestic
scenes—all opposed in ways for which the language of gender supplies
universal, transcendent sense. Home is the realm of the female soul;
under its sway, the domestic affections restore world-weary men's souls
and, beyond this service, remind us all of the soul's true home:

> Her angel voice his fainting soul can raise
> To brighter visions of celestial days!
> And speak of realms, where virtue's wing shall soar
> On eagle plume—to wonder and adore!
> And friends, divided here, shall meet at last,
> Unite their kindred souls—and smile on all the past. (*DA*, 164–65)

Yet these unities, kindred and divine, contend with some subversive lines
in Hemans's poem that limn the restrictions and deeper poverties of its
schemes of gender.

One point of stress, though its ideological commitments cannot allow
the poem to treat it as such, is a contradiction between the terms of this
spiritual function for women, and those that convey the extradomestic
expansions of male genius. Hemans means to anchor genius and its
attendant "Fame" in the nurture of the domestic affections, even gendering "Fame" and "Freedom" as feminine, as if to make them co-nurturers.
But her larger and more emphatic division of masculine genius and
feminine nurture reveals conflicting values. Consider the emblem of the
aspiring eagle:

> On Freedom's wing, that ev'ry wild explores,
> Thro' realms of space, th' aspiring eagle soars!
> Darts o'er the clouds, exulting to admire,
> Meridian glory—on her throne of fire!
> Bird of the sun! his keen, unwearied gaze,
> Hails the full noon, and triumphs in the blaze!
> But soon, descending from his height sublime,
> Day's burning fount, and light's empyreal clime;
> Once more he speeds to joys more calmly blest,
> 'Midst the dear inmates of his lonely nest!
>
> Thus Genius, mounting on his bright career,
> Thro' the wide regions of the mental sphere . . . (*DA*, 157)

Sustained by a feminine muse of Freedom and nurtured by the mother birds of the domestic nest, masculine Genius enjoys a freedom and energy in these lines for which the descent to the "lonely nest" of home, however calmly blest its joys, seems a death-in-life.

Indeed, the word *lonely* here has a deconstructive pressure. For in domestic bliss devoted to female healing of male souls, the result for women, Hemans finds herself saying (first in subordinate clauses and then in sustained meditations) is too frequently a depletion of her spiritual reserves. The praise of the woman's "angel voice" for its power to raise a man's "fainting soul" "to brighter visions of celestial days" (quoted above) is tellingly preceded by a notation that even as she "whisp[ers] peace" to these world-battered men, she must "conceal, with duteous art, / Her own deep sorrows in her inmost heart." A parenthesis a few lines later inscribes the necessary suppression of her own soul's pangs: "(Still fondly struggling to suppress *her own*)" (*DA*, 164). The italics are also Hemans's, a second graphic sign that presses hard against the parentheses that would contain their stress. By the end of the poem, her imagination is concentrating on the unequal economy that sustains gendered souls. In a significant shift, Hemans projects soul's ease for women—when gentle spirits "sooth her soul, / With soft enchantments and divine control"—into the world beyond death. Her "parting soul" becomes an "exulting spirit" as it "leaves her bonds of clay" (*DA*, 170–71).

This anticipation evokes traditional Platonisms that affect male poetics of the soul, too: this is the fundamental allegiance of *Alastor*, we recall, and it is an evolving one in Wordsworth's Christian orthodoxies. But where the schemes of their poems tend to reject the inconstancies of the feminine and nature together (reading one in terms of the other), the strains of "The Domestic Affections" keep both terms in view, exposing a culturally specific release for women from the "naturalized" domestic sphere that is supposed to ground their sense of soul. It is revealing that the poem ends with a celebration of the "Elysian clime" of heaven that is for women what the blessings of home are for men: an escape from the ravages of the world—but more specifically for the female soul, a delivery from the disappointments of the domestic sphere that cultural orthodoxy tells her is her heaven on earth:

> Yes! in the noon of that Elysian clime,
> Beyond the sphere of anguish, death, or time;
> Where the mind's bright eye, with renovated fire,
> Shall beam on glories—never to expire;

> Oh! there, th'illumin'd soul may fondly trust,
> More pure, more perfect, rising from the dust;
> Those mild affections, whose consoling light
> Sheds the soft moon-beam on terrestrial night;
> Sublim'd, ennobled, shall for ever glow,
> Exalting rapture—not assuaging woe! (*DA*, 171–72)

The affections of the soul on which women's social and cultural value is based now at least have a spiritual, if not a material, correlative and scope. It is only here that "th'illumin'd soul" enjoys a rapture paralleling that of masculine Genius in the mortal world. Young Felicia Browne felt this contradiction of venues and their attendant complications more than once. Writing of her admiration of the "noble Spaniards" in the peninsular campaign of 1808, she gushes, "my whole heart and soul are interested for the gallant patriots," but she then makes it clear that she realizes "females are forbidden to interfere in politics" (Chorley, 1:31).

What a girl's soul must do with this interest, if she is not to trespass into masculine glory and genius, is clear enough in one of Hemans's most anthologized poems in the nineteenth century, "Evening Prayer: At a Girls' School."[40] Contemplating this ritual, she superimposes the melancholy life that she knows awaits: "in those flute-like voices, mingling low, / Is woman's tenderness—how soon her woe!" The poem's refrain, "Therefore pray!" becomes a progressive descent into bitterness about the treacheries of domestic affection to the female soul: "Meekly to bear with wrong, to cheer decay, / And oh! to love through all things. Therefore pray!" If prayer is the language of the soul, Hemans's lesson is both explicit and devastating. For its deepest lesson is that the girls' future memory of these vespers will be their only nurture, "As a sweet dew to keep your souls from blight," their only relief amid all that "Earth will forsake."

If a woman's soul is moved beyond this forbearance, say, into civic heroism, Hemans's cultural orthodoxy tends to contain the potential transgression within an expanded field for the affections and to "correct" the expansion with tragic depletions. In "The Indian City," Maimuna, a Muslim widow on a pilgrimage to Mecca, is moved to passion when her son is slain by Brahmin children for having inadvertently wandered on to holy grounds.[41] Hemans evokes her grief in the image of a stilled, seemingly resigned soul—"her soul sat veil'd in its agony" (89)—and then turns this soul into a double soul whose division marks a site of transformation:

> And what deep change, what work of power,
> Was wrought other secret soul that hour?

How rose the lonely one?—She rose
Like a prophetess from dark repose!
And proudly flung from her face the veil,
And shook the hair from her forehead pale,
And 'midst her wondering handmaids stood,
With the sudden glance of a dauntless mood.
Ay, lifting up to the midnight sky,
A brow in its regal passion high,
With a close and rigid grasp she press'd
The blood-stain'd robe to her heaving breast,
And said—"Not yet—not yet I weep,
Not yet my spirit shall sink or sleep,
Not till yon city, in ruins rent
Be piled for its victim's monument.["] (90)

As compelling as this transformation is Hemans's insistence on representing it in the language of the soul, using this term to chart an emergence
from veiled stillness and passivity to an unveiled regal passion and a spirit
committed to violent action.

At the same time, Hemans's inhibition in the face of this kind of
emergence impels her to stabilize this eruption of energy by reinscribing
the gender of this secret soul of power. Although Maimuna's passion
inspires a war that wreaks the havoc she had pledged, her female soul
cannot survive its lost affections, "the yearning left by a broken tie."
Even as the city that destroyed this tie is itself destroyed, her fate joins
that of the vanquished city rather than the victorious armies; and the
barometer of this fate is her soul, now imaged as the prisoner of a walled
city on the verge of collapse:

Sickening she turn'd from her sad renown,
As a king in death might reject his crown;
Slowly the strength of the walls gave way—
She wither'd faster, from day to day.
All the proud sounds of that banner'd plain,
To stay the flight of her soul were vain;
Like an eagle caged, it had striven, and worn
The frail dust ne'er for such conflicts born,
Till the bars were rent, and the hour was come
For its fearful rushing thro' darkness home. (93–94)

In one stroke, this passage rewrites the gender and the fate of the aspiring
eagle of Genius and Freedom in "The Domestic Affections." Here, the
eagle is the caged soul, longing for release from the agonies of the worldly
triumph it had kindled; its most deeply desired soaring is a flight from life
to death. Escalating the conflict that strains "The Domestic Affections,"
"The Indian City" posits not the domestic nest but female life itself as the

prison from which the female soul seeks release. The only energy Hemans leaves to the woman warrior's soul is its brief arousal to a final expression of maternal love. Mourning her son's death on her own deathbed issues "a fitful gust o'er her soul again" that urges her to beg that they be laid to rest together (95).

Jewsbury's more heroic, "Roman" story of the female soul in grief is "Arria," but it is revealing that her cultural syntax, even so fortified, yields a similarly fatal figure.[42] Arria, "a Roman Matron," is imprisoned with her husband Pætus, whom she means to help die with Roman honor "by his own right hand." But already "[i]n soul and strength subdued" by his fetters, he merely expires, and it is left to "the wife and woman high" symbolically "to teach *him* how to die." This is the essential demonstration, Jewsbury implies, of "woman's soul" in its mode of heroic love:

> Ages, since then, have swept along;—
>   Arria is but a name,—
> Yet still is woman's love as strong,
>   Still woman's soul the same;
> Still soothes the mother and the wife,
> Her cherished ones 'mid care and strife:
> *It is not painful, Pætus*—still
> Is love's word in the hour of ill. (P. 124)

Whether in heroic sacrifice or in the meeker idioms of domestic affection, "woman's soul," in Jewsbury's imagining, bears a transhistoric and transcultural identity, its fundamental stasis as well as its endurance conveyed in her repeated *still*—and perhaps, in subversion of the poem's overt ideological commitments, tunable only therein with *ill*, a word that *still* contains both the level of conduct and letters. Burke, in a famous text that is the tacit backdrop for Jewsbury's emblem, hoped for no less heroism from the imprisoned "queen of France," whom he depicts as a "Roman matron" with both the dignity and the opportunities for suicidal honor borne by the compliment.[43]

For Hemans, the self-sacrificing passions of "a woman's soul" persist even when domestic affections are forsaken for life as an artist, and it is a sign of the conflict she herself felt that she repeatedly subverts her cultural identity as a poet with representations of women's art as a debased or impotent achievement. In "The Domestic Affections," recall, woman's art is delimited to the "duteous art" of self-effacement in the nurture of others, and Hemans's uneasiness about her work as artist yields more than one poem in which the soul of the woman artist accomplishes little more than discoveries of emptiness. The eponym of

"The Sicilian Captive" (*Records*, 172–79) is merely a singer, not an artist in any primary character; the trajectory is still one of self-cancelation, and her soul is the register. At first, as she sings of her lost home for her captors, her soul is invigorated by its theme:

> Faint was the strain, in its first wild flow,
> Troubled its murmur, and sad, and low;
> But it swell'd into deeper power ere long,
> As the breeze that swept over her soul grew strong. (P. 174)

Enchanting to her audience, the ultimate force of her art is its fatal effect on her. If singing evokes memories that inspire her soul—let "[t]hy soul flow o'er my lips again," she cries to Sicily (176)—such inspiration always contends with a soulful mourning that cannot be redeemed by a home so far away: "my sunny land! . . . Doth not thy shadow wrap my soul?" (175). The soul of the artist steadily declines and weakens in these shadows; when, recalling the "sweet sounds" of Sicily, the captive exclaims, "the soul to hear them faints in dreams of heaven away!" (177), the denouement is all but guaranteed. At the close of the song we are told (in the poem's last lines), "She had pour'd out her soul with her song's last tone; / The lyre was broken, the minstrel gone!" (179).

In the monologue of the sculptor, "Properzia Rossi" (which appears earlier in *Records* [45–54]), artistic creation emerges as a less than abundant recompense for the "deep affections that o'erflow / [Rossi's] aching soul" (51). Hemans's linear poetics write the story. The overflow of sense from line to line conveys this affectional force, while the grammatical richness of the word *o'erflow* itself utterly absorbs the artist's soul in a comprehensive grammar: the affections seem both to overflow from the aching soul and to flow overwhelmingly into it. An unsigned epigraph heralds this economy, its tenor explicitly diminishing any power of the soul devoted to genius and fame against the measure of all that has been lost:

> ————————Tell me no more, no more
> Of my soul's lofty gifts! Are they not vain
> To quench its haunting thirst for happiness?
> Have I not lov'd, and striven, and fail'd to bind
> One true heart unto me, whereon my own
> Might find a resting-place, a home for all
> Its burden of affections? I depart,
> Unknown, tho' Fame goes with me . . . (P. 47)

The contradictory strains of "The Domestic Affections" are here submitted to adamant evaluation by cultural norms. While the opposition between "happiness" and "lofty gifts" is a stock Romantic trope for the pains of genius, even of consciousness (everyone "understands" Manfred), Hemans unsettles the cliché by giving it a female voice. Rossi is exiled from happiness not just by genius but by the cultural contradiction of gender and genius.[44] In this contradiction, she, like the Sicilian Captive, can imagine no art for her soul purchased without her annihilation, and her monologue begins thus:

> One dream of passion and of beauty more!
> And in its bright fulfilment let me pour
> My soul away! (P. 47)

Again, Hemans's enjambment nicely tropes the flow of the soul-effacing desire.

For Romantic men, as we have seen, sex in souls typically involves schemes in which the feminine is evoked to nurture and complete a masculine soul—or if not, to suffer slander as the gender of every bafflement to such desire. Hemans and Jewsbury find themselves at cross purposes with these arrangements, but in their attempts to engage soulful discourse for their own poetics of desire, the dissonance of speaking as a woman entails a price. For Jewsbury's Julia, this is cultural alienation: Her love unrequited and her fame unsatisfying, yet still eager for adventure, she has to leave England for the sake of her soul. For Hemans, alienation is of the affections: Her poems not only repeatedly present women's souls as sites of frustrated affection, both lacking and yearning for the creative complement of a male soul, but their female epipsyches such as Rossi tend to reflect this desire in what Coleridge's letter describes as an "idle echo," a sterile "addition" rather than creative "combination."

Even so, the fuller narrative in which Hemans frames Rossi's dream of art subtly interrogates the negative cultural economy of woman's affection and the artist's soul. This has to do, in no small part, with the fact that Rossi's dream is not for art per se, but for art as the remedy and record (so a title-page note informs us [45]) of a fatally "unrequited attachment": "A painting by Ducis, represents her showing her last work, a basso-relievo of Ariadne, to a Roman Knight, the object of her affection, who regards it with indifference." This knightly shrug, while pathetic in the immediate narrative of Rossi's desire, is also, in the rhetoric of the poem's address to its reader, a stark sign of what a vain sacrifice art for affection would have been. Not only would abandoning her art not win happiness for her soul, but it would deny the only resource through which her soul gains, however fleetingly, a sense of self-possession and creative power. Although the poem devolves into a lament of the "aching soul," its middle section marks a brief interval of this access. Hemans softly but tellingly shifts Rossi's language into this register as Rossi describes her art taking shape (49):

> It comes,—the power
> Within me born, flows back; my fruitless dower
> That could not win me love. Yet once again
> I greet it proudly, with its rushing train
> Of glorious images:—they throng—they press—
> A sudden joy lights up my loneliness,—
> I shall not perish all!

Despite the brief bitterness about the "fruitless dower" of this lovelorn power, Rossi's language moves energetically into the lexicon of genius enjoyed by the aspiring eagle of "The Domestic Affections." And as she continues to express this enthusiasm, some of her terms (the work of the hand, the definition of the line, the infusion of self into art) seem to include not just the sculptor but also the poetry in which she is rendered:

> The bright work grows
> Beneath my hand, unfolding, as a rose,
> Leaf after leaf, to beauty; line by line,
> I fix my thought, heart, soul, to burn, to shine,
> Thro' the pale marble's veins. It grows—and now
> I give my own life's history to thy brow,
> Forsaken Ariadne! thou shalt wear
> My form, my lineaments; but oh! more fair,
> Touch'd into lovelier being by the glow
> Which in me dwells, as by the summer–light
> All things are glorified. (P. 49)

While Rossi's statue of forsaken Ariadne is clearly her mournful epipsyche and Rossi herself is such for Hemans, the unity of "thought, heart, soul" that Hemans briefly imagines for her work poses a tenuous suggestion of a different psychic economy: what women may create if the affections can inform and enjoy the bright work of art.

One of Hemans's last poems, written in the frustration of sickness, elevates and explicitly identifies with this imagined moment in Rossi's work. The "soul" of "Design and Performance" is given entirely to artistic inspiration and labor and, significantly, it is not gendered. The frustration is not of any domestic affection but of mortality itself:

> They float before my soul, the fair designs
> Which I would body forth to life and power,
> Like clouds, that with their wavering hues and lines

Portray majestic buildings:—dome and tower,
Bright spire, that through the rainbow and the shower
Points to th'unchanging stars; and high arcade,
Far-sweeping to some glorious altar, made
For holiest rites. Meanwhile the waning hour
Melts from me, and by fervent dreams o'er-wrought,
I sink. O friend! O linked with each high thought!
Aid me, of those rich visions to detain
All I may grasp; until thou see'st fulfilled,
While time and strength allow, my hope to build
For lowly hearts devout, but *one* enduring fane![45]

If, as Coleridge argues, there is a sex in souls, Hemans's design of the soul richly reconceives the ideologies of gender that grant only men's souls the privilege of desire and a claim to power. An important element of this design, in fact, is her incorporation of male-authored poetry. There are strains of Shelley's "Ode to Liberty," not only its language of the soul ("my soul spurned the chains of its dismay, / And in the rapid plumes of song / Clothed itself, sublime and strong" [5–7]) but also its visionary architecture: "a city such as vision / Builds from the purple crags and silver towers / Of battlemented cloud" (61–63). And at her sonnet's turn, there is a more resigned repetition of the crisis of vision at the end of *Epipsychidion* ("The winged words on which my soul would pierce / Into the height of love's rare Universe, / Are chains of lead around its flight of fire.—/ I pant, I sink . . . " [588–91]). There are also anterior recollections of Wordsworthian imaginings: "Earth has not any thing to shew more fair: / Dull would he be of soul who could pass by / A sight so touching . . . towers, domes, theatres, and temples" ("Composed upon Westminster Bridge"); and a subdued version of the heart-swelling vision given to his despondent Solitary ("Clouds of all tincture, rocks and sapphire sky . . . composing thus . . . that marvellous array / Of temple, palace, citadel, and huge / Fantastic pomp of structure without name" [*The Excursion,* 2.854–59]). These strains seem to some readers to mark Hemans as unoriginal, even "highly derivative,"[46] but we can grant their audibility a conscious design—something like a muted but no less reso-nant version of Jewsbury's appropriation of Shelley for Julia's voice. In this perspective, the prior texts participate in an intertextuality in which poetic performance is always engaged with something external. If Ro-mantic men gender the soul as feminine in order to explain and contain a decentered soul of inspiration, Hemans's intertextual inspirations amount to a similar acknowledgment of externality but without a troping in gendered terms. Other texts, like a soul outside, offer sources of inspirations that—to recall the terms by which Coleridge justifies a sex in souls—solicit a generative union with difference.

For a woman to write of sex in souls is to take on the question of what it means to write of the soul as a *woman*, to confront a literary tradition in which the female soul is contained by paradigms that mean to serve male privileges and interests. Some women are so impressed by this tradition that they internalize it as personal and cultural truth. To Wollstonecraft's biological heir, for example, who felt herself "nothing" in consequence of paternal disapproval and her husband's death, her mother's progressive speculations are unconvincing. "You speak of women's intellect," Mary Wollstonecraft Shelley writes to her friend Maria Gisborne,

I know that however clever I may be there is in me a vaccillation [*sic*], a weakness, a want of "eagle winged["] resolution that appertains to my intellect as well as my moral character—& renders me what I am—one of broken purposes—falling thoughts & a heart all wounds.—My Mother had more energy of character—still she had not sufficient fire of imagination—In short my belief is—whether there be sex in souls or not—that the sex of our material mechanism makes us quite different creatures—better though weaker but wanting in the higher grades of intellect.—(11 June 1835)[47]

Yet if she recoils from earlier Romanticism to retreat to the poorer safeties and comforts of orthodox hierarchies and the determinism of material mechanism (or what today we call essentialism), Jewsbury and Hemans put pressure on the terms that shape such understandings. Their writing shows how the very dislocation of female interest can also prove a productive ground for Romantic women: from a point of alienation, they may find themselves able to wonder about releasing spiritual poetics from a politics of gender, even enabled to imagine forms of desire neither dependent on nor limited by a sex in souls.

Already in the making in the early 1830s was another figure of design and performance, Sand's Lélia, whose sensational birth into print inspired the *Athenæum* reviewer to warn its readers that this heroine was "a monster, a Byronic woman—endowed with rich and energetic faculties, delicate perceptions, rare eloquence, fine talents, but no heart—a woman without hope and without soul" (646).[48] Published in this monstrosity was something Hemans had not yet imagined and Jewsbury only half did—the knowledge that women too could enter the romance of alienation, specifically by disdaining the "soul" assigned to them as the gendered bearer of cultural hope. This is a story that some post-Romantic women would explore more fully: "Beth was a poet herself—

& there was the reigning thought—No woman was ever such a poet as she w^d be," writes Barrett Browning in an autobiographical tale with some elaborations pertinent to the question of this essay: "when she grew up she w^d wear men's clothes. . . . One word Beth hated in her soul . . . & the word was 'feminine.' Beth thanked her gods that she was not & never w^d be feminine."[49] If Romantic women poets were not so confident, the persistent tensions of their texts generate an important cultural legacy for girls such as Beth, energizing her not only to reject the feminine "in her soul" but to find new gods to thank for this ungendering.[50]

Stephen Behrendt

Mary Shelley, *Frankenstein*, and the Woman Writer's Fate

Frankenstein is a woman author's tale of almost exclusively male activity, a tale whose various parts are all told by men. Women are conspicuously absent from the main action; they are significantly displaced (Agatha de Lacey, Safie) or entirely eliminated (Justine, Elizabeth, and the Creature's partially constructed mate). The only woman truly *present* in the tale is paradoxically not "there" at all: the unseen, silent auditor/reader Margaret Walton Saville (MWS), who exists only in Walton's letters. Walton's letters make clear that Margaret figures into his part of the tale as both confidante and confessor, much as Walton himself serves Victor Frankenstein. Indeed, Walton's explanations to Margaret of his own behavior suggest that he casts her in a role as *sanctifier*, whose province it is to hear, understand, sympathize, and approve (see Letter 2, for instance), rather in the manner of the roles in which Dostoyevsky later casts Liza in *Notes from Underground* and Sonia Marmeladov in *Crime and Punishment*. Walton manipulates his sister much as William Wordsworth encircles and silences his sister Dorothy in "Tintern Abbey": the brother's own future viability (which the text explicitly demands) is to be engineered precisely by the resonance of his own words in his sister's consciousness (ll. 134–59).

As "silent bearers of ideology" in Western literature and art, women have traditionally been made "the necessary sacrifice to male secularity," which finds its expression in materialistic public activity in a world that cannot—indeed will not—accommodate the woman of action.[1] Ellen Moers sees in Ann Radcliffe an alternative to both the intellectual, philosophical woman typified by Mary Wollstonecraft and the super-domesticated image of the submissive wife and mother extolled by earlier eighteenth-century culture. Moers claims that Radcliffe's vision of female selfhood involved neither the wholly intellectual nor the traditionally "loving" nurturant role but rather that of the traveling woman: "the woman who moves, who acts, who copes with vicissitude and adventure."[2] This very public role of the woman of action fits authors like Mary Darby Robinson and Helen Maria Williams, as well as the many Gothic heroines who, like Emily St. Aubert in *The Mysteries of Udolpho*, cope exceedingly well with continual reversals of fortune and circumstance. It is not, however, the model of experience embraced by Mary Shelley, who, despite her considerable travels and public activity, wrote in pointedly gender-specific terms in 1828 that "my sex has precluded all idea of my fulfilling public employments."[3] For modern readers her comment hints painfully both at the enculturated tendency of many women of the time—and today—to perpetuate women's oppression by discouraging public roles for women and at a narrowed and more biologically based rationalization of reserve on women's part.

In her important 1982 article, Barbara Johnson examines the troubled relationship among mothering, female authorship, and autobiography in *Frankenstein*, revealing some of the ways Mary Shelley associated authorship with monstrousness, and the products of authorship with the violent and unpredictable Creature. Anne Mellor has subsequently extended and refined the discussion in terms of Shelley's life and other writings.[4] My own reading is informed by their critical insights. I argue further that the initially well-intentioned and humane Creature resembles the idealistic author seeking to benefit her or his society, and so, tragically, does Victor Frankenstein. Both see their desires frustrated, however, as their intentions are first misunderstood and then misrepresented by others. Their interlaced histories thus pose a strong warning to authors—whether of literary texts or of cultural texts, such as revolutions—about the dangers of creating that which can destroy even its own author. The author must acknowledge the fact that her or his text's potential for mischief is at least as great as its potential for good. Because *Frankenstein*'s embedded lessons about the hazards of authorship bear particular relevance to the Romantic woman author, I shall here treat the novel as a touchstone as I examine some broader issues.

Although *Frankenstein* is a novel about *acts* and *actions*, it comes to us not in actions but in *reports* of actions, almost in the manner of classical theater, where much of the offstage action is represented only in verbal reports. The more contemporary parallel lies in Gothic fiction, in which the violence is often kept offstage and thereby rendered powerfully imminent, a menace whose physical manifestations are only barely held in abeyance by a combination of virtue, fortitude, coincidence, and plain good luck. In *Frankenstein* the reports are in fact frequently multilayered: they are reports of reports. The most heavily layered is Walton's report of Victor's report of the Creature's report of his self-education and experiences. Mary Shelley adds to this layering by beginning her novel in epistolary fashion, with a series of embedded reports that draw our attention to the writing acts of Walton and, by extension, to Shelley herself, both as original anonymous author and as the subsequently public, ex post facto authorial presence in the 1831 Introduction who reports on the novel's genesis. Moreover, in adopting the epistolary form of discourse, Walton adopts a genre long associated with *women's* writing. Just as he appropriates woman's procreative activity in creating his own "Creature," so does he appropriate the ostensibly uninhibited literary form (the letter form has been called "spontaneity formalized") that women—otherwise denied voice and hence access to male literary culture—"could practice without unsexing" themselves.[5]

To what extent does the nature of *Frankenstein* as a construct of words, rather than a direct representation of actions, embody the dilemma of the woman writer at the beginning of the nineteenth century? In what ways does the marginalization of women, their activities, and their perceived cultural worth figure in *Frankenstein*'s elimination or destruction of them? And what relation do these questions bear to the circumstances and the literary productions of other women writers of the Romantic period? Inherent in *Frankenstein* are some telling reflections of the ways in which women figured in the public world. In Mary Shelley's novel, women are occasionally the *objects* of discourse—most notably Margaret Saville, who cannot respond (or is at least represented as not responding), but also Justine and Elizabeth, whose responses to discourse aimed at them are in each case truncated by their deaths at the hands (in Elizabeth's case, quite literally) of the violent system of male authority within which the narrative is inscribed. When they are the *subjects* of discourse, on the other hand, they fare little better, for every woman of any importance who is spoken of in the main narrative is likewise destroyed: Victor's mother, Elizabeth, Justine, and the Creature's mate (who dies before even being "born"). In the public literary world of the time, the story is much the same. As objects of discourse, women were continually reminded of their "proper" and "natural" place in private familial and public extrafamilial interaction. The woman writer (who becomes herself an originator of discourse by publishing) is "represented" within public culture as an object of discourse when her work is reviewed by the (generally male) critic. But she is also translated into the *subject* of discourse when her literary efforts are indiscriminately interchanged with, or substituted for, her self—her individual person—within the public discourse of criticism.

Mary Shelley's first novel demonstrates that men's actions are typically either overtly destructive and therefore disruptive of social bonding or simply so thoroughly counterproductive that they result in paralysis, much as Walton's ship becomes immobilized in the ice. This message is repeated in one form or another in her subsequent novels and tales, and it appears in perhaps its starkest terms in *Matilda*, where the psychological and sexual oppressions are so powerful that they resist language's capacity to record them at all. The writings of Shelley and others reveal the consequences of the cultural pressures exerted upon the woman author, pressures whose cumulative weight often served either to drive women to misrepresent themselves by adopting the masculinist culture's literary conventions or to silence them altogether.[6] In the case of Mary Shelley—daughter of politically radical philosophers, wife of a particularly notorious radical artist, and member of a glittering literary circle—the residue of this enculturated sense of inferiority is startling. The terrible cost of her search for personal fulfillment in a permanent, secure relationship based equally upon affection and intellectual equality have been documented by her biographers. Sufficiently telling are two comments from her letters to two women, the first of whom (Frances Wright [Darusmont]) was herself an active political and social reformer transplanted in 1818 to America:

[W]omen are . . . per[pet]ually the victims of their generosity—& their purer, & more sensitive feelings render them so much less than men capable of battling the selfishness, hardness & ingratitude [which] is so often the return made, for the noblest efforts to benefit others.

In short my belief is—whether there be sex in souls or not—that the sex of our material mechanism makes us quite different creatures—better though weaker but wanting in the higher grades of intellect.[7]

The second remark, in which "weaker" clearly refers to physical strength and stature, comes from a letter that is unusual even for Mary Shelley in the violence of its self-deprecation. But Dorothy Wordsworth expressed her fear of disappointing Coleridge in much the same terms: "I have not those powers which Coleridge thinks I have—I know it. My only merits are my devotedness to those I love and I hope a charity towards all mankind."[8] John Stuart Mill expressed the nature of the dilemma when he wrote in 1861 that "all the moralities tell [women] that it is the duty of women, and all the current sentimentalities that it is their nature, to live for others, to make complete abnegations of themselves, and to have no life but in their affections."⁹ Comments like Shelley's and Wordsworth's provide compelling evidence of the validity of Mary Jacobus's much more recent observation that women's attempts to gain access to a male-dominated culture tend often to produce feelings of alienation, repression, and division: "a silencing of the 'feminine,' a loss of woman's inheritance" (27).

Indeed, expressions of self-disgust and self-hatred recur in the personal, private statements of Mary Shelley and other women who indulged their ambition (or, like Mary Robinson, Charlotte Smith, Felicia Hemans, and Shelley herself, their plain financial *need*) to enter the public arena of authorship. Entering explicitly into competition with the dominant caste of male authors, the woman writer seemed to violate not just social decorum but also the nature and constitution of her own sex. Not surprisingly, her efforts generated both anxiety and hostility among the male literary establishment, particularly when the woman dared to venture outside genres such as Gothic fiction that were more or less reserved for the heightened emotionalism expected of women writers.[10] It is instructive to remember that when Percy Bysshe Shelley composed a review of *Frankenstein* in 1818 his language implied that the author was male (perhaps, as was believed, Shelley himself).[11] Although this may have been yet another instance of Shelley's exaggerated, chivalric protectiveness toward his wife, the result was nevertheless to strip her of her authorship, even as she had been stripped of her early literary efforts in 1814 when the trunk containing her papers was left behind in Paris and subsequently vanished.[12]

I do not mean to minimize the growing impact women had on the Romantic literary market, either as authors or as readers.[13] But for nearly two centuries their place has been defined largely in terms of their relation to sentimentalism, which has had the effect of stereotyping the majority and effectively silencing the rest. By the later Romantic period it was becoming apparent that men no longer held quite the stranglehold on the literary scene that we have generally assumed. While publishing and criticism remained male-dominated fields, publishers especially were shrewd enough to understand their markets and to cater to the apparent tastes of a growing female readership, in part by employing women authors who addressed that readership. Nevertheless, the literary woman's activity remained circumscribed. Although women were free to write the literature of sentiment and were, in fact, encouraged to do so, the invitation did not customarily extend to the literature of science or, for the most part, of philosophy, political science, or economics. Indeed, the criticism of the would-be intellectual woman typically turned on assumptions about both the proper "nature" of women and the attributes that make them desirable to men, who are still the ultimate "consumers." This comment is typical: "[T]his woman had utterly thrown off her sex; when nature recalled it to her, she felt only distaste and tedium; sentimental love and its sweet emotions came nowhere near the heart of a woman with pretensions to learning, wit, free thought, politics, who has a passion for philosophy and longs for public acclaim. Kind and decent men do not like women of this sort."[14] The woman is Charlotte Corday, the famous man-killer; the account, from a Jacobin newspaper of the time. Such terminology recurs repeatedly in the English press and in the culture it both reflects and molds, and it suggests the extent to which the male establishment feared the "monstrous" advances being made by women. Like other novels (Smith's *Desmond* or Wollstonecraft's *Maria*, for example) whose rhetorical and thematic threads include the political, *Frankenstein* at once trespasses on "forbidden" territory and at the same time comments on the nature and consequences of that incursion.

The Romantic reading public's voracious appetite could consume authors as easily as their works, but their lack of access to the male-dominated, symbiotic twin industries of publishing and criticism made women writers particularly vulnerable. When Joseph Johnson hired Mary Wollstonecraft in 1787, he was taking an unconventional step, even though his decision was undoubtedly rooted more in pragmatic economic reasons than in progressive, gender-sensitive political ones; just back from France, she offered him both a contact (as well as a translator and editor familiar with the Continental literary milieu) and an intelligent author in her own right. Mary Darby Robinson's work for the *Morning Post* (which placed her squarely in the company of—and partly in competition with—Coleridge and Southey) offers another exception to the all-but-universal rule of male dominance. This overall dominance inevitably lent publishers and critics an inordinate power to silence the woman writer by denying her access to an audience or by so characterizing her efforts as to render them wholly unattractive to the inquisitive reader and thus to the prospective publisher of any subsequent efforts. Both of these forces stood poised to strike as soon as the woman writer overstepped the boundaries of propriety; they stood ready to step in "the moment she appeared to them as too palpably a manifestation of that monstrously capricious readership that has given birth to her" (Ross, *Contours*, 232).

This is not to say, however, that women poets (and women writers in general) were not acknowledged. Indeed, women poets seem to have been anthologized more frequently in the nineteenth century than they have been until recently in the twentieth, whereas women novelists like Ann Radcliffe, Charlotte Turner Smith, Amelia Opie, Jane Austen, and Mary Shelley, who *began* on the margins, achieved a more immediate and lasting enfranchisement. But the *manner* of that acknowledgment of women poets and of that anthologization tells its own tale. Let us take one example: Frederic Rowton's 1853 edition of *The Female Poets of Great Britain: Chronologically Arranged with Copious Selections and Critical Remarks.*[15] An enterprising editor and publisher, Rowton was active in such liberal causes as the Society for the Abolition of Capital Punishment. His anthology achieved a wide readership, both in England and in America, and there is no question that the volume called attention to women's contributions to England's poetic heritage. Nevertheless, Rowton's "critical remarks" typify the narrow post-Romantic characterization of women's writing in terms analogous to those in which women's "domestic" work was being characterized at the outset of the Romantic period. Rowton's comments on Felicia Hemans, for example, are illustrative:

She seems to me to represent and unite as purely and completely as any other writer in our literature the peculiar and specific qualities of the female mind. Her works are to my mind a perfect embodiment of woman's soul:—I would say that they are *intensely* feminine. The delicacy, the softness, the pureness, the quick observant vision, the ready sensibility, the devotedness, the faith of woman's nature find in Mrs. Hemans their ultra representative. . . . In nothing can one trace her feminine spirit more strikingly than in her domestic *home*-loving ideas. . . . No where, indeed, can we find a more pure and refined idea of home than that which pervades Mrs. Hemans's writings on the subject. (Pp. 386–87)

The delicacy that Rowton so admires in Hemans is in fact a recessive, deferential attitude that is more a critical overlaying, an interpretive imposition, than an essential quality of Hemans's verse. Just as female subordinates are kept in their "place" at the office by being called by first name (frequently in a diminutive form, at that) by supervisors whom they are expected to call by formal surname, so too is Hemans (and many others) "placed" by Rowton's condescending but nevertheless firmly authoritarian language, shored up by his "selection" of verse, which guarantees that the reader will see in Hemans precisely what Rowton intends. Interestingly, when H. T. Tuckerman wrote an introduction for the American edition of Hemans's *Poems* that appeared in 1853 (the same year as Rowton's anthology), he employed many of the same critical tactics, engaging in a form of "psychic defense" under the guise of critical appraisal. Such tactics, as Marlon Ross has demonstrated, "enable the critic to perform the crucial cultural endeavor of putting women in their natural and social place while ostensibly simply going about the mundane task of literary criticism" (*Contours*, 237).

The deferential, self-deprecating introduction or preface was a familiar literary fixture, whether it was employed by a Wordsworth or a Shelley in offering the world works that were proposed to be somehow "experimental" or adopted by a Mary Tighe (as in *Psyche*, 1805). But while readers seem to have "seen through" the affected posture when men employed it, they were more likely to regard that disclaimer, when women adopted it, not as a mere convention but rather as a statement of fact. And if the woman author failed to make the expected apologies, others stood ready to do it for her. Thus, the editorial introduction addressed "To the Reader" in later editions of Tighe's *Psyche, with Other Poems* assigns gender-driven terms to Tighe—and Tighe to them: "To possess strong feelings and amiable affections, and to express them with a nice discrimination, has been the attribute of many female writers . . . [but Tighe is] a writer intimately acquainted with classical literature, and guided by a taste for real excellence, [who] has delivered in polished language such sentiments as can tend only to encourage and improve the best sensations of the human breast."[16] Notice that the praiseworthy features—nicety, amiability, polish, sentiment—are intimately associated with such archetypal attributes of the Western female as cleanliness, orderliness, softness, and pliability. Even the exceptional (i. e., unfeminine) attributes—strong feelings, classical learning—are tempered by their being assigned to the support of essentially "feminine" concerns, the nurturing of the best *sensations* of the human heart chief among them. This sort of bracketing commentary is the norm for the period, both for the woman authors themselves and for the (male) interlocutors who felt compelled to speak for them in order to "introduce" them to their audiences.

Ironically, the notions of "home-loving" domesticity that Tighe's publisher, Rowton, and others sought to impose on women's writing have been succinctly summed up a century and a half later in—of all places—an anthropological study of dining etiquette:

If "a woman's place is in the home," her place implies all the "female" characteristics: interiority, quietness, a longing to nurture, unwillingness to stand forth, and renunciation of the "male" claims to authority, publicity, loudness, brightness, sharpness. These qualities have a multitude of practical applications; for example, they either make a woman altogether unfit and unwilling to attend feasts, or they influence the way she behaves while participating in them.[17]

Substitute "publish" for "attend feasts," and the fit is nearly perfect. Indeed, according to traditional Western (especially Anglo-American) etiquette, what could be less womanly, less feminine, than *public*-ation, which injects the woman into a visible world held to be as thoroughly and exclusively masculine an arena as that to which gentlemen adjourned after dining for cigars and port?

In exercises like Rowton's, ideology is represented as "natural" fact, and begging the question is then passed off as exposition. Elsewhere, Rowton observes of Hemans that "to *passion* she is well nigh a stranger." Unlike Byron (who is "indeed, of all others *the* poet of passion"), "affection is with her a serene, radiating principle, mild and ethereal in its nature, gentle in its attributes, pervading and lasting in its effects" (p. 388). And Letitia Landon (Maclean), whom Rowton explicitly compares (favorably) with Byron ("the Byron of our poetesses" [p. 424]) is nevertheless censured for treating materials and attitudes for which Byron was even in 1853 routinely praised—however cautiously. Rowton remarks of Landon's skill at portraying sorrow:

Persons who knew her intimately say that she was *not* naturally sad: that she was all gaiety and cheerfulness: but there is a mournfulness of soul which is never to be seen on the cheek or in the eye: and this I believe to have dwelt in Mrs. Maclean's breast more than in most people's. How else are we to understand her poetry? We cannot believe her sadness to have been put on like a player's garb: to have been an affectation, an unreality: it is too earnest for that. We must suppose that she *felt* what she wrote: and if so, her written sadness was real sadness. (Pp. 426–27)

Rowton's conclusions reveal a built-in ideological inability to credit the female poet with the imaginative capacity to *create* powerful moods or attitudes, a capacity attributed to a Wordsworth or a Byron without question. The male poet can create, invent; the female poet can only replicate and transcribe. Worse, Rowton extrapolates from his own faulty causal logic a narrowly moralistic (and predictably negative) literary-critical judgment: "This strong tendency towards melancholy frequently led Mrs. Maclean into most erroneous views and sentiments; which, though we may make what excuses we will for them out of consideration for the author, should be heartily and honestly condemned for the sake of moral truth" (p. 429).

We are dealing here with codes of behavior, with manners, considered within the sphere of literary production. Behaviors that are *tolerated* among male authors—even when they are disapproved—are intolerable in female authors. Morally reactionary critical responses to productions like *Don Juan*, *Prometheus Unbound*, or *Endymion* stemmed at least in part from a recognition that their authors were writers of substance and power, whose productions stood to shake up the conservative establishment on whose stability (and capital) the critical industry of the time had already come to depend. Women were writing powerful, socially volatile poetry, too; but rather than launch a comparable frontal attack on women writers like Mary Darby Robinson, Joanna Baillie, Charlotte Turner Smith, Letitia Landon, or even Hannah More, gender-driven criticism adopted the psychologically subtle device of *undermining* by misrepresentation, of assessing works in terms of their adherence to or deviation from presumed standards of "femininity." The male-dominated publishing industry and its accompanying critical establishment had, of course, a great store in preserving, codifying, *and enforcing* this construct of "the feminine" in writing, perhaps especially so in the field of poetry, which was, in the Romantic period, still the preeminent vehicle for "high" art. If the membership of the club could not be preserved indefinitely for males only, it could at least be stratified: separate, lesser rooms in the clubhouse could be apportioned to women to keep them out of the way.

Johnson and Mellor have helped us to see that Frankenstein's Creature shares the situation of Romantic women, marginalized and spurned by a society to whose patriarchal schemata they fail to conform. Moreover, the values and sensibilities typically assigned to women during the Romantic period are not unlike those that Shelley assigns the Creature, including instinctive responsiveness to Nature, the impulse toward emotional human bonding (especially apparent in the deLacey episode), and an experiential rather than an abstract empirical way of "knowing"—all of which are the heritage of eighteenth-century sentimentalism. In the pursuit of all of these impulses the Creature is thwarted, both by his irresponsible creator and by the members of the society that has produced Victor and countless others like him. That the Creature is not "beautiful"—another attribute stereotypically associated with women— indicates the seemingly deforming nature of nonconformity as measured by the standards and sensibilities of the dominant majority. Ironically, as the representative of the masculinist culture that places such a premium on physical beauty among women (note especially his descriptions of Elizabeth), Victor Frankenstein creates a being whose hideousness contravenes any proper instinctive and loving parental response on his part to the Creature as "child." He has created that which he abhors, a situation entirely analogous to what the masculinist social and political establishment wrought upon women, writers or otherwise, and with the same consequences: the victim is led to self-deprecation and ultimately self-destructive behavior. Likewise, the author who thinks highly enough of her work to publish it nevertheless compromises herself in publishing with it self-effacing, apologetic, or temporizing prefaces that devalue or even destroy the work that follows. This is a necessary compromise, it would seem, for those who would be heard at all. But the cost in honesty and self-esteem to the author is considerable.

Victor renounces the product of his activities when the creative seeks to usurp the procreative. Hence, physically destroying the Creature's mate is only an emblem of the real act of devastation implicit in Victor's actions: the demolition of those who will not retreat to passive, silent existence on the margins of human experience. Silent neglect, however, is an equally powerful response. This fact lends particular significance to a literary project Mary Shelley proposed in 1830 to John Murray III and to which he apparently turned a (predictably) deaf ear. Suggesting topics on which she might write for publication, she says, "I have thought also of the Lives of Celebrated women—or a history of Woman—her position in society & her influence upon it—historically considered. [*sic*] and a History of Chivalry."[18]

Did Murray simply assume that the market-driven "buying public" (despite the very large number of women *readers* in it) would be uninterested in a volume of prose about women, perhaps especially one about "Woman"? The topic itself was certainly not prohibitively unpopular: Hemans's *Records of Woman* had appeared in 1828, with a second edition the same year and a third in 1830, as Shelley must have known (although there is no mention of it, nor of Hemans, in her letters or journals of this period). The balance (or *im*balance) in Mary Shelley's query between the worthy and promising topic of the position *and* *influence* of women in society and the much "safer" "History of Chivalry" (in which women might be expected to figure as ornament rather than as agent) is unintentionally revealing of the cultural bind from which neither Mary Shelley nor any other woman writer of her generation could entirely escape. Certainly, when one considers the sentimental concessions to traditional expectations about gender and genre that mar *Records of Woman*, one cannot help acknowledging the truth of what Jennifer Breen says about women writers' dilemma of creating in their works a woman's point of view: they were forced by social pressure "to conceal the split between what was expected of them and what they actually felt."[19] Hence, most of the women in *Records of Woman* are, in fact, reflections of male social and cultural expectations only slightly displaced from their customary passive, recessive, nurturant roles to relatively more aggressive ones whose activity is typically generated by default, by the disappearance, death, or incapacitation of the male figure who would otherwise play the active role in the scenario (e.g., "Arabella Stuart," "The Switzer's Wife," or "Gertrude," whose subtitle, "Fidelity till Death," says it all).

One of *Frankenstein*'s lessons is that all creative activity (whether physically procreative or aesthetically/scientifically creative) drives individuals into seclusion and isolation and *away from* the salutary human interaction that is the proper objective of all human *action*. Shelley's introduction to the 1831 edition details the countersocializing aspect of her own experience as creative writer. That she chose to include that information and therefore to publicly detail her physical and psychological anxiety and her attempt to compete with the literary men who surrounded her is instructive, for her experience as a woman of words[20] ties her to contemporaries like Anna Letitia Barbauld, Jane Taylor, Mary Robinson, Ann Radcliffe, and Charlotte Smith, as well as to Dorothy Wordsworth, whose words were repeatedly appropriated by her brother in poems that for two centuries have blithely been regarded as "his." That still others, like Felicia Browne Hemans, unhesitatingly identified themselves by their married names (e.g., Mrs. Hemans, Mrs. Opie, or Mrs. Montolieu) indicates the extent to which they elected (whether freely or under cultural coercion) to reduce their actions and their identities to mere *words* (denoting marital status and recessive identity). What Stuart Curran says specifically of Felicia Hemans and Letitia Landon might be said of many of the women who were their contemporaries: In addition to the comfortable domesticity and sentimentality that may be glimpsed in their work, we can see also "darker strains," which include "a focus on exile and failure, a celebration of female genius frustrated, a haunting omnipresence of death."[21] This aspect of women's writing is as troubling today as it was two centuries ago, and it should not surprise us that intrusive contemporary commentators, editors, and anthologizers (like Frederic Rowton) attempted to deny the validity or even the meaningful presence of that aspect, either explicitly by branding it as subject matter inappropriate for women, in roundabout fashion by refusing to credit female authors with adequate imagination or intellect, or in slightly more covert fashion by calling their efforts on this front derivative from male models such as Byron.

Writing literature may be a form of communication, but it is decidedly not dialogue. Like Margaret Saville, the reader (or audience) is kept at a distance; functional interactive discourse with the author is precluded by the nature of the literary work of art. The one-sidedness of this arrangement is quite unlike the dialogic nature of the familiar letter (and I stress the adjective), a genre Mary Shelley seems to have much enjoyed.[22] The act of *literary* communication—the writing act and the production of a public, published text—distances both the writer and the reader from the subjective substance that the text mediates by means of language. In her preface to *Psyche* (1805), Mary Tighe presents a view of her work opposite to the one reflected in Shelley's 1831 reference to her "hideous progeny": "The author, who dismisses to the public the darling object of his solitary cares, must be prepared to consider, with some degree of indifference, the various receptions it may then meet."[23] Whether "hideous progeny" or "darling object," the fate of the published work is out of its author's hands, as is the author's private self, which soon becomes the property of critics and others who appropriate it by reading it both into and in the literary work, as is evident from this remark about Mary Darby Robinson's poetry:

Of Mrs. Robinson's general character, it can only be added that she possessed a sensibility of heart and tenderness of mind which very frequently led her to form hasty decisions, while more mature deliberation would have tended to promote her interest and worldly comfort; she was liberal even to a fault; and many of the leading traits of her life will most fully evince, that she was the most disinterested of human beings. As to her literary character, the following pages, it may be presumed, will form a sufficient testimony.[24]

Here again are the terms we have seen applied to Hemans and Tighe; they include the standard catalog of "feminine" virtues of softness, tenderness, and pliability, as well as the converse (and therefore culpable) traits of independence, immaturity, hastiness, and lack of foresight. The concluding sentence of the "Preface" makes perfectly clear the writer's rhetorical strategy: having detailed for the reader a literary life characterized by failures to behave "properly," both in life and in print, the writer injects the works themselves ("the following pages") into this pejorative context. Co-opted into disapproving of the author's life and life-style, the reader is invited to carry along that sense of disapprobation while reading the poetry. It is a classic tactic of reader manipulation and an unusually effective one, as history affords us ample opportunities to observe.

To create literary art is ultimately to falsify both the person and the *act*—whether external and immediate or internal and imaginative—that motivates the verbal text. It is not just a matter of producing fading coals, as Percy Bysshe Shelley suggests in *A Defence of Poetry*, but rather of burning up the raw material entirely. In the process the individual self gets burned up as well, consumed and extinguished. For the woman writer, no less than for the man, who and what one *is* gets superseded in the process of publication by the *words* that may represent—but more likely *mis*represent—that individual private entity. Fame devours person-hood, as Tennyson's Ulysses reminds us later when he ironically an-nounces that "I am become a name." In a "man's world," which is very much what the Romantic era was in England despite the presence of literary women in it, men are better able to overcome this dissolution of the self because they are the principal *actors* (act-ors) on the public stage, as well as the controllers of language and other cultural determinants. But because of their social, political, and cultural marginalization, wom-en have few resources for countering the extinguishing of the personal self. When they did write, as Susan J. Wolfson observes of Dorothy Wordsworth, their experiences frequently generated in their texts "coun-tertexts and spectres of defeat."[25]

Wolfson reminds us that in professing to "detest the idea of setting myself up as author" (p. 140) Dorothy Wordsworth effectively accepted the marginalized and *un*authoritative female role assigned her by the masculinist society epitomized in her brother and valorized by his public audiences. As journal keeper and documenter of domestic affairs both personal and public, rather than self-promoting, publishing author, she played out the culturally conditioned expectations of woman as domestic engineer, historical and social housekeeper, and minder of minor details of order and appearance. Nevertheless, Dorothy Wordsworth did write, both in prose and in poetry, and even her characteristic self-deprecating tone cannot entirely hide the clear strain in her writings of ambition and of longing for a more authoritative and self-expressive voice.[26] Much the same might be said about Mary Shelley, whose letters are filled with protestations against public visibility: "There is nothing I shrink from more fearfully than publicity— . . . far from wishing to stand forward to assert myself in any way, now that I am alone in the world, [I] have but the desire to wrap night and the obscurity of insignificance around me."[27] Despite her very considerable oeuvre, she often deprecated both her literary talent and her intellectual acuity by referring to her writing, as she once did to John Murray, as "my stupid pen & ink labors."[28]

Part of the Romantic woman writer's predicament involves what Sandra Gilbert and Susan Gubar have called the "anxiety of authorship"—the woman's radical fear "that she cannot create, that because she can never become a 'precursor' the act of writing will isolate or destroy her."[29] This is a potentially and often an actually crippling anxiety. And yet this fear need not be gender-specific to women. Sonia Hofkosh has demonstrated that no less "male" a male writer than Byron exemplifies the author who "dreads, as he desires, being read by others—a reading that rewrites him and thus compromises his powers of self-creation."[30] The problem is particularly acute for the woman writer, however, who in the Romantic period was working with only the bare thread of a literary heritage. Battling the powerful forces that everywhere reminded her of her cultural and intellectual marginality and the impropriety of her artistic aspirations—forces that fed (and rewarded) timidity and submissiveness—the woman writer was very like Mary Shelley's Creature. This gender-driven cultural stifling both of experience and of expression lies behind what Mary Jacobus, among others, sees as the themes of "dumbness and utterance" and of the powerful quest to fulfill an impossible desire (*Reading Woman*, 28).

We do well to catch in the Creature's history a glimpse of the history of the woman artist during the Romantic period—and indeed during much of the history of Western culture. What is at issue, finally, is the ongoing radical marginalization of the unconventional, a phenomenon as much political as social and cultural. The dominant social milieu severs communication with the Creature because neither its appearance nor its acts conform to the expectations of that majority culture. The society in which Frankenstein and Walton alike opt for the isolation of individual pursuits over the socializing impulses of human interaction proves to be the real agent in redefining the parameters of creative activity. Acts are replaced by words, activity by passivity, responsibility by the irresponsibly ambivalent, and individuality by abstraction. The person is dissolved.

Mary Shelley's first major literary project after Percy's death was *The Last Man*, which presents itself as a set of fragmentary papers—Sibylline leaves—that trace the vanishing of an entire civilization in a prolonged universal cataclysm. Since the indifferent universe of time and history effectively ends in the skeptical intellectual framework of that novel, all that remains to lend meaning to mortal existence are human interaction and human language systems, both of which, being temporal, are themselves inevitably doomed to end. The alternative to this desolate picture lies in Shelley's frequently iterated commitment to "an ethic of cooperation, mutual dependence, and self-sacrifice" as the means for salvaging individual and collective dignity and meaning from the wreckage of temporal human existence. She argued in work after work that civilization can achieve its full promise only when "individuals willingly give up their egotistical desires and ambitions in order to serve the greater good of the community."[31] But this situation leaves the writer in a particularly precarious position, with her or his printed words dependent for value on a community of readers to whom the author is nevertheless a stranger, whose language and *identity* is subject to gross misconstruing over time. Mary Shelley's life of Alfieri offers insight into her view of authorship, which itself seems to echo both Wordsworth's and Percy Bysshe Shelley's views: "The author has something to say . . . . An Author . . . is a human being whose thoughts do not satisfy his mind . . . he requires sympathy, a world to listen, and the echoes of assent. [The author desires] to build up an enduring monument . . . [and] court the notoriety which usually attends those who let the public into the secret of their individual passions or peculiarities."[32] But this is risky business, surely, for even if the assenting voice is loud and unified, the author still exposes her or his own autonomous personhood ("individual passions or peculiarities") for public view and public reading—or misreading. As the daughter of Wollstonecraft and Godwin and wife of Percy Bysshe Shelley, she would have appreciated more than most that the "sympathy" of which she writes here could be a rare commodity indeed among the early-nineteenth-century English reading public.

At the same time, though, to write is not just to yield authority but also to *take* it, to exercise it. In the preface composed for the anonymous first edition of *Frankenstein*, Percy Bysshe Shelley claims that the author has gone beyond what Erasmus Darwin and other speculative physiologists have postulated about the nature of life and "the elementary principles of human nature." Indeed, the author is presented as having surpassed not only these *scientists* but also other culturally ensconced male *literary* luminaries, including Homer, the Greek dramatists, Shakespeare, and Milton, as well as the two "friends" to whose conversations the story is said to owe. In her own 1831 introduction to *Frankenstein*, Shelley pointedly reminds us that her story originated with a set of conversations between Percy Bysshe Shelley and Byron to which she was essentially a silent auditor. Yet *hers* is the story that was completed *and* published *and* that became sufficiently popular to demand republication. Making her claim of authorship explicit, Mary Shelley in the process claims possession not only of the novel's language but also of the material—the apparently unremittingly *male* material—of its subject matter. Moreover, the new introduction constitutes a gesture of authority by which her own authorial voice supersedes the ventriloquistic voice of her dead husband in the preface. By 1831 she had, after all, survived both Shelley and Byron, and the popularity of her novel had far exceeded that of her husband's works and had rivaled and in some quarters even surpassed that of Byron's.

The Last Man extends some of the issues I have already raised in terms of *Frankenstein*. Is the author's role (whether the author be female or male) merely to record the real or invented acts of others? That is, after all, what Mary Shelley turned to in her later years when she wrote the lives of eminent *men*. The *historian* characteristically steps *out* of the history she or he writes, functioning as nameless, invisible recorder, although even in the best of cases an element of fiction enters—or is inserted—into the writing of history. This ostensibly detached role appears to have become increasingly attractive to Mary Shelley, who in 1834, while working on her contributions to the *Lives of the Most Eminent Literary and Scientific Men of Italy, Spain, and Portugal*, wrote at length about her imagination's fleeting visitations and suggested that, as Wordsworth wrote in the "Intimations" ode, the years that bring the philosophic mind provide recompense (though not necessarily so "abundant" as the poet regards it in "Tintern Abbey") for the imagination's fading: "I hope nothing & my imagination is dormant—She awakes by fits & starts; but often I am left *alone* (fatal word) even by her. My occupation at present somewhat supplies her place—& my life & reason have been saved by these "Lives"—Yes—let the lonely be occupied—it is the only cure."[33]

And yet is not this consuming indulgence in words both the goal and the supermarginalizing consequence of authorship generally—to be reduced to *words*, to be captured, "pictured," and read not as person but as textual construct, as a sort of shadow existence, a phantasm of the reader's own distorting imagination?

The author constantly runs the risk of being made into a fiction by the reader who formulates or extrapolates the author from the text. The woman author is "read" within a system of culturally encoded patriarchal authority over which she has virtually no control but within which she is expected to express herself. She is thus deprived at once of subjectivity, creativity, and autonomy. The assessment not just of Romantic women's writing but also of the cultural and intellectual position of the woman writer in general underscores the urgency of Annette Kolodny's observation that what unites and invigorates feminist criticism is neither dogma nor method but rather "an acute and impassioned *attentiveness* to the ways in which primarily male structures of power are inscribed (or encoded) within our literary inheritance."[34] Worst danger of all, one runs the risk of becoming an accomplice to the substitutional fictionalization of the "real" (the actual, autonomous, personal, and historical individual) self by the very act of writing. For the text that results from that act contains the self that the reader may reformulate and reconstruct in a living lie that reflects not the author but the *reader*, who has, in the act of reading her, appropriated her and torn her to pieces, much as Victor Frankenstein first assembles and then tears to pieces the Creature's mate.

Virginia Woolf suggested that George Eliot's decision to combine womanhood and writing was very costly indeed; as Mary Jacobus observes, it was a mortally significant decision that entailed "the sacrifice not only of happiness, but of life itself" (*Reading Woman*, 29). Women writers are particularly sensitive to the conflict between the "domesticity" that society expects of them and their own authorial aspirations for public fame, Marlon Ross writes, precisely because "the conflict is so palpable in their private lives and in their poetic careers" (*Contours*, 289). Mary Shelley understood the personal cost of authorship, writing of it to Trelawny that "I know too well that that excitement is the parent of pain rather than pleasure."[35] Writing, especially for publication, is an act of society, of civilization: a surrender of the autonomous self and identity to, and ostensibly on behalf of, the collective public. But as Rousseau had foreseen, the impulse toward formal civilization brings with it a radical reduction of one's options and, for the writer, "an enclosure within the prisonhouse of language" (Mellor, *Mary Shelley*, 50). One becomes what one writes, to paraphrase Blake, even as one writes what one is. In this endlessly revolving cycle one becomes imprisoned in temporality and topicality; one is reduced, finally, to a cipher, to a sheaf of papers, to reports of actions—or to reports of *ideas* that purport to be actions.

Like her contemporaries, Mary Shelley wrestled with the assault upon the personal ego inherent in the public response to one's formal writing. She wrote—after 1822 primarily because she *had* to, to support herself and her son—and only occasionally did she allow herself to stare back at the potential uselessness of it all: "What folly is it in me to write trash nobody will read— . . . I am—But all my many pages—future waste paper—surely I am a fool—."[36] At more optimistic and self-assured moments she could at least find consolation in the *activity* of writing, even if it was merely a matter of filling the hours.

That Walton finally redirects his ship toward the south (and symbolically toward warmth and society) at the conclusion of *Frankenstein* might indicate that he has learned from his experience, were it not that Walton does not choose freely in the matter but rather accedes in the face of a mutiny. I suggest that the practical struggle to be true to oneself and to one's ideals and aspirations—for the woman writer as for the man Arctic explorer—inevitably involves compromise and with it the reduction and subjection of one's essential self to a report embedded in words. Literature traditionally introduces us not to authors but to their words, the words by which they represent impressions of their ideas and of the "selves" in which they live their days. Living with the diminished self whose record is the journal of papers that makes up the novel will haunt

Walton, even as the Creature haunts the obsessive-compulsive Victor Frankenstein (who is no victor at all but the ultimate cosmic loser). But so too must the writer—woman or man—inevitably be haunted by the specter of herself or himself reduced to a cipher, to a construct of words, the work itself becoming a "hideous progeny" that dissolves the author as self, as living, acting entity. Whatever the inherent formal value of the literary product, it nevertheless both mutilates and misrepresents its author. In this sense, among others, it seems to me entirely valid to read in *Frankenstein*, as in much of Romantic women's writing, the enigmatic warning that creativity may be hazardous to one's health—indeed to one's entire existence.

Mitzi Myers

De-Romanticizing the Subject

Maria Edgeworth's "The Bracelets," Mythologies of Origin, and the Daughter's Coming to Writing

*Had I a son as much my friend, or as worthy of my friendship nothing would be
wanting to my domestic felicity.—Richard Lovell Edgeworth to Maria Edgeworth,
3 February 1785*

*I was very sorry to hear from [Richard Lovell Edgeworth] that he has lost his favourite
Daughter, HONORA, the image of her Mother, but, as he says, superior both in beauty
and understanding.—James Keir to Erasmus Darwin, 15 March 1790*

*A new era opens with the juvenile romances of Miss Edgeworth . . . which had all the
charm of a Protean introspection of the personages. . . . [H]ad her works been published
anonymously, one would have pronounced the writer to be a travelled citizen of the
world, with the experiences of a man and the sensibilities of a woman.
—Alexander Innes Shand*

I

*G*ood little girls don't have any fun. In the Romantic era, so the critics tell us, they're all little girls lost, with no access to power and pleasure
and no desire of their own. Herself and the story she tells about it mostly
invisible, the female child is scarcely seen, much less heard. A lack, an
absence, at best a male poet's muse or colonized project, the feminine
Other panders to masculine desire; even the erotic "Belle Dame Sans
Merci" fades fast. The only good Romantic heroine is, like Wordsworth's

Lucy, a dead one. Akin to rocks and trees, she holds no dialogue with feminine readers or feminist critics. In stories composed specifically for good little girls, so the literary histories recount, the results are still more disastrous. Nigel Cross's examination of paraliterary London presents a dreary picture of nineteenth-century women writers for children under the rubric of the "female drudge." Gillian Avery categorizes the largely female writers of Georgian juvenile fictions as typically down-at-the-heels governesses out to make a pound and vent their grievances against girl nature through punitive tales. Yet more murderous than masculinist poets, women writers of the late-eighteenth- and early-nineteenth-century moral tale are said to constitute narrative itself as repression. Browbeating juvenile readers with didactic morals, authorial mothers sugar-coat the bitter pill of gender restraint and coerce girl readers into accepting a repressive death-in-life of passivity and powerlessness.

This essay challenges such literary and critical traditions with a feminist reconfiguration of Romantic literary history, a privileging of the child construed from the woman writer's perspective. The metanarrative of childhood that dominates the appropriation of Romanticism for juvenile literature and pedagogy is, literally, a master narrative—the Romantic story of the emergent male self. This story eclipses the girl's growing up and edits out the women who wrote about her. Although my object here is to historicize one child writer, my argument implicitly criticizes the standard representation of the child reader in literary histories too. It's always assumed that, like Wordsworth, Lamb, and Coleridge, any red-blooded youngster prefers fantasy, fairy tales, and sensational chapbooks to stories about everyday life. Book 5 of *The Prelude* is the poetic locus classicus; Geoffrey Summerfield's *Fantasy and Reason* is the most entertainingly outrageous apotheosis of Wordsworth as childhood's savior. Indeed literary historians and critics have long validated that appropriation by misreading women's juvenile fictions as defective because they don't mythologize the child as men do. Mostly ahistorical and androcentric, narratology hasn't offered much help with the pleasure, play, and child power that women writers of the past encode in their tales for the young, either. This essay, then, is about the Romantic daughter's empowerment through language, through her capacity to tell her own tale. It's the story of one little girl's entrance into Romantic literature, not as insentient rock or visionary muse but as a thinking writer, a child at once playful, philosophical, and needy, whose narratives call into being the self and the social world she desires.[1]

In the family romance of literary history, Maria Edgeworth (1768–1849) always plays the neglected sibling—effaced by her sister author

Jane Austen when she writes feminocentric fiction like *Belinda* (1801)
and *Helen* (1834) and erased by her brother writers Sir Walter Scott and
William Wordsworth despite her priority in regional tales and in the
imaginative re-creation of childhood.[2] Still more important in accounting
for Edgeworth's diminished literary standing is her own real-life father,
Richard Lovell Edgeworth, who looms almost as large in histories and
biographies as in his daughter's imaginative accounts of him. In her story
of how she became a writer, composed almost forty years after her
juvenile debut—a story appropriately embedded within her continuation
of Richard Lovell's autobiography—the father affords both cause and
content of his daughter's extraordinary nineteenth-century success. She
likes to picture herself as her father's partner, writing to please him and to
popularize his innovative educational ideas for an audience beyond the
family circle.[3] Although literary histories still forget Maria Edgeworth's
importance in her day—and she was the Romantic period's premier
British woman writer—critics always remember Richard Lovell Edgeworth.[4] For the past century, what little discussion the daughter's work
has received focuses on the father: did the child's identification with the
parent empower or impede her literary authority?

Whether critics construe the author as Daddy's girl positively or
negatively, they pay surprisingly little attention to Maria Edgeworth's
juvenile writing and to the circumstances of its composition. Yet the
juvenile Edgeworth demonstrates a gift for being in two places at once,
simultaneously child and adult, masculine and feminine, that queries her
customary labeling as unproblematic Daddy's girl. Taking "The Bracelets," an early and important autobiographical fiction, as a site for
feminist rethinking of Romanticism's mythologies of origin, my essay
reassesses the relation between the child's "I" and the adult's voice,
between women's subjectivity and the masculine Romantic subject, the
strong psyche of poetic self-assertion.[5] As the tale of a young girl writing
for both child and adult readers, writing *as* both child and adult, the
story and the familial context from which it emerged suggestively illustrate the multiple positions that women writers of juvenilia necessarily
inhabit.

Calling into question critical history's accepted truths about masculine
and feminine imaginings of literary childhood, this essay also aims at
demystifying the generic mythologies of origin that impede revisionary
reading of juvenile Romantic literature by women. Except for Jane
Austen—and perhaps we can now add Mary Wollstonecraft and Mary
Shelley—female authors of the Romantic period remain marginal to
literary history and to the literary canon, no matter how important they

were in their own time.[6] But most neglected of all are women whose audience was young and whose medium was realistic narrative. Even though most of the female authors who made standard authorial lists like the *Dictionary of National Biography* and the *Cambridge Bibliography of English Literature* wrote for children as well as adults, juvenile literature remains peripheral to our contemporary reconceptualization of the canon. Especially is this true of the Romantic period: the history and criticism of children's literature have always been dominated by that criticism's special version of Romantic ideology, and even Romantic scholars who deconstruct that ideology continue to perpetuate the myth that William Wordsworth gave birth to the modern child, with Blake, Coleridge, and Lamb as attendant midwives.[7]

Recent critics of Romanticism have increasingly preferred to situate their work outside the universalist claims to truth, art, and selfhood promulgated in the name of the male Romantic canon. Gender and politics, for example, are increasingly factored into studies of adult poetry, as the recent proliferation of work revising and debunking conventional "Romanticism" attests; few critics now totalize the "self" as one and indivisible any more than they do "woman."[8] But a pedagogical version of a restrictive Romantic ideology that essentializes childhood, creativity, and the educational process is still the norm in historical studies of children's literature.[9] Reading fairy tales (which were not originally for children) and fantasy as childhood's natural food, literary histories construe children—persons differentiated by gender, class, race, and historical locale—into The Child, an idealized locus of regressive yearning. And despite the current ferment in elementary pedagogy and the emergence of children's literature as an increasingly sophisticated discipline, its practitioners still proclaim Wordsworth the visionary father of Romantic childhood.[10] In contemporary juvenile literature and pedagogy, *The Prelude* is read as simultaneously the story of a literary apprenticeship—a coming to writing—and the formation of a self, unified, coherent, individuated, transcendental—and masculine. Literary historians traditionally privilege the gratifications of this visionary child of nature, asocial and presumptively male, over the pleasures of the literate child-in-community endorsed by the female tradition; women writers' fondness for empirical observation of everyday life and their realistic emphasis on social growth through interaction with others are typically read as stultifying repression. Even the few recent critics who notice alternative feminine traditions of juvenile storying and self-representation usually judge them from within a Wordsworthian frame of reference. My essay decenters the two hagiographies that mythologize masculine and adult origins: the ahistorical acceptance of Wordsworth as both the progenitor of the modern child and its best representative, which still structures the canon and determines what counts as literary childhood, and the paternal narrative that dominates Edgeworth studies.

This essay, then, proposes a triple paradox. First, rather than seeking a "new" subjectivity in adult Romantic poems *about* the child (a poetry that outlines the "contours of masculine desire"), we need to reexamine a female tradition of prose fiction written *about*, *for*, and occasionally *by* the child. Second, by contextualizing these fictions, we discover a critical awareness, progressive and pro-woman, that's sometimes in advance of adult women's fictional forms.[11] We can historicize female desire outside the ritual dance of the adult novel's courtship plot, and we can integrate the desires that women writers encode in juvenile genres with specific changes in aesthetic practices. Vernacular language, fresh attitudes to the child, and what women writers like to call the "romance of real life" are everywhere in juvenile literature long before Wordsworth proposes them as poetic innovation. It's not men's poems but women's "minnikin volumes" that first conflate psychic growth with the naturalistic rendering of common life.[12] Women's interest in "small objects, and small errors" implies an aesthetic—quotidian and egalitarian—as well as a morality predicated on the communal significance of domestic acts ("Bracelets," 42).[13] The third mythology of origin that I consider heretically is the relationship between paternal literary authority and the daughter-writer. As a teacher of writing, I know that successful apprenticeship works not like a master-slave relationship but like the reciprocal economy of gift exchange; as a teacher of children's literature, I recognize that juvenile writing is an inherently transgressive genre, one that insists on writers and readers canny enough to be in two places at once, to play both child and adult. Renegotiating the familiar dualism of paternal fiat and filial "anxiety of authorship," I want to read "The Bracelets" as a fable of feminine, fatherly, *and* familial identity: to consider how the father might be formed and informed by the pupil he instructs, to notice how the daughter's narrative works to constitute the emotional solidarity she desires.[14]

What is "The Bracelets" about? Or rather, what's the "why" of this tale about Cecilia and Leonora, two competing schoolgirl heroines; Mrs. Villars, a benign mother-teacher who spends most of the story on the sidelines; and an absent father and brother who appear only in Cecilia's reflections?[15] If twentieth-century juvenile groups and games get pigeonholed into dichotomous sex categories, historically situated stories like "The Bracelets" are more readily reduced to whatever narrative

moment polarizes masculinity and femininity.[16] Thus, Edgeworth's ambiguous two-part fiction is readily tidied into a conflict between boys'
generous options and girls' curbed aspirations. "The Bracelets" deals
with a precocious and difficult young girl's twin desires for affiliation and
achievement: Edgeworth's child character wants to win, and she wants
everybody to love her too. Cecilia yearns to succeed, to have her work
earn the prize as the best her school produces. Like most female intellec-
tuals, she's ambitious for the "A," or in this case, the ornament that's
tangible proof of her intellect and industry, the bracelet with the teacher's
picture that every pupil covets. But like Maria Edgeworth herself, Cecilia
desperately wants her teachers and her little comrades to care for her too;
the more her touchy temper alienates others, the more she determines
that she'll make them love her. She herself proposes the trial for a second
bracelet, an eighteenth-century popularity contest in which all of the girls
cast secret votes for the schoolfellow they love most, whose award is
emblematically woven of her classmates' hair.

Throughout the story, Cecilia is contrasted with Leonora, her best
friend and strongest rival, who is as serene and even indolent as Cecilia is
anxious and energetic, and with little Louisa, the school's youngest pupil,
who does not yet have to face all of the questions that trouble girls
growing up in Georgian England. Cecilia's choices are also measured
against those of her brother George, the favorite companion of her
earliest years. Although the reader never meets George or Cecilia's father,
the masculine freedoms that they stand for have conditioned Cecilia's
impatient character and constitute the story's subtext. A motherless
child, she has been brought up more like a boy than a girl, so even her
virtues become "such as were more estimable in a man, than desirable in
a female" (42). Summarized thus baldly, the story can and has been read
as a straightforward account of the constraints of gender identity, a
narrative of girlhood's victimization that demonstrates yet again wom-
en's relegation to the passivity and powerlessness of the private domestic
sphere. Stripped of the lived context that generated the narrative, "The
Bracelets" comes off as an ideological hat trick. The missing brother gets
the goods, the sister resigns herself "to a life with and among other
women," and Edgeworth herself is faulted for representing female domestic life and failing to imagine alternative social arrangements: the
author's fiction "effectively banishes any suggestion that Cecilia's needs
or desires might transcend her circumscribed situation."[17]

Instead of recuperating androcentric Romanticism's dismissal of good
little girls and their domestic tales, I argue here for an alternative feminist
reading that monitors the complexities of Edgeworth's narrative. For if

we engage "The Bracelets" as an exemplary feminine fable of identity formation and emergent authorship, we are also working toward a different metanarrative of literary childhood that counts women in and (multiply) de-Romanticizes the "subject." Setting aside interpretive traditions that define the "bracelets" of female juvenile storying as handcuffs and bondage instead of links, rewards, and gifts, I want to see the tale, as Edgeworth does, through the eyes of the desiring little girl.[18]

II

Once upon a time, there was a little girl who never grew taller than four feet, seven inches, even though she was stretched on a machine to draw out her muscles when she was at boarding school. Besides being dwarfish, she was plain, awkward, and high-strung. Her father didn't love her mother much, so he was gone from home a lot, once for two years, taking her older brother, her favorite playmate, with him to France. When she was only five, her mother died giving birth to another sister, and her father came home. She was impressed with the man in black even though she didn't recognize him. In a few months she had a new stepmother, who was very beautiful, very brilliant, and disinclined to spoil little girls who had been allowed to run wild. They all went far off to Ireland to live, where she and her brother and sisters soon had a new sister and then a new brother. She felt very much unloved and very unhappy. She wanted attention, so she smashed glass, cut up furniture, talked back to grown-ups, and even threw tea in their faces. She was so unruly that at seven she was separated from her elder brother, her companion in naughtiness, and sent back to England to Mrs. Latuffiere's boarding school at Derby. There she discovered that she was smart and that even if her schoolmates didn't like her best, she could enthrall them with the stories she retold or improvised, like the one about the adventurer who disguised himself by wearing the mask of a dead man's face.

In the miniature world of the school, she was always watching characters and analyzing motives; she began early to hone those skills in penetration and observation that startled and delighted her adult audiences years later when she became a famous novelist. She learned to impress her teachers and her parents by being good, and she found that a lot of being good was being good with words. She realized that she possessed leadership abilities and exchanged her timidity for vivacious chatter whenever anyone loved her enough to listen. She stayed at Derby till she was twelve, seeing her family only on holidays. She wrote letters home because she wanted to belong, and eventually she was assigned fiction too, like completing a well-known Arabian tale that her father had begun, with her own version.[19] She soon thought of writing as generative, as something that changes people and makes things happen. She grasped that little girls could get happiness, maybe even love, by giving pleasure through words. With her letters and her stories, she was inventing for herself a crude version of what Lewis Hyde terms gift-exchange, a dialectic of giving and receiving that connects one to a community, an imaginatively and emotionally charged communal world made tangible in the transfer of the gift.[20]

The plain little girl's beautiful stepmother got sick and died, leaving her father so devastated that he wrote his eldest daughter a remarkable letter from beside the corpse. He praised his wife's "timely restraint" of her deviant stepdaughter and her unalterable justice, "yielding fondness towards you only by the exact measure of your conduct," and he urged his child to become "ambitious of that valuable praise which the amiable character of your dear mother forces from the virtuous and the wise." Since he understood his daughter as talented but volatile, he urged her to choose her friends wisely, to regulate her behavior, and to continue "the desire which you feel of becoming amiable, prudent, and of USE" (Edgeworth, *Memoir*, 1:7).[21] A few months after the first stepmother's death, her father married the stepmother's sister. The schoolgirl was sent from Derby to Mrs. Devis's fancier establishment in London, where she developed such serious eye trouble that the doctors feared she would go blind.[22] When she was fourteen, she went home to Ireland for good.

Sometimes the teenager thought of herself as a child; sometimes she delighted in self-consciously acting the adult educator: "Proteus=like I assume different shapes."[23] The little half brother born in 1782, the year they went home to Ireland, was given to her as her very own pupil, and she dubbed herself a serious writer as she translated Madame de Genlis on education. She alternated between playing her father's son and his daughter. Her headstrong older brother had also been sent away to an English school, but he had soon gone to sea. Since he had deserted ship in the Far East and no one had heard of him for years, her father taught his sister to manage the family estate and took the serious step of disinheriting his eldest son in 1787 (the same year "The Bracelets" was apparently written). Richard Lovell never much favored the children of his first unhappy marriage, except Maria, who was as ambitious and determined to make herself loved as was her own Cecilia in "The Bracelets." He wrote off her elder brother Dick early on, although this first son's rather feckless career was mostly the result of his father's failed experiment in recapitulating *Émile*; when Dick died young in 1796, his parent remarked coolly that it was a good thing "that he has retired from the scene."[24] Since the eldest daughter was getting her absent brother's training in estate business, as well as the paternal educational attention due to an obviously talented pupil, she probably had more intimate involvement with her father in the first few years after her return to Ireland than she commanded later as one among an ever-increasing number of siblings. Yet her contemporary letters to her schoolmate Fanny Robinson resonate with insecurities, her need to be remembered and loved, her desire to be happy; her family members weren't from the beginning always the dearest friends they came to be in later years.[25]

With the death of Richard Lovell Edgeworth's second wife and beloved intellectual partner, Honora Sneyd Edgeworth, the twelve-year-old stepdaughter Maria found the father-daughter relationship that she defines as central to the emergence of her "authorship self" (Butler, *Maria Edgeworth: A Literary Biography*, 278).[26] As "The Bracelets" and many family documents suggest, the dead Honora's consumptive daughter, also named Honora, would have been a formidable rival had she lived past 1790, and in 1787, when Maria's story apparently was written, she was very much alive. Recounting the young Honora's "extraordinary beauty, her early genius, and the exalted character with which she impressed all who knew her," the family memoir also notes her angelic temper, her unusual maturity, and the fortitude under suffering that impressed everyone as much as her looks—and she was so dazzling that waiters at inns stood transfixed when she traveled with her aunt (Edgeworth, *A Memoir of Maria Edgeworth*, 1:16–17). Richard Lovell calls Honora "my most excellent daughter," "admired and adored" by all her family, the fitting heir of her "incomparable" mother (Richard Edgeworth, *Memoirs of RLE*, 2:128).[27] "What does Honora want? She wants [i.e., lacks] a fault," her father said of her, and after she died, he promised all of his other daughters, "I will never reproach any of you with Honora. I will never reproach you with any of her virtues" (Harriet Jessie Butler and Harold Edgeworth Butler, eds., *The Black Book of Edgeworthstown and Other Edgeworth Memories 1585–1817* [London: Faber and Gwyer, 1927], 164; Edgeworth, *A Memoir of Maria Edgeworth*, 1:18). Instead of Maria's penchant for witty allusion and talking "nine miles an hour," Honora had a gift for abstract definition and mathematics, which delighted her mechanical-minded father. When friends feared she might turn out "too *reasonable*, or too reasoning," Richard Lovell set out to excite her love for literature and to develop her imagination. Since he felt that genius was cultivated rather than born, he saw no reason why she shouldn't share Maria's literary as well as her parents' scientific talents.

With her "serious simplicity and dignity," this "most uncommon and superior creature" took to the sublime: Antigone's resolution to bury her father herself was her favorite, no doubt for its rhetoric of filial piety (Richard Edgeworth, *Memoirs of RLE*, 2:123–28; Edgeworth, *Memoir*, 1:35). By the time she was twelve, Honora was also writing tales as surprise presents for her father when he was away on visits or business, just as her older sister did. Richard Lovell lavishly praises one of them, a fairy tale called "Rivuletta—a Dream," in the chapter on geometry he wrote for *Practical Education*, the family manual for parents published in 1798, and Maria reprints the story as reading matter for her autobiographical child character Rosamond in her *Early Lessons* (1801).[28]

Another of Honora's stories, an untitled manuscript among the family papers at Oxford, strikingly parallels the themes that Maria develops in "The Bracelets"; it too shows girls displaying their work for public adjudication.[29] Like "The Bracelets"—and perhaps written during the same paternal absence—Honora's 1787 tale thematizes daughters as competing artists and sisters as simultaneously rivals and friends. Honora's fragment about feminine identity and creativity actually borrows from another early story of Maria's, an Eastern-style parable written a few years earlier, around 1784. Honora's tale concerns sisterly emulation and obliquely critiques the father, like "The Bracelets," but it's framed like a continuation of Maria's "The Mental Thermometer," in which a wise old man discloses the secret of life—a magical device that measures happiness—to his protégé: the tube ironically self-destructs when the young man generously gives it to a savant who yearns to experiment. Like Maria's fable, Honora's grapples with the philosophical question of what makes people happy. Devoid of dramatic action or dialogue (always Maria's strong suit), Honora's tale presents two daughters, Cordelia and Clarissa, who vie for a "small prize" to be awarded by their parent for the best picture. Both sisters "lay their performances before their father," who rewards Cordelia for her ingenious idea: she has painted Clarissa's heart. The winner tactfully reminds her father that the tribute is supposed to go to the best art work; so Clarissa gets the victory because her painting was better executed, but Cordelia earns the father's special commendation. Like young Honora herself in the family accounts, Cordelia is an idealized abstraction of daughterly intelligence, generosity, and devotion. Negligible as fiction, Honora's story is nevertheless invaluable as familial romance. Together, the Edgeworth sisters' tales elucidate the dynamic and interactive network of family relationships and affective ties that make their narrative orderings make sense—what we might call the domestic ecological system.[30]

III

"The Bracelets" isn't central to my account of the female author's coming to writing because it's Maria Edgeworth's most engaging or most accessible story for juveniles, lively and accomplished though it is, but because it's one of her earliest to survive and one of her most revelatory.[31] It's an ambitious and ambiguous tale composed when the author herself was still teenaged, though she had already been thinking of herself as a writer for some years. It was being shown to friends in October 1787 and was probably written that year, about the same time that Maria's older brother Dick was disinherited and the younger half sister, Honora the second, added imaginative writing to her intellectual repertoire with her own welcoming stories for her father's return. What does "The Bracelets" look like as the desiring daughter's narrative when it's embedded within this family romance? How does it read as an adolescent author's surprise gift to the author of her being?[32] How does the deficient daughter become the good girl who achieves what she desires through the tales she creates? What interpretations of the construction of gender and the constitution of the self does she offer? In what ways does the narrative work to generate the community and mutuality that it thematizes?

"The Bracelets" belongs to the long-lived tradition of the school story initiated in English children's literature with Sarah Fielding's *The Governess; or, Little Female Academy* (1749), a genre very much alive and well even now. Edgeworth's tale delicately revises and transforms the women's educational tradition to which it belongs, which includes English thinkers like Mary Wollstonecraft, whom Edgeworth studied closely, and French writers like Madame de Genlis, whom Edgeworth knew very well indeed, having translated her predecessor's manual for parents in 1782 as part of her own literary apprenticeship. A school story may seem the most obvious resource for a fledgling writer with little experience to fall back on, but surprisingly, amateur authors reveled in dream-world fantasies of sentimental courtship devoid of critical edge or realistic detail. Schoolboys and schoolgirls wrote hundreds of unpaid contributions for late-eighteenth-century English miscellanies, but Robert D. Mayo's survey of original magazine fiction finds "not one . . . about daily life in an academy or college, the cruelties of headmasters, or the adventures or misadventures of boarding-school misses" (353).[33] Jane Austen's juvenilia evade the conventions of sensibility Mayo describes by parodying them; Edgeworth's precocious tales sidestep the clichés of "feminine" writing by naturalizing childhood.

Edgeworth's self-reflexive tale both builds on a female tradition of juvenile writing—the genealogy of wise women and moral mothers toward which I've gestured—and strikingly revises it by focusing on the friendships and psychic strategies of girls at school; the story renders juvenile interiority as feminine, taking the child's part, not the adult's. Edgeworth replaces the myth of an isolated male subjectivity self-engendered amid nature with a subjectivity that is collective and culturally constructed. Unlike Madame de Genlis, she doesn't obscure the developing subjectivities of her maturing heroines by superimposing an omnipotent and almost omnipresent maternal dialogue. (Like Rousseau, Genlis goes in for spying on her charges and manipulating their learning via tricks.) Unlike Wordsworth, Maria Edgeworth doesn't figure the child's movement from innocence to experience as lost paradise, either. Her school is no gynetopia, and what one Victorian reviewer calls her "unblinking" portraits of child life are still capable of startling modern critics who expect all nineteenth-century juvenile writers to be reassuringly sentimental.[34] Edgeworth's schoolgirls confront realistic problems and pleasures; they face tough "metaphysical" questions of what happiness counts most—the term is Edgeworth's—and they have to decide how to achieve the happiness they desire themselves: how to think and "invent" for oneself is always her leitmotif. Maria Edgeworth grew up in a period saturated with search-after-happiness literary conventions popularized by Johnson's *Rasselas* and Oriental tales in the *Rambler* like "Seged."[35] Cecilia's trials mockingly miniaturize the potentate Seged's grandiose plans for a perfectly happy day, and "The Bracelets" has passages of Johnsonian moralizing that Edgeworth avoids in later stories. But the precocious writer who thought of herself as a "philosopher" at fifteen was sharp enough to fuse the schoolgirl worries and the abortive experiments in adult drama that fill her early letters with a more malleable form, a juvenile narrative newly structured around the developing subjectivities of the little heroines. Edgeworth invests the miniature world of little girls' lived experience with affective and aesthetic resonance, legitimating and dignifying childhood's vernacular and homely specificities with her penchant for "Dutch" detailism. She is among the very first to make the child's thought processes central to a story and, in foregrounding the trifles of everyday child life, to democratize her aesthetics as well as her ethics.

Edgeworth's narrative learns from, transcends, and personalizes *The Governess*, the precursor of the realistic juvenile story. Fielding locates her little girls in a circumstantially realized world and endows them with lifelike characters and believable voices. Years later in Richard Lovell's

"Address to Mothers," which prefaces Maria Edgeworth's *Continuation of Early Lessons* (1814), her father (like everyone else of his generation) remembers with fondness Mrs. Teachum and her little female academy, as readers of "The Bracelets" would be expected to do.[36] Fielding opens with a glorious fight, a juvenilized mock epic battle à la her brother's *Tom Jones*: her little scholars rip and tear one another's frocks, caps, and hair until Jenny Peace, the eldest pupil, steps in and resolves their dispute over an apple. The rest of the volume consists of rather static sections in which each pupil is described by the narrator and then gives her own confessional history.[37] All relate their past faults and demonstrate that they've learned Fielding's lesson of social happiness in community. After the initial fray, *The Governess* devotes its energies to exemplifying its epigraph from *A Midsummer Night's Dream*: sisterly friendship and "union in partition." Fielding's morality is secular, hedonistic, and feminine. So is Edgeworth's, but she doesn't portray the shift from disharmony to community as instantaneous and unproblematic; she dramatizes and psychologizes it, giving her young heroines real moral dilemmas to resolve.

Most important, unlike Fielding, Edgeworth lays no ban on ambition for girls. Since Mrs. Villars's endowments fit her for "the most difficult, as well as most important of all occupations—the education of youth," her twenty little pupils are always "good and gay." They're also frankly "emulous" and encouraged to be so (3). Indeed, "The Bracelets" is about competition for excellence, which Edgeworth's model teacher stimulates by an annual prize and holiday on the first of May (a date conventionally associated with children's pleasure, power, and play).[38] "The Bracelets" thematizes the direction that emulation should take, as exemplified in the two bracelets: part one's prize for school achievement and part two's prize for "amiability," the peculiarly resonant eighteenth-century term that subsumes all of those affective qualities leading others to love the possessor and enabling her to live harmoniously in community. Edgeworth's counterpoint of two prizes, two heroines, and two ways of being in the world isn't just another conventional story about curbing female rebelliousness. Instead, the novelette vividly embodies an adolescent's conflicting emotions about what kind of daughter she wants and needs to be if she is to achieve happiness in "this little society" (4). Cecilia and Leonora are the top candidates for both prizes, and Edgeworth develops their contrasting characters and effects on others in psychological terms almost too elaborate for a child's tale. The self-representational Cecilia has an "active, ambitious, enterprising disposition," which is not presented as a bad thing in itself, but she is vain: she cares too much what other people think. Leonora (whose name is a variant of "Honora") is "contented, unaspiring, temperate"; she's proud, meaning she relies on her own judgment and approbation, so she's more independent of others than Cecilia is (5). Edgeworth's chapter "Vanity, Pride, and Ambition," for the parental manual *Practical Education* (1798), composed almost a decade after the story, underlines the fact that Cecilia's vanity and Leonora's pride aren't just the garden-variety flaws of the moral tale; rather, they stand for two ways of relating to that most important of all qualities in Edgeworthian epistemology, psychology, and ethics: sympathy, the approbation of others. Edgeworth depicts a subjectivity constructed in community, with life's happiness depending on the "pleasures of sympathy" and the "suffrages of others."

It's important to notice that Cecilia's fault is not ambition or emulation or her wish for knowledge and philosophical self-command. Her aggressive desire to improve herself in everything she undertakes is validated by the tale's plot, by the reader's interior view of the heroine, and, importantly, by the rare appearances of the school's head and surrogate mother, Mrs. Villars, at the conclusion of each section. Nowhere does the story encourage passivity or suggest that Cecilia's need to achieve and improve must be curbed. The gendered faults that Cecilia commits are transgressions against affiliation, as emblematized in the story's pervasive interest in gifts—especially appropriate for a tale intended as a present, an affective link between writer and reader. Cecilia's troubles begin with her initial triumph of winning the first bracelet and are worked out in a charged language of justice (associated with Leonora) and generosity (Cecilia's favored term). Giddy with "spirits and vanity" at having beaten all of her competitors, Cecilia leads the crowd rushing down the garden steps to enjoy their holiday, accidentally knocking down little Louisa and smashing her mother's brand new gift (8). She may not be able to help breaking Louisa's china doll, but to make fun of its decapitation is unfeeling—though the reader, like Cecilia's band of followers, has to smile too when the head careens grotesquely down the steps. Cecilia can't bear Leonora's criticizing her for having laughed, and worse yet, she suspects Leonora loves Louisa best. She's so vexed she spoils all the "plays" the little girls devise, so they exclude her from their ninepins, circle dances, and threading-the-needle: "she was thrown out" (11–12). Jealous, she loses her temper when she finds Louisa picking strawberries to cheer up Leonora and flings the little girl's intended gift over the hedge. Then she's really sent to Coventry, trapped in an arbor ashamed and alone while the others whisper and mock and huddle mysteriously together to avoid her contamination. Even Leonora tells her she must have a "bad heart." Poor Cecilia doesn't have a clue as to what this is, except "it is something which every body hates" (20, 28).

Perhaps because Edgeworth got in hot water more than once at school for indulging her "turn for ridicule" at the expense of others, readily owned up to her early defects of temper, and felt at times that "no one liked me" when she was a student, Cecilia's plight is presented with irony and sympathy.[39] No wonder Mrs. Villars is startled to find Cecilia sobbing on the heap of turf she'd playfully named her throne, sure that everybody dislikes her, instead of enjoying "one of the happiest days of your life" (22). Mrs. Villars reassures Cecilia that no one so eager to give others pleasure and to improve herself could possibly have a "bad heart." All she need do to be a star companion as well as a star pupil is to add good temper to good nature, bearing with other people's foibles and acknowledging her own without always having to be right. It's just a matter of gradually changing one's habits.[40] So Cecilia gives herself a motive; since she knows ambition is her "most powerful incentive," she thinks up the second prize and Mrs. Villars applauds the scheme (33). The girls decide on the bracelet of their own hair and plait the multi-colored strands themselves. Marilyn Butler misremembers when she writes that "the headmistress announces that she means to award a second prize" and that the very qualities that let Cecilia win the first time now stand in her way (53). So does Christina Edgeworth Colvin when she remarks that because Cecilia is motivated by vanity, "she did not succeed" (197). The story always keeps the spotlight on the girls themselves, and its conclusion ingeniously makes it possible for everyone to "win."

Edgeworth's literary biographer suggests that Leonora marks the birth of the "Edgeworthian heroine," gentle, modest, and domestic yet secure and strong in herself, as well as greatly valued by the tightly knit circle around her—the woman Maria wanted to be and felt she wasn't (Butler, *Maria Edgeworth: A Literary Biography*, 54).[41] There certainly is such a female figure apparent throughout Edgeworth's works—she once remarked with amusement that someone had admired her "clean" heroines—but Maria Edgeworth often entertains rather mixed feelings toward her.[42] She complains that she can't stand "good young men" and can't do a thing with them, and the Edgeworthian heroine isn't immune. Cecilia may be full of faults, but like Edgeworth's other fallible auto-biographical child heroines, she's invariably interesting. Leonora's pervasive association with justice, her rather tepid avoidance of wrongdoing, and her squeamishness in a sickroom don't win the reader's heart; and surely Mrs. Villars is right in finding the cruelty of branding Cecilia with "bad heart" quite uncalled for.[43] As the attitudes of her schoolmates and the narrator's loaded language show, Leonora is not presented unequivocally as the perfect "feminine" heroine, though the few critics who have noticed the story like to label her that way.

The constellation of values each girl stands for matters so much to Edgeworth that she returns to it again and again. Indeed, from the point of view of the hypothetical child reader, the story's chief weakness is its philosophical comparative analysis of the two girls. Because she needs approbation, Cecilia's vanity makes her more dependent on others and "more anxious to please" than Leonora. Leonora is most eager to avoid doing wrong; Cecilia, the most ambitious to do what's right. Cecilia's a leader, though not much loved at the story's start; Leonora's loved but "too indolent to govern" (5–6). Impatient Cecilia is always in a hurry: she can't close a door without banging it, lets her imagination run away with her, and is forever hurting somebody's feelings when she doesn't mean to. She has good nature and loves to give her companions pleasure, but Leonora has good temper and can bear and forbear. More restrained, Leonora is uniformly just and equable, not "liable to be misled by the indiscriminate love of admiration." Because her character is so consistent and unvaryingly kind, she gets the "esteem and passive love" of her companions, which is to say that they don't want to offend her, but they're not anxious to oblige her either. Leonora's justice extorts esteem, like a tax; Cecilia's good acts are rewarded, perhaps beyond their actual merit, because generosity begets generosity. Cecilia, in contrast, inspires "active love" because she actively shows love for others. Justice demands that Leonora be esteemed, but active love arises spontaneously from particular acts of kindness; it's connected with a "feeling of generosity rather than with a sense of justice" (43–44). Edgeworth knows that such reflections are over the heads of young readers and obliquely apologizes for it, but the very creaky apprenticeship in "The Bracelets" makes the extended comparisons of the two girls particularly interesting: this is Edgeworth's own personal scale of values. She learned forethought and rational self-command as she grew older, adding Leonora to her natural Cecilia, as it were, but affective values—what she calls "that magnetic sympathy of liking"—always mattered far more to her than anything else.[44] Her public reputation as the utilitarian bluestocking, chilly and just, always tickled her; she was at home and at heart always the desiring child, needy for love and active in expressing it.

The story's second part, "The History of the First of June," transforms competition into reconciliation. Determined to make everybody love her so that she'll get the prize, Cecilia hasn't rested a minute in her canvassing. She has abated her violent temper and changed the course of her habits, substituting her "powers of pleasing" for her "abilities to excel." She needs to win the popularity contest so that she can generously make up with Leonora, rather than having to because it's the "necessary tribute to justice or candour." Grown more amiable, Cecilia is more desirous than ever to do what's right, but "she had not yet acquired sufficient fear of doing wrong. This was the fundamental error of her mind." It's important to notice that the story identifies Cecilia's error as arising from her having been brought up like a boy by her father, but it's equally important to observe that her problem isn't the "enterprizing, independent spirit" she's insensibly acquired from her father's rearing her with her brother (40–41). Something more complicated is going on here than a lesson in standard gender ideology, especially since Edgeworth is already anticipating the mythology of origin that she elaborates in her conclusion to her father's autobiography in 1820: the wishful notion that her father had educated her and cared for her from the very start, instead of first ignoring her and then shipping her off to boarding school for years.

Cecilia's brief remembrance of her brother George also suggests Edgeworth's discomfort with the plight of her brother Dick, who *had* been brought up by his father from earliest childhood, only to be rejected when he turned out to be a human experiment that didn't work. Almost shockingly frank in his memoirs, Richard Lovell admits that he first applied *Émile* uncritically and then neglected his oldest son when he got too interested in engineering projects at Lyons, but parental error didn't absolve Dick from becoming a responsible adult. Richard Lovell wasn't partial to his children just because they were his; Dick was on probation for most of his short life and died about the time "The Bracelets" was published in 1796. When the story was taking shape almost a decade earlier, he hadn't been heard from for some time, so he was being officially erased from the familial circle. His sister always regarded him and his considerable talents with the liveliest affection, and she responded with delight when he surfaced a few years later, enjoying immensely his brief visits and sure that he'd redeem himself by future achievements. She wrote sadly after one visit that she missed the laughs and fun since he'd gone back to America (Butler, *Maria Edgeworth: A Literary Biography*, 126). But she also knew that she was the apprentice in estate management that her brother would have been in the normal course of events, that she was, in important ways, now her father's eldest daughter *and* his eldest son. Implying a fantasy as well as a fear of such restitution, the story firmly identifies Cecilia with the father; because of his training, her virtues "consequently became such as were more esti-mable in a man, than desirable in a female." Even Cecilia's "impatient disposition" gets attributed to the father's instruction, wrapped in a fictitious masculinity. In depriving Cecilia of maternal nurturance and documenting the ill results, "The Bracelets" may well suggest as much about Dick, the defective son brought up by men, as about the daughter (41–42).

In contrast to Cecilia's paternal identification, the equable and just Leonora is firmly mother-identified. In this way the two girls complement each other; together with Louisa, youngest of the classmates and school pet, they form a microcosmic family—a small circuit of simultaneous rivalry and community. Conveniently, only Cecilia and Leonora have had the measles that confines Louisa on the day that decides the contest between the red (Cecilia's) and the white (Leonora's) shells. Simul-taneously friend and surrogate daughter, little Louisa is the focus for the dual heroines' display of affiliative skills and maternal nurture. Edge-worth had two very young sisters at this time, but little Louisa, every-body's darling, probably derives from Sarah Fielding's youngest pupil, Miss Polly Suckling, "the Play-thing and general Favourite of the whole School" (*Governess*, 312). Neither of the older girls is the perfect nurse. Leonora is impeded by too much sickly sensibility; Cecilia tires the sufferer with her bustling and eagerness to amuse. As Edgeworth jokes of herself, Cecilia was "born impatient"; she's identified too with the au-thor's quick wit and quick step, her readiness to laugh, her delight in exuberant activity.[45] When she finds the old traveling peddler on the step, she instantly dashes downstairs to procure his entry. Justice demands that she replace Louisa's broken china doll, but generosity and vanity prove her undoing. Luckily, the peddler has one mandarin; price, three shillings. (Like Jane Austen's characters, Edgeworth's little girls and boys live in a real world where money matters; the reader always knows how much they have and what they spend it on, and many of her plots dramatize how they manage to earn what they need to save a pet or a parent.) Unluckily, the peddler also has a handsome Flora, crowned with roses and carrying a basket of flowers, in her own mahogany case complete with tiny lock; but she costs a half-guinea, and Cecilia has but six shillings in the little silver box that serves her as coin purse. When the peddler offers to take the box in lieu of the missing money, Cecilia suffers a warm conflict indeed, for the keepsake box is a gift from Leonora, a token of the special friendship that formerly existed between them.

Because she can never be satisfied with "only common justice" in restoring the smashed doll, Cecilia is seduced; she sells Leonora's box to

buy Louisa's love and her schoolmates' admiration: "have I not a right to
do what I please with it?" (51–52). But of course she doesn't, as the
story's pervasive symbolism of gifts makes clear: keepsakes aren't autonomous possessions but links that bespeak solidarity and interconnection.
They stand for an intersubjective selfhood that knows itself in relation to
others. Interestingly, as theorists of the gift remind us, Cecilia's (and the
author's) prejudice for generosity over justice is sound—justice is like
paying back in a market economy—but she has confused the generosity a
gift should encode with her own vanity. An expensive china collectible
originally destined for the display cabinet of a lady, the Flora is not really
designed to be a child's playmate but to gratify the possessor's—or the
giver's—ostentation. Edgeworth, like Wollstonecraft before her, is dubi-
ous about dolls as toys in any case, because they slot girls' behavior into
conventional forms and don't teach them to use their minds. While
Cecilia is showing off the Flora to the admiring crowd preparatory to
presenting it to Louisa, Leonora, in ironic counterpoint, is buying the
silver box from the peddler for Louisa, because it's just like her former
gift to Cecilia. Since Louisa has scratched her initial at the bottom,
Leonora at once figures out that it's the same box, but she doesn't tell and
she makes Louisa keep quiet too.

Infatuated with her own vanity, Cecilia exhibits the Flora in every
possible attitude to Louisa's admiring eyes, but she can't get rid of the
reflection that she's sold what she promised to keep forever and made "a
parade of my generosity" on top of it (61). Cecilia first cheers herself up
with George's example of intrepid confession and swears she'll tell all,
but how can she when the prize is to be awarded momentarily and she's
worked so hard to change herself? And Cecilia *has* changed and "wonderfully improved within this past month," Leonora admits to herself
even as she laments that they are no longer "always together, the best of
friends and companions; our wishes, tastes, and pleasures the same" (64–
66). Since Leonora knows that Cecilia really wants the prize, which
matters less to her than the restoration of their friendship, she urges
Louisa to put in a red shell instead of the white one she wants to vote.
Cecilia, she knows, isn't really jealous, just more anxious to succeed and
to please: "when she no longer fears me as a rival, she will again love me
as a friend." While Leonora is vexing the voters by dawdling upstairs
with Louisa, Cecilia, consumed with "absolute anxiety" to win this
simple prize of love, is energetically constructing an outdoor bower all by
herself and showing everybody—again—how much she cares for their
preference (69–70). Yet at the very moment when the contest is a tie, she
gives her own shell vote to Leonora. Then Mrs. Villars shows up with

Louisa's vote—in the silver box, much to Cecilia's discomfiture—and the Flora too; since Leonora insists that Louisa give her vote to Cecilia, the child wants to show that she hasn't been bought. But Cecilia won't take the little girl's red shell because Leonora has been so generous, nor will she take Leonora's vote instead of Louisa's; she owns up to her lapse. By virtue of the former rivals' mutual generosity, little Louisa gets the prize, and, significantly, Mrs. Villars, who knows all about the selling of the box, gives Cecilia the honor of bestowing the bracelet: she deserves the reward because she *has* improved. "For one fault I cannot forget all your merits, Cecilia" (78). Cecilia and Leonora are best friends again, everybody respectfully admires Leonora, and Mrs. Villars reminds Cecilia that she doesn't, as she mistakenly thinks, need to be still more generous but to be just and "invariably consistent" (78–79).

The story's ostensible gender lesson is that, unlike her brother George, Cecilia can't disregard "all small objects, and small errors . . . as trifles" by frankly confessing her flaws and winning parental approval for her candor (42). Edgeworth's aesthetics and ethics alike certainly work to valorize the detail—the cultural mattering of the "trifles" in little girls' lives. Indeed, "The Bracelets" is in part a playful exemplification of serious philosophical questions in juvenile guise: the two prizes for merit and amiability—Adam Smith's two "great characters of virtue"—probably derive from Edgeworth's enthusiastic recent reading of *Theory of Moral Sentiments*.[46] Yet Edgeworth's aesthetics of the detail is less a statement about the restrictions of female life than a manifesto for a clear-sighted and unsentimental women's art, for in both its emplotment and its original destination as paternal gift the story permits the heroine—and the author—to get what they want via narrative confession. Mrs. Villars, the pedagogic authority figure, makes her appearance only to conclude the two parts of the story. Each time she occasions the heroine's self-dramatizing revelation of shortcomings and her desire to improve. Each time she absolves Cecilia, loving her, warts and all—a narrative modeling within the story of the desired paternal reading response outside the story. Sophisticated in both its self-reflexivity and its deployment within the family circle, "The Bracelets" justifies Cecilia's actions and character, shows that the sisterly competitor and the father aren't perfect either, and demonstrates for the paternal audience what the effect of the story ought to be. As philosophers and investigators of children's storytelling alike remind us, narratives of self and others are rhetorical as well as expository: amid the jostling desires of family politics, children must make a case for themselves. They learn to tell the "right" story of mitigating circumstances, getting what they want while minimizing conflict with siblings and parents.[47] Self-storying creates a reality of its own, in life as in art.

Composed in secret as a gift for the father, Edgeworth's story of daughters and sons, female friendships and rivalries, and the formation of feminine subjectivity in community both idealizes and critiques the educational practices of the parent whom it addresses. Writing for herself and for the father who is the narrative's intended first reader, Edgeworth rearranges an adolescent's conflicting emotions about her place within her family into a narrative that relieves her anxieties about identity: how to be the daughter her father wants and yet replace the son he's lost, how to be like that son and yet not risk his fate. The profile of Cecilia offers an analysis of the character's strengths, weaknesses, and psychic injuries that's strikingly insightful for a young author and, when her paternal upbringing is identified as the problem, strikingly interrogative too. Cecilia embodies both threatening and threatened emotions for Edgeworth: the impetuous temper that offends others and the chief defect of Maria's character as identified by Richard Lovell Edgeworth, the "inordinate desire to be beloved" (Butler, *Maria Edgeworth: A Literary Biography*, 477n).[48] Uniting the young Maria's extreme eagerness to learn with her extreme eagerness to please, Cecilia's behavior *is* the father's doing, though not exactly in the terms the tale narrates. Odder instances come to mind (like Mary Shelley's sending William Godwin her novel about paternal incest), but "The Bracelets" makes a surprise gift for the father that is indeed surprising.

Unlike critical readings of *The Prelude* as a story of the apparently autonomous, self-determining little boy, Maria Edgeworth's "Bracelets" is an intertextual and intrafamilial story of the little girl—the self as cultural and narrative construct. "The Bracelets" isn't a sad story about learning to accept not being a boy; it's about what kind of girl to be and how to get what one wants in a world that's experienced as intersubjective and communal. Since the tale can be read as a parable about emergent female authorship as well as feminine identity formation, Edgeworth's shrewd self-assessment is, in multiple ways, an apprentice story recording the pleasures and pains of interdependence. It's not just a narrative about juvenile desire and agency; it's also a tale in which the writing of the narrative itself empowers the adolescent author, calling into being what the writer desires: the subjectivity and social world grounded in mutuality that the story represents. Whereas Wordsworth's dual consciousness of child and adult is most typically retrospective, Edgeworth's favorite literary paradigm is proleptic and predictive: the author's narrative ordering works as a transformative act to change the writer's reality and the situation in which the story is received. Maria Edgeworth the adult writer is often read as the unproblematic celebrant of domestic happiness, but the juvenile desiring daughter is not so much reporting on the family as an already existing entity as working to create that family community through her collaborative narratives. If Cecilia is in many ways the young Maria as she was, a nineteen-year-old author who can cannily fictionalize that self's errors and mend her ways is also writing herself into a different identity and a different reality. In her life, as in her story, Edgeworth learned how to take criticism and profit by it, how to control her temper, how to "improve" herself and so get the love from others she needed to survive. When Edgeworth closes the first part of the story with Cecilia's hasty petulance offending her classmates yet again—"How far she succeeded in curing herself of this defect, how far she became deserving of the bracelet . . . shall be told in the History of the First of June"—the plot of the story predicts the plot of the life, and neither has an unhappy ending. On his deathbed her father told her that "no daughter since the creation of the world had ever given a Father more pleasure."[49] The adult male Wordsworth poeticizes the "Child [a]s father of the Man"; the adolescent female storyteller plays narrative mother to her future adult self and to her father as she wants him to be, as well as to her young protagonists and juvenile family readers.[50]

Re-creating the network within which "The Bracelets" realizes its fullest meaning, I've granted Maria Edgeworth's rich and revealing tale the same critical attention long accorded male Romantic writers. In articulating the web of familial, literary, and cultural relations that shaped Edgeworth's literary apprenticeship and subsequent career, I've underlined the uses of children's literature for the woman writer. Reading the girl's construal of her own subjectivity and the author's coming to writing as interconnected stories, I've offered a model of her achievement that values instead of deprecating her lifelong fondness for literary child-ship. I won't claim for Edgeworth an outré status as the madwoman in the nursery, but I do argue that women's juvenile writing is sophisticated, revelatory, and culturally significant. It is at once the most neglected genre in the reconceptualization of early-nineteenth-century literary history and possibly one of the most relevant to our contemporary rethinking of how literacy and literature shape subjectivity. But attending to such narrative apprenticeship and to the ecology of discursive and familial systems within which a girl comes to write does more than enrich our understanding of one writer and tale. Since current research on a variety of fronts suggests that selves—or in modern parlance, subjects—come into being through the stories they tell about themselves, Romantic women's juvenilia offer a lively and overlooked resource for considering female self-fashioning. Exploring their multiple positions of child and adult, we realize how complex these practices of self-representation actually are and how the telling of the narrative itself enters into the formation of identity so that storying is both a way of knowing and a way of making things happen. We may also wish to ask whether an allied complexity exists in Romantic writing by men. When we seek to answer the question of how women write the female subject into literary identity, we are also investigating originary moments of cultural formation. We recognize how the subject and subjectivity are historically and culturally constructed, and we see women writers, readers, and protagonists *also* recognizing this textual constructedness—not as passive victims of cultural givens but as makers of narratives and models of reality that contribute in turn to the reality of their participants. If Edgeworth's "The Bracelets" is a fiction about learning something, as most children's stories are, the lessons it teaches are remarkably complex—for the protagonists, for the author, for the original paternal and familial audience, and for postmodern feminists reimagining the Romantic canon, too.

Part Two

Textual Strategies

William McCarthy

"We Hoped the *Woman* Was Going to Appear"

Repression, Desire, and Gender in Anna Letitia Barbauld's Early Poems

I take my title from William Woodfall's 1773 review of *Poems* by Anna Letitia Aikin, later Mrs. Barbauld.[1] It is a piece both admiring and muddled, in almost equal proportions. Few have praised *Poems* more highly than Woodfall did: "In some of the pieces we have a smoothness and harmony, equal to that of our best poets; but what is more extraordinary, in others, we observe a justness of thought, and vigour of imagination, inferior only to the works of Milton and Shakespeare" (54). But on one score Woodfall found the poems disappointing. They seemed to him insufficiently "feminine": "We hoped the *Woman* was going to appear; and that while we admired the genius and learning of her graver compositions, we should be affected by the sensibility and passion of the softer pieces." He wished "that she had marked, from her own feelings, the particular distresses of some female situations," that "she had breathed her wishes, her desires, and given, from nature, what has been hitherto only guessed at . . . by the imagination of men" (133). This perceived failure to represent "the *Woman*" Woodfall attributes to Barbauld's having been educated by her father: "she . . . has . . . trod too much in the footsteps of men . . . : if she had taken her views of human life from among her female companions . . . we should have been as much enchanted with her feminine beauties, as we are now . . . astonished by the strength of her imagination, the variety of her knowledge, and the goodness of her heart" (137).

In our time, commentators have shifted this ground slightly and have declared the poems, along with Barbauld herself, disappointingly unfeminist. In part they have been influenced by Mary Wollstonecraft's scorn of one Barbauld poem, "To a Lady, with some painted Flowers," as an example of "the language of men" that degrades women.[2] In part they have been influenced by a letter printed by Lucy Aikin, Barbauld's niece and first memoirist, in which Barbauld deprecates the wisdom of founding a college for women.[3] Citing both Wollstonecraft and this letter, Marilyn Williamson brusquely declares Barbauld "no feminist" and her position on the question of women's intellectuality "almost retrograde." Citing this letter, Marlon Ross holds that "a woman who cannot grant women absolute equal rights with men also cannot grant them the right to write freely from the dictates of their own desire"; the poems themselves suffer from "the limits of Barbauld's feminism."[4]

From Woodfall to Ross, despite its changed vocabulary, the charge is the same: Barbauld neither writes "as a woman" nor affirms womanhood in her writing. The charge, I shall argue, is false. It expresses a spurious essentialism, the idea that there is a "natural" (as Woodfall would say) female view of human life that a person biologically female would adopt if she were not perverted by education. The antidote to this notion is historical inquiry; to understand the relation of Barbauld's work to feminism and gender, we need to study the codes in which matters of gender were encrypted in her time. I reserve for a later page consideration of Wollstonecraft's response to Barbauld, for her response forms part of an attack on the very feminism which, as I read them, Barbauld's poems embody. In contrast to Wollstonecraft, other women found *Poems* thrillingly woman-affirming. Thus "Mira," in the *Gentleman's Magazine* (1774):

> Hail, charming Aikin, hail! thy name inspires
> My glowing bosom with congenial fires.
> Oh! could the Muse her tuneful aid impart,
> And teach to speak the raptures of my heart . . .

Thus Mary Scott, in *The Female Advocate* (also 1774):

> How fair, how beauteous to our gazing eyes
> Thy vivid intellectual paintings rise!
> We feel thy feelings, glow with all thy fires,
> Adopt thy thoughts, and pant with thy desires.

Introduced to *Poems* at age fifteen, Mary Darby (later Robinson) "read them with rapture; I thought them the most beautiful Poems I had ever seen, and considered the woman who could invent such poetry, as the most to be envied of human creatures." In *The Scottish Village* (1786), Hannah Cowley celebrates "glowing BARBAULD," "powerful Barbauld," her "fervors" and her "magic glass."[5] For these readers, Barbauld was "a woman speaking to women" and expressing strong emotion. They were moved by the poems' construction of female passion and a female subject; unlike Marlon Ross, they appear to have recognized Barbauld's texts as signs of female desire.

I propose to follow their lead and to explore Barbauld's early poems for the woman who eluded Woodfall and still eludes feminist commentators.[6] I begin by decoding several poems for Barbauld's motives and personal "themes," to illustrate a way of reading them that discloses those themes and explains their disguises. I then consider the poems as feminist texts, finding topics in them that align them with particular kinds of feminism. Finally, I examine Barbauld's constructions of "woman" in the poems, arguing for a feminist understanding of her need to idealize the female in the way she does. At each stage, I read Barbauld's texts biographically, that is, as traces of a subject who was their efficient cause. The case against Barbauld is based on a biographical reading: the presumed inadequacies of her poems are traced to presumed personal failings. The corrective to this bad biography must be better biography. That may seem to imply appeal to "personal" documents (letters, diaries) rather than "literary" ones like poems, but in Barbauld's case it does not. In her case, relatively few "personal" documents survive; apart from some anecdotes by her niece (to which I shall indeed appeal), the main evidence of her youthful subjectivity is her poetry. As I construe them, the poems are Barbauld's experiments in constructing her own subjectivity.[7]

Because Barbauld constructs her subjectivity in terms of gender, the biographical is necessarily the political. Self-construction, however privately carried on, entails entry into a public discourse; or, as Mary Poovey has put it, "because gender roles are part of familial, political, social, and economic relationships, the terms in which femininity is publicly formulated dictate, in large measure, the way femaleness is subjectively experienced." *Poems* thus has a place in the big debate about gender—specifically, about "woman"—that occupied public discourse in the last quarter of the eighteenth century. William St. Clair has observed, following Foucault, that the outpouring of books on the subject of female education and conduct between 1785 and 1820 argues that "women were . . . a problem in Britain" throughout those years; and G. J. Barker-

Benfield persuasively holds that "the culture of Sensibility" was a culture dominated by concerns about gender roles.[8] In Barbauld's own life "woman" was similarly a problem: her early poems document her resentment of woman's restricted fate, her imaginative resistance to that fate, and her efforts to conceive a more satisfying idea of her gender. Moreover, in publishing her self-constructions Barbauld performed the political act of inciting other women to observe and emulate. The responses of women readers of *Poems* suggest that they experienced Barbauld's imaginings not as constraints upon, but rather as liberations of, their own subjectivities.

"The Daughter of a Presbyterian Clergyman"

That Woodfall found "the *Woman*" absent from *Poems* is surprising, for "woman" is literally written all over them. Twenty of the thirty-three published poems are addressed to, mention by name, or incorporate as an internal character a person of female gender.[9] Less immediately obvious but nevertheless noticeable is their tendency to gender nouns feminine, not only conventionally feminized nouns such as the soul, nature, pleasure, the earth, the spring, nations and countries, liberty and virtue but even comparatively unexpected nouns such as "the bird of Jove" (i.e., the eagle). In the concluding poem of the volume, "A Summer Evening's Meditation" (poem 58), ten of fourteen explicitly gendered nouns in the first-edition text (the one reviewed by Woodfall) are feminine. Woodfall himself censured one of those genderings as mistaken: "there is . . . a slight mark of seeming inattention, where the . . . writer speaks of Saturn in the feminine." He calls this an "offense," albeit a minor one, "against ancient mythology" (*Monthly Review*, 136n), and in so doing he exposes his own bias. The "Meditation," as we shall see, is virtually a gynetopia, but the only female noticed by Woodfall is noticed because, according to patriarchal booklore, she should be "he" and is thus an "error."[10]

Gender pronouns, however, probably did not interest Woodfall. What he wished for were personal confessions, much as Marlon Ross wishes for endorsements of desire. These wishes need not have been disappointed. The poems swarm with signs of "the personal": the first-person pronoun abounds, usually signifying authorial subjectivity; a footnote to "On the Death of Mrs. Jennings" (poem 17) identifies Mrs. Jennings as "The Author's Grandmother"; passages in "The Invitation" (poem 4), describing the Duke of Bridgewater's Canal and Warrington Academy, situate the author geographically in Lancashire and politically in Protestant Dissent; "Mrs. P——" (poem 3), "Miss B*****" (poem 4), "Miss R——" (poem 8), and "Lissy" (poem 39) all appear to signify the author's intimate friends. The poems actually invite a biographical reading, even as they also slightly repel it by making the signs of the personal only partially intelligible ("Mrs. P——," not "Mrs. Priestley"). The effect of half-disclosure is to make the poems seem not really meant for the public eye; our relation to them seems that of overhearers of private musings. This privacy itself may signify gender because in gender convention (and in much social practice) the private was the realm of woman.

Woodfall, who knew something of Barbauld apart from what he saw in *Poems,* in fact initiated reading them biographically. He footnoted lines 61–62 of "The Groans of the Tankard" (poem 38), "Unblest the day, and luckless was the hour / Which doom'd me to a Presbyterian's power," with the remark "Miss Aikin is the daughter of a Presbyterian clergyman" (*Monthly Review,* 56n). The Tankard is speaking, but Woodfall's note seems to assign its groans to Barbauld herself. In so doing, whether or not Woodfall understood it, his note points to a deeply personal theme of Barbauld's poems: resentment against repression, amounting to imaginative insurrection. His note also intimates the nature of the code in which the poems inscribe her personal themes: displacement or, in rhetorical terms, allegory. "The Groans of the Tankard" is a fine point of departure for both topics.

In this burlesque poem, the Aikin family tankard interrupts dinner with a miraculous complaint of ill usage. Once the vehicle of port and ale at City feasts and ecclesiastical manses, it has been degraded by its Presbyterian owners to a mere water pitcher. Its lament includes brief but luxuriant description of the gustatory pleasures enjoyed by "the portly Alderman, the stately Mayor," "the gouty Dean, / Or rosy Prebend" (39, 70–71), from which it has been exiled. Because the poem is burlesque, the opposition between the past and present lives of the Tankard courts an ironic reading of the Tankard's groans, one in which Presbyterian purity and sobriety contrast favorably with Establishment booziness and loose living.[11] This contrast is by no means trivial to Barbauld; elsewhere she identifies vigorously with Presbyterian Dissent, victimized as it was by a bigoted and licentious Establishment. But in "The Groans of the Tankard" that is only one strand of resentment, and it provides cover for a deeper resentment of Presbyterian Dissent itself—of the very sobriety which, in the ironic reading, is Presbyterianism's honorable distinction. Presbyterianism, the Tankard complains, is joyless, anti-sensual; the Tankard is

Fated to serve the Puritanick race,
Whose slender meal is shorter than their grace;
Whose moping sons no jovial orgies keep;
Where evening brings no summons—but to sleep;
No Carnival is even Christmas here,
And one long Lent involves the meagre year. (63–68)

Unequivocally, albeit humorously, this poem ratifies *appetite*. At the dinner hour, desire, in the form of hunger, simply overwhelms an entire system of values:

'Twas at the solemn, silent, noon-tide hour,
When hunger rages with despotic power,
When the lean student quits his Hebrew roots
For the gross nourishment of English fruits,
And throws unfinish'd airy systems by
For solid pudding and substantial pye,
When hungry poets the glad summons own,
And leave spare fast to dine with Gods alone . . . (5–12)

Synecdochically represented by "Hebrew roots" (a pun that links learned philology with low diet) and "airy systems" is the curriculum of study at Warrington Academy. The snub to Milton in line 12 ("spare Fast, that oft with gods doth diet" ["Il Penseroso," line 46]) generalizes to the Dissenting tradition of high-minded seriousness, of which Warrington was the latest and most ambitious effort. The fact that the "lean student" is male further generalizes to gendered provisions for education in patriarchal society. Even the desire acknowledged by these lines is male: men are also allowed to drop their pretensions and feast. Only at "our sober meal" (13) is desire stinted.

Whose desire? The Tankard's, and the Tankard is implicitly gendered female. It is feminized by being given words that parody the speech of Pope's Thalestris to Belinda after the rape of the lock. Was it for this, Thalestris asks, that your sexuality was cultivated? Was it for this, demands the Tankard, that I was born?

Did I for this my native bed resign,
In the dark bowels of Potosi's mine?
Was I for this with violence torn away,
And drag'd to regions of the upper day?
For this the rage of torturing furnace bore,
From foreign dross to purge the bright'ning ore?
For this have I endur'd the fiery test,
And was I stamp'd for this with Britain's lofty crest? (53–60)[12]

A second feminizing move is Barbauld's allusion, in line 5, to a poem by David Mallett, "The Ballad of William and Margaret." At "the silent, solemn hour, / When night and morning meet," Margaret's ghost appears at William's bedside to reproach him for faithlessness.[13] The Tankard utters its—or rather, her—reproach at "the solemn, silent, noon-tide hour."

The character whom the Tankard reproaches—the counterpart to William in the ballad—is the Presbyterian to whose power she is subject, and that person, in Woodfall's reading and in mine, is a character never named in the poem, the Rev. John Aikin.[14] The poem suggests that his faithlessness consists of stinting his daughter's appetite and barring her from the studies of men. The stinting of appetite may be both literal and figurative. It is literal in that, as Barker-Benfield observes, control of desire for food was strongly urged on women: "moralists pushed inexorably against women's . . . expressing appetite."[15] It is figurative if "appetite" is generalized to include other desires, such as hunger for education. The poem protests, but at its close repression is reinstituted. The Tankard's groans are quelled by the appearance of another female,

> An ancient Sybil furrow'd o'er with years;
> Her aspect sour, and stern ungracious look
> With sudden damp the conscious vessel struck;
> Chill'd at her touch its mouth it slowly clos'd,
> And in long silence all its griefs repos'd . . . (82–86)

In terms of the poem's fiction—it is dinnertime, and the meal is just over—this crone might be a servant, come to clean up. But why should the Tankard be made to feel guilty ("conscious") by a servant? And what is she feeling conscious about, unless about her rebellion? Rebellion against a parent is, of course, punishable by a parent; logically, then, the "sour" female who represses complaint is the poet's mother.[16] Commenting on this poem, Woodfall, in another moment of muddled insight, speaks of Barbauld's "chastised and regulated genius," from which he would not have expected her to succeed in burlesque (*Monthly Review*, 57). His words are surprisingly apt, in view of the poem's close. Chastised and regulated, the Tankard shuts up.

A similar but more prosperous insurrection, one not punished by an internalized parent, is the ode "To Wisdom" (poem 32). Perhaps its greater success results from its being more heavily encoded. In appearance, the poem simply replays Milton's "L'Allegro," banishing the wisdom that only frowns and inviting pleasure in its place:

> But if thou com'st with frown austere
> To nurse the brood of care and fear;
> To bid our sweetest passions die,
> And leave us in their room a sigh;
>
> . . . .
>
> WISDOM, thine empire I disclaim,
> Thou empty boast of pompous name!
>
> . . . .
>
> Hail to pleasure's frolic train!
> Hail to fancy's golden reign!
> Festive mirth, and laughter wild,
> Free and sportful as the child! (7–10, 15–16, 19–22)

But one of Lucy Aikin's anecdotes promotes a more pointed reading. Barbauld, she says, wrote the poem in protest against a ban by the Warrington Academy tutors on amateur theatricals.[17] In this context, "Wisdom" acquires a new, more specific meaning: it virtually personifies the Academy's authorities—who included her father—and thus transforms the poem into an outright repudiation of them. ("Care and fear" are particularly suggestive in this reading, for the Rev. John Aikin was noted for his caution, even timidity: "He is alarmed at every thing," his colleague Joseph Priestley remarked.)[18] Construing "Wisdom" as Barbauld's code name for the local patriarchy is encouraged by an unpublished poem regretting the departure from Warrington of a Mr. and Mrs. Edwards, apparently as a result of conduct that offended the tutors (poem 45).[19] To Barbauld, they are still a "blest pair" in whose company she delights; she loves them for the very gaiety and "careless[ness]" that probably led to their exile, and she sighs for their return "tho Wisdom frown." "Wisdom" serves as a code name for the tutors by metonymy, in congruence with its more customary meaning. Barbauld "patriarchalizes" the word, making it a blocking agent and an object of resistance. In both poems it is placed in opposition to pleasure, and in both its repressive opposition is resisted.

In the published poems the personal is (not surprisingly) encoded in displaced forms so that to read the poems biographically is to allegorize them. Two unpublished poems give us the personal without displacement, although at a price: instead of displacing, they idealize. One of them, "To [her brother] Dr. Aikin on his Complaining that she neglected him" (poem 7; 1768), fills a gap at the center of "The Groans of the Tankard": it tells what birthright Barbauld felt herself to have been cheated of. Apologizing to her brother (who is at Manchester studying surgery) for neglecting his letters, she asserts her utter freedom from "angry thoughts" and "envy" (35) and traces their mutual love to their

earliest years. But in the very act of denying envy, she repines at the fate
patriarchy assigns to her gender, a fate so different from John's:

> Those hours are now no more which smiling flew
> And the same studies saw us both pursue;
> Our path divides—to thee fair fate assign'd
> The nobler labours of a manly mind:
> While mine, more humble works, and lower cares,
> Less shining toils, and meaner praises shares.
> Yet sure in different moulds they were not cast
> Nor stampt with separate sentiments and taste.
> But hush my heart! nor strive to soar too high,
> Nor for the tree of knowledge vainly sigh;
> Check the fond love of science and of fame . . . (48–58)

Compare "stampt" here with the Tankard's "stamp'd . . . with Britain's
lofty crest": both signify one's condition at birth. The Tankard was born
to a better fate than it has met. Likewise Barbauld: by birthright she was
as capable as John of enjoying literary and medical education. However,
she now feels guilty for desiring them and tries to accept her "bounded
sphere" (60).[20] The other unpublished poem, "On Mrs. P[riestley]'s
Leaving Warrington" (poem 1; 1767), is a lamentation at losing two dear
friends, Joseph and Mary Priestley, to whose house she has been in the
habit of making day-long visits:

> How oft the well-worn path to her abode
> At early dawn with eager steps I've trod,
> And with unwilling feet retired at eve,
> Loath its approach unheeded to believe.
> Oft have I there the social circle joined
> Whose brightening influence raised my pensive mind,
> For none within that circle's magic bound,
> But sprightly spirits move their chearful round.
> No cold reserve, suspicion, sullen care,
> Or dark unfriendly passions enter there,
> But pleasing fires of lively fancy play,
> And wisdom mingles her serener ray.
> Not in that form those stern forbidding airs
> Which seated on the Cynic's brow she wears
> To damp the spirits, each gay hope controul,
> And check the unguarded sallies of the soul,
> But drest in easy smiles with happy art
> She builds the surer empire in the heart. (37–54)

Barbauld's representation of the "sprightly," "chearful" Priestley household may owe something to contemporary idealizations of the "middle-
class family" as a locus of happiness (for example, in Adam Smith's

Theory of Moral Sentiments [1759]); however, lines 37–45 also suggest a felt contrast between their household and her own, a place of "reserve, suspicion, sullen care" where "wisdom" operates as "controul" and restrains her spontaneity. For her, the Priestleys represent the freedom to be spontaneous; her eager visits to them and reluctant returns home enact the same opposition as that between pleasure and wisdom in "To Wisdom."

The woman who can be inferred from these poems and whom I identify with Barbauld the poet is emotionally conflicted, struggling against strong parental and cultural repressions of her energies. Sometimes she is able imaginatively to overthrow the repressions; at other times they resubjugate her. The struggle takes various forms, some of them far displaced. In one form, the overtly political metaphorically represents the personal or simply admits the personal by congruence. Thus, "Corsica" (poem 9; 1769) and "The Times" (poem 10; c. 1769, unpublished) espouse oppositionist causes and insurrectionary acts in the public sphere. It is not, however, simply the cause of Corsican independence that makes Barbauld's "raptur'd fancy" burn (31). The idea of struggle for freedom itself excites her:

> It is not in the force of mortal arm,
> Scarcely in fate, to bind the struggling soul
> That gall'd by wanton power, indignant swells
> Against oppression; breathing great revenge,
> Careless of life, determin'd to be free. (102–106)

Obliged in the end to acknowledge Corsica's defeat by superior numbers, she proceeds, characteristically, to feminize it, this time by simile:

> . . . So strives the moon
> In dubious battle with the gathering clouds,
> And strikes a splendour thro' them; till at length
> Storms roll'd on storms involve the face of heaven
> And quench her struggling fires. (188–92)

The suppression of Corsican nationalism is thus likened to the suppression of the female. Finally, Barbauld herself closes the poem with a move that envelopes a "private," "female" meaning within a public, political one:

> There yet remains a freedom, nobler far
> Than kings or senates can destroy or give;
> Beyond the proud oppressor's cruel grasp
> Seated secure; uninjur'd; undestroy'd;
> Worthy of Gods: The freedom of the mind. (197–201)

This is a compensatory move, asserting an ideal substitute for a failed reality. Hermeneutically, it speaks to two audiences at once. To one, including Woodfall, it speaks the language of Milton ("the mind is its own place") and thus situates Barbauld in a well-defined male tradition of ethical-political discourse. To the other, readers of Mary Astell or Lady Chudleigh, it speaks the language of early feminist quietism: the conclusion that, in Astell's words, since women cannot obtain power in this world, "our only endeavour shall be to be absolute monarchs in our own Bosoms."[21] Thus, Barbauld smuggles her personal themes into these poems under the label of a public discourse. To the reader of "Corsica" who, like Woodfall, is prepared only to hear Milton, there will seem to be no woman in the poem.

Elsewhere, protest against Establishment repression of Dissent is the vehicle of her complaints. Barbauld is ambivalent in her relation to Dissent; although she resents its self-denial, rationalism, and emotional low temperature, she also identifies with its deprivations at the hands of the Establishment. In "The Invitation" (poem 4), allegorizing the legal obstacles raised by the Establishment against Dissenters' education, she figures Dissent as an eagle, gendered feminine, impeded in her flight by a phallic figure, a snake (99–104). In the same poem, her expressions of enthusiasm for Warrington Academy compare in wistful enviousness with her praise of her brother's achievements in "To Dr. Aikin . . . " (poem 7). She intimates that she might appreciate the opportunities open to Warrington students more than they do:

> Ye generous youth who love this studious shade,
> How rich a field is to your hopes display'd!
> Knowledge to you unlocks the classic page;
> And virtue blossoms for a better age.
> Oh golden days! oh bright unvalued hours!
> What bliss (did ye but know that bliss) were yours?
> With richest stores your glowing bosoms fraught,
> Perception quick, and luxury of thought . . . (111–18)

In a "Prologue to the Play of Henry the Eighth, spoken by a Warrington Student in his morning Gown" (poem 30, c. 1772, published 1790), she constructs a contrast between the ancient universities and humble Warrington that parallels the contrast, in "To Dr. Aikin . . . ," between her brother's life prospects and her own. Against the towers and bowers of "illustrious Oxford" and the "growing pride" of Cambridge (3–5), she sets Warrington's "far humbler structures . . . unknown to fame," which "fondly aspire to bear the muses name" (15–16). By analogy, Warrington's relation to the Establishment resembles that of female to male opportunity. The parallel structurings of privilege and denial ("illustrious" and "nobler" against "humble[r]" and "fond[ly]") in the two poems—undisplaced in "To Dr. Aikin . . . ," displaced onto Warrington

in the "Prologue"—implicitly align women with Dissenters and patri-
archies with Establishments. Here in the "Prologue" and in her later
pamphlet *An Address to the Opposers of the Repeal of the Corporation
and Test Acts* (1790), Barbauld anticipates Virginia Woolf, who in *A
Room of One's Own* and *Three Guineas* figures the second-class status
of women in terms of the scanty educational provisions made for them by
a patriarchy that lavishes treasure on the instruction of its sons.

Once sensitized to Barbauld's pattern of displacement, we can see it in
contexts apparently far distant from the biographical. "On the Back-
wardness of the Spring 1771" (poem 18) tells in its figuration a tale of
mutilated, grieving womanhood. The rainy spring resembles a woman
pilgrim "whose wounded bosom drinks her falling tears" (14). If we
assume that Barbauld's grief and sense of "mutilation" arose from her
experience of parental "controul" and denial of opportunity, this poem
appears to enact child–parent relations. The poem's last stanza, a plea to
"indulgent nature" to let spring happen, sounds like a child's plea to a
withholding parent. "Indulgent" is one of Barbauld's favorite words in
Poems; in "The Invitation," in a typical use of it, she flies from winter's
rigor to "brighter climes, and more *indulgent* skies" (22; my emphasis).
Such passages may be seen as metaphors for harsh and kind parenting—
for the "controul" she had endured and the spontaneity she craved.

Perhaps the only undisplaced form in which a young woman would
feel licensed to articulate emotional turbulence in the first person was the
religious poem. "An Address to the Deity" (poem 2) avows "the waves
of grief," seemingly chronic, and the "headlong tide" of "impetuous
passion" (13, 14). It can avow them because it also surrenders them,
longingly, to the "controul" of the superparent. While her family's control was marked by reserve, suspicion, and care, God's is that of an
indulgent father:

> His spirit, ever brooding o'er our mind,
> Sees the first wish to better hopes inclin'd;
> Marks the young dawn of every virtuous aim,
> And fans the smoking flax into a flame:
> His ears are open to the softest cry,
> His grace descends to meet the lifted eye;
> He reads the language of a silent tear,
> And sighs are incense from a heart sincere. (27–34)

Imagining this parenting, Barbauld permits herself a moment's regression
to infancy: "Thus shall I rest, unmov'd by all alarms, / Secure within the
temple of thine arms" (69–70). Although religious discourse commonly
trades in fantasies of infantile regression, this poem may still be treated

hermeneutically in the same way as "Corsica"; its public discourse of God is an envelope for Barbauld's fantasies of happier relations with her parents. Again, in "Hymn to Content" (poem 52) she prays to be "no more by varying passions beat" (13) and to be stilled into stoical indifference. Here the admission of turbulence is licensed by the avowed wish to escape it, a move that had a respectable (and distinctly female) lineage, including, most famously, Elizabeth Carter's translation (1758) of Epictetus, whose work counseled the conquest of passion by self-command.

Read biographically, Barbauld's poems give an impression of reiterated, restless efforts to deal with the same knot of life themes. Their core motive is grief and anger at the deprivation of birthright inflicted by her family's and her culture's oppressive construction of "woman." The complaints they raise are encoded to elude detection by the wrong parties. Because the poems were written for and to Warrington people and circulated in the very milieu of which they complain, we could hardly expect otherwise. Barbauld's way of circulating them tended to emphasize their character as "messages" even while it also often displaced them from herself. Many were sent in letters to her intimate friend Elizabeth Belsham;[22] others were deposited in places where they would be found later. The most famous of the deposited poems is "The Mouse's Petition" (poem 19), left in the cage of a mouse that Joseph Priestley had captured for use in an experiment. In the "person" of the mouse it pleads, quite simply, for freedom; it asks for equal treatment under Priestley's code of political liberty, which "spurn[s] a tyrant's chain" (10). No doubt Priestley took the poem literally (he is said to have released the mouse); but had he known Anne Finch's poem "The Bird and the Arras" (1713), he might have divined that fables of animal entrapment are a tradition of feminist complaint. Encoded in these various ways, Barbauld's poems lend themselves to duplicitous readings, often, although not exclusively, along gender lines. Thus, William Woodfall could admire them for carrying on in the tradition of Milton, oblivious to the signs in them of "the *Woman*." From the ecstatic responses of "Mira," Mary Scott, Mary Robinson, and Hannah Cowley, it would appear that they understood Barbauld's encodings as the postcards from the volcano that they are.[23]

"We . . . Pant with Thy Desires"

The cardboard antifeminist image of Barbauld, purporting to be based on her biography, is a figure of repression pure and simple, an enemy of women's desire. A more thorough biographical reading discloses a far more complicated and interesting woman—and in at least one important respect, a feminist. In a culture that imposes upon women a narrow range of permissible desires and limited means of expressing them, to insist on asserting desire may be, ipso facto, a feminist act.[24] Barbauld's insurrections against repression all assert desire. The objects of her desire vary and thus imply various traditions of feminism. In "The Groans of the Tankard" and, more explicitly, in "To Wisdom," the object of desire is pleasure—a more oppositional demand, given the historical tendency of Presbyterianism (of which the Tankard reminds us), than it may seem today, when pleasure (or what at least usually passes for it) appears politically banal. In "The Invitation" (poem 4), Barbauld calls upon her friend Elizabeth Belsham to leave the town and join her in pursuing the pleasures of a Lancashire spring:

> From glittering scenes which strike the dazzled sight
> With mimic grandeur and illusive light,
> From idle hurry, and tumultuous noise,
> From hollow friendships, and from sickly joys,
> Will DELIA, at the muse's call retire
> To the pure pleasures rural scenes inspire? (9–14)

Pleasure is allegorized as a "smiling goddess" whom they will pursue wherever she may lead, through forest or mead or hill or glade, and whom they will never lose because "she cannot fly from friendship, and from you" (33–38). In a twist on the traditional moral exhortation *surge, age* (arise, get going), Barbauld urges her friend to "haste away, / And let us sweetly waste the careless day" (52). This single line epitomizes important Barbauld concerns. *Careless* is a word central to Barbauld's youthful poetic vocabulary; almost always used honorifically, it contrasts with *care*, as in "the brood of care and fear" ("To Wisdom," 8) and thus opposes the patriarchal ideology encoded in the word *wisdom*. "Waste" is gloriously self-indulgent: an exhortation to *haste* that we may *waste* implicitly summons up everything for which Protestant Dissent stood, to snub it utterly. (The gesture is analogous to the gesture in "The Groans of the Tankard" that summons up Milton in order to snub him.) Barbauld is seeking not "improvement," not "profit," not power nor responsibility nor rationality, nor even "seriousness"; she is seeking pure enjoyment. Her ethic here resembles that of Aphra Behn's poem "The Golden Age" (1684), in which the only injunction is "to pursue delight," and in our own time that of Marilyn French's *Beyond Power*. This kind of feminism, writes French, "abjures the self-sacrifice . . . patriarchy demands from women, offering instead an ideal of personal integrity and pleasure; it condemns the pursuit of power, stratification, and the repudiation of the body and feeling that patriarchy instills in the public world, offering instead an ideal of felicity."[25] In their short compass, Barbauld's lines indeed do all this. The town's "glittering scenes," "mimic grandeur and illusive light," encode the public world of power and stratification in which women have no place; the invitation to Delia to form a gynetopia of two (or rather three, including Pleasure) repudiates patriarchy. Feeling is present in Barbauld's love for her friend, and body is honored by the sensuous image of pleasure lying "*wrapt* in careless ease" as in a garment (29; my emphasis).

Although Barbauld's language of pleasure is chaste, it is by no means drained of sensuousness or eroticism. Two of her favorite words, *soft* and *sweet*, serve as shorthand for a range of sensory delights. They can eroticize discourse otherwise seemingly unerotic, as in "Verses written in an Alcove" (poem 39), where these two words, together with the pulse of the lines, suggest quick-breathing anticipation:

> Now the moon-beam's trembling lustre
>   Silvers o'er the dewy green,
> And in soft and shadowy colours
>   Sweetly paints the checquer'd scene.
>
> . . . .
> Choral songs and sprightly voices
>   Echo from her cell shall call;
> Sweeter, sweeter than the murmur
>   Of the distant water fall.
>
> . . . .
> Soft, as when the evening breezes
>   Gently stir the poplar grove;
> Brighter than the smile of summer,
>   Sweeter than the breath of love. (1–4, 21–24, 29–32)

The poem appoints a tryst in the alcove, at night, with "Lissy" (Elizabeth Rigby, whose "love creating wiles" are celebrated in another poem [poem 44, unpublished]). Barbauld eroticizes her friendship with Lissy as a way of figuring the delights of that friendship—more probably, of female friendship in general.

The most apparently erotic of the poems are the six "Songs" (poems 22–27). Because they are love songs, they are highly conventionalized and codified, and their eroticism is largely notional. The subject position in most of them is generically male, and the objects of the passions represented in most of them are generically female. First published in John Aikin's *Essays on Song-Writing* (1772) and written in correspondence with him about love songs as a genre, they have a "theoretical" character, as if designed to demonstrate various postures of amorous discourse. There is probably also a measure of dry humor in them; Barbauld has something of Dryden's taste for extravagance verging on parody. Nevertheless, the songs give scope to her genuine desire for passionate rhetoric, for representing hyperbolic emotion. Thus, the "marks" of true love (according to song 1) include being "all bath'd in tears," lying "whole ages at a beauty's feet," "kneel[ing]," "languish[ing]," "implor[ing]," and still adoring "tho' she disdain": "It is to do all this and think thy sufferings sweet." The lover in song 4 is carried away by destructive passion as a sailor is carried out to sea by the storm surge and drowned. Song 6 envisions a lover who has heedlessly cultivated a passion for a young girl that, now that she is grown, utterly dominates him. To represent his state, Barbauld indulges herself in the language of "Oriental" despotism:

> But now despotic o'er the plains
> The awful noon of beauty reigns,
>   And kneeling crowds adore;
> Its beams arise too fiercely bright,
> Danger and death attend the sight,
>   And I must hope no more. (19–24)

The extravagant irrationality of these assertions, their studied imprudence and cultivated rhetoric of self-immolation, must have been highly attractive to a person brought up on rational guard against the "sallies of the soul"; they are best regarded as exertions of a secularized religious enthusiasm.[26] That the subject position of these songs is generically male rather than female is almost inevitable. No "respectable" woman in the late eighteenth century could have addressed such language to a male (other than God or Jesus); in a woman's text, the rhetoric of erotic passion had to be encoded in a form that makes it appear male.[27]

The poems also evince a sporadic but intense interest in childbirth. In "To Mrs. P[riestley], with some Drawings of Birds and Insects" (poem 3), this interest is displaced onto the insects, which await their birth in a "heaving tomb" that "distends with vital heat" (78). Their birth is likened to two scenes in Tasso's *Gerusalemme Liberata*, here conflated by Barbauld into one:

> So when Rinaldo struck the conscious rind,
> He found a nymph in every trunk confin'd;
> The forest labours with convulsive throes,
> The bursting trees the lovely births disclose,
> And a gay troop of damsels round him stood,
> Where late was rugged bark and lifeless wood. (85–90)

The births follow an act analogous to sexual penetration. This passage, which occurs apropos insects, could give point to Richard Polwhele's horror in *The Unsex'd Females* (1798) at the idea of teaching women natural history; in his view it was a provocation to eroticism.[28] In another Barbauld poem (a "character" of Mary Enfield, published posthumously [poem 46]), a woman who bore twins is figured as an orchard tree, "heavy . . . with fruit" (3). Emphasizing "lovely fruit" (7), "ruddy orchards" (8), and "twin apples blushing on a bough" (9), the poem images the childbearing woman as luxuriantly sensual.

Pleasure and eroticism are not, however, the only objects of desire in Barbauld's poems. In "Corsica," desire is explicitly political: to be free of domination, to be empowered. Lines 102–106 (quoted above) generalize the demand for liberty in terms that could embrace young women in Lancashire as well as male insurgents in Corsica. More than that, the poem's figure of Liberty is amazonian: "the mountain goddess," a female athlete who "loves to range at large" in "lonely scenes / Of unquelled nature," "and on the iron soil / Prints her majestic step" (68–69, 75–77). The sheer power implied by the language of *printing* a step on *iron* soil is noteworthy. Indeed, the female in "Corsica" is a notably powerful person, whether encoded as Liberty or—her other incarnation—as Virtue. A virago, she revels in scenes of storm and combat:

> . . . then her tow'ring form
> Dilates with kindling majesty; her mien
> Breathes a diviner spirit, and enlarg'd
> Each spreading feature, with an ampler port
> And bolder tone, exulting, rides the storm,
> And joys amidst the tempest.
>
> . . . .
> . . . The bold swimmer joys not so
> To feel the proud waves under him, and beat
> With strong repelling arm the billowy surge;
> The generous courser does not so exult
> To toss his floating mane against the wind,
> And neigh amidst the thunder of the war,
> As virtue to oppose her swelling breast
> Like a firm shield against the darts of fate. (146–51, 160–67)

The two last lines image female joy in aggressive action, in terms anticipating Monique Wittig's *Les Guérillères* (1969).[29] To appreciate just how thrilling these visions of female athleticism must have been to Barbauld and her women readers, we need only recall the impediments to movement with which eighteenth-century women were encumbered. The suppression of bodily activity in girls was, of course, part of their training to be "ladies."[30] In the figures of Liberty and Virtue here and in that of "my soul" in Hymn 5 (poem 37), exhorted to awake and arm herself for Christian battle, Barbauld compensates for the restraints imposed on her gender with robust fantasies of free and powerful movement. That women readers responded to these fantasies is perhaps indicated by Elizabeth Benger's praise of Barbauld in *The Female Geniad* (1791): "she *rambles* o'er the bounties of the globe."[31]

The greatest female freedom of action in *Poems* is found in "A Summer Evening's Meditation" (poem 58), an extraordinary poem in the traditions both of Anne Finch's "A Nocturnal Reverie" and of *Paradise Lost*; indeed, it seems to marry them. Like Finch and also as in her own "Alcove" verses, Barbauld claims the night poetically for women, as the time when (in Finch's words) "tyrant *man* doth sleep." At the poem's opening, Diana, rising while the sun ("the sultry tyrant of the south" [1]) sets, "impatient for the night, . . . seems to push / Her brother down the sky" (9–10; cf. Barbauld's all but avowed envy of her brother). Contemplation is up and about; she is a female who spends her days in dark, hidden places (grottoes or deep woods), feeding on "thoughts unripen'd by the sun" (22) but who at night comes into her own. The stars emerge, at once a sensuous experience by virtue of their beauty and also an accession of knowledge, for they speak divine wisdom to her who watches them.[32] As the poem's narrator contemplates the stars, relishing their beauty and pondering their meaning, she dares to wish to explore them nearer. No sooner is the wish formed than she soars upward, sailing "on fancy's wild and roving wing" (72) past the moon and the planets, launching "fearless . . . into the trackless deeps of space" (81–82), even "to the dread confines of eternal night . . . Where embryo systems and unkindled suns / Sleep in the womb of chaos" (93, 96–97). Her language in this recalls, of course, the Miltonic Satan's journey upward from Hell through Chaos to Earth (*Paradise Lost*, 2:910 ff). Apparently, she is appropriating the Miltonic sublime for a feminist "sally of the soul." Yet in a way, Satan's rebellion against the deity is an archetype of Barbauld's various insurgencies against patriarchy; like him, she will not stay in her assigned place. Having dared thus greatly, the poem backs down at its close. She ceases flight, "abash'd" (111), and returns to earth. Even so, the poem ends with a permitted (because religiously authorized) orgasm of pleasure as she imagines what heaven will offer hereafter "to my ravish'd sense" (121).

In Barbauld's poems, then, desire takes the form of compensatory fantasy. What in life she is denied or discouraged from doing Barbauld asserts in imagination. That the assertions themselves are displaced or variously compromised signifies that the texts in which they occur should be construed as emotional battlegrounds or, in the phrase of materialist feminism, "sites of conflictual discourses." To see them merely as static embodiments of fixed positions (and those positions "unfeminist") is to perpetuate the remarkably unperceptive notion set down long ago, by Henry Crabb Robinson, to the effect that "the felicity of [Barbauld's] life consisted in a passionless serenity of mind," a state that "is not the element of poetry."[33] This notion still lives in Marlon Ross's claim that Barbauld's poetry is limited by her alleged unwillingness to endorse female desire. In fact, Barbauld's mind was neither passionless nor serene. It was turbulent, and a main source of its turbulence was gender.

"The Sunshine That Laughs on Her Brow"

The poem that Mary Wollstonecraft scorned, "To a Lady, with some painted Flowers" (poem 55), likens the lady to "flowers sweet, and gay, and delicate" (3), distinguishes flowers, a "luxury," from "loftier forms" to which "rougher tasks [are] assign'd" (7–9), and closes by asserting that "[her] best, [her] sweetest empire is—to please" (18). "On this sensual error," complains Wollstonecraft, " . . . has the false system of female manners been reared, which robs the whole sex of its dignity, and classes the brown and the fair with the smiling flowers that only adorn the land. This has ever been the language of men."[34] Even apart from this poem, many of the other constructions of "woman" that we encounter in *Poems* cannot avoid striking us as proleptic of the Victorian "angel in the house." Miss Rigby (poem 8) is an example: honored as a caregiver whose breast is a "pillow" for her declining mother's head (28), she is even called an "angel" (9). Susannah Barbauld Marissal (poem 40) is praised for a sweetness and innocence that feminists today would regard as idiotic; we want something altogether tougher. To say this is, of course, to come up short against the ideological demands of feminist textual commentary today. If we mean to be historians, however, we must be willing to situate the constructions of "woman," so persistent in Barbauld's early poems, not among our discourses but among the discourses of their culture. Further, to understand why Barbauld persisted in constructing these particular ideas of woman, we need to imagine the role they played in her construction of her self.

Because Barbauld's early poems predate the *Vindication* by twenty years, the discourses among which we must situate them do not include Wollstonecraft. Rather, Barbauld's constructions can be seen as reactions against previous or contemporary constructs of "woman" that Barbauld herself would have regarded as misogynist. Her insistence on women's friendships, for example, and on celebrating so many of her friends, looks like a direct response to James Fordyce's *Sermons to Young Women* (1766). She deeply resented Fordyce's insinuation that women's friendships are not sincere (a hoary topic of misogyny) and was tempted "to have burnt the book for that unkind passage."[35] But the writer whom she most answers probably is Pope. Her intimate knowledge of his poems is written all over hers, in the form of echoes and allusions such as the one in "The Groans of the Tankard" to *The Rape of the Lock*. Implied by Pope's Belinda, whose eyes are "unfix'd," is an idea of woman as light-minded and unsteady;[36] his essay "Of the Characters of Women" dwells on the supposed incoherence of the female character (or even its nonexistence) and on women's alleged abundance of incontinent, whirling, wasteful energy. In some quarters today, the idea that woman cannot be fixed to any character may have a satisfyingly Foucaultian ring, for we have learned to distrust category divisions as engines of cultural control; in the name of human liberation (from race, class, and gender), we are exhorted to "refuse what we 'are.' "[37] There is some irony in a development that can make Pope's misogynist ideology look retrospectively chic. For Pope, "female caprice" signified not the liberation of woman but her inferiority; it was evidence of the "weaker," "softer" material of which woman was made, "matter too soft a lasting mark to bear."[38]

Barbauld could reply to the Popean aspersion in several ways. She could oppose it, counterasserting female integrity and coherence in terms similar to those in which Pope constructs such ideal figures as the "good Critic" or some other character that reconciles oppositions instead of being torn apart by them. Several poems practice this reply. Mary Priestley (poem 1) reconciles Popean opposites in possessing at once "so cool a judgment, and a heart so warm" (26). Barbauld's cousin and sister-in-law-to-be, Martha Jennings (poem 41), is utterly regular and rational, speaks only "sense and truth," and betrays but one ruling passion, a "generous" excess of love. Sarah Taylor Rigby (poem 42, unpublished) is "prudent, *tho* gay, and active, *yet* serene"; an unnamed lady's handwriting evinces her combination of strong judgment and easy manner, "correct *though* free, and regular *though* fair" (poem 51; my emphases in both). Elizabeth Rowe the poet reconciles "the Christian's meekness and the Poet's fire," and like Pope's good Critic in *Essay on Criticism*, she is "learned without pride" (poem 57).

These "pattern[s] of a female mind" (Barbauld's phrase, poem 40) do not lack precedent, even in satires on women, as Felicity Nussbaum has demonstrated;[39] but whereas in satires—including Pope's "Of the Characters of Women"—the "pattern" woman serves as a rare and scarcely saving exception to the general wreck of the sex, in Barbauld she is the only kind of woman. Where the satires depend on a dialectic in which pattern women are used as sticks to beat the rest of their sex, Barbauld's aim in constructing pattern women appears to be to rebuke that dialectic. From her poems, one might imagine that every woman she knew was a pattern. This holds true even for a certain Mrs. Fenton, whom Barbauld calls "ill fated Flavia," whose history would classify her in satire or homily among the "fallen" and therefore as a typical blot on her sex: she was seduced in youth and abandoned.[40] Barbauld, however, does not renounce her and sympathizes with her sufferings; moreover, she hails Flavia as a heroine who refuses to be defeated by misfortune. Flavia

> Not only bore her wrongs, but strove to hide;
> The griefs she could not quell, she scornd to own,
> And drew resources from herself alone.
> Her active mind above her fortunes rose,
> And smil'd superiour to a weight of woes. (Poem 48, unpublished)

A second kind of reply to Pope would be to revalue his terms, promoting "soft" (still feminized) and demoting the (masculinized) honorifics "strength," "firmness," and so forth. This kind of move, of which there is a long feminist tradition, amounts, as Marilyn French (following Julia Kristeva) observes, to an attempt "to alter the symbolic dimension of women's position, and the 'sociosymbolic contract' imposed on them" (*Beyond Power*, 454). Although she did not invent it,[41] this is Barbauld's preferred move. (A narrative version of it is the opening of "A Summer Evening's Meditation," where, as we saw, the harsh, masculine sun is expelled in favor of the gentle, feminine moon.) The poem in praise of Susannah Marissal (poem 40) provides the archetype: "soft," "sooth[ing]," "innocent," "endearing," "kind," "pure" and "good"; she is explicitly valued above wealth, wisdom, beauty, or "brutal strength" on the principle that "goodness only can affection move." We can see here another example of the feminism that, like Marilyn French's, would reverse the culture's preference for power over pleasure.

In her poems Barbauld usually associates the female with softness, and softness she always associates with pleasure; "To a Lady, with some painted Flowers" is fairly typical, though a bit more aggressive than the others. (There is a suggestion of *épater* in the last line's dash: "Your best, your sweetest empire is—to please."[42]) The constellation of honorifics that compose "Verses written in an Alcove"—"soft" and "sweet" pri-

marily, in practically every possible grammatical form—not only sensual-
ize that poem but also feminize it. And like "The Invitation," it too is an
intimate gynetopia made up of Barbauld, one female friend, and a
goddess, here "that other smiling sister, / With the blue and laughing
eye" (45–46), probably personifying Mirth. *Smiling* and *laughing*, words
almost as important in Barbauld's early poems as *soft* and *sweet*, should
remind us that pleasure need not be passive: the enjoyment that Barbauld
wants to associate with woman is outgoing and jovial. In "The Invitation," pleasure itself is feminized as a "smiling goddess." In another
poem, her friend Elizabeth Belsham is composed of spring, sunshine, and
joy:

> But the sunshine that laughs on her brow
> Unclouded shall ever remain;
> Ease, Wit, and the Graces reside,
> With Betsy the joy of the plain. (Poem 5, unpublished)

The Rigby sisters, whose actual gaiety seems to have alarmed the Warrington tutors, are celebrated in two unpublished poems for the very
frivolity that the tutors condemned. The younger, Elizabeth ("Lissy" of
the "Alcove"), "stands like the laughing year and breathes delight." Her
exuberant good health and happiness alone are antidotes to Barbauld's
"pensive mind": "Bloom on her cheek and pleasure in her eye / Sorrow
and care are chear'd when she is by" (poem 44).[43]

The female figures on whom Barbauld confers her honorifics are all, of
course, idealizations, all "pattern[s] of a female mind." Once we understand Barbauld's usual form of psychic defense—compensatory fantasy—
we can understand these idealizations as so many distress signals. The
true subtext of her notorious letter about women's education is that
Barbauld was not easy in her gender—that, in many respects, she hated
being "woman" as "woman" was constructed in her culture.[44] Unhappy
with her mother, unhappy with what she was being compelled to become,
she compensated, as adolescent girls classically have compensated, by
idealizing other actual women (friends or relatives) into possibilities of a
more satisfying self.[45] "Pensive," socially awkward, and depressed in her
life, she envisions women who laugh, frolic, and charm. For her, hedonism is a necessary component of feminism. The laughing woman is such
a central figure in these poems because she combines so many of Barbauld's life themes. She is spontaneous, able to indulge "the unguarded
sallies of the soul"; she is a pleasure seeker and giver, in opposition to
Presbyterian "care and fear" and stinted senses; and she is, not least, at
ease in her gender.

This last point, perhaps the most important to Barbauld, is, of course, the most problematic for modern feminism—or even for Wollstonecraft's feminism. The same type of objection can be brought against Barbauld's pattern female as has been brought against the late eighteenth-century "feminization of sensibility" itself by some feminists today: "if women were valued for natural, intuitive feeling, so were children and idiots."[46] Barbauld is vulnerable to the criticism that she makes her ideal of woman in purely oppositionist reaction against Presbyterianism, so in seeking to undo its particular deprivations she embraces a conventionally impoverished construct of the female. (Indeed, in one poem she herself identifies pleasure as "the portion of th' inferior kind" ["To Mrs. P(riestley) . . . ," 94].) On the other hand, there are many rooms in the house of feminism, and Wollstonecraft is not its sole proprietor. Take Barbauld's flower-woman, for instance: if classing "the brown and fair with the smiling flowers that only adorn the land . . . has ever [meaning "inevitably," "essentially"?] been the language of men," what would Wollstonecraft have made of Monique Wittig's lesbian warriors, who compare their vulvas to violets?[47] Whatever position one takes on the political wisdom of basing a feminism on "only those metaphors and parts of experience that have already been ceded to women" (French, *Beyond Power*, 455), it must at least be granted that a discourse of flower-women like Barbauld's is not *essentially* "the language of men." It can be appropriated as well by women who identify strongly with women.

We should also be careful, puritans as we ourselves tend to be, not to scorn Barbauld's constructs merely because they identify the female with pleasure. We need to ask, first, pleasure for whom? In Barbauld's poems the answer is usually clear: pleasure for the subject herself, for woman. A comic poem published posthumously, "Bouts Rimés in Praise of Old Maids" (poem 16; 1770?), because it is comic can, as usual, assert the point more directly:

> Hail all ye ancient damsels fair or Brown,
> Whose careless minutes dance away on Down,
> No houshold cares your free enjoyments Saddle,
> Thro' life's wide sea your lonely skiff you Paddle . . . (1–4)

There follows a list of evils from which the old maid is free: lovers, wedding bells, nurses attending "with Caudle and with Cake" ("Too dearly bought when liberty's at Stake"), fickle and drunken husbands, dying children, "squalling brats." And the poem concludes, grandly: "In pleasure's free career you meet no Stop, / Greatly alone you stand without a Prop" (15–16).[48]

Not that this is Barbauld's last word on "woman." There is a third response to Pope's aspersion of the female: to revalue his notion of woman as a bundle of restless, crazy energy to construct a figure of powerful and purposeful woman—roughly, to see Atossa in "Of the Characters of Women" not as a termagant but as an amazon. To be sure, Pope himself might have called her an amazon and damned her precisely for that character. The problem of revaluation here is greater than with "soft," for energy itself is forbidden to women, and softness is not. In the late eighteenth century, however, together with the "feminization" of culture we see also a tendency to what might be called the "amazonizing" of woman: stories of women who smuggled themselves into army regiments and fought alongside men become topical, and in other ways women come to be imagined in men's roles.[49] Whether the amazon figures in Barbauld's poems result from a revaluation of Pope is impossible to say, but the figures are there: Liberty and Virtue in "Corsica," as we have seen, and "my soul" in Hymn 5. Another is Sarah Vaughan, wife of the patriot Samuel Vaughan. In her "character" (poem 14, posthumously published) elements of the amazon mix with a figuring of woman's domestic roles of wife and mother: Vaughan is likened to "the mighty mothers of immortal Rome" (4). This poem seeks both to "domesticate" the amazon and to "amazonize" the domestic. Strenuous moral agents, Barbauld's amazon figures all exert themselves in scorn of pleasure. Presumably, they would have been more to Wollstonecraft's taste, embodying as they do the kind of feminism that emphasizes moral agency.

It would be nice if we could date Barbauld's poems to construct a satisfying progression from "lower" to "higher" versions of woman and thus represent Barbauld as waxing consistently "stronger" in her imaginings. The arrangement of *Poems* for publication tends, in fact, to do that, since it places in the last position "A Summer Evening's Meditation," a poem in which the woman's pleasure and her power are one. But *Poems* does not reproduce the order of the poems' composition, and for many of them the order is unknown. In any case, the "growth of strength" paradigm is itself an idealization, one favored by the political tradition of optimistic individualism. It is probably better biography to see Barbauld's various constructs as just that: various. She returns to the subject because it is vital to her to do so, but she does not necessarily build on previous imaginings; rather, because she is in deep conflict on all of these subjects she takes different, sometimes contradictory, positions. Alternatively, her various imaginings could be construed as so many different angles of attack on her ongoing problems. They could be understood as her tacit recognition that (to quote Marilyn French one more time) feminists, confronted as they are with massive patriarchal resistance, "must shift and parry, [and] demonstrate imagination, spontaneity, opportunism, and joy in the quick jab" (*Beyond Power*, 487).

Barbauld's feminism can be seen, finally, to give her an important place in Romanticism as well. Her relation to both is bound up with the principal psychic defense encoded in her poems, compensation fantasy. Deprived in life, she seeks in imagination the opposite of her condition. Constrained by the "bounded sphere" ("To Dr. Aikin . . . ," 60) of cultural womanhood as she knows it, she envisions bursting out of it by active opposition; condemned by religion and gender to "controul" and plain living, she revels in ideas of hedonism. Compensation fantasies were necessary to women in a culture that constructed "woman" as a stinted, mutilated being, denied her birthright. As women entered upon the scene of writing in ever greater numbers in the late eighteenth century, it is not surprising that what they committed to paper were precisely such fantasies. The movement that later came to be identified with Wordsworth and his circle began with women committing to print their (inevitably, in this context) feminist fantasies of compensation. In a true history of Romanticism, Anna Letitia Barbauld would be counted among its genuine founders.[50]

Anthony John Harding

Felicia Hemans and the Effacement of Woman

The sentiments are so affectionate and innocent—the characters of the subordinate agents . . . are clothed in the light of such a mild and gentle mind— the pictures of domestic manners are of the most simple and attaching character: the pathos is irresistible and deep.—Percy Bysshe Shelley

ffection, innocence, domesticity, pathos—the passage quoted in the epigraph above could almost be from a contemporary assessment of Felicia Hemans's *Records of Woman*, but it was actually written about *Frankenstein*. Percy Bysshe Shelley seems to be reassuring himself and us that Mary Shelley's novel is not, after all, wholly outside the bounds of women's discourse, despite its lurid subject matter and unwomanly preoccupation with violence and death.[1] It is one of those moments when the force of social expectation as it affects the reception of women's writing, even writing of a distinctly new and disturbing kind, becomes tellingly apparent.

Yet the shocking juxtaposition of domestic affection and death that made *Frankenstein* seem so disturbingly "unwomanly" is also present in Felicia Hemans's work.[2] Death, in her poems, is not so much the enemy of domestic affection as the necessary dark backdrop against which the affections show their true brightness. At times, death virtually becomes a kind of guarantee of the significance of a life, particularly of a woman's life. The very pervasiveness of this ethos in Hemans's work, an ethos in which a woman's life is more worthy of memorializing the more it is played out against the backdrop of another's death and most especially if it finds its *own* highest realization in death, exposes to the modern reader the power of social expectation, of the social construction of gender.

In Hemans's poetry, domestic affection, or what Kurt Heinzelman has referred to as "the cult of domesticity," is so often not a counterbalance to violence and death nor a refuge from them, as it seemed to be for Percy Bysshe Shelley in his reading of *Frankenstein*, but a value that inexorably demands violence and death as its perfect tribute. Heinzelman's definition of the "cult of domesticity" is worth quoting at length:

[T]he belief that the household is the site of value not merely or even primarily because of what it produces in the economic sense but because it provides the place where the individual personality may grow and the occasion to discover in that growth a way of integrating self and society, family and polis. . . . The cult of domesticity was a replacement for or sublimation of the family as a viable, self-sustaining economic entity; it thus depended upon a division of female and male labor in which commodity production came to be seen as the masculine activity while female economic activity was regarded as reproductive, whether literally in the case of childbearing or metaphorically in the form of service-based employment such as nanny, maid, governess, or indeed houseworker in general.[3]

In glorifying the ethic of female self-sacrifice and linking it in many poems (particularly later in her career) with the heroic deaths of women as sacrifices to the domestic ideal, Hemans delivers a new version of the Romantic hunger for transcendence, a version that purports to compensate women for their unpaid labor and the relative obscurity of their lives as nurturers and caregivers. Read "against the grain," however, Hemans's texts reveal the terrible price of the "cult of domesticity."

For rarely in Hemans does a woman's life earn significance on its own account. Its significance more often derives from its relationship to the transcendent, to the afterlife—that is, to what is *absent from it*. Death, not life, is the veil that must not be lifted. That Hemans does not set out to challenge received values (as Mary Shelley does, in some respects at least) makes her work all the more interesting, for she gives full expression to the seductiveness for women of this ethic of self-sacrifice. Yet whatever Hemans's intentions may have been, her poems expose the destructive potential of the prevailing metaphysic just as relentlessly as *Frankenstein* does.

Records of Woman, the title of Hemans's 1828 collection, seems promising enough to the reader hunting for forgotten literature by Romantic women writers. This should be, it seems, a treasure trove of women's experience, a sort of verse rival for Matilda Betham's *Biographical Dictionary of the Celebrated Women of Every Age and Country*

(1804). So often, however, the tone in which these poems document
women's life experiences disappoints us. It cannot be their sentimentality,
for sentiment is exactly the point in so many of the poems; and in any
case it is not right to permit Fielding, Sterne, and Dickens their sentimentality but object to it in Hemans. Rather, it is the total absorption of
Hemans's women by values that appear to us patently hostile to women's
individual identity and destructive of any intrinsic significance their lives
may have.

In "Madeline: A Domestic Tale," a young Frenchwoman leaves her
mother to sail for America with her new husband. The parting of mother
and daughter is described in language that is almost biblical in intensity.
In an odd reversal of the prodigal son story in Luke 15 the daughter, at
parting, "fell upon her mother's neck, and wept" (Records of Woman,
146). In America, the husband dies, and the daughter contracts a fever
that threatens her life until, in a skillfully managed surreal moment fusing
fevered dream with actuality, she gradually realizes that her mother is
there to save her and take her home. The fact that the mother's appearance at her daughter's sickbed is described in such a way as to appear
miraculous and that the moment when her daughter recognizes her is
described as one of "true and perfect love" (149) indicates that motherhood is here given all of the sanctity of the strictest religion. Wordsworth
never represented the power of mother-daughter bonding so convincingly, but the mother in Hemans's poem is idealized rather than individu-
alized; she is never given a name, even though the story is as much hers as
it is Madeline's. Indeed, the poem seems to suggest—contrary to its own
ostensible moral—that women's personal lives and identities stand to be
doubly obliterated, for if tragedy and death do not obliterate them, time
eventually will: "we trace / The map of our own paths, and long ere
years / With their dull steps the brilliant lines efface, / On sweeps the
storm, and blots them out with tears" (147). The whole point of this
"domestic tale" is that individuality is sacrificed to the mother-daughter
relationship, and the poem permits no doubting of the primacy of that
relationship, any more than, say, a George Herbert poem permits the
reader to doubt the existence of God. To lament the effacement of
individuals' lives by time and tragedy and then to contribute to that very
effacement by having a character become all *mother* and nothing else
seems to us not only inconsistent but a condoning and compounding of
the socially sanctioned oppression of women. It seems to confirm the
opinion of a recent writer that our culture "idealizes motherhood but
holds real mothers in contempt" (Griffin 41).[4]

Dorothy Mermin has identified this problem accurately in a recent essay: "[W]hen women write, what is conventional or figurative in men's writing can seem awkwardly real . . . women's renunciations of worldly ambition go smoothly with the grain of social expectation, not interestingly against it: rather than making a real choice, they seem to be accepting their inevitable lot."5 There is much truth in this, yet for me Mermin too easily abandons the cause and risks consigning writers like Hemans, especially, to the limbo of the once popular but now unreadable. Why should what is "awkwardly real" be automatically less interesting than what is "conventional or figurative," even though it may embarrass us or demand of us a different kind of reading? And may there not actually be considerable interest for a modern reader in what appears to "go smoothly with the grain of social expectation"?

The poem "A Spirit's Return," in *Songs of the Affections* (1830), provides an instructive instance of what Mermin calls the "awkwardly real" and the way it can be read *against* the grain of social expectation. The speaker is a woman whose life on earth holds no value or interest for her, whose every hope is set on a transcendent world until she falls in love, and then her absorption in the man's identity is total. The poem makes it abundantly clear that she accepts the man's perceptions as definitive of reality: "There was no music but his voice to hear, / No joy but such as with *his* step drew near; / Light was but where he look'd— life where he moved . . . " (7). The man dies, and by the sheer power of love she calls up his spirit to reassure her that the relationship can continue beyond the grave. This ghost is no Lorenzo with sepulchral voice. The ghostly lover's speech is harmonious and angelic, but the narrator is filled with "the sick feeling that in *his* far sphere / *My* love could be as nothing!" (13). Her love, or rather her total absorption in his construction of reality, has left her with no existence of her own on this side of the grave. Her love and therefore her identity can be validated only in death. All of the significance that might belong to her as a person is, as it were, postponed or transferred to the afterlife. Romantic love and more especially the complete dependence of romantic love on the metaphysic of transcendence denies the woman in "A Spirit's Return" any positive status or significance in *this* world. The difference between this poem and Shelley's "Adonais," which ends on a similar note of passionate yearning for another world, is that in Shelley's poem the speaker's surrendering of earthly hope strikes us as tragic, the renunciation of the world as an act of intrinsic public and individual significance, but the woman's does not seem tragic because from the very beginning she had no identity that was not purely defined in absence.

Such absorption and obliteration of woman's existence in a destiny that is presumed to be of greater significance is equally apparent in other poems from the 1830 collection about heterosexual love ("The Vaudois' Wife," "Thekla at Her Lover's Grave," "The Image in the Heart") and in poems on motherhood ("The Charmed Picture" and "The Tomb of Madame Langhans"). In these poems it is death alone that validates the woman's significance, either because her lover has died and so ensured that his love for her, and hers for him, cannot change or because the woman has died and in the act of dying is identified with one or another noble cause. The female archetype that dominates *Songs of the Affections* is clearly the Mater Dolorosa. At the tomb of Madame Langhans, who has died in childbirth, the speaker feels "[a] solemn joy" and "a sense / Of triumph, blent with nature's gush of weeping, / As, kindling up the silent stone, I see / The glorious vision, caught by faith, of thee" (*Songs of the Affections*, 90). One of the few poems in the volume that is even moderately positive about *life* is "The Fountain of Oblivion," in which the speaker, longing to drink a forgetful draught from the fountain, changes her mind at the last moment but only because she decides that memories of the past are all she has on which to form an idea of the afterlife and those who are now enjoying it: " 'Tis from the past we shadow forth the land / Where smiles, long lost, again shall light our way . . . " (137). It is for the sake of the dead that she must remember her own past life.

Susan Wolfson has suggested that an element of therapeutic fantasy can be seen in some of Hemans's later poems, which "repeatedly fantasize escape . . . by destroying adult domesticity before it can even begin." Wolfson cites as one example "The Bride of the Greek Isle," in which Eudora, a proud young Greek, is carried off by pirates on her wedding day. She avenges her abduction and the murder of her fiancé by setting fire to the pirates' ship, turning it into her own funeral pyre. As Wolfson points out, it is not simply that Eudora, though a woman, consummates a heroic act of vengeance; it is that "the deeper plot projects a release from marriage and from enslavement alike" (unpublished ms., 7–8). Whether or not the story is fantasized escape from domesticity on Hemans's part, however, "The Bride of the Greek Isle" clearly also belongs in the category of poems that seem to validate violent death as the epitome of womanly self-sacrifice.

This unforgiving ethic, granting significance to woman's life only when it is sacrificed to the equally depersonalized idealizations of heterosexual love and of motherhood, has its clearest expression in an odd and little-noticed poem among the "Miscellaneous Pieces" in *Records of Woman.* "The Image in Lava," as Hemans explains in a note appended to the poem, is about "the impression of a woman's form, with an infant clasped to the bosom, found at the uncovering of Herculaneum" (307). Neither the woman nor her baby has a name. Excavation of a group of small houses, the homes of ordinary citizens, in the ancient Campanian city of Herculaneum, destroyed by the eruption of Vesuvius in A.D. 79, had begun in 1823. (Work was interrupted by the attempted revolution but resumed after the restoration of the king of Naples in 1824.) To judge by the frequency of reports in the *Times* of London, there was considerable interest in England in both the Pompeii and Herculaneum sites. At Herculaneum, before 1823, only a royal villa had been excavated, in the early eighteenth century under the patronage of King Charles III of Naples.[6]

Hemans could therefore represent the recently discovered "woman's form" as that of an anonymous *bourgeoise*, her sole known relationship being that of mother to the infant she clasps: "Haply of that fond bosom, / On ashes here impressed, / Thou wert the only treasure, child! / Whereon a hope might rest" (308). The eruption of Vesuvius has reduced this woman's existence to an appealing simplicity, effacing everything about her but her role as mother. Unlike, say, Joan of Arc or Properzia Rossi the sculptor, whose lives are celebrated elsewhere in the collection, this woman warrants memorializing not because of any special characteristics that belong to her as an individual but just because she was a nursing mother. Though an ordinary and anonymous citizen, she has achieved significance by becoming (unwillingly) a permanent symbol of a privileged social value. At the same time, the poem claims special significance for this "trace" of woman's existence, because, thanks to the instantaneous immortality bestowed by the volcanic eruption, it has outlasted the empire under which she lived. Empires decay, but this symbol of motherhood endures:

> Temple and tower have moulder'd,
>   Empires from earth have pass'd,—
> And woman's heart hath left a trace
>   Those glories to outlast! (307)

The poem, then, does propose a scheme of value that explicitly counters the military conquest and statecraft we normally associate with the Roman Empire. "Domestic affection" is triumphantly validated, resurrected; the nineteenth-century allocation of a separate realm and discourse to women based on the division of life into public and domestic duties is found to be reflected back to Hemans's time from a Roman household of the first century A.D.[7]

Yet the modern reader is unlikely to feel that this positive celebration

of a "trace" left by women's experience can compensate for the obliteration of the woman's own self. The poem neatly illustrates the problems
faced by those wishing to retrieve the neglected voices of women of the
Romantic period, particularly the voices of those who, like Hemans,
recorded woman's experience without challenging the social paradigms
by which that experience was defined. The woman's existence is recorded
but at the cost of the complete obliteration of her actual identity and the
reduction of her social being to one relationship and one function:
motherhood.

It is possible to envisage an alternative and more positive feminist
interpretation of Hemans's work, one emphasizing her resistance to
patriarchal notions of identity and her affirmation of women's own sense
of themselves. Rather than stressing the obliteration of women's identity
by a patriarchal ideology, this approach would see in Hemans a subversion of male modes of self-definition, of "temple and tower," by a kind of
volcanic eruption in which the dissolution of personal identity is the
triumph of a deeper female knowledge. "The Image in Lava" would then
qualify as a kind of "writing in white ink" (in Hélène Cixous's famous
phrase), writing that does not confront male self-definition directly but
inscribes a wholly other kind of signifying process, where boundaries of
self and symbols dissolve and only joyous play remains.[8] Such an approach could also appeal to the feminist psychoanalysts who argue that
women's lack of a rigid sense of self—their supposedly "more flexible or
permeable ego boundaries"[9]—constitutes a strength; that it is only *misrepresented* as a weakness in patriarchal culture, that woman's ability to
put her nurturing and caregiving role ahead of the requirements of a rigid
self-definition is an entirely positive trait, and that it is in fact the *male*
who is weak, since he is perpetually vulnerable to fear of whatever seems
to threaten his sense of himself, whether it be emotion, death, or merely a
more successful male rival.

The dangers of this approach are perhaps sufficiently obvious. Whatever the secret attraction of the loss of self, dissolution, and absorption into the irresistible powers of earth, the lava-flow of nonbeing—
especially compared to the alternative, the absurdly vulnerable temples
and towers of patriarchal religion and militarism—Hemans's poem historically epitomizes the way in which the temptations of self-sacrifice
were exploited to persuade women that motherhood and self-denial
guaranteed them significant lives—but only in the transcendent hereafter.
Second, the characterization of women as somehow naturally having
weak ego boundaries essentializes woman's nature, as a value system
independent of and unaffected by the social order and its cult of domes-

ticity. It is perhaps more instructive—more revealing of the nature of Hemans's resistance to effacement—to look for pressure points, those points where we can see momentarily emerging a concept of gender and gender roles different from the conventional one. If we wish to trace a literature of resistance hiding somewhere in the seemingly collaborationist work of the poet who wrote "The Stately Homes of England,"[10] we might look at those poems—and there are some—in which an overt transgression of gender boundaries takes place.

One such transgression of gender boundaries occurs in *The Forest Sanctuary*. The narrator, a Spaniard who has fled to North America to escape religious persecution, recalls watching his dearest boyhood friend, Alvar, being marched to the stake to be burned as a heretic. With Alvar are his two beautiful sisters, Theresa and Inez, whom the Inquisition has found equally guilty; they are to be burned in the same auto-da-fé. As might be expected, Hemans gives full play to the pathos of the sisters' plight, first describing them as "flowers" whose beauty has suffered from their long imprisonment. However, the description of Theresa introduces a new note, that of tragic heroism. What is remarkable about this passage is that several images and concepts that the male Romantics consistently claimed as masculine—"energy," "fire," "prophecy," a "kindled eye"— are here invoked to characterize the dignified courage shown by the woman as she defies the power of the church:

> It seem'd as if her breast
> Had hoarded energies, till then suppress'd
> Almost with pain, and bursting from control,
> And finding first that hour their pathway free:
> —Could a rose brave the storm, such might her emblem be!
>
> For the soft gloom whose shadow still had hung
> On her fair brow, beneath its garlands worn,
> Was fled; and fire, like prophecy's had sprung
> Clear to her kindled eye. (20–21)

What is especially striking about this description, too, is that Hemans explicitly connects Theresa's brave and impassioned stance with the more conventionally "feminine" resources of affection and relationship, which are emphatically contrasted with the Byronic emotions a man might have felt in such a situation—scorn, pride, and "sense of wrong":

> It might be scorn—
> Pride—sense of wrong . . .
>   yet not *thus* upborne
> She mov'd . . . .

> And yet, alas! to see the strength which clings
> Round woman in such hours!—a mournful sight,
> Though lovely!—an o'erflowing of the springs,
> The full springs of affection, deep as bright! (21)

In other words, Theresa's ability to face martyrdom with resolute dignity
is ascribed to a specifically female kind of strength, even while the images
that describe her defiance are drawn from the predominantly masculine
vocabulary of energy and prophecy ("masculine" in the male Romantics'
scheme of things). This emphasis on the woman's courage in the face of
death is balanced on the other side of the gender divide by the way the
male narrator expresses profound paternal tenderness toward his young
son, whom he has brought with him into exile to protect him from the
violence of the Inquisition (7, 49). If *The Forest Sanctuary* shows a
woman as capable of showing courage equivalent to any man's though
arising from different, specifically female, sources, it also shows a man
capable of tenderness like a woman's, though, again, based on a different, specifically male role. It has to be admitted, however, that both
Theresa and the narrator are portrayed as exhibiting these unconventional qualities only under exceptionally dire conditions and that (as in "The
Bride of the Greek Isle") the woman's heroism is still a heroism of self-
sacrifice and is in some sense for the sake of a male value system.

Another instance of the images of fire and prophecy being reappropri-
ated for the female poet occurs in "The Rock of Cader Idris" (one of the
"Welsh Melodies"). The poem is based on an old Welsh tradition that a
bard who spends a night on the summit of Cader Idris will have the gift
of poetic inspiration when he wakes, unless he is unlucky enough to die
or go mad instead. The speaker, who has obviously survived this gruel-
ing initiation, claims the masculine Romantic attributes of "immortal
flame," "voice," and "power." Although the poem is clearly spoken in
the persona of the male bard, there is a sense in which (as in Blake's
Milton) the precursor's voice is appropriated by the neophyte, in this case
female: "I awoke to inherit / A flame all immortal, a voice, and a
power!" (*Poetical Works*, 253).

As in many of Hemans's poems about a male literary tradition,
though, the rearticulation of the bardic voice conceals something more
traditionally feminine, a scene of reading. It is through *texts* that the
tradition of Cader Idris descends to Hemans. Such a scene occurs also in
"Tasso and His Sister" (a poem based on a couple of sentences in
Germaine de Staël's *Corinne*) in a quite literal way. Tasso's sister is
depicted reading aloud, to her children, Tasso's poetry—the deeds of
Tancred and Godfrey. In the sixth stanza of the poem, Tasso himself

suddenly stands before her, dressed as a poor pilgrim. His health, his reason, everything but his poetic gift has been destroyed by his long imprisonment. In several senses this is an epiphanic moment for Hemans's readers. The mother, surrounded by her attentive, wondering children, reads the text of her brother the poet ("words of power" they are called in the second stanza), and the sentiments that the poet appropriated for his text are realized once more, in the reader and her hearers. As if in proof of the power of this woman's reading, the poet himself materializes before them. The woman's reappropriation of the brother-poet's sentiments, her creative rereading of his text, not only arouses wonder in the children who hear it but in a literal sense reunites the family that had long been divided by the tyrannical power of the state. This in itself suggests the special way in which Hemans's work may occasionally verge on a kind of literature of resistance. Tasso—for the male Romantics, an icon of the solitary poet's courageous resistance to arbitrary power—is almost literally resurrected by the force of a *woman's reading* but not (this time) as a solitary bard or Byronic hero but as member of a family. Poetry's "words of power" are placed at the service of family, not the mere exaltation of the solitary gifted male; and the exhausted, half-mad Tasso, worn out by his struggle against tyranny, seems a timely image of the male Romantic cult of genius, now at the end of its tether, yielding to a different, more humanizing and socializing conception of the place of poetry and the conditions of its production.

Mellor comments on Hemans that "having accepted her culture's hegemonic inscription of the woman within the domestic sphere, Hemans's poetry subtly and painfully explored the ways in which that construction of gender finally collapses upon itself, bringing nothing but suffering, and the void of nothingness, to both women and men" (*Romanticism and Gender*, 142). I do not dispute that it does that, nor even that it is more truly characteristic of her poetry to do that, but I want to suggest here that it might sometimes have been received as achieving something more positive: the affirmation of a different way of valuing women's powers and of a correspondingly different poetic.

However, no alert reader can ignore the ways in which Hemans's poetry can be seen to collaborate with the existing social order, even to justify it, while her subtext reveals quite starkly the terrible price this social order exacts of women. One embarrassing fact to be faced— embarrassing at least for those feminists who consider the recuperation of previously ignored or marginalized texts to be an important part of the feminist project—is that Hemans, while marginal to the Romantic canon of today, was not exactly marginal in her time. Hemans was destined to be read as not a margin but a center, the embodiment of that hearth and home that would send forth Englishmen to subdue the world and to which the lucky ones would return, at least in thought, to remind themselves of why they were fighting or contracting malaria and typhoid in foreign parts. And yet, of course, this center was not a center of power, in the normal sense of the word. Political and economic power lay elsewhere and, moreover, needed what Hemans came to symbolize, a focal point around which loyal sentiment could gather. Judith Lowder Newton has argued convincingly that the increasing emphasis between 1800 and 1840 on the importance of women's "influence" was actually an attempt to assure middle-class women that "they *did* have work, power, and status after all"; their work was to "mitigate the harshness of an industrial capitalist world."[11] This division of labor is clear in an 1850 *Westminster Review* article, "Woman's Mission":

> [T]o warm, to cherish into purer life the motive that shall lead to the heroic act— this is her genius, her madness, her song flowing out, she knows not how, going she knows not whither, but returning never again. The woman . . . differs from man then in this—in possessing a greater capacity—a greater genius to influence. She influences through no direct exercise of power, but because she must. Influence breathes from her, and informs every thing and creature around, and we are only conscious of it by its results.[12]

But crediting women with power through influence effectively devalued all of their other capacities and denied women self-definition: a woman was to be identified by her services to others (Newton, *Women*, 4).

"The Image in Lava," "Tasso and His Sister," *The Forest Sanctuary*, and other such works cannot be put forward as "feminist" poems; but perhaps they belong in a feminist canon. "The Image in Lava," like "Madeline: A Domestic Tale" and other poems in *Records of Woman*, precisely reveals the social construction of gender at the same time that it confidently affirms the triumph of the "female" traits of love and parental affection over the imperial male order, symbolized by the "temple," "tower," and "cities" now moldering in dust. This is not to say that Hemans's work can now survive only as somehow typical of contemporary social attitudes, the sort of thing that might be cited as "background" to the study of Mary Wollstonecraft or Emily Brontë. Her poems would not hold the interest they do if they did nothing other than "go smoothly with the grain of social expectation." The strong sentiments in these poems are conveyed through an always competent and sometimes brilliant lyric and narrative art. To us, Hemans's women may seem to be singing in their chains, but they do sing—and the very attractiveness, the quasi-religious discipline, of the ethic of self-sacrifice that pervades *Records of Woman* and *Songs of the Affections* contributes largely to the aesthetic value of her work. But it is an aesthetic value that we are bound to experience differently. As Jan Mukařovský lucidly puts it,

The work of art itself is not a constant. Every shift in time, space or social surroundings alters the existing artistic tradition through whose prism the art work is observed, and as a result of such shifts that aesthetic object also changes which in the awareness of a particular collective corresponds to a material artifact—an artistic product. . . . It is natural that with these shifts of the aesthetic object, aesthetic value also changes rather frequently.[13]

The pathos of Hemans's "The Image in Lava" is not only in the event that it records, the death of a woman whose life ended abruptly and tragically in A.D. 79, but in the fact that the poem itself is a trace left by Hemans's own effacement by a discourse that compelled her to comprehend woman principally on the terms established by the needs of the bourgeois family, which she sees impressed on the volcanic mud of Vesuvius. Like the embarrassing fact of Anne Killigrew's smallpox, meticulously recorded by John Dryden in his poem of praise to her (Mermin, "Women Becoming Poets," 353–54), Felicia Hemans's effacement may strike us now as having to do less with a strictly personal tragedy than with the recognition that women's reality is an imposed reality. We can recognize in the obscure woman of Herculaneum and her "dark fate" an image emblematic of Hemans's own situation and her own literary fate.

Judith Pike

Resurrection of the Fetish in *Gradiva, Frankenstein,* and *Wuthering Heights*

*In his reading of the photograph as a fetish, Christian Metz says that the photo allows for the "possibility of a lingering look," which is not possible in film because of its continuous movement.[1] While the use of a close-up shot by some cinematographers or video's capacity to still a single frame allows for that extended gaze, what is perhaps more essential to the fetish is less the "lingering look" than the inanimate quality of the fetish.[2] Motion pictures may have revivified the image in a way not possible for photography or for any of the visual arts, but this very animation at the same time dispossessed the spectator of a certain voyeuristic pleasure. The fetish, as Parveen Adams notes, "has the qualities of suspense, the frozen, arrested quality of a photograph, the something fixed to which the subject constantly returns 'to exorcise the dangerous consequences of movement.'"[3] However, when that movement cannot be exorcised and the inanimate quality of the fetish is threatened and it acquires a most unexpected mobility, there is often a radical transformation in which the fetish is no longer viewed as an object of pleasure but rather is perceived as something unsettling or even abject.

Unlike the myth of Galatea and Pygmalion, in which animation rendered the object more alluring, other literary works have shown us that animation profoundly threatens the viability of the fetish. Freud's reading of *Gradiva* provides the theoretical framework to analyze the dread provoked by the revivification of the fetish, but Romantic literature had already introduced us to the problematic of the fetish through the writings of Mary Shelley and Brontë. And in *Frankenstein* we witness one of literature's most dramatic portrayals of the threat of revivification when Victor Frankenstein's prized object attains "the dangerous consequences of movement."[4] Thereafter, the majority of the novel describes Frankenstein's relentless pursuit of his creature to arrest that very movement. *Wuthering Heights* offers us another example of the revivification of the fetish in the scene of Lockwood's nightmare of the ghost/corpse at the window. Brontë's novel ultimately exposes the fetish of the female corpse, which has an entire literary and cultural heritage as a perverse fantasy that represses the dread of the unsublimated dead/female body. Both Shelley and Brontë offer us a powerful cultural critique of Western civilization's fetishization of the dead body, in particular the dead female body. Yet it is not the corpse alone that the fetish seeks to repudiate, but as we shall see in Freud's analysis of *Gradiva*, it is often the fully animated female body that generates the fantasy of the body arrested in suspended animation.

While the inanimate quality of the fetish is essential, Adams also notes that there can be "live" fetishes, in which the body is frozen in suspense. She takes the example of Masoch's *Venus in Furs*, in which the female protagonist is transformed into a live fetish by assuming the various poses of a statue, a photo, or a painting, which "capture the gesture midway and this is the moment of suspense" (252). Freud's study "Delusions and Dreams in Jensen's *Gradiva*" (1907) offers us another provocative example of the essential relation between the fetish and arrested movement. In Jensen's novel (1903), an ancient Roman bas-relief, which captures the suspended gesture of a young woman walking, overpowers the imagination of a young archeologist, Norbert Hanold. The young archaeologist becomes so fixated with the image of the girl's feet that he has a plaster replica made, but the central conflict in Jensen's novel arises with the archaeologist's search for a live "Gradiva." Once he discovers an animate "Gradiva," the woman provokes profound ambivalence rather than pleasure and threatens the viability of this fetish. Freud relates how, although there was a great urge to touch his live "Gradiva" to ensure that she was not a mere delusion, "an equally strong reluctance held him back even from the very idea."[5] Though Freud suggests that Hanold's reluctance was grounded in the fear that he suffered from delusions, a more critical reading of this scene reveals that a greater anxiety arose from the possible discovery that this woman was indeed far too real. Freud's failure to read this scene more critically might in part be due to the fact that, at this point in his career, he had not as yet worked out a thorough study of the fetish and was more concerned with an analysis of dreams and delusions. Before the publication of "Delusions and Dreams," Freud had developed only a preliminary notion of the fetish in "Three Essays on the Theory of Sexuality" (1905), in which he simply discusses the issue of overvaluation and substitution of the fetish for the original or "normal" sexual object. This very early concept of the fetish, which makes no mention of the role of ambivalence, is completely consistent with his reading of fetishism in "Delusions and Dreams." However, ten years later, in "Repression" (1915), Freud introduces the idea of a splitting of the "instinctual representative," which in "Fetishism" (1927) is more fully developed and is shown to relate to the element of ambivalence operational in the fetish.

In "Delusions and Dreams" we see ambivalence operating most dramatically when the young archaeologist uses the pretext of a pestering housefly to plant "a vigorous slap" (9:27) upon Zoe, his new found "Gradiva," to test her physical reality. Twenty years later the significance of this slap comes to light when, in "Fetishism," Freud explains that the fetishist's relation to his prized object not only stimulates pleasure, erotic or otherwise, but it can also generate a certain amount of displeasure. For while the fetish functions as a means of disavowing lack (for Freud, maternal castration), the fetish also simultaneously becomes a marker of that lack, a kind of psychic tombstone. Thus, one's pleasure is always tinged with potential disgust or ambivalence; the experience of one's "special" object is always threatened by the recognition that it also functions as a signifier of a lack. Freud describes how this oscillation between disavowal and affirmation of lack is played out in the fetishist's radical shifting from adoration to abuse of that object: "the divided attitude shows itself in what the fetishist does with his fetish, whether in reality or in his imagination. To point out that he reveres his fetish is not the whole story; in many cases he treats it in a way which is obviously equivalent to a representation of castration" (21:157). Without the knowledge of his later work, Freud misses a crucial element when he interprets Hanold's slap as an affectionate gesture, arguing that in childhood he would do a little "bumping and thumping" (9:31) with his little playmate Zoe. Yet in the end he acts very much in the way Freud later describes the fetishist's abuse of his revered object.[6]

While animation threatens the viability of the fetish, there is also a moment in the text when there is the possibility of its restitution. Hanold asks Zoe to lie down and assume the frozen pose of a relief; looking "as peaceful and beautiful as marble," Zoe has become Gradiva (9:62). Immobile, asleep, without the possibility of an exchange of the gaze and without subjectivity, Zoe can restore the power of the fetish. Yet in the end, Hanold gives up the fetish for romantic love, which for Freud marks Hanold's cure, for he has rediscovered "normal" erotic urges. While the return to life of the fetish as a *tableau vivant* was threatening, Freud suggests that the "triumph of love" (9:40) has the power to dismantle that threat or at least sublimate it through the discourse of romantic love.[7] However, without the philter of romantic love, the resurrection of the fetish becomes a menacing object that must be destroyed.

The Resurrected: Nights of the Living Dead

Were we to take this fetishistic intrigue with the frozen poses of the body one step further, we might begin to see why the figure of the human corpse has become such an alluring fetish throughout the history of both literature and the visual arts. Although most fetishes are but part objects—Gradiva's foot, the saint's finger, the Host, or swatch of blue velvet—the fetish of the *exquisite corpse* presents itself as a complete and more integral body, which more effectively allows for the repudiation of castration/lack.[8] Thus, this fetish can conceal its metonymical status more convincingly than can any part object. Yet while the fetish of human corpse has an uncanny allure, it also has the potential to be a most powerful threat; whereas the exquisite corpse resting serenely on its deathbed evokes pleasure in the spectator, the reanimated corpse awakens a powerful dread that brandishes itself in our psyches.

Mary Shelley captures this dread when she resurrects her Monster and transforms the exquisite corpse of the eighteenth century into a menacing *sublime corpse* that resists fetishization.[9] By setting her novel in the eighteenth century, Shelley not only distances herself from earlier Gothic novels set in medieval landscapes, but she also calls into question the aesthetic category of the sublime that was at the heart of both eighteenth-century aesthetics and Romanticism. While both Burke and Kant investigate the aesthetic potential of the terrifying and destructive faculty of the sublime, Shelley explores more fully its transgressive potential.

Burke argues that the sublime "is conversant about terrible objects, or operates in a manner analogous to terror" but that there remains a certain aesthetic distance from that terror.[10] "When danger or pain press too nearly, they are incapable of giving any *delight* [emphasis added][11], and are simply terrible; but at certain distances, and with certain modifications, they may be, and they are delightful" (36). Although Burke repeatedly stresses that terror and danger are essential components of the sublime experience, terror ultimately must be held in abeyance. For Kant, the danger evoked by the sublime moment is to a far more radical degree sublimated by the "supersensible faculty" of reason, which elevates our imagination to a higher faculty in a transcendent moment and again ensures an aesthetic distance. What is so original about Shelley's text is that it presents us with two very different representations of the sublime. In her descriptions of Frankenstein's treks through Chamonix and the French Alps, we find a portrayal of the sublime experience consistent with Kant's transcendental notion of the sublime. Frankenstein describes how the "sublime and magnificent scenes" elevated him "from the littleness of feeling" to some higher faculty (92) and how "the sight of the awful and majestic in nature had indeed always the effect of solemnizing my mind" (93). For Frankenstein these sublime moments, though "awful" or terrible at first, have a recuperative potential that allows for aesthetic distance and even tranquility.

In contrast to this more conventional portrait of the sublime, Shelley offers us the experience of the *sublime body*, which is far more transgressive and does not allow Frankenstein "the effect of solemnizing" his mind. Moreover, Shelley's invention of this sublime body inaugurates a profound break from another eighteenth-century aesthetic, that of the romantic cult of mourning and the fetishization of the dead body. *Frankenstein* presents us with a critical reading of the romanticization of the dead body as a perverse male fantasy that produces sublime corpses rather than exquisite ones.

Laboring in the "unhallowed damps of the grave" (53), Frankenstein was on his way to creating an exquisite corpse that befits what Philippe Ariès calls "the Age of the Beautiful Death" (409–74). Frankenstein even describes how he had chosen the finest body parts, though oversized, to create a stunning new species of men. Before its animation, this creation was not only nonthreatening but was looked upon as a specimen of beauty, an exquisite corpse(s):[12] "His limbs were in proportion, and I had selected his features as beautiful" (56). Yet while hovering over this creature, ready to "infuse a spark of being into the lifeless thing," the doctor was filled with dread (56). Inanimate, it was beautiful; endowed with life, it became monstrous and inspired a sublime terror devoid of the aesthetic distance envisioned by the Enlightenment. This sublime corpse evoked a sublimity that would offer none of the recuperative powers found in the sublimity of the Alpine vistas; for the rest of the novel Frankenstein struggles, fruitlessly, "to exorcise the dangerous consequences of movement" that had transfigured his exquisite specimen into a sublime corpse. Yet the more Frankenstein attempts to exorcise this movement, the more excessive and even compulsive it becomes; the Monster's superhuman ability to traverse space accentuates this compulsive movement.

The creature is horrifying not only in the animation of his limbs, but also in the movement of his "dull yellow eye": "It was already one in the morning; the rain pattered dismally against the panes, and my candle was nearly burned out, when, by the glimmer of the half-extinguished light, I saw the dull yellow eye of the creature open" (56). Although both Metz and Adams focus on the agency of movement and its relation to the constitution of the fetish, movement is not the only threat to the fetishist's pleasure; there is also the threat of the visual. In Freud's account of fetishism, the visual plays the most crucial role. The moment the child catches view of the dread scene, his vision is arrested; the fetish then steps in to erase that moment by trying to freeze the moment before the dreaded sight. Sight, then, is the agency that causes such dread, yet it is also through sight, through another look, that the fetish can be constituted.

In Shelley's text, the visual dimension is further complicated by the opacity of the creature's gaze. Bearing no reflection, this "dull yellow eye" returns a blank, "castrating" gaze that resists identification. Later Frankenstein is awakened from a nightmare "by the dim and yellow light of the moon, as it forced its way through the window shutters" (57); the yellow eye has been transformed into a phantasmagoric gaze of the moon, redoubled by the creature's actual gaze above his bed. By the end of this passage, Frankenstein has mentally transformed his creature into a "demoniacal corpse" even though it has done nothing more than look upon its creator, perhaps with the wonder of a child and no more. And in the next passage the creature is no longer referred to as either a "demoniacal corpse" or as "the wretch," but as a *Thing*: "it became a thing such as even Dante could not have conceived" (57). One cannot help but notice that this final twist comes in the aftermath of Frankenstein's dream of his dead mother: just as he kisses his beloved Elizabeth, she turns into his mother's putrefied corpse. Once again Shelley presents us with a critical response to the idealization and fetishization of the exquisite corpse: for Frankenstein's nightmarish vision of the maternal Thing ultimately becomes transfigured into that nameless wretch from which he flees.

As Freud has noted, that which has been repressed becomes repeated. The attempt to exclude or repress the maternal is exemplified by the creation of a being through the male birth of science. Unlike his later work, which was based on a purely masculine model of science, Franken-

stein began his studies by reading the works of the alchemists Cornelius
Agrippa, Albertus Magnus, and Paracelsus. Evelyn Fox Keller writes that
Paracelsus's science includes both the maternal and the feminine: "Indeed, the hermaphrodite and the marital couple provide the basic images
of the writings and iconography that the alchemists left behind. In
depicting hermaphroditic union, sexual union, or simply the collaborative effort of man and woman, their graphic images represent the conjunction, or marriage, of male and female principles that was central to
hermetic philosophy."[13] When Frankenstein entered the university, he
studied mainstream scientific academia and "attended the lectures and
cultivated the acquaintance of the men of science of the university" (49).
It is in this setting that he abandons his alchemical studies along with the
feminine and the maternal; the latter, of course, survive to haunt Frankenstein's dreams.

The fact that the repressed returns is perhaps less interesting than the
form that this return takes. For Lacan, the return of the repressed figures
as the automaton. Whereas Lacan refers to the automaton as the insistence of the sign, we might also read Shelley's Monster as a kind of
automaton that embodies this insistence in his compulsive pursuit of
Frankenstein. The association between the Monster and an automaton
may be a convenient one, but it may also be one that Shelley herself had
thought of while conceiving of her creature. By the end of the eighteenth
century and the beginning of the nineteenth, when Shelley was writing,
the very same experiments in science and technology that launched the
industrial revolution were producing a proliferation of toy automata.
Only two years prior to writing her novel, Shelley saw the highly nota-
rized exhibit of Swiss horologist Jacquet-Droz's automata, a mechanized
human figure called "The Scribe," at an exhibit in Neuchâtel.[14] But while
Shelley's own "automaton" has certain sociohistorical roots, I find that
the figure of the automaton plays an even stronger role in terms of the
automation of the psyche, as demonstrated by the return of the repressed.
For in *Frankenstein* what is repressed by the young scientist reappears as
the compulsive drive and libido of his creature.

In his discussion of the automaton, Lacan goes one step further and
asserts that beyond this automaton there is another more terrifying
encounter—with the real: "The real is beyond the *automaton*, the return,
the coming-back, the insistence of the signs, by which we see ourselves
governed by the pleasure principle. The real is that which always lies
behind the automaton, and it is quite obvious, throughout Freud's research, that it is this that is the object of his concern."[15] Lacan points
out, however, that this encounter with the real is always a missed encoun-

ter and one that is inassimilable in our waking life (55). Dreams offer a
mere glimpse of this encounter: "Is not the dream essentially, one might
say, an act of homage to the missed reality—the reality that can no longer
produce itself except by repeating itself endlessly, in some never attained
awakening?" (58). Although Frankenstein calls his creature a Thing, his
dream reveals that there is a far more traumatic Thing—the encounter
with the real of the maternal body, which is experienced in his dream as a
traumatic vision of incest and necrophilia. If, as Lacan argues, we experience the real as a missed encounter, then dreams, like literature, allow for
the possibility of that encounter to take place in our waking life.

While the scientist's fetishistic hunt through charnel houses for the
perfect body parts promises an exquisite corpse, this quest is quickly
exposed as a monstrous male fantasy. At the time Shelley was writing, the
prevailing representation of death was epitomized by beatific death
scenes, which, as Ann Douglas notes, domesticated the dead by sentimen-
talizing and immortalizing them.[16] An entire industry and ideology of
death had emerged with the cult of mourning: there was a mass proliferation of mourning portraits and consolation literature, and the rural
cemetery movement was on the rise.[17] The grotesque dead body and the
charnel houses of former times, which portrayed death too vividly, were
replaced by romantic and sentimentalized images of the spiritualized
"dearly departed" and by rural cemeteries that mistook themselves for
pantheistic landscapes.[18] We see one instance of this sentimental portrait
of death in a scene where Clerval tries to console Frankenstein after
William's death. "'Dear lovely child, he now sleeps with his angel mother!'" (71). He is not a corpse but a "gentle form" that will be put to rest
in Nature's bosom. Shelley debunks this conventionalized portrayal of
death and the cult of mourning by presenting the reader with the terror of
the unsublimated dead body. Although both the dream of the putrefied
maternal body and the description of the Monster's "shriveled complexion and straight black lips" (56) offer compelling portraits of the unsublimated dead body, perhaps the most dramatic example of Shelley's dismantling of the fantasy/fetish of the exquisite corpse is the creation of the
Monster's female counterpart: the monster's own fantasy of a compatible
female "exquisite" corpse turns into a brutal atrocity when Frankenstein,
in a wild fury, dismembers the half-finished body and leaves its remains
scattered on the floor. Some thirty years after Shelley wrote *Frankenstein*,
Emily Brontë's *Wuthering Heights* challenged Western culture's fetishization of the dead body. Brontë's novel, however, begins not with the
promise of an exquisite corpse but with the traumatic encounter with
the *real* dead body, represented by Lockwood's dream of the corpse at the

window. The rest of the story, I would argue, is an attempt to repress this event by embedding in the text a new narrative, which exorcises the horrific body of the specter through a tale of romantic love. Once again, we discover that it is through the guise of romantic love that the indecent female dead body can be transformed into the fantasy of the exquisite corpse.

However, although Brontë incorporates this rhetoric of romantic love into her novel, she also presents a critical reading of romantic love. Her critique is most powerfully exemplified by Lockwood, a rather inept and squeamish romantic whose fantasy of the exquisite corpse is revealed as precisely that, a fantasy. Brontë demonstrates that this fantasy is not just the product of the naïve romantic but that it is deeply embedded in the cultural imagination; even her other, less naïve characters, such as Heathcliff and Nelly, re-create this fantasy as a means to repress the dread of the female corpse.

Corpse at the Window: Hauntings in *Wuthering Heights*

This is a strange book. It is not without evidences of considerable power: but, as a whole, it is wild, confused, disjointed, and improbable; and the people who make up the drama, which is tragic enough in its consequences, are savages ruder than those who lived before the days of Homer.—Examiner (London), 8 January 1848

When *Wuthering Heights* was first published in 1847, the critics' response was strikingly similar to Lockwood's own response to Wuthering Heights as a strangely interesting place inhabited by something wilder and more savage than his own naïve and clichéd romanticism could fathom. One critic wrote: "*Wuthering Heights* is a strange sort of book, baffling all regular criticism; yet it is impossible to begin and not finish it."[19] This critic was much bolder than Lockwood, who is unable to finish his narrative after his second visit to Wuthering Heights; his housekeeper, Nelly, must take it up for him. Both narrators have a certain fascination with the strangeness of the Heights, but like Brontë's early critics they resist looking too closely at its *real* nature. J. Hillis Miller suggests that the reader, too, must struggle with a double guilt of either refusing to look far enough or else of looking too far:

The double guilt of Lockwood's narration as of any critic's discourse is the following. If he does not penetrate all the way to the innermost core of the story he tells, he keeps the story going, repeating itself interminably in its incompletion. This is like the guilt of the one who keeps a grave open, or like the guilt of a sexual failure. On the other hand, to pierce all the way in is to be guilty of the desecration of a grave, to be guilty, like Heathcliff when he opens Cathy's grave, of necrophilia.[20]

Miller adds that while everything must be brought out, it must also be given a "decent burial" (p. 71). I would instead argue that the desire for a decent burial is precisely that which keeps the story "repeating itself interminably in its incompletion."

While Heathcliff may penetrate further than either Lockwood or Nelly, Heathcliff also resists going too far. Indeed, his desecration of Cathy's grave does not "pierce all the way"; rather, it is merely an alibi to give her a decent burial in his own imagination as an exquisite corpse. The "proper" burials narrated by Lockwood, Nelly, and even Heathcliff only prove to be "premature burials." These narratives function as missed encounters with the real/corpse, which is why, I argue, the story repeats itself. Although Lacan says that the dead (such as Hamlet's father) return because they haven't received a proper burial, we must make a distinction here between a *proper* and a *decent* burial. Although Claudius gave Hamlet a decent burial, it was not a "proper" one. A proper burial, in the original etymological sense of the word *proper*, meaning one's "own particular," is quite different from a decent burial enacted not for the dead but for the survivors who appropriate the dead. In a decent burial, the dead body becomes the property of the living— Nelly, Heathcliff, and Lockwood—who refigure that body as an exquisite corpse. For this reason the undead, like Cathy, return when their bodies have been too hastily appropriated. Although she returns to ask the outsider Lockwood for a proper burial, he is too decent a fellow for such a task, and like the others he immures her in another narrative that yet again represses the grotesque dead body.

Ironically, when Lockwood first pays a visit to Wuthering Heights, he stops to admire the grotesque figures that ornament the exterior of the house: "Before passing the threshold, I paused to admire a quantity of grotesque carving lavished over the front, and especially about the principal door, above which, among a wilderness of crumbling griffins, and shameless little boys."[21] But Lockwood is far more resistant to the aesthetic of the grotesque than this passage suggests. At the novel's beginning he reads himself as a dark romantic figure when he identifies himself and Heathcliff as "such a suitable pair" (45), as if they were kindred souls; but Lockwood's naïve romanticism later causes him great embarrassment when he mistakes "a heap of dead rabbits" for an idyllic scene of some nestled kittens (52). Such misreading represents Lockwood's resistance to the real. Carol Jacobs argues that, as an outsider, Lockwood fails to read *Wuthering Heights-as-text* (Jacobs's term) though he "makes repeated efforts to force his way into the penetralium."[22] Yet the real intruder is not Lockwood, as Jacobs suggests, but the corpse at the window; this corpse must be expelled from *Wuthering Heights*-as-text. When Lockwood experiences the penetralia of this house in the form of his dreams, he violently resists. Instead, he struggles to reconstitute *Wuthering Heights*-as-text as a decent text, one that has the proper name rather than the grotesque carvings over its portal.

Lockwood presents himself not only as the narrator of this text but also as a participant. Brontë, however, provides us with an early clue of his inability to be anything more than a voyeur at a safe distance or, in other words, a secondhand narrator of a framed text. The one biographical piece Brontë gives us about her narrator concerns his aborted romantic liaison, which is quite telling. While on vacation at the seacoast, Lockwood was struck by a woman who, he says, was "a most fascinating creature, a real goddess" but only "as long as she took no notice of me" (48). Once she returned his glances, he "shrunk icily into [himself], like a snail, at every glance retired colder and farther" (48). While Lockwood is in the position of voyeur, he enjoys himself; but as soon as the woman "looked a return," he is threatened. Although in this instance Lockwood could flee her gaze, it will return and repeat itself in his dream of the corpse at the window. In his waking life he either flees what he finds terrible or, as with the dead rabbits, mistakes the grotesque for the beautiful, but his dreams are invaded by "indecent" elements unassimilable in his waking consciousness.

Feeling safely enclosed in his paneled bed at the Heights, "secure against the vigilance of Heathcliff, and everyone else," Lockwood is ironically least secure against the vigilance of his own unconscious. After his troubling dream about the Reverend Branderham's sermon, he hears a branch knocking on the window. The noise so upsets him that he thrusts his hand through the window to grab the branch whereupon his "fingers closed on the fingers of a little, ice-cold hand!" (67): "The intense horror of nightmare came over me; I tried to draw back my arm, but the hand clung to it, and a most melancholy voice sobbed, 'Let me in—let me in!'" (67). Although she has caught him by surprise, this specter is not all that terrifying with her "most melancholy voice." In this scene *Lockwood* is by far the more terrifying and sadistic figure: "As it spoke, I discerned, obscurely, a child's face looking through the window—terror made me cruel; and, finding it useless to attempt shaking the creature off, I pulled its wrist on the broken pane, and rubbed it to and fro till the blood ran down and soaked the bedclothes; still it wailed,

'Let me in!' and maintained its tenacious grip, almost maddening me with fear" (67). James Kavanagh argues that the violence in this scene is symptomatic of Brontë's text: "The deliberate cruelty of Lockwood's response is particularly striking, and yet it is symptomatic of much that will follow in *Wuthering Heights*. Indeed, a persuasive sadism saturates the novel's discourse."[23] Wade Thompson also suggests that an "extraordinary sadism" along with a "preoccupation with infanticide" underlies Brontë's text.[24] Both critics correlate the novel's violence to an infanticidal impulse, but Kavanagh holds that Lockwood's sadistic response is linked to a repressed sexual urge: "the object of fear in a nightmare is also an object of desire—an intense and taboo desire, which therefore evokes the fear of intense retribution" (23).

While I agree with these critics' observations about the sadistic vein in Brontë's novel, I think that Lockwood's response to the figure at the window involves more than just repressed sexual desire or infanticidal fantasies. Lockwood's horror is also symptomatic of the cultural horror of death and the need to reconstruct the dead body as an exquisite corpse that can be fetishized. What provoked the "intense horror of nightmare" was not so much the element of surprise as the touch of the ice-cold hand. This corpse is not an immobile and passive "still life" but all *too alive* with its "tenacious grip."

The profound dread of a fully animated corpse, as we have already seen in *Frankenstein*, is a dread that is not only provoked by "the dangerous consequences of movement" but also by the gaze. As Brontë has already illustrated for us, Lockwood is quite susceptible to the dangerous consequences of the gaze, in particular a woman's gaze. It is not the hand alone that makes him react so brutally. "Terror made me cruel," he says, the terror of "a child's face looking through the window." Only after he is caught by this look does he behave so violently. This look and the child-corpse embody the drive of the return of the repressed, which persists—"still it wailed, 'Let me in!' "—beyond the grave.

In his final struggle, Lockwood erects a barricade against this creature by piling a pyramid of books against the window. Yet language and the symbolic order are no security against the eruption of the real. Even after constructing his textual barricade and plugging up his ears, he still hears "the doleful cry moaning on!" (67). Lockwood, like critics who merely want to read *Wuthering Heights*-as-text, resists the tenacious grip of the real, which persists even if we plug up our ears.

From another perspective, Jacobs argues that perhaps the text subverts Lockwood's texts. Instead of Lockwood's being the interpretative agent of texts crucial to the text of *Wuthering Heights*, it is *Wuthering Heights* that dreams of Lockwood as its antagonist, struggling against him "to define a space for its own fiction" (65). Although insightful, this interpretation still reads the scene from a textual and linguistic perspective. The intrusion of the corpse into the text is precisely that other domain of the real that cannot be reduced to a textual dimension. Jacobs's interpretation repeats the same mistake made by other critics who privilege the written inscription of Hareton Earnshaw's name over the extralinguistic images of "a quantity of grotesque carvings" and the "wildness of crumbling griffins" that crown the portal of Wuthering Heights. Before his dream, Lockwood glosses through a text with "the inscription—'Catherine Earnshaw, her book'" (62). He wants to decipher Catherine *as* inscription, as text: "An immediate interest kindled within me for the unknown Catherine, and I began, forthwith, to decipher her faded hieroglyph" (62). While she returns in the space of a dream, Lockwood's violence is not enacted against a book. Although he is, at first, haunted by the repetition of her name scratched in the ledge ("a name repeated in all kinds of characters"), glaring in white letters "as vivid as spectres—the air swarmed with Catherines" (61), he doesn't awake to discover that he has violated these inscriptions. In his dream his terror is not provoked by the "spectres" of white letters but by the child's touch, voice, and look—extensions of the body. While body images haunt Lockwood, he seeks refuge in inscriptions and texts. Later, when Lockwood visits with young Cathy and discovers that she has no books to read, he says to her "'take my books away, and I should be desperate!'" (331). Lockwood even tells her that most of his books are "written on my brain and printed in my heart" (332). Lockwood's dread is not of books or of hieroglyphs but of the corpse's real body—the very locus of his violence.

While Lockwood struggles to barricade the window shut, Heathcliff passionately flings the window open, pleading for Catherine's return:

> He got onto the bed, and wrenched open the lattice, bursting, as he pulled at it, into an uncontrollable passion of tears.
> "Come in! come in!" he sobbed. "Cathy, do come. Oh do—*once* more! Oh! my heart's darling! hear me *this* time—Catherine, at last!" (70)

Lockwood, who only minutes ago was raving himself, watches Heathcliff soberly; he deduces that his own compassionate nature, decent fellow that he is, allows him to overlook the folly of this man's raving. Feeling fully awake and having reassumed his narrative voice, he concludes in a lighthearted tone that this "spectre showed a spectre's ordinary caprice; it gave no sign of being" (70). Although he may be trying to spirit away his own anxiety by reducing the evening's events to a mere whim or caprice, his own words betray him: *caprice* comes from the Italian *capriccio*, meaning "head with hair standing on its end," which, of course, is a sign of terror and horror.[25] So even as Lockwood tries to use language to repress the horror of the spectacle, the repressed only returns, here as a rather revealing case of overdetermination.

Unable to assimilate his experience at the Heights, Lockwood piles up a new series of books when he asks his housekeeper, Nelly, to narrate a story. Not only does Lockwood try to reason away the significance of his dreams as "the effects of bad tea and bad temper" (64), but as Jacobs notes, he refuses any further mention of them. "He organizes his explanation by suppressing all further mention of the dreams and by linking the subsequent events into a simplistic causal chain. A sleepless night and a difficult journey through the snow bring on a bad cold. The illness, in turn, incapacitates him, and so he calls in the housekeeper to entertain him with her tales" (*Uncontainable Romanticism*, 62).

As Freud often points out in his work on hysteria, when the patient cannot acknowledge or verbalize a traumatic experience, it becomes inscribed on the body as a hysterical symptom. Thus, perhaps Lockwood's "gruel cold" is not so much a consequence of his snowy journey home as of his traumatic evening at the Heights. Bedridden, Lockwood then seeks solace in Nelly's romantic narrative of Catherine and Heathcliff, which becomes the vehicle to reconstruct the real corpse into a fetish. After Lockwood's troubling night, Nelly will continue surveillance of *Wuthering Heights*-as-text and guard against any further intrusions.

As "patriarchy's paradigmatic housekeeper," Nelly must clean up the mess left by Lockwood in the bedchamber.[26] The corpse at the window must be taught docility. As patriarchy's domestic she must domesticate the female corpse and make it decent for viewing, especially for the likes of Lockwood. In order to guarantee that propriety be maintained, Nelly usurps the young woman's own *proper* control over her own body, which becomes the property of another. In eighteenth- and nineteenth-century literature it is quite often the domestic in families of means who dresses the corpse and puts on the final touches.[27] Although domestics are seemingly minor characters, they have an important role as patriarchy's housekeepers, whose final surveillance of the female corpse ensures that the dead heroine can have a decent viewing.

Although Nelly may not have literally dressed the corpse, her narrative of Catherine's death certainly arranges the body in "a gentle dream" that is meant to be an antidote to Lockwood's nightmare. Her narrative acts to exorcise Catherine's unruly corpse from the text's central narrative and substitute for it a more domesticated body, more befitting Nelly's "moral meal." As Kavanagh suggests, Nelly is the phallic mother who acts as the agent of patriarchal law: "Despite Nelly's projection of herself in the role of benevolent, protective mother, trying to shield the innocent children . . . , the subdued sadism of her phallic-maternal control is symptomatically present in her own crucial interventions in this narrative" (*Emily Brontë*, 40). One of the most obvious instances of Nelly's phallic-maternal control comes in the scene of Catherine's final illness. After her husband, Edgar, has forbidden her to see Heathcliff again, Catherine shuts herself in her room and refuses to eat. While Edgar hides in his study with his books, Catherine "fast[s] pertinaciously" in the hope that her husband will repent and forgive her (158). After several days of fasting, she begins to fear that she is dying and asks for some food. Nelly remarks that this might be a ploy on Catherine's part to get Nelly to say something to Edgar: "I believed no such thing, so I kept it to myself" (158). Her allegiance here is obviously not to her mistress but to her master, and she refuses to disturb him for such a trifling feminine matter as the preliminary signs of anorexia. She is not the "benevolent, protective mother, trying to shield her children" but the disciplinarian whose role is to domesticate the feminine creature. While Catherine uses her body, albeit in negative and self-destructive ways, as a vehicle of revolt against her husband's attempts to domesticate her, power over her own body is ultimately usurped by Nelly.

Before Nelly gains complete control, Catherine rages in what Nelly calls a brain fever. Her last resistance to this phallic mother is written off as madness: "Tossing about, she increased her feverous bewilderment to madness, and tore the pillow with her teeth, then raising herself up all burning, desired that I open the window. We were in the middle of winter, the wind blew strong from the northeast, and I objected" (160). Gilbert and Gubar remark that Nelly is the "keeper of the house who shuts windows" (*Madwoman*, 292). The shutting of windows becomes the narrator's most important task, for as Lockwood discovers, open windows—both textual and architectural—invite the threat of outside elements: dreams, the undead, or madness. While Nelly tries to subdue Catherine, Catherine's "delirious strength much surpassed mine"; Nelly admits that "she quite masters me" (164–65). Catherine's mastery, however, is never recognized as legitimate but rather as "delirious" and symptomatic of madness. Yet in her delirium she sees quite clearly the pernicious nature of this phallic mother when she envisions Nelly as a withered old hag who has betrayed her: "'Nelly is my hidden enemy— you witch! So you do seek elf-bolts to hurt us!'" (166). Nelly only dismisses this as a "maniac's fury" and goes off to get a doctor. When the doctor asks her how such a "stout, hearty lass" could have fallen so ill, Nelly again attributes her condition to an aberration of a mind "filled with all sorts of strange ideas and illusions" (167). Catherine's "strange ideas" do not fit into patriarchy's narrative, so Nelly, as patriarchy's watchdog, excludes her from any legitimate discourse by turning her into another madwoman in the attic.

The scene of Catherine's "delirium" also exposes a fissure in Lockwood's and Nelly's later narratives of Catherine's death and final domestication. Catherine is bewildered by the deathly image that she finds reflected back to her in the mirror: " 'Don't you see that face?' she enquired, gazing earnestly at the mirror. And say what I could, I was incapable of making her comprehend it to be her own; so I rose and covered it with a shawl" (161). Try as Nelly does to veil this cadaverous face, Catherine is not so easily fooled: "It's behind there still!" (161). Although the shawl falls off, Nelly's narrative of Catherine's death will serve to permanently resituate it.

Appropriately enough, we learn of the actual events of Catherine's death through a double narrative. Just before her death is described, Brontë decides to have Lockwood take up the narration again. Suggesting that Nelly's text is distasteful and unrefined, Lockwood vows to "extract wholesome medicines from Mrs. Dean's bitter herbs" (191), although she was "on the whole, a very fair narrator"; he will continue the story "in her own words," but his version will be "a little condensed" (192). We will never know what he has edited from Nelly's story but only that Lockwood's extracts are more "wholesome medicines." Together the two narrators re-form Catherine into a wholesome antidote to the corpse at the window.

On the eve of her death, Catherine still shows some signs of defiance, even though her metamorphosis into an exquisite corpse has already begun. She is no longer described as a "stout, hearty lass," as the doctor had pictured her, but befitting the tradition of feminine death, she is becoming etherealized. Nelly observes that "there seemed unearthly beauty in the change" (192): "The flash of her eyes had been succeeded by a dreamy and melancholy softness; they no longer gave the impression of looking at the objects around her; they appeared always to gaze beyond, and far beyond—you would have said out of this world" (193). Whereas the "stout, hearty lass" could resist this phallic mother, as an unearthly beauty she is no threat. By disembodying her, Nelly also disempowers her. However, before Catherine is completely spirited away, she offers a final resistance to Nelly during Heathcliff's last visit. Nelly says that the two of them "made a strange and fearful picture" (195) and that "her present countenance had a wild vindictiveness in its white skin, and a bloodless lip, and scintillating eye" (195). Interestingly, Catherine's cadaverous face, with its vindictive gaze, is strikingly similar to Nelly's description of Heathcliff after she discovers his corpse: "His eyes met mine so keen, and fierce, I started; and then he seemed to smile" (364). Present in both accounts is the terror of the cadaverous gazes—her "wild vindictiveness" and his fierce look. And yet what is perhaps even more disarming is that these "corpses" have something too alive about them, something excessive. There is an uncanny scintillation, that dangerous spark in Catherine's eyes or Heathcliff's smile that disquiets the romanticized portrait of death as a peaceful slumber. While Nelly gives Catherine's corpse a more ethereal countenance, Heathcliff's corpse bears a mocking countenance that she cannot erase. She is able to shut the window, but she cannot shut away his sneering gaze of exultation. Heathcliff's corpse has something too animate about it: "I hasped the window; I combed his black long hair from his forehead; I tried to close his eyes—to extinguish, if possible, that frightful, life-like gaze of exultation, before any one else beheld it. They would not shut—they seemed to sneer at my attempts, and his parted lips, and sharp, white teeth sneered too!" (365). The male corpse can be buried with a disfigured sneer, but the female corpse must be given a decent burial as an exquisite corpse.

Body Snatchers

In contrast to the defiant and raving Catherine, Nelly's final portrait of Catherine presents a most docile figure. While Heathcliff stands outside dashing his head against a tree, Nelly stands over Catherine's corpse, nusing on its ethereal quietude: "No angel in heaven could be more beautiful than she appeared; and I partook of the infinite calm in which she lay. My mind was never in a holier frame, than while I gazed on that untroubled image of Divine rest" (201). Nelly's "memorial" to Catherine goes beyond a mere sentimentalization of this dearly departed. Not only has she finally domesticated Catherine by turning her into an angel, which in one stroke both disembodies and desexualizes her, but more important, she has appropriated her corpse for her own "infinite calm." Whereas Miller finds Heathcliff's opening of Catherine's grave a desecration, I find Nelly's appropriation of Catherine's body more like the act of a body snatcher or a grave robber. Catherine's natural body has been substituted for by another body, a sublime body. Even Heathcliff, who supposedly desecrates Catherine's grave, is guilty of no such crime as Miller suggests. He does indeed open up Catherine's coffin, but like Nelly he fails to see the real corpse. He too finds a sublime body:[28] "I got the sexton, who was digging Linton's grave, to remove the earth off her coffin lid, and I opened it. I thought once, I would have stayed there, when I saw her face again—it is hers yet—he had hard work to stir me; but he said it would change, if air blew on it, and so I struck one side of the coffin loose—and covered it up—not Linton's side, damn him!" (319).

Although Nelly calls Heathcliff "wicked" for having disturbed the dead, the hermetic seal is never really broken. Before the seal protecting this sublime body can be broken, Heathcliff rapidly closes up the coffin to inhibit the body's decomposition. Unlike Hindley's corpse, which was described as "carrion" only moments after his death, Catherine's body appears immune to decomposition. Heathcliff asks Nelly the details of Catherine's death ("Did she die like a saint? Come, give me a true history of the event. How did—" [203]), and he finds his answer when he exhumes her body. She did indeed die like a saint: one of the church's prerequisites for canonization is the immutability of the saint's body.

As Miller points out, the act of reading *Wuthering Heights* is a resurrection, "an opening of graves or a raising of ghosts" (70). However, what we find is that the opening of these graves and the raising of ghosts in this text is the very means by which the female body is exorcised from the text. Her body is snatched and replaced, first by the sublime body and then later by a benevolent ghost. To fulfill her domestic duties, Nelly not only must resurrect the sublime female body but she also must resurrect the undead. The question, though, is how to raise a ghost that will not haunt or inspire dread, like the ghost in Lockwood's dream. Nelly's task, then, is to raise the dead without provoking the threat of the undead. Romantic love becomes the very vehicle to pacify the living dead. At the end of the novel, Catherine is no longer roaming about alone; the old man "has seen two on 'em looking out his chamber window" (366). Catherine and Heathcliff become the romantic couple whole unto themselves.

This is the order of the romantic novel. However, Brontë's novel does not offer such a simple solution. Although Nelly says, "I believe the dead are at peace" (366), she is not so convinced of this herself. She also says that the boy who saw the ghosts *probably* made them up, and *yet still* she is afraid: "He probably raised the phantoms from thinking, as he traversed the moors alone, on the nonsense he had heard his parents and companions repeat—*yet still*, I don't like being out in the dark, now—

and I don't like being left by myself in this grim house" (366; emphasis added). While Nelly has taken care of the dead, she fails to exorcise all signs of the undead from Wuthering Heights. She ends on a very ambivalent note. She tries to maintain her belief in the fetish of the exquisite corpse peacefully asleep; *yet still* there is that remainder of doubt. Nelly's narrative functions both to construct a fetish and, at a structural level, *as* a fetish. On the one hand, Nelly disavows the possibility that her sleeping beauties might in fact be the living dead, haunting the moors, awaiting their proper obsequies. Yet still, she does not want to be in the "grim house," and thus she acknowledges her own doubt. Her narrative reveals a splitting of the narrative. Since Nelly's narrative could not remedy this split, this task is left to Lockwood. Standing before their graves, he "wondered how anyone could ever imagine unquiet slumbers, for the sleepers in that quiet earth" (367). Lockwood's last statement, like Nelly's, also fails to disavow completely the possibility of the dead returning. This is quite ironic, for Lockwood had already imagined unquiet sleepers in his dream of young Catherine.

Putting to rest this dream of "unquiet slumbers" becomes Lockwood's final attempt to give the corpse at the window a decent burial. However, these attempts prove to be only premature burials. With Brontë's novel, we realize that the exquisite corpse is *always* the result of a premature burial: these narratives become missed encounters with the real/corpse, and thus the story repeats itself. While Lockwood and Nelly have completed their narratives, the story itself becomes repeated in unauthorized versions as "idle tales" of the "country folks" (366). Catherine's ghost will continue to circulate like idle tales and gossip, for as we have seen with Sade's Justine, the sublime body has multiple lives. What both Shelley and Brontë have shown is that these sublime bodies do not always remain exquisite corpses. Their multiple lives are, in fact, sustained by the drive of the return of the repressed—the drive of the undead, awaiting their proper burial.

Part Three

Nationalism, Patriotism,
and Authorship

Jeanne Moskal

Gender, Nationality, and Textual Authority in Lady Morgan's Travel Books

$\mathcal{L}$ady Morgan herself described the difficulty of her roles as woman writer and as Irish patriot; in her time, "to be a woman was to be without defence, and to be a patriot was to be a criminal."[1] I will argue that Morgan, one of the first popular British women travel writers, defends herself against the charges of woman and patriot by embracing and utilizing the marginal. In one of her most controversial works, *France*, Morgan uses textual "marginalia" such as prefaces, footnotes, appendices, and quotations to construct an appearance of masculine authority, authenticity, and scholarship. Morgan also embraces the marginal and "criminal" role of Irish patriot, a role that triangulates her observation of the English occupation of France by inserting Ireland into the equation. Embracing this "criminal" role of Irish patriot creates the psychological compensation of constructing her authority along recognizable masculine lines, springing as it does from identification with her father, and paradoxically defending her against the more serious charge of being a woman writer. At the same time, it permits her the refuge of the feminine role of advocate for another's cause, one of the few cases in which patriarchy finds women's anger justifiable.[2] In accommodating masculine models of authority and in presenting herself as her father's daughter (and as the titled wife of Sir Charles Morgan), Morgan presents a figure less likely than, say, Mary Wollstonecraft to satisfy present-day seekers of foremothers who successfully resisted patriarchal constraints. Nonethe-

less, her mix of revolutionary politics, accommodation to gendered conventions of authorship and authority, and venture into a genre new to
women provides an example of the social and psychological complexities
confronting Romantic women writers: she shows the implications of one
Romantic woman writer's travel literature for the cultural history of both
liberal nationalist politics and gender identities.[3]

Morgan's tendencies in *France* to split textual authority and to identify
herself as an Irish patriot arise from the circumstances of her life. Morgan
was born Sydney Owenson, probably in 1776. Her Irish father, Robert
Owenson, married her English mother, Jane Hill, while trying to make an
acting career for himself in Shrewsbury. After their mother's death in
1789, she and her sister Olivia attended a Huguenot school in Clontarf,
near Dublin, forging an early connection with French culture. When her
father's theater, the National, went bankrupt, Morgan declared that she
could support herself, Olivia, and her father by writing novels and by
working as a governess. Her third novel, *The Wild Irish Girl*, received
considerable attention, and Sydney was invited to join the household of
the Marquess and Marchioness of Abercorn. There she met Dr. Charles
Morgan, the family physician, whom the Abercorns wanted her to marry
despite her reluctance. The Abercorns arranged to have Dr. Morgan
knighted, providing an added inducement. Sydney and Sir Charles married in 1812 and settled in Dublin, where they lived for twenty-five years.
Robert Owenson died that same year, inflicting the greatest loss Morgan
had suffered, yet freeing her from caring for her father in order to travel
with her husband and add travel writing to her career as a novelist. From
their Dublin base the Morgans traveled to the Continent four times,
Morgan writing her travel books and several more novels. While in
Ireland, the couple endured an attack on the legitimacy of Sir Charles's
title. Despite her satisfaction with Catholic emancipation in 1829, she
found Ireland tiresome; on receiving her government pension for literary
services in 1837, the Morgans moved to London, where he died in 1843
and she in 1859.

If Morgan is remembered now, it is for her novels, particularly the
four Irish "National Tales": *The Wild Irish Girl* (1806), *O'Donnel*
(1814), *Florence Macarthy* (1818), and *The O'Briens and the O'Flaher-
ties* (1827).[4] But to her contemporaries, both friend and foe, a major part
of her achievement consisted of her three travel books: *France* (1817),
Italy (1821), and *France in 1829–30* (1830). Her *Italy* was praised by
Byron as "fearless and excellent" and by Mary Shelley as singularly free
from the usual British prejudice against Italians.[5] Moreover, *Italy* was
placed on the papal *Index* and banned by Germany and by Austria,

which governed five of the seven states of Italy—prohibitions that helped its sales in England and even in Italy (*Memoirs*, 2: 89–90). But above all it was the first travel book, *France*, praised by Lafayette as the best contemporary work on France, that caught the tide of postwar taste and made Morgan's contemporary reputation.[6] *France* unashamedly promoted the cause of the French Revolution, excusing its excesses and lionizing Napoleon and his achievements while denigrating the corruption of the Bourbons. It is a disorganized work, in two volumes, sporting topically named books: in volume 1, "Peasantry" and "Society"; in volume 2, two books on Paris, then "The French Theatre" and "Eminent and Literary Characters." The text proper is followed by four appendices on law, finance, medicine, and political opinion written by Sir Charles Morgan with the help of Lafayette.

Published simultaneously in English and French, *France* achieved considerable success, with four English editions, two French, and three American coming in rapid succession (*Memoirs*, 2:55, 74, 80).[7] In addition to the admiration of many, *France* also met with vilification. Its sympathetic portrayal of Napoleon and the French Revolution provoked the ire of the conservative British reviewers; Morgan was ridiculed by the *Quarterly Review* in what Byron called "perhaps as bitter a critique as ever was written."[8] Her liberal political opinions in *France* provoked William Playfair to write an entire travel book in refutation, *France as it is, not Lady Morgan's France* (1819), which condemned the French Revolution and Morgan's supposed naïveté. And her literary opinions condemning French neoclassical drama provoked controversy as well; Stendhal recounted, "as soon as *France* appeared, hosts of people proceeded to massacre or energetically defend [Racine]," the controversy continuing in Charles Dupin's attack, *Lettre à Lady Morgan sur Racine et Shakespeare* (1818), and in the approval of French Romantics, who later hailed Morgan as their champion.[9]

"To Be a Woman Was to Be without Defence": Paratext and the Anxiety of the Woman Writer

The numerous attacks on Morgan's *France* suggest the vulnerability of the woman travel writer. Important feminist works by Sandra M. Gilbert and Susan Gubar, Margaret Homans, and Mary Poovey have examined the anxieties of Romantic women novelists and poets who deviate from the patriarchal ideal of feminine propriety and silence. These critics ascribe Romantic women writers' ambivalences to a longing for the self-assertion of writing, a fear of becoming the monsters that patriarchy identified with deviant (i.e., writing) women, a longing to conform to the ideal of feminine propriety, and a fear of being silenced themselves in writing about a feminized, silent Mother Nature.[10] Morgan herself recounts an incident illustrating the fear of being unsexed: Tom Moore "exclaimed bitterly against writing-women, even against the beautiful Mrs. Norton. 'In short,' said he, 'a writing-woman is one unsexed'; but suddenly recollecting himself, and pointing at me, said to my sister, 'except her,' (me) whom, in all his works, he had passed over in silence" (*Memoirs*, 2:403–404).

Even though the popularity of women novelists such as Frances Burney and Ann Radcliffe provided some bulwark of precedent for the budding woman writer of Morgan's time, the woman *travel* writer faced the additional stigma of the woman traveler. We have inherited a cultural tradition that associates travel with sexual freedom (as Byron's *Don Juan* attests). Fynes Moryson, a Renaissance traveler, provides an early example of the patriarchal position that travel is incompatible with female virtue: "women for suspition [*sic*] of chastity are most unfit for [travel]," despite the fact that "the masculine women of the Low Countries" travel for trade. Like the women novelists analyzed by Poovey and Gilbert and Gubar, women travelers, in Moryson's account, unsex themselves to become "masculine women."[11] John Donne provides a more familiar example. In "A Valediction: Forbidding Mourning," the male speaker, about to depart for travel, compares his soul and his wife's to a compass: "Thy soul, the fixed foot, makes no show / To move, but doth, if th' other do." The wife stays home, like Homer's Penelope, and anchors her husband's travel. This tradition was cited in critics of the practices of eighteenth-century travel, when conservative male writers warned that traveling women may be seduced by or—more threatening still—seduce the men they meet (Black, *The British*, 110). Taking the evidence of such writers, historian Eric J. Leed has recently concluded that Western culture pervasively links men with mobility and women with "sessility" (or place), making travel an inescapably gendered and gendering activity (111–29). Morgan's friend, Elizabeth Patterson Bonaparte, the deserted wife of Napoleon's brother Jerome, corroborates this sense of the general disapproval of women travelers: in Geneva, Madame Patterson Bonaparte writes that "there exists, too, an *esprit de corps*, or *de coterie*, appalling to strangers,—I mean, to *woman* strangers, for men are *les bien venus partout*" (emphasis in original; *Memoirs*, 2:110). And Mary Wollstonecraft, who traveled to Scandinavia in 1795, encapsulates the paradox of the woman travel writer: her Norwegian host "told me bluntly that I was a woman of observation, for I asked him *men's questions*" (Wollstonecraft's emphasis).[12] Wollstonecraft's authority as an observer depends on her asking questions recognizable as significant, defined as questions asked by men, usually about politics, economics, and so forth. Yet she is proud to be recognized as "a woman of observation," maintaining a feminine identity despite the threat that the activity of travel (and later of writing) might "unsex" her.

However, during the Romantic period, despite the persistent stereotype, more women traveled abroad. Before about 1750, British women had rarely traveled to the Continent and even more rarely to other destinations, a condition that explains the fame of Lady Mary Wortley Montagu's *Turkish Letters*, circulated in manuscript from the 1730s and published in 1763, the year after her death. William Lucas's guidebook, *Five Weeks' Tour to Paris, Versailles, and Marli* (1750), instituted a change in travel practices by formalizing an abbreviated Grand Tour for the middle classes, in which women participated accompanied by their families, usually fathers or husbands (Black, *The British*, 128) After the Romantic period, the increase in women traveling accelerated further with the establishment of Thomas Cook's group tours in the 1860s, which enabled "respectable" women to travel abroad in nonfamilial groups. Romantic women travel writers thus confront the double bind articulated by Wollstonecraft: proving themselves competent women ("women of observation") despite the fact that competence is recognized only in masculine terms (when they ask "men's questions"). In her first travel book, *France*, Morgan negotiates that double bind by splitting her book into a proper text and what Gerard Genette calls "paratext"—all typographic material that surrounds a text without being part of the text: chapter headings, title, page numbers, illustrations, and—Morgan's favorite paratextual device—footnotes. She thus summons masculine authority in the paratext while simultaneously exiling it to the margins to keep pristine the propriety of the main text. Morgan's reflections on her early life reveal a similar attempt to negotiate an uneven sense of her own authority over feeling and language:

All, that literary counsel, acquirement, and instruction give to literary composition, was, in my early career of authorship, utterly denied me. . . . [I] was inevitably destitute of that command of language, which books and reflection only give. . . . [E]xcept when I had to give utterance to some strong feeling, (for *feeling always finds it own language*), I was often, as the sportsman's phrase is, "at fault." *Conscious of the poverty of my vocabulary, I frequently borrowed a word, or adopted a phrase* . . . not for its precise application or intrinsic meaning, but simply "pour orner mon langage." (Emphasis added)[13]

On the one hand, Morgan expresses confidence in feeling, conventionally gendered as feminine, that "finds its own language," while on the other she expresses anxiety about vocabulary, which is associated with "literary counsel" and "books," the prerogatives of men's education.[14] Moreover, she enacts the same anxiety by adopting the explicitly male "sportsman's phrase" and by closing with the French quotation, ambiguously both an achievement of male education and a conventional accomplishment of gentlewomen.

It is particularly appropriate to see *The Wild Irish Girl* as a precursor to the travel books on France and Italy, for, as Joseph Leerssen observes, *The Wild Irish Girl* itself draws from contemporary travel books about Ireland, travel books that had recently become more sympathetic to Irish nationalism. *The Wild Irish Girl* is one of the first appropriations of that pro-Irish discourse into the novel.[15] In *The Wild Irish Girl* (1806), Morgan forged an early version of a woman writer's authority by splitting text and paratext, the defense she later used in the travel books. The text of *The Wild Irish Girl* is composed of letters written by a Horatio M——under the pseudonym Henry Mortimer. Horatio, the son of an English owner of Irish land and very much a "man of feeling," falls in love with Glorvina O'Melville, "the wild Irish girl."[16] The paratext consists of numerous footnotes (and sometimes notes on the footnotes). While only some of the footnotes are explicitly attributed to "Ed." or "Edit.," their pervasive presence creates a persona of the (presumably female) editor, effusively demonstrating the editor's knowledge of Irish lore.[17] The editor comments on Irish customs and language, being particularly anxious to liken the Irish to the ancient Greeks and to the biblical patriarchs (e.g. 1:119n, 1:148n, 2:194n).[18] Footnotes prevent the reader from dismissing the plot as mere sentiment by guaranteeing the veracity of the editor and anchoring the plot and characters in "objective" facts. When recounting the plight of a peasant who helps Horatio and who has not eaten in twenty-four hours, a footnote hammers the point home: "In this little scene there is not one word of fiction" (*WIG*, Pandora ed., 13n).[19] When Horatio laments the ills of absenteeism, a footnote quotes the denunciation of absentee landlords' agents as "a horde of tyrants" from *An Enquiry into the Causes of Popular Discontent in Ireland* (*WIG*, 1:96n), underlining and literally underwriting the authority of Horatio's statement. Finally, the editor repeatedly cites numerous works on Irish culture, such as Edmund Burke's *Letter to a peer of Ireland on the Penal Laws against Irish Catholics* (1781), Joseph Cooper Walker's *Historical Memoirs of the Irish Bards* (1786), Sylvester O'Halloran's *Introduction to the Study of the History and Antiquities of Ireland*

(1772), and Arthur Young's *A tour through Ireland with general observations on the present state of that kingdom* (1780).[20]

Leerssen has demonstrated that the prolific footnotes maintain the high sentiment of the plot by exiling Morgan's learned digressions to footnotes ("Ireland Romantic," 213). But the implications of this splitting for construction of a woman writer's authority have not been discussed. Though Morgan writes these letters ostensibly as a man, the author's sex was known from the name, Miss Owenson, on the title page of the first and subsequent editions. As a result of this explicit display of learning in the paratext, the footnotes return authority to the female as editor, whereas the text proper complies with conventions that deprive female characters of agency and authority while investing the male with these qualities. In the main text, ascribed to the male "Henry Mortimer," Glorvina is the embodiment and repository of Irish culture, who can be sought but cannot herself seek. But the agency and authority of Morgan as Glorvina emerges in the footnotes, a return of the repressed. (This identification of Morgan with Glorvina lasted much of her life, as most of her friends addressed her by that name.)

Shari Benstock, in an important article on footnotes and authority, has claimed that footnotes in novels extend textual authority by enlarging the fictional context, whereas footnotes in critical works delimit the works' authority.[21] Benstock's claim at first seems appropriate to Morgan's novel. But Benstock further claims that literary notes playfully, consciously divide the text against itself. While this second claim may be true for the male writers Benstock treats (Fielding, Sterne, and Joyce), who have confidence in their right to be authors, it rings false for Morgan, whose footnotes in *The Wild Irish Girl* extend the context of the romantic fiction by shoring up the author's status as an authority on Ireland, supporting the text's claims, not dividing against them. *The Wild Irish Girl* employs footnotes to supplement the text, not to undermine it, and to advance the woman writer's claim to authority; text and notes create the impression of the same voice singing in two different modes. Ironically, however, much of this authority is mustered by quotations from male authorities.

Morgan's authority is both (conflictedly) feminine and straightforwardly nationalist. Significantly, Morgan summons up specifically *Irish* authority in *The Wild Irish Girl*, an authority that follows a pattern of cultural nationalism described by Anthony Smith:

The cultural dimension of nationalist movements has two aspects: a populist and Rousseauan [*sic*] nostalgia for the simplicity and sturdiness of agricultural life, which embodies in pristine form the essence and inner virtue of the community, uncontaminated by urban luxury and corruption; and an academic, scholarly component, which is not only useful in undergirding the historic claims of the movement before the bar of world opinion and sceptical authorities, but can also provide the whole nationalist enterprise with legitimacy based on scholarly research. . . . Hence the proliferation of historical, philological, ethnological, socio-demographic, art-historical, musicological, and other forms of historicist enquiries, and the appeal of nationalism for those engaged in such enquiries.[22]

Morgan's *Wild Irish Girl*, in its peculiar mix of sentimental text and copious footnotes, exemplifies both of the cultural nationalist tendencies Smith discusses. (By contrast, her 1811 novel, *The Missionary*, enacts its nationalist agenda by displacement to an East Indian setting, rather than with numerous footnotes.) New nations are trying to establish legitimacy in ways that resemble new writers, so the struggle to "legitimate" Ireland and the struggle to "legitimate" the female author follow overlapping strategies. Moreover, this specific Irish identity is linked with her identity as her father's daughter. The father-daughter relation is preeminent in the novel. Before the arrival of Horatio, the relationship of Glorvina to her widowed father, O'Melville, the Prince of Inismore, is exclusive. She is undeniably his favorite; the prince "keeps up the old Irish customs and dress, letting nobody eat at the same table but his daughter, *not even his Lady, when she was alive*" (*WIG*, 1:124; emphasis added). Having sustained her own mother's death at the age of thirteen, Morgan projects back in time the fantasy of possessing the father exclusively *before* the mother's death, implying that the father preferred her over the mother in the oedipal rivalry. Further, she presents this favoritism as a quintessentially Irish custom, foregrounding the national identity that links her with the father.

The importance of Irishness and of the identity as her father's daughter is underscored by the biographical material. As the daughter of the impecunious Irish actor Robert Owenson, Morgan had strong encouragement to write. She hoped to delight her "papa," to relieve his financial embarrassments, and to provide for his old age (*Memoirs*, 1:148, 134). In her play, *The First Attempt, or Whim of a Moment* (1807), Morgan combined these goals by writing the part of a "stage Irishman" specifically for her father, a part he played with gusto. And finally, the advocacy of Irish causes enabled her to identify with her father's Irishness, as oldest daughters frequently are allowed to identify with their fathers in families with no sons.[23] During the daughterly stage of her life, the ambition to write posed little threat to the desire to conform to feminine propriety; as Morgan wrote in 1803, "I am *ambitious*, far, far beyond the line of laudable *emulations*, perhaps beyond the power of being happy. Yet the

strongest point of my ambition is to be *every inch a woman*" (*Memoirs,*
1:230; original emphasis). The goal of woman writer poses no threat to
the Irish daughter.

The transition from daughter to wife in 1812, made irrevocable by
Robert Owenson's death that same year, exacerbated Morgan's crisis of
authority in *France*. Morgan initially found marriage threatening to
authorial—and patriotic—identity, even though it promised wifely fulfillment. Early in the marriage, she wrote: "As to me, I am *every inch a
wife*, and so ends that brilliant thing that was GLORVINA" (*Memoirs,* 2:5;
original emphasis), expressing the fear of losing her identity both as the
author of *The Wild Irish Girl* and also as the incarnation of its heroine,
but also the ambivalent hope of being "every inch a wife." She wrote to
Morgan that in marriage she feared leaving the country she loved (*Memoirs,* 1:452, 456) and, in declaring her intention to marry, melodra-
matically seemed to renounce her family and career: "*My whole soul is
yours!* Father, sister, friends, country, all are forgotten, and I enter again
upon life with you. . . . I give up my career of pleasure and vanity to sink
into privacy and oblivion; *and the ambition of the authoress and the
woman is lost in the feelings of the mistress and the wife*" (*Memoirs,*
1:497; first emphasis Morgan's, second added). No longer, it appears, can
she be ambitious for both womanly (now wifely) and writerly goals. One
letter suggests a remedy for the loss of her ambition: "We shall write a
novel together" (*Memoirs,* 1:484), a dream of joint authorship achieved
only in the travel books. However, as events proved, the poor reception
of Sir Charles's book, *Sketches of the Philosophy of Life* (1818), criticized by religious authorities for its skepticism, caused him to retire from
general practice, keeping only his appointment to the Marshalsea Prison
in Dublin (*Memoirs,* 2:23).[24] Finding herself in a family context that
invited public ridicule, a context in which her career outshone her husband's, Morgan's venture into the masculine genre of travel literature in
writing *France* posed a challenge, for she was simultaneously forced to
answer that threat to convention by maintaining her feminine propriety
by means of the newer, more fragile identity as wife rather than as
daughter. As in *The Wild Irish Girl*, paratext in *France* exemplifies the
authority exiled from the proper text, but in *France* that authority stays
exiled in the margins, split off much of the time from the image of proper
femininity that Morgan presents.

The physical appearance of *France* also caused comment, if not controversy. The book does look peculiar. It proliferates paratext such as
prefaces, appendices, footnotes, and another kind of boundary material
that Genette does not include in his definition of paratext, namely,

quotations from other languages (Morgan quotes in French). The front matter in the second edition of *France*, which followed six weeks after the first, includes two prefaces by Morgan and an advertisement by her publisher, not quite balancing the four appendixes by Sir Charles. On the book's pages, French and English compete for space: many pages contain italicized, untranslated quotations in French; indeed, many pages are entirely in French. M. Thomas of Philadelphia, a prudent American publisher, translated all of the French passages in the second and subsequent American editions of *France*. Furthermore, numerous pages are typographically divided between text and footnotes, the notes often running parallel beneath the text for several pages, and sometimes taking over a page completely. Even though substantial footnotes were popular, even conventional, underwriting Maria Edgeworth's *Castle Rackrent* (1800), Walter Scott's *Waverley* (1814), and Byron's *Childe Harold's Pilgrimage*, Morgan's practice was considered quite excessive. Henry Colburn, the publisher, hoped that in a new article "the *notes* would not be too long or too numerous, it being her peculiar tendency to pile up all her loose lying materials into notes as long as the text" (Morgan's *Memoirs*, 2:190; original emphasis). Morgan's critics derided her paratext, claiming that in her French quotations she used the language affectedly and ignorantly, that her husband's appendixes were mere "makeweight to the literary cargo which his lady . . . was bound to deliver," and that in her notes she "remembers too frequently the conversations that she had with individuals of all ranks," unwittingly employing spies who fooled her.[25]

The prefaces demonstrate Morgan's nervousness under the purview of her critics. She defends herself against the *Quarterly Review*'s attacks on her novels and in them her "licentiousness, profligacy, irreverence, blasphemy, libertinism, disloyalty, and atheism." She writes: "As [the *Quarterly*] foretold, I am become, in spite of the 'seven deadly sins' it laid to my charge, 'not indeed a good writer of novels,' but, I trust, 'a respectable,' and, I am *sure*, 'a happy mistress of a family'" (*France* 1:xi; original emphasis). Morgan's quotation of the *Quarterly* seems peculiarly ironic. On the one hand, she seems to exult in her acquisition of a title, for she has thereby fulfilled beyond expectation the role of respectable mistress. On the other hand, she allows the *Quarterly* to define the terms of her success, not as author but as a proper wife (however much the *Quarterly* continued to criticize her later). The assertion of a proper, relational identity persists in the preface, as Morgan justifies her voice by invoking her husband's consent: "In a work which bears the sweeping title of '*France*' . . . it would be a strange solecism to omit all notice of the jurisprudence, medical science, and finance of that country; subjects connected with its most vital existence, but far beyond my limited sphere of enquiry. At my request my husband has undertaken to furnish some sketches on these points" (1:xi–xii). In creating such a division of labor, her own text and her husband's appendixes, Morgan appears to conform to the gendered conventions of the genre. Indeed, many of the travel books by men that preceded Morgan's were dominated by such "masculine" topics: Nathaniel Wraxall's *Tour through the Western, Southern, and Interior Parts of France* supplemented his *History of France under the Valois* (1777). Arthur Young divided his *Travels during the years 1787, 1788, and 1789; undertaken with a view to ascertaining the cultivation, wealth, resources, and national prosperity of the Kingdom of France* (1792) into a journal that recounts his travels and a section of "General Observations," mostly economic. And Dr. Martin Lister's *Journey to Paris in 1698*, which included an entire section on medicine, had recently been reprinted in John Pinkerton's well-known *General Collection of the best and most interesting Voyages and Travels in all parts of the world* (1807–14).[26] (In rather a different conception of how to divide labor by gender, Mary and Percy Bysshe Shelley's *History of a Six Weeks' Tour* mixes her journal and letters with his letters and lyric poem "Mont Blanc," ending, as does *France*, with the masculine voice.)

The split between feminine propriety in the text and masculine authority in the paratext does not hold throughout, however. Morgan's text demonstrates her awareness that she has ventured onto largely "masculine" territory, as she explicitly addresses her predecessor male travel writers, Arthur Young and John Scott. Young had argued, in his *Travels*, that the French peasants were naturally industrious but lacked national policies that contributed to their prosperity; Morgan agrees (*France*, 1:12). She disagreed, however, with John Scott's claim in *A Visit to Paris in 1814* (1815) and *Paris Revisited in 1815* (1816) that the French deserved defeat because they had no sound principles (Maxwell, *English Travellers*, 265). In reply, Morgan praises the French peasantry as primitive, intelligent, and frank (1:25, 33, 74), particularly refuting Scott's complaint that France had too many beggars and praising the enforcement of the mendicancy laws. Nonetheless, these forays into the masculine arenas of politics and economics remain embedded in Morgan's anxieties and assertions of feminine identity. She prefaces her discussion of the *corvée* by calling her work "the production of a few scattered fragments" (1:7), implicitly deferring to Sir Charles's appendixes.

In addition to the prefaces, the footnotes and the quotations in French provide prolific paratext. Ostensibly, these materials function to bolster the travel book's claim to authority by authentically rendering the impression of the moment. In the preface she explains that the frequent recurrence of French sentences and dialogues, which "break up and disfigure the text . . . arose from my anxiety to give impressions with all the warmth and vigour with which I received them" (1:vii). One curious feature of the French quotations is the catholicity of political sentiment; she quotes all three of the main political parties: the *ultras*, who wanted absolute monarchy; the Constitutionalists, who favored the current constitutional monarchy; and the Independents, both Liberals and Bonapartists (Suddaby and Yarrow, *Lady Morgan in France*, 24–25). For example, she quotes an ultraist "woman of rank, talent and education" who approved of the secrecy of the notorious *lettres de cachet* because it prevented public disgrace of a family (1:214). In another incident, she quotes a soldier's praise of Napoleon, stressing her authenticity and authority: "I have at this moment before my eyes one of these 'veteran youths' as I once beheld him, describing the evacuation of Paris" (1:252–53). Morgan reproduces, and corroborates, his approval of Napoleon. Many of these conversations and anecdotes in French are moved to the footnotes, the location of most authority, and marked as authentic; for example, "I literally copy the jargon of loyalty as I took it down, *de vive voix*, in my journal" (1:200n).

This receptivity to all political persuasions and mustering of authority by means of "literal" transcription is undercut, however, by Morgan's insistence on maintaining a persona more in keeping with proper femininity: the persona of a titled celebrity, the title derived from her marriage and her celebrity derived partly from her authorship. The speakers she quotes are most often fellow guests at parties she attends, and this emphasis on her own celebrity—a theme she mentions too often—tends to trivialize her exposure to such a range of opinions. The most forthright example is this: "It has frequently occurred to me to have witnessed the most opposite discussions, and listened to the most contradictory opinions, in the course of the same evening; *assisting* at a *royalist* dinner, drinking ultra tea, and supping *en républicaine*. I have thus graduated on the political scale, from the extreme of loyalty to the last degree of rebellion" (1:230; original emphasis).

The undercurrent of vanity over her own social currency has the unfortunate effect of making the numerous quotations of political sentiment serve not only the purpose of bolstering the masculine claim to authenticity and authority but also to provide evidence that Morgan has fulfilled the role of Sir Charles's wife, the "happy mistress of a family," that the *Quarterly* set out for her. In stressing the entertainments in which these sentiments occur, she minimizes their political status. Morgan, then, attempted to redefine a version of feminine, wifely authority in *France*, not entirely successfully, by adapting her familiar technique of footnotes to splitting the text from the paratext.

"To Be a Patriot Was to Be a Criminal": The Political Triangle of England, Ireland, France

As my analysis of *The Wild Irish Girl* suggested, Morgan found a refuge from the anxiety of the woman writer in the roles—for her, indistinguishable—of Robert Owenson's daughter and of Irish patriot. This second defense in *France*, the role of Irish patriot denouncing English oppression of France and Ireland simultaneously, has its roots in the family triangle. The conflicts of the Anglo-Irish were mirrored in her own family situation, Irish father and English mother: "My first point of society was to behold the conflict between two unequal minds—the one (my mother) strong and rigid—the other weak and yielding; the one strong to arrest dispute—the other accelerating its approach" (*Memoirs*, 1:430). Contrary to gender expectations but matching political expectations, the English mother possesses strength while the Irish father is weak, exhibiting only the capacity to rebel against preexisting authority in accelerating the approach of dispute. Morgan clearly associated the mother and her Englishness with despotism: When her mother invited clergy over to discuss religion, she was "the Protestant Pope among them all!" who "exercised a despotic influence to the full stretch of her very limited power" (*Memoirs*, 1:76, 77), a portrayal foreshadowing Morgan's portrayal of England in *France*. Her repression of the connection to the mother is suggested in her letters: "*I do not like* women, I cannot get on with them! . . . except the excessive tenderness which I have always felt for my sister. . . . *Devancer son sexe* is as dangerous as *devancer son siècle*" (*Memoirs*, 2:28). Nonetheless, Morgan in part attributed her own strong advocacy on behalf of the Irish to the feminine tendency to identification: "The accidental circumstance of being born and educated in a land stamped with the impress of six centuries of degradation—the natural tendency of a female temperament to a prompt, uncalculating sympathy—and the influence of that stirring quality called indignation (as often constitutional as a moral affection)—gave a direction to my feelings, and a colour to my mind and writings, which from my 'youth upwards' have remained unchanged and indelible" (Morgan, quoted in Newcomer, *Lady Morgan the Novelist*, 80). In fact, the role of patriot provided both protection from and subversion of conventional women's roles, for, as Ina Ferris has observed, Morgan genders the categories of patriotism and politics in her maxim: "Politics can never be a woman's science; but patriotism must naturally be a woman's sentiment."[27] In the explicit claim of Morgan's self-justification, even the acceptable feminine role of patriot, which a respectable woman would take gladly, had been declared "criminal." However, implicitly, Morgan clears a space for herself to speak on political matters, by claiming it as only the (feminine) role of patriot, safely occupied by a daughter.

This family situation clearly took a political cast, as Morgan explicitly connected her father with the cause of Irish nationalism:

At a moment when Irish nationality was rising above the level of unavailing complaint; when Irishmen hawked their grievances as beggars hawk their sores; when the glorious body of Irish volunteers became the Praetorian bands of the land, not to impose, but to break her chains; my father snatched the epithet and gave his theater the name of "National." He was backed by some of the best men of the time; patriots, in the best sense of the word. (*Memoirs*, 1:66)

Thus, Robert Owenson acted in the spirit of contemporary Irish nationalism, his founding of a theater recognized by his contemporaries as a patriotic act. Moreover, he embodied for his daughter the essence of the Irish character, "[setting] about his theatrical reformation with all the zeal and all the indiscretion of a true Irishman" (*Memoirs*, 1:66). France and Frenchness had a place in the Anglo-Irish family constellation, making a national triangle in the family situation. On the personal level this tie was reinforced in a couple of ways, as Robert Owenson claimed a connection with the Bordeaux family of French vintners and became a wine merchant based on that connection (*Memoirs*, 1:26–27). Moreover, Morgan attended a Huguenot school, where all conversation was carried out in French (*Memoirs*, 1:105). On the political level, Ireland's ties with France had long consisted in a common antipathy to England, one wave of Irishmen, the "Wild Geese," having emigrated after the Battle of the Boyne (1690) to royalist France, followed by another wave of United Irishmen defeated in the 1798 rebellion.[28]

Further, the literary circles Morgan found in British-occupied France replicated the political triangle. Irish novelists Maria Edgeworth and Charles Maturin enjoyed considerable popularity among the French; Thomas Moore's *Irish Melodies*, widely distributed in French, inspired Hector Berlioz's *Mélodies Irlandaises* (1829), while his *Lalla Rookh* was made into a French opera by Félicien David in 1862. Every novel by Morgan appeared in French translation, getting mixed reviews. Raifroidi notes that the French admired *The Wild Irish Girl* for its description of an "Ireland positioned in the ocean at the far corners of the world."[29] In addition, several Irishwomen conducted salons in Paris in the postwar period: Mary Clarke, Lady Blessington, and Mme Belloc, the translator of Byron and Thomas Moore. Among all of them Morgan was lionized, as the *Journal de Paris* records: "[E]lle a été courue, fetée, adorée dans nos cercles."[30] Thus, in some measure, French recognition of her celebrity compensated for the hostility of the English press and the fragility of Morgan's titled status.

One significant example of Morgan's political triangulation appears in her somewhat forced but long-extended comparison of France and Ireland in a metaphor of gardens. She writes that the finest flowers in France are to be found in the gardens of the peasantry, names several flowers, and remarks on the pride the gardener takes in his work. Then she exclaims:

Oh! when shall I behold, near the peasant's hovel in my own country, other flowers than the bearded thistle, which there waves its "lonely head," and scatters its down upon every passing blast; or the scentless shamrock, the unprofitable blossom of the soil, which creeps to be trodden upon, and is gathered only to be plunged in the inebriating draught, commemorating annually the fatal illusions of the people, and drowning in the same tide of madness their emblems and their wrongs. (*France*, 1:47–48)

The *Quarterly Review* singled out this passage for particular ridicule, probably because of its Irish patriotism, though ostensibly for its effusion of emotion.[31] Appended to this feminine expression of sentiment, a note follows in the scholarly style of *The Wild Irish Girl*: "It is an annual custom in Ireland to drown the shamrock in whisky, on St. Patrick's day, a festival commemorated by every species of barbarous revelry." However, unlike *The Wild Irish Girl*'s endorsement of all Irish culture, here the text proper's digression on Irish affairs focuses on politics ("the fatal illusions of the people") as the cause of their deplorable habits of drunkenness. These botanical metaphors acquire additional resonance in the context of Gerald Newman's observation that eighteenth-century thinkers frequently reconciled cosmopolitanism and nationalism in the metaphor of the garden: "the civilized world as a great international community, a garden as Herder pictured it, to which all the varying flowers, the English rose and German Kaiserblume as well as the French fleur-de-lis, contributed in some measure."[32]

Another example of the double vision of Ireland and France occurs when, after describing the French peasants' equally polite attitude to their fellow peasants and to their social superiors, Morgan exclaims:

Oh! in listening to their sensible questions, and frank replies, how often, and how unavoidably, have I contrasted their deportment with that of the peasantry of my own country, where a whole population seems condemned to exhibit, in their unregulated conduct and manners, the extremes of lawless resistance, and of groveling servility;—where he, who for some trifling benefit to-day kneels in the dust at your feet in exaggerated gratitude, with *"long may you reign! may you have a happy death!"* (for power and death are familiar images to the Irish mind) will perhaps, tomorrow, in the midnight meetings of his wretched hovel, in the desperation of poverty and inebriety, plan the violation of your property, or the destruction of your life. Slave of his passions, and victim of his wrongs; in good or ill, equally governed by their tyranny, he re-acts upon the policy which made him what he is, with a faithful, but frightful influence. (*France,* 1:67–68; original emphasis)

France, which has benefited from the care of Napoleon, fosters sensible and frank peasants, while Ireland has become servile under English despotism and absenteeism. Here Morgan explicitly addresses the English oppressors of Ireland, mentioning the threat the Irish offer to "*your* property" and "*your* life." Again, she distances herself from the groveling servility of the Irish working classes. Thus, Morgan exhibits an ambivalence in the political triangle (distancing herself from the Ireland whose cause she advocates), which may echo ambivalence fostered in the family triangle, in which love for the mother clashes with defiance of her despotic English authority, defiance underwritten by the Irish father and his potential to threaten.

French Fathers: Lafayette and Denon

The role of daughter, closely allied for Morgan with the role of Irish patriot, provides surer authority in the displaced father figures of Lafayette and Denon, both of whom had particular salience for the Irish. Lafayette's leadership in both the American and French revolutions combined the ideals of both the republican Irish in the South, who admired France, and the Northern Irish, who found the example of America more compelling. Moreover, Lafayette supported Irish nationalist movements (O'Tuathauigh, 21). In addition to his significance as an ideal, Lafayette befriended and consistently encouraged Morgan personally, as Lloyd S. Kramer has observed.[33] His friendship invited Morgan to cast him as a father. Lafayette was in his sixties when Morgan met him. In book 1 of *France,* Morgan borrows Lafayette's paternal and Irish authority by using his presence in France to frame her own: "I was one morning, in the summer of 1816, walking under the venerable towers of Chateau la Grange, and leaning on the arm of its illustrious master, general the marquis de la Fayette (and who would not boast of being supported by that arm, which raised the standard of independence in America, and placed her banner above the dungeons of France?)" (1:19). Here Morgan's daughterly identity is formed by "leaning" on Lafayette's arm; her Irish-patriotic identity is underwritten by mentioning his American and French heroism. Prior to this passage, Morgan has mentioned no other relationships or traveling companions, nor has she narrated her journey.[34] Therefore, the presence of Lafayette temporarily stabilizes the narrative of the main text, while it also characterizes the author as an authority: "Who would not boast of being supported by that arm?" Morgan's pattern of triangulation, inserting Ireland into the discussion of England and France, also occurs in her praise of Lafayette as a landowner and benefactor of the peasants of La Grange; as Kramer writes, "These idyllic country relationships differed so dramatically from Morgan's perception of the behavior among the absentee landlords in Ireland that she could make her own social argument by simply describing Lafayette's tours of his farm" (55). Lafayette's status as protector is explicitly paternalized in a later section of *France*, where Morgan writes: "We found General La Fayette surrounded by his patriarchal family,—his son and daughter-in-law, his two daughters . . . and their husbands; eleven grand-children." (2:302). The *Quarterly Review* criticized Morgan for this particular misplaced modifier, "patriarchal," but the slip of the pen suggests the word's importance to her, for Lafayette gave her and Ireland the legitimacy of his support and was eager to do so.[35]

Similarly, Morgan's friendship with Baron Dominique Vivant Denon (1747–1825), director-general of museums under Napoleon from 1804 to 1815, had resonance for an Irish nationalist.[36] Denon, a key figure in Napoleon's expedition to Egypt in 1798, would remind the Irish reader of Napoleon's failure to liberate Ireland; the Irish had expected substantial military support in their May 1798 rebellion, but instead Napoleon sent only a few troops to County Mayo while he departed on an expedition to Egypt. While accompanying Napoleon on this expedition, Denon sketched many of the monuments of Egyptian art, often under enemy fire; he published the results in a travel book, *Voyages dans la basse et la haute Égypte* (1802).

While Napoleon's expedition to Egypt required exculpation in the eyes of many Irish, as a loyal "daughter" of Denon, Morgan implicitly justified Napoleon's expedition to Egypt by suggesting its cultural rather than its military value, its value as a means of acquiring cultural treasures appropriate for the Louvre:

> When the French army, after crossing the burning desarts of Africa, came within view of the mighty ruins of ancient Thebes, it halted unbidden, and, by one electric and spontaneous emotion of awe and admiration, the soldiers clapped their hands, as if the conquest of Egypt was completed; as if, to behold the gigantic remains of this great city, had been the sole object of their long and painful labours, their glory, and their reward. This is one of the grandest images, which human affections have ever presented to the contemplation of the poet or the philosopher. France was then free and covered with glory, she was for a moment susceptible of the sublime, and *she was worthy of the spoils her bravery had won*, and which taste could thus feelingly appreciate. (*France* 2:25–26; emphasis added)

Here Morgan uses the occlusion of the actual Egyptians living at the time, a practice common in travel books that serve colonialist interests, in order to emphasize the Western encounter with the unmediated art treasures of Egypt's past, unencumbered by its present—a tendency that, Edward W. Said has observed, characterizes much European treatment of the Middle East and which has underwritten many museums' acquisition of art (Said, 80–89). Morgan's insistence that the French deserve to be the custodians of art treasures of Italy takes on an added bite in light of the political triangle we have been examining, for the British were involved in a parallel dispute over art custody in the case of the Elgin Marbles. Lord Elgin finally arranged to have the cultures and bas-reliefs from the Parthenon shipped to England in 1812, where they languished during a controversy over their authenticity, finally being purchased by the British government and placed on display in 1816, the year of Morgan's visit to France.[37] Against this backdrop, she clearly implies that the French, due to their political ideals, deserve this distinction, whereas the English do not. Denon's worthiness, as director-general of museums, is also implied.

Morgan persists in this theme of proper custody of art works by addressing an especially painful condition of the Congress of Vienna: loss of trophies won by Napoleon, particularly the withdrawal of the art treasures collected by Napoleon from Denon's Louvre (supervised by English troops) and the removal of the Venetian horses from the Place du Carrousel (Maxwell, *English Traveller*, 272ff.). In John Scott's view, the French richly deserved these two humiliations, due to their rallying around Napoleon for the Hundred Days after his return from Elba in 1814. Morgan, by contrast, stresses the French nation's fitness as custodian for the art treasures of the world out of daughterly loyalty to her friend Denon (Elkington, *Les Relations*, 116–7).

Napoleon Redefined

Including Morgan's *France* in our view of Romanticism provides a sense of the disparate portrayals of Napoleon by contemporary British writers, a topic I can sketch here only briefly. One familiar portrayal of Napoleon accords with a major strand of the Romantic ideology, the ideal of the autonomous self, an ideal particularly embodied for the male Romantics in Prometheus and Napoleon. For example, Percy Shelley's sonnet "Political Greatness" (1821), despite its lament of Napoleon's failure, makes clear the grounds of the ideal from which Napoleon fell:

> Man who man would be
> Must rule the empire of himself; in it
> Must be supreme, establishing his throne
> On vanquished will, quelling the anarchy
> Of hopes and fears, *being himself alone.*

Byron displayed considerable ambivalence about Napoleon's titanic isolation, at times claiming "that what he most likes in [Napoleon's] character is his want of sympathy,"[38] but writing in *Childe Harold's Pilgrimage* that

the great error of Napoleon, 'if we have writ our annals true,' was a continued obtrusion on mankind of *his want of all community of feeling for or with them*; perhaps more offensive to human vanity than the active cruelty of more trembling and suspicious tyranny.

Such were his speeches to public assemblies as well as individuals; and the single expression which he is said to have used on returning to Paris after the Russian winter had destroyed his army, rubbing his hands over a fire, "This is pleasanter than Moscow," would probably alienate more favour from his cause than the destruction and reverses which led to the remark. (Emphasis added)[39]

Byron's distaste for Napoleon's want of sympathy comes through in this note, but as Marlon Ross has demonstrated, the continuity of Napoleon and Prometheus form part of the male Romantic poets' myth of self-possession, the desire to trope literary enterprise as masculine in the light of an increase in women poets and women readers. In *Childe Harold's Pilgrimage*, Ross observes, "the poet's quest for self-possession and the conqueror's quest for world possession . . . [turn] into the other with dizzying rapidity."[40] The "titanic" portrayal of Napoleon, then, mirrors the poet's (illusion of his) autonomous identity.

Morgan offers not a titanic Napoleon but a communal, nationalist Napoleon. Her portrayal retains the lionization of the Napoleon who fostered the widespread Irish hope that Protestantism would be extinguished forever in 1825, a hope generated by Pastorini's prophecy, first published in 1771, and later meshing with Irish hopes of a French invasion. In this millenarian context, the Irish cast Napoleon as a deliverer in poems such as these:

> Even though many people who do not fear justice
> Believe that there is no help or protection available to them;
> Still, the leader will come from France without delay
> And he'll take the English down a peg or two—that's Bony.

And:

> As Grainne was wandering along the sea shore,
> For seventy weary long years and more,
> She saw Bonaparte coming far-off at sea,
> Saying rowl away, my boys, we'll clear the way
> So pleasantly.[41]

Although Morgan cannot, in 1816, entertain such hopes, her portrayal of Napoleon retains the communal and nationalist cast; he is the leader of an army, and, surprisingly, a member of a family. In a note to the passage about Napoleon's approach to Thebes, quoted above, Morgan expands on the exquisite taste of the entire French army and particularly of its leader Napoleon:

See Denon's Travels.—The progress of the French army through the wastes and among the ruins of Egypt, was occasionally characterized by traits of great grandeur and sublimity. The soldiers, under the command of Dessaix, spontaneously broke their order of march, and halted before Tentyra, in endless admiration of its grandeur. The enthusiasm, both of officers and of men, was exhibited in an ever ready assistance to the artists, and the members of the Egyptian Institute. But history has not, perhaps, an image more magnificent to offer . . . than that of Buonaparte, as yet young, as yet known only by the glory he had acquired, lost in contemplation before the mighty pyramids of Cheops; and, in the presence of the enemy's army, pointing to these gigantic monuments, as he addressed his soldiers in words, sublime as the objects which inspired them—"*Allez, et pensez que, du haut de ces monuments, quarante siecles nous observent*" [Soldiers, remember that from the height of these pyramids forty centuries look down upon you]. (*France*, 2:26)

As in the vindication of Denon, Morgan here is anxious to stress Napoleon's taste. Yet significantly she revises the conventional association of individual isolation with the sublime. Her Napoleon conforms to one condition of the sublime familiar from Burke's *Enquiry*, that the observer appropriates the object's sublimity for himself, for his words are as "sublime as those objects which inspired them." However, unlike Burke's model, Morgan's Napoleon speaks directly to an audience, functioning as a teacher of taste as well as the leader of an army. Napoleon here is not the solitary viewer but the leader of an army and a nation, defined relationally.

Morgan's advocacy of Napoleon remained strong throughout her *Italy* (1824), which lacks the political triangulation of *France*. Unlike *France*, *Italy* seldom mentions the Irish-English situation, except to argue for religious toleration (1:65n, 1:235) and to challenge England's self-righteousness following Waterloo (1:87, 137).[42] Morgan retains a purpose similar to that of *France* (1817), declaring that the goal of the book is to trace the effect of the French Revolution on Italy (1:30). As in *France* (1817), she more or less equates the French Revolution with Napoleon, and her tracing of the effects of the French Revolution consists mostly in a vindication of Napoleon. The fact that Napoleon's relation with Italy was imperial, unlike his national leadership of France, may well have challenged Morgan to revise her estimate of Napoleon in the light of her nationalist sympathies. Indeed, there is some material to this effect: she denounces empires throughout history, including Napoleon's (1:3-4), calls him an invader (1:44), and remarks wryly that Italian art treasures paid for improvements in Paris (1:63-64). But as Morgan writes of the treasures looted from a Turin church, her admiration of Napoleon reveals itself as well: "Some [treasures] have gone to stem the incursions of the Po, others to raise the noblest of its bridges; and some have even found their way to Paris, and have contributed to clear the noxious purlieus of the Tuileries, and to build the beautiful *rue de Rivoli*, the monument of the French conquest over the royal pleasure-grounds of Turin" (1:63-64). Napoleon may have looted the church, but he put the money to better uses by making civic improvements in Italy as well as in Paris. Morgan makes the ironic suggestion that Napoleon, by building bridges, out-pontiffs the pope. Despite her slight protest over Napoleon's use of Italian loot to clean up Paris, she clearly values those improvements. Most tellingly, she rewrites the referent in her final sentence about "the monument of the French conquest over the *royal pleasure-grounds* of Turin," to imply that Napoleon conquered not the church, her original referent, but the site of idle pleasure associated with royalty.[43] All in all, whatever criticism Morgan offers with one hand, of Napoleon as the invader of Italy, she neutralizes with the other by declaring Napoleon's actions justified in the overthrow of monarchy or in the preservation of culture; Napoleon is another example of the patriarchal figure who resists the enemies of liberty, in Ireland or in Italy. She notes with pride that Napoleon created a waiting room for tributary kings, thus justly humiliating them (1:69). She defends the French army against the charge leveled by John Chetwode Eustace in *A Tour through Italy, exhibiting a view of its Scenery, its antiquities, and its monuments* (1813) that they looted Turin's libraries; Morgan claims that the French restored numerous books to better condition (1:73). Eustace further charged that Napoleon's troops shot at *The Last Supper* and damaged it, but Morgan replies that, in fact, Napoleon himself protected the painting by ordering a copy to be made (1:135–37). In passing she notes Napoleon's improvements in education for women and foreigners (1:195–96) and claims that Napoleon converted Milan from a city of brick to a city of marble (1:121). Morgan's ambivalence toward Napoleon as emperor of Italy may be summarized in her epithet naming France's campaign against Italy "France's splendid degradation" (1:46n). The entire note reads:

The campaigns of Italy, under the Directory and Consulate, were well worth all the Imperial battles fought in the days of France's splendid degradation. The pass of Mont St. Bernard stands unrivalled in military history. The artillery was dragged up the heights by sheer strength of arm, by efforts almost superhuman. Pecuniary motives for exertion, proffered by the General, were rejected by the army. The soldiers, one by one, climbed through the crevices of the ice-rock, and in five hours they reached the convent of St. Peter. The descent was yet more perilous. The infantry cut short the difficulty by sliding on their backs down the ice. The First Consul followed their example, and, in the sight of his army, slided [*sic*] down an height of two hundred feet. (1:46n)

This note, too, demonstrates Morgan's conflicted construction of self as authority in her works' boundary materials. Morgan's identification with Napoleon, as with Lafayette, positions her as both military authority and as one dependent on and protected by (male) military authority. In fact, Morgan exults in her reception by the Bonaparte family in Italy, visiting in Rome Napoleon's sister Pauline, Princess Borghese; Cardinal Fesche, Napoleon's uncle; and Madame More, Napoleon's mother. Morgan writes:

The Palace of the Princess Pauline Borghese . . . [is] the most hospitable house in Rome . . . . Lucien and Louis Bonaparte, though they have fine palaces, live exclusively in the bosom of their family. But by far the most distinguished and interesting of that family is the venerable mother of Napoleon. Retaining great remains of the most brilliant beauty, dignified in adversity as she was moderate in prosperity, her thoughts and feelings have now but one sole object—the prisoner of St. Helena. (3:51)

The effect of all Napoleon's relatives in Italy is to stress Napoleon's relational identity, as the member of a family and particularly the son of a mother. Morgan's friendship with Madame Patterson Bonaparte and her sympathy with her over her desertion by Napoleon's brother did not affect her admiration for Napoleon, for Madame Patterson Bonaparte herself was still a Bonapartist, despite all of her betrayals by the family (*Memoirs*, 2:503).

Morgan's writing career was not entirely free of the desire for achievement, troped as mastery and conquest, that Ross has observed in the male Romantic poets. In fact, Dixon writes that till the end of her days, she tended to see her achievements, like an Indian brave, as scalps or conquests. However, the metaphor of conquest is particularly apt for the genre of travel writing—Wordsworth wrote of the genius as Hannibal crossing the Alps—and Morgan served as one of the pioneers of the genre, as Dixon observes, despite her abandonment of the travel book on Germany: "she had long ago given up the thought of making a book on that country, to range with her *Italy* and *France*. Another race of writers, younger and less scrupulous than herself, had rushed into the field which her genius had first laid open to feminine adventurers" (*Memoirs*, 2:466). Meanwhile, the travel books on Italy and especially on France had illustrated the overlapping political and literary struggles of a woman writer from Ireland who set out to establish her own authority and her nation's in a political and cultural context that denied the legitimacy of both.[44]

Richard C. Sha

Expanding the Limits of Feminine Writing

The Prose Sketches of Sydney Owenson (Lady Morgan) and Helen Maria Williams

*B*y the late eighteenth century in Britain, the "ideological work" of such female accomplishments as sketching was to "keep women out of harm's way" by teaching them the value of industry and "attachment to the home," as Maria Edgeworth put it.[1] Helen Maria Williams and Sydney Owenson Morgan not only harnessed the power of the "sketch" to confer the cachet of an appropriate and "ladylike" accomplishment on their prose sketches, but they also envisioned the sketch as a genre capacious enough to permit some reflection on the very notions of femininity that demanded that women sketch and not write. Calling their written works sketches was a strategy by which they, on the one hand, insisted on their amateur status and denied that their works were in competition with the more finished works of men and, on the other, began to manipulate the boundaries between masculine and feminine. My strategy here will be, first, to demonstrate how the sketch helped to keep women in the private sphere, and, second, to show how Morgan and Williams invoked, if only to resist, such strictures on feminine propriety and sketching. Indeed, both writers deployed the sketch to conflate the public and private spheres that it was intended to separate. By making history more accountable to individual experience and emo-

tional intensity, moreover, they resisted the general devaluation of feminine sensibility, a term suggesting a kind of witless emotional reaction,
arguing instead that the French Revolution and English despotism of the
Irish had made feminine sensibility, despite its problems, a historically
necessary remedy to such violence. At times self-conscious of the fact that
the rhetoric of sensibility was excessive, even artificial, Williams and
Morgan turned to the iconicity of the sketch in an effort to contain that
excess, harnessing the immediacy and seeming naturalness of the image
to heighten the reader's perception of objectivity *and* to move their
readers to action.[2]

I

Although commonly thought of as "innocent amusements," female accomplishments such as sketching were in part an ideological ploy to keep
leisure-class women attached to the home. With the rise of middle-class
domestic servants and decreasing emphasis on manual labor for women
came a new stress on female accomplishments, such as needlework,
sketching, music, and dancing.[3] In the anonymous *The Polite Lady, Or a
Course in Female Education* (1769), a mother exhorts her daughter to
become an "accomplished woman" and informs her that "no young lady
deserves this honourable character without a competent knowledge in
the art of drawing."[4] In *Letters on Education* (1790), Catharine Macaulay enlisted the aid of such "innocent amusements" to help ladies "of
fortune . . . get rid of time."[5] Likewise, Erasmus Darwin argued in his
1797 *Plan for the Conduct of Female Education* that "as ladies in polite
life have frequently much leisure time at their disposal, it is wise for them
to learn many elegant as well as useful arts" like drawing and "sketching
with the needle" in their early years; "this will make them appear less
solicitous to enter the circles of dissipation, and to depend less on the
happiness of others." As one of the principal female accomplishments,
sketching became, as Maria Edgeworth would phrase it in her enormously influential *Practical Education* (1801), a "ticket of admission to
fashionable company." Speaking of accomplishments in general, Edgeworth argues that such skills should "cultivate those tastes which can
attach them to their home."[6] And to demonstrate further the usefulness
of these accomplishments, Edgeworth cites a mother who exclaims: "I
should wish my daughter to have every possible accomplishment; because accomplishments are so charming resources for young women,
they keep them out of harm's way, they make a vast deal of their idle time

pass so pleasantly to themselves and others!" (3:5) To show how such accomplishments might keep a lady "out of harm's way" and preserve her virtue, Edgeworth offers a lesson in exemplary history: that of Madame Roland, who was executed for complicity in inciting revolt against the Jacobin control of the French Convention and who resourcefully occupied her time with drawing while in prison. To illustrate her point, Edgeworth includes this lengthy journal entry from Madame Roland:

> I then employed myself in drawing until dinner time . . . the study of the fine arts, considered part of female education should be attended to, much less with view to the acquisition of superior talents, than with a desire to give women a taste for industry, the habit of application, and a greater variety of employments; for these allow us to escape from ennui, the most cruel disease of civilized society; by these we are preserved from the dangers of vice, and even from those seductions which are far more likely to lead us astray. (3:13–14)

Because Madame Roland became deeply involved in her husband's political affairs and was executed, she would seem to represent the antithesis of Edgeworth's ideal woman. If we place Madame Roland's journal entry, written near her death, in the context of her history, we find that her conviction that drawing has an overtly moral purpose has come about all too late. Edgeworth seems to suggest that had Madame Roland recognized the virtues of drawing before she had become involved in her husband's political affairs, she might have been spared the guillotine. Sketching might have literally kept her "out of harm's way."

At the same time that women were supposed to acquire accomplishments such as sketching, they were warned not to exhibit their drawings publicly—at least not beyond the confines of an intimate and often female coterie—lest approbation fill them with pride. Public display would serve only to jeopardize female modesty: the very linchpin of their morality.[7] Hence, Octavia Stopford announced in the preface to her *Sketches in Verse and Other Poems* (1826) that "they were not originally written for publicity, but were principally composed for a domestic circle."[8] Maria Edgeworth thus warns that accomplishments should be considered only as "domestic occupations" and "not as matters of competition, or of exhibition, nor yet as the means of attracting temporary admiration" (3:20). Hannah More would put it more bluntly, arguing that a woman's talents are not "instruments for the acquisition of fame"; rather, such ambition is "subversive of her delicacy as a woman, and contrary to the spirit of a Christian."[9] More makes it clear that public display might call into question both a woman's status as a woman and as a Christian. By insistently defining the female sketch in terms of privacy, utility, morality, application, and industry, conduct-book writers sought to ensure that women understood that sketching was not a venue for expressing emotions more sincerely and spontaneously than men did. But for Helen Maria Williams and Sydney Owenson Morgan, the sketch was much more than the conduct-book writers envisioned.

II

In her four-volume *Letters Containing a Sketch of the Politics of France and of the Scenes Which have Passed in the Prisons of Paris* (1795), Helen Maria Williams uses the sketch and letter to insulate her feminine persona from masculine politics in part because, as Mary Poovey has observed, politics was the least appropriate realm for women in the eighteenth century.[10] Indeed, Williams's very title insinuates generic boundary lines of the letter and the sketch between self and subject matter. Because her letters merely "contain a sketch of politics," politics would seem not to figure prominently in the work. Moreover, the sketch and the letter's alleged privacy perhaps allowed women to record desires that might have been otherwise silenced by social codes.[11] Williams again explicitly links these genres in her 1801 *Sketches of the State of Manners and Opinions in the French Republic Towards the Close of the Eighteenth Century in a Series of Letters*, where she attempts to counter what she called the "censure which has been thrown on writers of the female sex who have sometimes employed their pens on political subjects."[12] Because the cruelty and horrors of the Terror she must describe might do violence to feminine propriety, Williams further invokes the iconicity of the sketch in ways that allow her to frame and contain her subject pictorially. Emphatically not a sustained reflection, her work is purportedly more casual, haphazard, and spontaneous. "I would require the pencil of a master to trace in all its dark colouring that picture," she claims (2:64). "Master" here seems especially appropriate.[13] Whereas a "master" might be able to render a finished painting, Williams can offer only incomplete sketches.

Nonetheless, by repeatedly suggesting how women's capacity to feel makes them more capable of understanding liberty than men are, Williams lends women the authority to speak on such matters. Rather than seeing women's capacity to feel as being at odds with intelligence and courage, Williams argues that they are mutually reinforcing. In this regard, she revalues sensibility so that it becomes an antidote to "female weakness" (1:41).[14] While men abandoned their friends who were imprisoned by the revolutionary committees, "shrinking back in terror" from the prisons, "women, in whom the force of sensibility overcame the fears of female weakness" refused to cast off their friends (1:41). With men, by implication, sensibility lacks the force to overcome cowardice.

Using the verbal sketch to help her manipulate an iconographical tradition that already had feminized liberty, Williams further naturalizes liberty as feminine so that she may not only commodify this "masculine" subject—she transformed one year of postrevolutionary history into four volumes—but also to argue that the revolution had gone awry because men did not fully understand liberty. Indeed, she lambastes Jacques-Louis David, the master painter himself, who "instead of cherishing that sacred flame of enlightened liberty . . . was the lacquey of the tyrant Robespierre" (2:74). She figures liberty as the feminine soil that nurtures fruit: "as no weeds are more pernicious than those which arise in that soil from which good fruit alone should have sprung, so no crimes have exceeded those which the tyrant and fanatic have created in the name of freedom" (1:256). And she later claims that the "daemon of Jacobinism . . . had transformed the cradle of infant liberty into a den of desolation and carnage" (4:128). If liberty is like a nurturing soil that bears fruit and like an infant in a cradle, then who might better care for it than women?

Williams grounds this female attachment to liberty in the "superior sensibility of the female mind" (1:213) and in women's strong sense of attachment to others: "While men assume over our sex so many claims to superiority, let them at least bestow upon us the palm of constancy, and allow that in the fidelity of our attachments we have right of pre-eminence" (1:40–41).[15] Although she does not seem to be asking men for much of a concession, the logical consequences of this argument later become clearer. If women are granted fidelity, then might they not be more "faithful" to philosophical ideals as well as to personal relations? She thus shows dozens of exemplary women who unite sensibility with courage, women whose "hearts are pure and uncorrupted by the world" (4:58). For instance, she praises Charlotte Corday for having "imbibed a strong attachment to liberty" (1:128), and she extols Madame Roland for her "most ardent attachment to liberty" (1:195). What makes Roland even more remarkable to Williams is that she recognizes the abuses that have been committed under liberty's name. Upon mounting the scaffold, Roland "lifts her eyes to the statue of Liberty . . . [exclaiming] Ah Liberty! how hast thou been sported with" (1:201).

Men, by contrast, often lack such attachment. Indeed, a woman's heart and her strong attachments were an even more historically necessary palliative to the Terror, given her view that "stupefied Terror had frozen every heart" (1:225). "Tender sympathies," she mourns, have been "so long repressed by the congealing stupefaction of Terror" (3:2). Although her defensiveness betrays her recognition that by the mid-1790s sensibility was suspect, she considers what the world would be without it.[16] Williams notes that the "fury of these implacable monsters," namely, the male leaders of the Revolution, "seemed directed with particular virulence against that sex, whose weakness man, by nature, was destined to support" (1:215). Williams suggests that it is because women embody the very capacity for feeling that leaders give up in their quest for power that they have become victims. At the trial of Marie Antoinette, for example, Williams observes Robespierre's horrified recognition of Marie Antoinette's ability to "excite the sympathy of the public in her last moments" (1:155). Recognizing the effacement of all outward signs of sensibility, Williams announces, "it [then] required the most daring courage to be humane, and when to be cruel was to be safe" (1:13). Indeed, among all of the revolutionary committees, Williams observes, "there was not as much pity to be found 'as would fill the eye of a wren'" (1:13). By contrast, Williams relates an anecdote about an Englishwoman in France who sends her daughter, Charlotte, home for her own safety. By calling attention to the fact that even the dog howls in lamentation every time he hears Charlotte's name, she seems to ask what it means when animals show more humanity than men.

Williams argues that one important reason men abuse liberty is that they let ambition and power replace their capacity to feel. "It is melancholy to see what monsters men may be transformed by the possession of power." (3:14). Even worse, she adds, "with what eternal regrets must the lovers of Liberty feel, that her cause should have fallen into the hands of monsters ignorant of her charms, by whom she has been transformed into a Fury, who brandishes her snaky whips and torches" (2:212). As men with power become monsters, they remake the goddess of liberty into their own image, violently disfiguring her. And when men falsely try to understand liberty as an abstract logical principle as opposed to a passion, they can coldly perpetuate horrors under its name. Hence, Williams lambastes the "frigid composure of a calculator reasoning hypothetically," referring to Lequino, a man "who weighed with calmness the advantage or disadvantage of butchering five hundred thousand men" (3:14). And hence she excoriates Fouquier Tainville for having "feasted his heart on the despair of his victims whom a breath from his polluted lips sent every day to the scaffold" (4:41–42) and Robespierre for refusing "to soften his obdurate heart" (3:145). Praising Marc-David La Source, a man who was her fellow prisoner and former member of the

National Convention, as a notable exception to these men, Williams writes that in him "Liberty was less a principle than a passion" (1:42).

III

Sydney Owenson Morgan, the first woman to receive a pension (£300) for "services to the world of letters" (in 1834), completed *Patriotic Sketches of Ireland* (1807) in six weeks, seizing upon the formal openness of the sketch to exercise her verbal facility.[17] She also exemplifies how a woman could use the genre of the sketch to signal feminine propriety, while at the same time renegotiating the boundaries of that propriety so that it might include space for feminine assertion even in political matters. In an early letter to her lifelong friend Alice Lefanu, Owenson declares her adherence to propriety: the "strongest point of my ambition is to be every inch a woman."[18] Suggesting both overt display and desire for rank, "ambition" here nevertheless becomes double-edged. By dressing ambition in feminine clothes, Morgan on the one hand makes it appear more proper and on the other calls attention to the fact that women were not supposed to have it. She continues, admitting that "seduced by taste to Greek and Latin, I resisted lest I should not be a very woman. And I have studied music rather as a sentiment than a science, and drawing as an instrument rather than an art lest I should become a musical pedant, or masculine artist" (Campbell, *Lady Morgan*, 52). In her preface to *Patriotic Sketches*, she further exploits the propriety conveyed by the sketch. The self-taught Lady Morgan was mindful of her "limited talents" (xi) and triply marginalized position. She wrote, "as a woman, a young woman, and an Irish woman; I felt all the delicacy of undertaking a work which had for the professed theme of its discussion, circumstances of national import, and national interest" (ix).

But she cleverly meanders between the Scylla of humility and the Charybdis of having ventured into a masculine province by insisting that her work is not political; rather, it is "patriotic": "politics can never be a woman's science; but patriotism must naturally be a woman's sentiment" (xii). Echoing her earlier comment that she had studied music "rather as a sentiment than a science," Morgan opposes masculine science and feminine sentiment, if only to revalue them. Suggesting an elevated thought influenced by emotion, "sentiment," despite its feminine modifier, marks a site where feelings and intellect converge. Insofar as both "sentiment" and "sensibility" both presuppose what Janet Todd calls "emotional susceptibility" (*Sensibility*, 7), they become virtual synonyms. Nevertheless, Morgan argues that women have a natural claim to patriotism because "it is inseparably connected with all those ties of tenderness which the heart is calculated to cherish . . . the fondness of the child, the mistress, the wife and the mother" (xii). At once she has acknowledged her proper place—not in politics—and transgressed it. Moreover, in feminizing patriotism—by literally exorcising the *pater* from patriotism—she predicates her authority to speak about it on very traditional feminine roles, thus investing women with a greater power to speak on such matters than men.

Morgan's sketches are remarkable for the ways in which they play with the notion of female propriety. Her first sketch suggests that it is nothing more than an innocent picturesque description of scenery: "the scenery which environs the town of Sligo is bold, irregular, and picturesque . . . a perfect landscape" (15). The sketch is almost formulaic: the reader's attention is called to "lofty mountains," winding roads, "dreary heaths," and perhaps most important, "a bold and continued mass of rocks through which nature, time, and art, seem to have cut a deep and narrow defile" (16). This last detail provides the roughness required of the picturesque. Claiming that "I have copied with the same rude simplicity with which they were drawn in the moment of passing observation" (17), Morgan insists that her sketches are merely copies.

At the end of this first sketch, however, Morgan transforms this copied picturesque landscape into an emblem of transience. While Sligo is now an opulent commercial town, her parent city, Ballysidore, is a "ruinous and wretched village." Morgan then boldly foretells that "the vicissitudes of those two little places present us an epitome of the fate of all earthly states . . . . the rise, climatric [*sic*], and fall of every empire." With this pronouncement, she also foregrounds England's colonization of Ireland. That she utters these words only seven years after the Union of England and Ireland, a union that on the surface implied equality between the two countries, makes her remarks all the more transgressive. She then goes so far as to end this sketch by heralding the "transitions of power from the mighty to the lesser" (20).

By the middle of the first volume, Morgan's initial invocation of traditional notions of femininity looks increasingly calculated to make her sketches seem appropriately demure. Once alerted to this strategy, readers understand that one project of her *Sketches* was to convert the Irish landscape into the ne plus ultra of the picturesque and sublime in an effort to convince her audience that these "scenes are never to be viewed with indifference" (28). Indeed, she boldly asserts that the charms of the Irish landscape exceed those of Italian scenery (16). Once Morgan has made her audience feel passionately about this painterly landscape and has made it clear that the Irish, if not more than the Italians, have culture and the arts, she begins to argue that the Irish do not deserve English oppression: "But the government which they, the Irish [common people], loved, was still counteracted . . . for it was ever, as it is now, the singular destiny of Ireland to nourish within her own bosom her bitterest enemies, who with a species of political vampyrism, destroyed that source whence their own nutriment flowed" (84–85). What the countries share, in Morgan's view, is not in any sense of the word a "Union." Although the Act of Union of 1800 promised an equal partnership between England and Ireland, Morgan argues that England does nothing more than drain the blood of its victim.[19] By appropriating this gothic image, Morgan confers upon her pronouncements the rhetorical force of psychological terror. By such means she also manages to exploit a form that is to a great extent historically marked as feminine and apolitical—the sketch—to the end of excoriating England.

Thus, if the sketch offered women writers the cachet of feminine propriety, it also enabled Morgan and Williams to reflect on their roles as female historians. More specifically, these writers legitimate the place of women in history writing by arguing for the centrality of emotional intensity in any historical narrative. This is not to say, however, that both writers did not exploit the shared iconicity of writing and sketching to confer truth on their versions of history. Williams insists she was an eyewitness to the scenes she describes, giving "such detail, as can only be learned on the spot" (1:255). By such means, she impresses her narrative with the authenticity of the site itself. Mary Russell Mitford would likewise insist, in her *Our Village: Sketches of Rural Character and Scenery*, that "her descriptions have always been written on the spot, and at the moment, and in nearly every instance with the closest and most resolute fidelity to the place and the people."[20] The value of her sketches is not contingent upon her skill—or lack thereof—but on truth. At times, Williams refers to herself as a mere "transcriber" (2:52). And she opens her third volume by announcing, "My pen, wearied of tracing successive pictures of human crimes and human calamity pursues its task with reluctance" (3). Her inaugural verb, *trace*, which denoted both to draw and to copy (*OED*), when followed by *pursue* reinforces the idea that all she is doing is copying the lines of the original historical pictures, even though she "wearies" of doing so. Her own mediating presence and the mediating effect of language are thus partially effaced.

Yet if these writers invoke the iconicity of the sketch to suggest their objectivity, they also use the sketch's declared spontaneity to redefine historical truth in such a way that feminine sensibility becomes an essential component of truthfulness; that is, spontaneity or the illusion thereof becomes a vehicle for the display of sensibility. Williams's strategy is to exploit the culturally accepted notion that women were naturally suited for faithful copying so that she can extend the range of feminine fidelity to include not only faithfulness to objects delineated but also to personal relations and to principles. Hence, she announces at the outset of her sketches that "if the picture I send you of those extraordinary events be not well drawn, it is at least marked with the characters of truth, since I have been the witness of scenes I describe, and have known personally all the principal actors" (1:2). Williams continues, "Those scenes, connected in my mind with all the detail of domestic sorrow, with the feelings of private sympathy, with the tears of mourning friendship, are impressed upon my memory in characters that are indelible" (1:2–3). When coupled with her image of the mind as a surface on which scenes are engraved, her choice of "characters"—suggesting an engraved or printed mark (*OED*)—hovers between language and image and works to suggest that the verbal sketches she presents to her readers are the same as those impressed upon her mind; that is, before her memory can mediate these pictures, they are delineated before us. What by implication makes these characters so indelible and therefore incapable of being altered or manipulated is her own capacity for feeling. She hopes, then, that her sketches will have the same indelible effect on the mind of her audience.

Morgan indirectly redefines historical truth to include feminine sensibility by reconsidering the gendering of artistic line and color: the former, appealing to the intellect, is thought masculine; the latter, being potentially deceptive and sensuous, is thus feminine. Jean Hagstrum touches upon Pope's linking of color and women to their mutual disadvantage: both are "falseness, fancifulness, transience."[21] Arguing instead that color remains truthful and that women's sensibility makes them more capable of coloring, Morgan revalues it. No longer is color ornamental or peripheral: "I was . . . aware that in the historic page, recent details, and existing circumstances of Irish story, lived many a record of Irish virtue, Irish genius, and Irish heroism, which the simplicity of truth alone was sufficient to delineate; many a tale of pathos which women's heart could warmest feel and truest tell, and many a trait of romantic coloring and chivalrous refinement, which women's fancy fondest contemplates and best depicts" (x). Rather than opposing color and truth, Morgan renders them mutually reinforcing. The "simplicity of truth" not only includes "tales of pathos" and "romantic colouring," but these emphatically feminine qualities are the sine qua non of truth. Even the weight of her syntax leans toward coloring. Her choice of "fondly contemplates" once again asserts the compatibility of feeling, coloring, and intelligence. Indeed, it is women's very receptiveness to color that allows them to be the best and most honest delineators. Morgan continues, "in preference to a cold detail of flat realities," I allowed "fiction to weave an airy web to draw the brightest tints of her variegated tissue from the deathless coloring of truth" (x-xi). Without color, history remains both cold, potentially embalming its subject matter, and flat, lacking depth and contour; history so delineated lacks any rhetorical power.

If Morgan and Williams stress feeling and description it is because they recognize how the Terror and what we now call colonialism can stifle, if not expunge, humankind's faculty for feeling. Whereas Williams saw how male leaders of the Terror were threatened by female sensibility, Morgan points to another historical threat to sensibility: "That mind indeed must be endued with great native strength, over which a certain peculiarity of situation holds no influence; which can breathe the spirit of liberty beneath the lash of despotism, be true to nature where art only reigns, and . . . disdain to graduate its sentiments and opinions on a scale proportionably contracted" (48). Despotism contracts the sphere of sentiment and opinion, almost to the point where they are snuffed out.

More critically, by disabusing their readers of the idea that history is over and done with and by demanding the exercise of readerly sensibilities, Morgan and Williams remind their often female audience of their potentially active role in history. Because they recognize both that history is more than a process of recovery of what really happened and that the present is itself a moment in history, they seek to activate their audience's potential to change history. In this regard, they call attention to the image's greater capacity over language to elicit emotional response. Williams, for instance, recalls a moment in her imprisonment when she gazed longingly on an image of a sublime landscape. "How often," she exclaims, "while my eyes were fixed on that canvass [sic] . . . did I wish for wings of a dove, that I might flee away and be at rest" (1:37). She informs us that "all the objects on the tapestry are indelibly impressed on my memory" (ibid.).

Wanting to harness the sensuous immediacy and naturalness of the image, Williams and Morgan further call attention to the unfinished state of their sketches. By stressing a causal relationship between understanding recent events and shaping the future, they remind readers to take responsibility for what will happen. Morgan thus offers "sketches" of the Irish poor to allow her audience to feel their injustices. Claiming that the causes of poverty are political rather than moral, she depicts the "helpless and wretched groupes [sic] struggling along the high roads . . . while frost-bitten limbs of . . . infant companions drew tears to their eyes" (74). Arguing that these peasants "embraced beggary as the only alternative to want and famine," she describes her own response to these pitiful images: "when the strained eye of sorrowing affection has followed the father and the husband, even till fancy gives what distance snatches from view, the mother closes the door of her desolate cabin" (ibid.). Because indifference harms the social fabric at large, she must combat it: "POLITICAL philosophy by extending the mind's eye to the whole great scale of civil society, and demonstrating the close-linked dependencies of its remotest parts, affords to the benevolence of the human heart, and the comprehension of the human understanding, a social system, gratifying to the feelings of the one, and ennobling to the faculties of the other" (33). Perhaps because women embody sensibility, they are less likely to become indifferent. Once the heart again becomes the very crux of the social system, women have the central role in political philosophy of stimulating the indifferent.

Morgan's habitual stimulation of her viewers' sensibility is designed to encourage them to do what they can to end oppression of the Irish poor. Similarly, Williams insists that her readers fill in the gaps of her sketches: "every heart can feel, and every imagination can fill up the picture" (4:73). Her insistence on "every" makes this community universal, implying that everyone, providing they have a heart, will fill in her sketch in a similar way. Not only does she remind readers that she was an eyewitness, but she recognizes how her iconic language conveys the illusion of presence; that is, by placing her verbal sketches before her readers, she makes them virtual eyewitnesses. Although she has been "compelled to wound your feelings" by "dwelling on images of dismay, " she adds, "how faint is the impression which I have conveyed to you at a distance, of those local emotions which are felt at the spot" (4:1). She insists, "I need not describe what he related to me of the scene—your heart will readily fill up the picture" (2:228). The iconic metaphors here work to appropriate for language the sensuous immediacy of the visual representation.

Lest her English readers become complacent by dismissing her sketches because they describe a distant topography, Williams concludes her sketches on France with a plea to her readers to do what they can to uphold the cause of liberty in Britain and to do away with slavery. Although the English might simply charge the French with barbarism and dismiss this entire history, Williams writes, "Ah let us, till the slave trade no longer stains the British name, be more gentle in our censures of other nations! I know not how that partial morality can be justified, [that] . . . while it pours forth the bitterness of human crimes in France, sanctions them in Africa" (4:176–77). She then offers an image of "a wretched African, torn forever from all he loved" (177), once again imploring her readers to feel this injustice. "With all the feelings of an Englishwoman at my heart, a heart that glows for the real honour of my country, I pour the fervent wish . . . that she may reject with indignant scorn that execrable traffic of which humanity is the barter" (178). She suggests that anyone with feelings must also deplore such travesties.

Sydney Owenson Morgan and Helen Maria Williams, then, stress the reader's responsibility to complete their historical sketches so that all readers become active participants in a community based on mutual feelings of the heart. Although they recognize that feminine sensibility is not without its problems, they realize that without it, history lacks the rhetorical force to precipitate change. They thus turn to the iconicity of the sketch to confer on their written words the power to affect their readers.

Moira Ferguson

Janet Little and Robert Burns
The Politics of the Heart

⟡

$\mathcal{B}$orn in 1759, also the year of Robert Burns's birth, Janet Little became known as the "Scotch milkmaid" after she published a volume of poems in 1792 with this cognomen on its title page. Like the designation "ploughman poet," which was invariably used to describe Burns, the "Scotch milkmaid" registers both Little's working-class status (she was first a family servant and later a dairy superintendent) and her identification with other Scottish laboring-class poets, who then enjoyed a wide audience among working- and middle-class people as well as gentry like Frances Dunlop, who became the patron of Little and Burns. As James Boswell shrewdly advised, Little dedicated her volume of poems to twelve-year-old Flora Mure Campbell, countess of Loudoun.[1] The countess of Loudoun's powerful name, Burns's assistance, and Dunlop's vigorous campaign for subscribers netted about seven hundred subscriptions. Little's dedication specifies her class and her gratitude: "To the Right Honourable Flora, Countess of Loudoun. The following Poems are with Permission, Humbly Inscribed, by Your Ladyship's Ever Grateful, and Obedient, Humble Servant, Janet Little."

After this dedication and a poem that commends the young countess, her munificent family, and fine estate, the rest of the volume has nothing to say about its wealthy patrons. Instead, Little's poems chronicle poverty, woe, the toughness of laboring women, and (more obliquely) the reality of working life at the castle. The cultural messages embedded in these poems, some of them overt, others submerged, reflect Little's precarious status as a woman from the laboring class who aims to enter the public arena of letters. She protects her vulnerable class position by offering tributes to Burns that imply their solidarity as working-class Scottish poets. But she also masks a subtle critique of Burns in seemingly benign, conventional lyrics. The reasons for Little's antagonism are both simple and complicated. On one level, she dislikes Burns's modus operandi toward women, for which he was rebuked by the Mauchline Kirk session in Ayrshire to which he belonged. On another, she recognizes and resents his comparative political and social freedom. For although she is a Scot who sympathizes with Burns's Jacobinism, her gender and her occupation require a degree of conformity not asked of Burns, who remained Frances Dunlop's friend and protégé even after he wrote derisively of the guillotined French king and queen.[2] In the repressive political climate of Scotland during the French Revolution, Burns could dissent more freely than Little could. Even so, Little's veiled judgment of Burns's sexual libertinism barely conceals her attraction to a man whose class and cultural identity were so much like her own.

In part because Frances Dunlop encouraged contact between the two poets,[3] in 1789 Little wrote a cordial verse letter to introduce herself to Burns as a fellow laborer: "I felt a partiality for the author, which I should not have experienced had you been in a more dignified station . . . I shall, in hope of your future friendship, take the liberty to transcribe them."[4] As someone whose class origins were even humbler than Burns's—her father was a hired laborer, his a tenant farmer—Little would have appreciated the struggle Burns endured to become recognized as a poet whose life was one of "thwarted progress as well as of sturdy rooted vitality."[5] Titled "An Epistle to Mr. Robert Burns," Little's poem commends Burns by adding his name to the distinguished lineage of Scottish vernacular poets, including Allan Ramsay.[6] She eulogizes Burns's ability to captivate an audience of different classes, and lavishly praises his nature poems: "To hear thy song, all ranks desire; / Sae well thou strik'st the dormant lyre" (161). She praises Burns's dedication to Gavin Hamilton "[i]n unco' bonny, hamespun speech" (161) and mocks the lavish dedications of "servile bards wha fawn an' fleech, / Like beggar's messin" (161)—dedications like her own to a countess. With patriotic spirit, Little speculates that English men of letters passionately envy Burns's poetic genius. Thus, she imagines that Joseph Addison, Alexander Pope, and Samuel Johnson are distraught with jealousy at the plough-boy who sings "wi' throat sae clear, / They in a rage, / Their works wad a' in pieces tear / An' curse your page" (162). She even praises Burns's poems in praise of "Scotch Drink" and "Earnest Cry and

Prayer": "An' weel ye praise the whiskey gill." No matter how blunt her own quill might become in praising him, that praise, she insists, will be accorded him "frae ilka hill" (162). All she can do, she humbly confesses, is "blot thy brilliant shine" with her "rude, unpolish'd strokes" (163). She ends by asserting that she will stop extolling his talents; instead she will pray for all mortals to dispense blessings "with an indulgent care / To Robert Burns" (163).

Burns's reply is polite but unforthcoming about this poem. Later he writes Dunlop instead and uses his allegedly untutored social manners to excuse his lack of response.

I had some time ago an epistle, part poetic and part prosaic, from your poetess, Mrs. J. L——, a very ingenious but modest composition. I should have written her, as she requested, but for the hurry of new business. I have heard of her and her compositions in this country; and, I am happy to add, always to the honour of her character. The fact is, I know not well how to write to her: I should sit down to a sheet of paper that I knew not how to stain. I am no dab at fine-drawn letter-writing.[7]

Exhibiting a nationalist sentiment yet more, Little foregrounds her gratitude for the honor Burns brings to Scotland in another poem, "Given to a Lady Who Asked Me to Write a Poem." After discussing the difficulty of writing "in royal Anna's golden days, / Hard was the talk to gain the bays," she launches into those who "got near [Parnassus'] top: that little fellow Pope, Homer, Swift, Thomson, Addison, an' Young."[8] Almost immediately, she declares that Samuel Johnson shows them all up:

> But Doctor Johnson, in a rage,
> Unto posterity did shew
> Their blunders great, their beauties few.
> But now he's dead, we weel may ken;
> For ilka dunce maun hae a pen,
> To write in hamely, uncouth rhymes;
> An' yet forsooth they please the times. (114)[9]

Patriotically parodying and avenging Johnson's critique of Scottish society, she identifies Burns as an overreacher (like herself) "sous[ing] his sonnets on the court." Here Little uses a concrete image for her activities as a domestic servant. In addition to its meaning of "pouring," "souse" also means sloshing from a pail or a bucket. It may also have another forceful association since "souse" means, in dialect, to strike a blow. If Johnson were still alive, she protests self-mockingly, he would have had material for another anti-Scottish *Dunciad*:

> But what is more surprising still,
> A milkmaid must tak up her quill;
> An' she will write, shame fa' the rabble!
> That think to please wi' ilka bawble.
> They may thank heav'n, auld Sam's asleep:
> For could he ance get a peep,
> He, wi' a vengeance wad them sen'
> A' headlong to the dunces' den. (114)

Unlike Burns, she concludes, a "rustic country queen" like herself has no
such versatility. Little maintains this self-parody until the last line, when
she turns the parody against the English Johnson. Through her use of
"queen," a common word for "girl" in northeast Scots, Little invokes the
contemporary debate over writing in Scots. She challenges those who
disparage the vernacular.[10] Her stated detachment from Burns only
serves to enhance their connections because Burns is her reference point,
while her firm use of "wise" affirms a strong sense of female capacity:

> Does she, poor silly thing, pretend
> The manners of our age to mend?
> Mad as we are, we're wise enough
> Still to despise sic paultry stuff. (115)

Burns's talent, she affirms, is to please "a' denominations," instruct
people in love, set forth deft though pithy political commentary, and
intimidate critics.

Little wrote a second poem about Burns, entitled "On a Visit to Mr.
Burns," when she traveled to meet him at Ellisland in Dumfriesshire, near
where she was born, a visit negotiated through Dunlop's good offices.
Unfortunately, Little arrived on an inauspicious day, when Burns had
fallen off his horse, named "Pegasus" in the poem. Her response oscil-
lates between delight in his presence and commiseration at his condition.
Little's recollections of the visit—her poem to Burns read unmediated,
we assume, by a public enamored of Burns—express astonishment at her
good fortune in meeting Scotland's top-ranked contemporary poet: "Is't
true? or does some magic spell / My wond'ring eyes beguile? / Is this the
place where deigns to dwell / The honour of our isle?" (111) Now she
stands in his presence, she coyly asserts, he is no longer "bequeath[ing]
her a poignant dart" (112). She deplores his present injured condition
with a reminder that human life constantly meshes joy and sorrow, while
lauding his lyrical prowess. In token of her fascinated fervor, Little
dialogizes some dependence on Burns and perhaps some fear of his
power and dominance.

In "To My Aunty," the speaker recalls a dream in which her poems are widely published and critics pounce on her alleged imperfections. As the critic whom everyone wishes to please, the figure of Tom Touchy is modeled on Burns, whose "characteristic touchiness and pride" David Daiches has described.[11] If he wants a line scratched out, they do so. No one—Jack Tim'rous is the example given—wants to oppose this "foremost man": "So much he fear'd a brother's scorn, / The whole escap'd his claws untorn" (166). When James Easy barely whispers that he likes the poem, Touchy denounces him abusively—at which point the speaker awakes. Although nothing about the critics' debate centers specifically on a female poet, the speaker asserts the vulnerability of all poets, including herself. From her always precarious position as a servant and a female poet, Little imagines Burns's support against antagonistic critics.

Unfortunately, the Tom Touchy of "To My Aunty" was and remained a fiction. The real Burns freely criticized Little's poems during a visit to Dunlop in December 1792. She angrily replied to Burns's harshness in a letter: "How did I upbraid my own conceited folly at that instant that had ever subjected one of mine to so haughty an imperious critic! I never liked so little in my life as at that moment the man whom at all others I delighted to honour. . . . I then felt for Mrs. Richmond (Jenny Little), for you, [Burns] and for myself, and not one of the sensations were such as I would wish to cherish in remembrance."[12]

Unlike the dedicatory poem to the countess, the next poem in Little's *Poems*, "To Hope," emphatically denotes the world as an unmitigated "scene of dole and care." The narrator is severely divided against herself, as if she started off intending to placate and ingratiate herself with the conservative wing of the reading public and her Tory patron only to be taken over by repressed feelings of anger. At a highly generalized level, she discerns disappointment everywhere. Evidence of anguish saturates the poem, not least when the speaker proclaims that hope's favor "shall ever / alleviate my wo" (28). Hope illuminates our "dark and dreary way, . . . bend[s] our steps to heav'n, [and] stem[s] the trickling tear." Hope, too, "decorates the chain" of marriage. Though illusory, "we all thy flatt'ring tales believe, / Enamour'd of thy art" (30). Everyone hopes. She ends by focusing on hope's power to cancel the terror of death— almost as a cover-up—and a realistic view of an unhappy world.

Much as Little must conceal her discontent when she applauds aristocratic generosity, so must she suppress her antagonism toward Burns. In "On Happiness," she marshals a discourse against the character of the libertine. Little was herself a respected member of a Dissenting congregation in Galston, a few miles from Mauchline, where Burns attended an Old Light Calvinist church. She was also a respected dairywoman whose responsibilities increased as Ayrshire's reputation for cheese grew.[13] These associations direct her critique of Burns, whose drinking and libertinism are awarded separate personas. In "On Happiness," a poem that extols religion as the institution whose "force alone can soothe the anxious beast" (35), she attacks those whose immoral way of life prevents happiness.

The libertine, like the drunkard in the poem, never knows happiness and is left with "cruel disappointment's rage, / Remorse, despair, the inmates of his soul" (34). Toward the close of her litany of people whose lives preclude happiness, Little mentions lovers who feed on illusion and married couples beset by a "thousand ills . . . and . . . bitterness & wo" (35). All concur: "Successless is the search; / to nobler objects henceforth bend your view" (35). This religious advice entails recognizing where one belongs. Little's speaker observes that divine law alone brings "content and calm serenity" to her "humble station." A faint disdain for superiors who lead hard, irreverent, licentious lives echoes throughout. Little alludes to Burns's notorious confrontation with Kirk authorities in 1786, when the Mauchline Kirk Session in Ayrshire, to which Burns belonged, rebuked him (a time-honored practice in the Sunday church service) for fornication. Burns had persistently challenged Scottish religious practices with a "common-sense humanitarianism that stressed salvation by good works."[14] He especially deplored the domination of the people by the Kirk.[15] After being censured for getting Elizabeth Paton pregnant, Burns penned a poem to celebrate the birth, defiantly entitled "Welcome to a Bastard Wean."[16]

Nonetheless, Little still has to be wary about attacking Scotland's new standard-bearer. In questioning Burns's way of life, she confines her resentment to nuance and allusion. For one thing, she projects her objections to womanizing onto women from another era who denounce men like Burns.[17] She provides a critical framework for Burns's actions by documenting in pastoral verse the experiences of vulnerable women, she pens direct addresses to Burns that subtly remind readers of his conduct toward women, and she compares the early-eighteenth-century religious poet Elizabeth Rowe to the outspoken Lady Mary Wortley Montagu:

> As Venus by night, so Montague bright
>   Long in the gay circle did shine:
> She tun'd well the lyre, mankind did admire;
>   They prais'd, and they call'd her divine. (153)

So pure was Rowe, however, that national morality altered:

O excellent Rowe, much Britain does owe
    To what you ingen'ously penn'd:
Of virtue and wit, the model you've hit;
    Who reads must you ever commend.

Would ladies pursue, the paths trod by you,
    And jointly to learning aspire,
The men soon would yield unto them the field,
    And critics in silence admire. (154)

By citing Rowe last and applauding her as the most significant model for women, Little relegates Lady Mary's energetic intellectual and social life to second position. This praise for Rowe's virtue at the expense of Lady Mary's raciness may reflect a middle- and upper-class standard of femininity that excludes Little herself. Unprotected by her station, Little is vulnerable to the blandishments of charming seducers like Burns.

In a cluster of neoclassical poems from Delia to Alonzo, fashioned much like the *pastourelle* that tells of and warns against smiling, fraudulent seducers, Little echoes Burns's poems to warn against his poetic charm. In their subtly feminized reworking of Burns's masculinist tropes, these poems articulate sexual disquiet by exposing the male manipulation of women that Delia cannily rejects. Little's Alonzo first addresses Delia as the "empress of my heart" to whom "I'm urg'd to vent my pure untainted flame." Alonzo graphically confides that his "swelling sighs your kind attentions claim." Flattering her, with no intention of marriage, Alonzo is a smooth-talking rake. He begs her to "hasten" to his arms, resign her "heart and hand," and render them in the eyes of all the muses, a "happy pair" (184–85).

Delia recasts Alonzo's Edenic allusion by recalling Eve's role in the loss of Eden. Ironically, she recommends that he learn from Adam "lest some fond nymph your pleasures all expel." She ends with an encomium on celibacy that complements Little's attacks on marriage elsewhere in the volume:

A single life we find replete with joys.
The matrimonial chain I ever dread.
A state of celibacy is my choice;
Therefore Alonzo never can succeed (187).

In a second poem, "From Delia to Alonzo. Who Had Sent Her a Slighting Epistle," Delia beats her would-be cunning suitor at his own game, while flattering his great wit and learning. She leaves his machinations and ribaldry to the reader's imagination. Alonzo sings more sweetly than Philomel, Delia avows, and flies on Pegasus, a horse with the same name as the one on which Burns, poetically, took a hard tumble. Then she cleverly mediates her tribute, almost with a sense of eighteenth-century camp:

> That dire, deceitful creature man . . .
>   is fill'd with mazy wiles;
> His count'nance stor'd with fickle smiles:
> His flatt'ring speech too oft beguiles
>   Pure innocence; . . . (189)

Pointedly invoking facts in Burns's life, Delia refers to Alonzo as "[t]he laureate of our days," and goes on:

> 'Tis pity, sir, that such as you
> Should agriculture's paths pursue,
> Or destin'd be to hold the plough
>   On the cold plain;
> More fit that laurels deck'd the brow
>   Of such a swain . . .

Delia plays with Alonzo, too, as he has with her, by speculating that he might turn out to be famous: a future age might be "[s]truck with the beauties of your page, / Old Scotia's chieftains may engage / Your name to raise" (190). Last, Delia trivializes Alonzo's "weak attempts" at a "ponderous theme." Regretting that love never rests within her—a knock at his rakishness—she forthrightly stresses that she would never entertain a guest who would give her pain (suggestively unspecified) and ends with the sexually ambiguous statement: "I wish you, sir, so much distress'd, / Soon well again" (191).

Most telling of all is Little's poem "On Seeing Mr.——Baking Cakes." The significant blank name in the title is identified in the opening line. The "Mr. Blank" of the title turns out to be Rab, the name by which Robert Burns was and is still known throughout Scotland: "As Rab, who ever frugal was, / Some oat-meal cakes was baking" (171). This baker crumbles before a young female poet: "a crazy scribbling lass, / Which set his heart a-quaking. / I fear, says he, she'll verses write, / An' to her neebors show it" (171). These words replay Burns's earlier diffidence toward Little and predict his post-publication critique of her poems. By eliding the silent signifier verses and sexuality to the cake, the baker implicitly blends Burns's talent with his personal designs on women. He affects not to care because everyone likes his wares.

Rather than have customers simply glance at his cakes, the baker prefers them to be touched and invites any female passer-by to "Put out her han' an' pree them" (172). Polyvalent and heavily suggestive, *pree* is a Scots word that ranges in meaning from experience or taste to partake of or kiss. The sense of "to sample" is also relevant. The so-called cakes are eagerly received by the lasses. And although Mr. Blank runs away, he cries out that he has "cakes in plenty." Moreover, he can supplement the cakes with "[b]aith ale and porter, when I please, / To treat the lasses slily" (172). The last stanza suggestively recalls the evolving legend of Burns as a man who periodically impregnates women:[18]

> Some ca' me wild an' roving youth;
> But sure they are mistaken:
> The maid wha gets me, of a truth,
> Her bread will ay be baken. (172)

The speaker's embedded excoriation of Burns's carousing was a popularly held attitude, in part governed by Calvinist views. Janet Little herself was an ardent Burgher.[19] Frances Dunlop highlights contemporary objections to Burns in one of her letters to him: "A gentleman told me with a grave face the other day that you certainly were a sad wretch, that your works were immoral and infamous, that you lampooned the clergy and laughed at the ridiculous part of religion, and he was told you were a scandalous free-liver in every sense of the word."[20] Burns retorts cavalierly, insisting on his right to remain silent, while claiming the privilege of foregrounding male exploits in his poems, regardless of the reader's gender. Burns wants simultaneously to titillate and respect prescribed female delicacy.

In all of these poems Janet Little sets herself a difficult task—to be judicious in public and yet subtly embed her critique of Burns. In "Given to a Lady," for instance, her commentary about the charity of the aristocracy intersects veiled hints about Burns's fornication that pinpoint her ambiguity regarding Scotland's republican hero. Little applauds Burns's genius and his egalitarian politics, as well as his depiction of nature and reactionary critics, yet seems to disapprove of Burns's nonmarital relations with women.

Little's second poem to Burns suggests an attraction for Burns that collides with her opposition to his sexual conduct. Put more bluntly, Janet Little's understated challenge to Burns is freighted with unstated feelings for the poet whose seductive attentions to women she so vehemently deplores. Specifically, the tribute she writes to Burns on the day of his mishap suggests an attraction for the carousing poet that collides head on with her opposition to his moral license. Her playful characterization of Burns as a charmer of women who has woven a magic spell over her precedes a sexually laden stanza in which an eroticized discourse of dreams unconsciously erupts: "Oft have my thoughts, at midnight hour, / To him excursions made; / This bliss in dreams was premature, / And with my slumbers fled" (111).

The reality of the poet's situation, the presence of Jean Armour (Burns's wife), his accident, and the pain he suffers from a broken arm directly confront the milkmaid poet, who initially appears awestruck. In letters to Burns, moreover, Frances Dunlop divulges on more than one occasion the importance Janet Little attaches to meeting the famous poet:

> But talking of praise, I ought to tell you Jenny Little says you are very stupid, did not come and see her when you were at Mauchline. She is sure she would not grudge going five times as far to see you. Nay, had she not been lame she might have seen the house you lived in and the reeky spence where you wrote the "Vision." I am almost hoping this will not find you at home, that you will be set out for Ayrshire to carry home your wife and son. Should that be the case, I flatter myself you will not grudge to come a little further, either to see Jenny or me. You may trust to female vanity that each will appropriate a sufficient part of the compliment to herself. Indeed, you have experience how ready I am to catch at every instance of kindness or regard from one whose esteem I value so highly.[21]

It is not just Burns who has fallen and suffers pain; Janet Little has fallen. Hence, her multivalenced sentiments about human fate comprising "alternate joy and wo" and, perhaps more to the point, her erotic, anguishing last stanza: "With beating breast I view'd the bard; / All trembling did him greet: / With sighs bewail'd his fate so hard, / Whose notes were ever sweet" (112). Her boldness and delight in watching this domestic scenario of pain and intimacy, which implies a cathected relationship with Burns, renders her insensitive to some of Burns's personal and professional needs. It is arguable that Burns did all he thought possible.[22] Moreover, Dunlop's vigorous conservatism and her disapproval of Burns's behavior might suggest some influence on Janet Little's supposedly free choice of subject. Dunlop tells Burns of Little's observations on his stoicism: "I greatly applaud that strength of mind which enables one to surmount bodily pain to such a manly pitch of fortitude as to chat at seeming ease and tranquility, as Jenny tells me you did, and entertain others with great kindness and good humor."[23]

Yet as Janet Little learns from Burns's toughmindedness, her emotional and cultural ties to him intensify. In her reactions to Burns's poetry, she sees the gap between what she thinks is the condition of her existence—that employers and patrons treat her well and respect her needs—and her real condition of existence: that she is permanently condescended to and patronized. Little's personal negotiations with Burns help her construct her identity and, by extension, show her how she might oppose that construction through social verse and cultural confrontations. And there is a further hard edge to these illuminations that Burns might have provided.

Look at it this way: Attuned to the sexual vulnerability of women, Little knows that a fallen woman was virtually unemployable (and employment itself was difficult enough.)[24] In other words, Little might be discussing, via Burns, her apprehensions about the precarious position of women in her own class. Unable to expose sexual exploitation openly, and keenly aware of the difficult life that awaited laboring women who "fell,"[25] Little could mention such common practices only through the guise of neoclassical or carefully distanced discourse. Even so, Little uses Burns as a target. She broaches subtextually, from a female point of view, what the kirk elders were authorized to execute in front of the congregation: a public assault on Burns for fornication.

Burns, moreover, can claim freedoms not available to Little. He can insert versions of his rebellion against sexual and class mores in his poetry, whereas class and gender restrictions bar Little from declaring her anger or using, as Burns does, the idioms of her class and experience to express outrage at male-female relations. Instead, she often adopts English diction and often uses rigid, restrictive verse forms.[26] Paradoxically, Burns may have helped Little see these constraints. His prestige and presence gave her a certain kind of permission to explore the contradictions she saw. And because she recognized some of these complexities, she may have attacked Burns's sexual conduct less openly than she might otherwise have done.

As an upholder of the kirk and laboring-class values, Janet Little seems to have tolerated a difficult relationship with her famed plowman compatriot, Robert Burns. She sides with him on democratic principles and the people's rights, and she shares a knowledge of poverty that locates them in a similar relationship to middle- and upper-class people, but she flinches from his treatment of women. But given Burns's popularity, even a fantasy of opposition to the local hero was scarcely permitted. Moreover, Little needs to sustain friendships with affluent people, her class antagonists—though not necessarily personal ones—to bolster her standing as an artist. She prides herself on her art and is prepared to fight for acceptance or a chance to display it. To negotiate these varying vantage points, Little employs a form of dialectical reasoning by expressing difference while forging several informal alliances.

Thus, despite her Presbyterian umbrage at Burns's high jinks and anti-Kirk machinations, Janet Little guarded her opinions. Her praise of Burns's genius allowed her to move between the poles of conservatism and less conventional assertions of gender and class equality. Because Little was a laboring woman and a poet, her cultural solidarity with Burns challenged the conservative values she had assimilated. The reservations she expresses about Burns thus enable her to attack her class superiors indirectly. But even Little's indirect critique has its limits. Invariably, her poems betray traces of an elite culture's influence. As a self-styled "crazy scribbling lass" fused with Dunlop's "rustic damsel," notwithstanding her pragmatic use of passivity, Little cannot efface the textual influences of those she is obliged to placate and those she seeks to condemn.[27] But she is used to such complexity, even inured. Like Burns, she espouses unorthodox religious views; she is a dissenting Burgher in Presbyterian Scotland, a follower of the famed secessionist, the Reverend Ebenezer Erskine.[28] As a Burgher, Little finds liminality part and parcel of her life. She is always a maid and a woman, with limited resources at her disposal for dissolving certain vantage points. In several poems, she presents herself modestly to preserve the "correct," self-effacing demeanour expected of her.

In the final poem in the volume, "To A Lady Who Sent the Author Some Paper With a Reading of Sillar's Poems," she again deprecates herself as untalented. But rather disarmingly, and perhaps with a self-effacing wit, she also notes that this poem is the last in a two-hundred-plus-page volume, then proclaims, somewhat ironically, that she will cease being a poet:

> And lest with such dunces as these I be number'd
> The task I will drop, nor with verse be incumber'd;
> Tho' pen, ink and paper, are by me in store,
> O madam excuse, for I shall ne'er write more.

Robert Burns's maleness affords him a range of poetic subjects denied to Janet Little. In that sense, Little's mandated thematics reflect her gendered class solidarity with such predecessors and contemporaries as working-class poets Mary Collier, the washerwoman, and Ann Yearsley, the "milk-maid poet."[29] How did she feel, we wonder, soliciting help from Burns and Boswell, relying on Dunlop for diverse favors, and then petitioning a twelve-year-old countess to clear the ground for publication? Since this triumvirate represents quite antinomic values, Little is obliged to navigate through rather diverse ideological waters, the Scylla of archconservatism on one side, the Charybdis of fornication (which she deplores) and competition on the other. Individually, these supporters and patrons reflect a many-sided self that she can develop; collectively, they deny her rights and expropriate her freedom.

A female cultural activist with a complex public self-representation, Janet Little recognizes the vulnerability of her social position and gender. She voices herself into the public arena, in some senses, as representative: to wit, as a cottar's daughter, a laboring-class woman, a servant, a dairy supervisor, and a poet, she occupies multiple though conflicted and assailable positions that overlap, coalesce, and separate, concurrently closed- and open-minded, at once involuntary and controlled. This matrix of values and her social conditioning, in other words, yield deep and understandable tensions and double-edged meanings. While allying herself with labor and against gender exploitation, she joins battle on both fronts, recognizing Burns as a class ally, as a sexually attractive male. At another level, attuned to the economic and cultural precariousness of her life, Little is an agent of traditional values, simultaneously dedicated to hierarchy and exclusion, complicitous in one way or another with those who dominate her socially. Janet Little is withal a Romantic woman and poet, who, like Mary Collier and Ann Yearsley, forges a career during a difficult revolutionary era, in the midst of the personal and class tensions that mark her 1792 volume of poems.

Part Four

Performance and the Marketplace

Catherine B. Burroughs

"Out of the Pale of Social Kindred Cast"

Conflicted Performance Styles in Joanna Baillie's De Monfort

$\mathcal{I}$n 1929, Virginia Woolf wrote that "it scarcely seems necessary to consider again the influence of the tragedies of Joanna Baillie upon the poetry of Edgar Allan Poe."[1] Yet more than sixty years later, discussions of Baillie's influence on writers who lived during or beyond the Romantic period are relatively rare.[2] The author of twenty-six plays,[3] pages of poetry, and a number of play prefaces in which she articulated her theory of theater and drama, Baillie has suffered the fate of nearly all of the remarkable women who wrote for and about the theater between 1798 and 1832: their contributions have, until recently, been forgotten, neglected, or dismissed. In Baillie's case, this fate is all the more striking given that a number of her contemporaries readily acknowledged her significance.[4] Mary Berry, to whom a copy of Baillie's first volume of plays was sent in 1798, summarizes the tone of the early responses to Baillie's work: "everybody talks in raptures (I always thought they deserved) of the tragedies and of the introduction as of a new and admirable piece of criticism."[5] The "rapture" of Elizabeth Inchbald survives in the introductory preface to Baillie's tragedy *De Monfort* in the *British Theatre* series (1806–9): "Amongst the many female writers of this and other nations, how few have arrived at the elevated character of a woman of genius! The authoress of 'De Monfort' received that rare distinction, upon this her first publication."[6]

Published anonymously in 1798 with two other plays that comprised the first part of Baillie's three-volume series called *Plays on the Passions* (1798–1812), *De Monfort* dramatizes what would become Baillie's abiding critical interest throughout her writing career, the relationship between "the closet" and public staging. In exploring this relationship, the dramaturgy of *De Monfort* sets in conflict two styles of performance that competed for audience attention during the late eighteenth and early nineteenth centuries: the mode of statuesque stasis cultivated by the French neoclassicists and the emotive school of acting characteristic of German Romanticism.[7] These acting styles are embodied in the social performances of the two major characters in *De Monfort*, a sister and brother who struggle throughout the play to enact each other's vision of the ideal gendered person. Jane De Monfort, portrayed as the epitome of perfect womanhood by the standards of middle-class London society during the Romantic era, performs with carefully controlled gesture and speech; even her simple costume evokes the classical acting mode associated with Sarah Siddons and her brother John Philip Kemble, both of whom starred in *De Monfort* when it was first staged in 1800.[8] In contrast, De Monfort's inconsistent and erratic performances are filled with *Sturm und Drang*, anticipating the style of acting popularized by Edmund Kean in his fiery portrayals of Elizabethan and Romantic heroes when he made his stage debut in 1814. (Kean, like Kemble, also appeared as De Monfort, in 1821).

The dramaturgical tension that results from the play's conflicting acting modes suggests Baillie's ambivalence about prescribing a particular style of performance for characters navigating her fictionalized social settings. While her dramatic theory clearly expresses a preference for a more emotive, psychological style of acting, conducive to performing closeted passions in public arenas—a style that could be labeled, in the context of the Romantic period, feminine—Baillie's prefaces enact a conflict similar to that of her title character. Just as De Monfort struggles with how to perform his gender identity correctly for public audiences while still giving vent to his closeted emotion, so in her preface writing Baillie enacts her own conflicts with how to "be" a successful playwright. Despite the fact that many of her male colleagues heralded the closet as a retreat from the vulgarities of the public stage, Baillie argued that full-fledged theatrical productions could help her determine how successfully she had brought the drama of the closet into public view. Her whole body of work may be read as an attempt to negotiate the space between text and performance—between plays read and plays acted—while also negotiating a dramaturgical ambivalence about the performance of gender on and off the stage in the late eighteenth century.[9]

Elsewhere I have noted that Baillie's first play preface, the "Introductory Discourse" to the first volume of *Plays on the Passions* (1798), uses the trope of the closet to articulate her vision of what she believed was a new kind of play, one that focuses on the closeted passions in "an infant, growing, and repressed state"[10] in order to trace their development to full-blown, mature expression.[11] For Baillie, the closet is the location of some of the most interesting theater, because here one may observe how public and private identities diverge. The closet is not, as the term came to be associated with the Romantic blank verse dramas, the site of the unperformable, the disembodied, or the only read. For in contrast to a number of her contemporaries for whom the closet play signaled a retreat from the stage, Baillie struggled to disassociate herself from the antitheatrical sentiment that permeated Romantic criticism. This struggle makes her theory important for closet drama revisionists, who have recently begun to argue against the traditional dismissal of closet plays as undramatic and unactable. These theorists view closet drama, by virtue of its anomalous position in theater history, as indispensable to their reconsideration of the traditional use of critical terms and categories. Michael Evenden, for example, has sought alternative models of theatrical staging in the closet plays of Seneca, Roswitha, Byron, Stein, and Brecht, recognizing that the closet play offers theater historians a genre whose very dramaturgy raises questions about the relationship between performance and theoretical endeavor.[12]

Appropriately, in an era that famously dichotomized the activities of playreading and theatergoing, Baillie attended in the prefaces and letters that she wrote after 1804 to the boundaries that separate dramatic literature into "drama" (playscript) and "literature." Often, she expressed her regret that even her most loyal fans (with the general exception of Walter Scott) did not readily identify her as a playwright of the theater. In an earlier letter (1804) to William Sotheby she had urged against "setting me aside as a closet writer" because a "play certainly is more perfect for being fitted to play upon the stage as well as the closet,"

and why should I not aim with all my strength to make my things as perfect as possible, however short I may fall of the mark. Don't be afraid that I shall injure them as reading plays on this account. It is endeavouring to suit pieces to the temporary circumstances of particular theatres, and not to the stage in general that injures them in this way. One who never expects as long as she lives to see a play of her own acted, and who never intends to offer a play to any theatres under their present management, is not very likely to do her works much harm by keeping the stage in her eye.[13]

Indeed, Baillie's prefaces show her negotiating the space between what Harry Berger has described (in reference to contemporary Shakespearean criticism) as "New Histrionicism" and "conventional armchair reading";[14] her theoretical interest in the movement between closeting and uncloseting passion finds a parallel in her characters' negotiation of several identities as they discover the difficulty of performing a single socially sanctioned gender role. In order to navigate what Count Freberg in *De Monfort* refers to positively as "the culture of kind intercourse" (3.2, 90)—an ideology that extols politely superficial behavior so as to reinforce rigid class and gender distinctions[15]—some of Baillie's characters choose performance modes that demonstrate how gender identity may be viewed as a theatrical "act."[16]

The relationship between performance style and gender in Baillie's plays is clarified by Judith Butler. Butler draws upon phenomenology to assert that the successful social actor, like the theater performer, has managed to memorize a script in which the boundaries for the performance of gender identity have been carefully delineated. This circumstance occurs as the result of an often arduous process similar to the rehearsal period preceding a play in which a culture's "directors" shape the body of the social performer to meet spectatorial demands. Butler stresses the community effort behind this project to remind us that one does not perform his/her identity in isolation—as a role put on and discarded as easily as one might exchange a theatrical costume. Rather, the performance of gender constitutes and is the product of a complex act shaped by many people. Butler exposes the difficulties inherent in resisting cultural imperatives to perform gender in scripted ways, as well as suggests how one might gain greater control over one's performance of gender in the course of any social interaction.[17]

Moving from Butler's postmodernist feminist perspective back to *De Monfort* brings into focus the play's equation of socially successful characters with carefully prescribed ways of acting gender. It also reveals those moments when characters in *De Monfort* alternate between several social postures as a means of exerting cultural critique. This alternation does not in itself reveal a recognition that "the truth or falsity of gender is only socially compelled and in no sense ontologically necessitated" (Butler, "Performative Acts, 528), but it does signal the dramaturgy's preoccupation with identity as performative. For it is in the improvisational moment—in that instant when a character experiments with a variety of performance modes—that he or she can be said to express an unease or weariness with, or even a distrust of, traditional social performance methods. Although this essay does not have space to discuss explicitly the development of a "feminine" or "feminist" theory of Romantic acting and the cultural implications of that development, it points toward such an exploration by locating in Baillie's plays a debate about performance style and its corresponding assumptions about gender identity.

Baillie's overt commentaries on acting appear primarily in 1812, when she wrote her preface to the third volume of *Plays on the Passions*, but they are also forecast in 1798, in the "Introductory Discourse" that she attached to the series' first volume. Baillie valued the "natural and genuine acting" cultivated in the smaller "country theatres" because this mode allowed for "that variety of fine fleeting emotion which nature in moments of agitation assumes" ("Preface to the third volume of *Plays on the Passions*" [1812], 232–33). Such emotional "variety" was the central focus of Baillie's "passion plays." As an antidote to the "exaggerated but false" (232) acting style encouraged by the large auditoriums of Covent Garden and Drury Lane, Baillie argued for the preservation of rural training grounds that would develop in actors a method analogous to "a rough forest of our native land," to the "oak, the elm, the hazel . . . the bramble" and the "humble cottage" ("Introductory Discourse," 6). Her theory of performance, with its vision of secret souls coming uncloseted, certainly cried out for the acting methods of the impassioned Edmund Kean rather than the emotionally distant Kemble, and, in effect, *De Monfort* predicts Keanian acting through its portrayal of the title character. Indeed, according to Jeffrey Cox, Baillie's plays may be read as investigating "the ways in which . . . the acting style of Mrs. Siddons entrap[s] women within conventional forms of emotional response" (*Seven Gothic Dramas*, 57). By speculating how "the gradual unfolding of the passions" ("Preface to the third volume," 232) might occur within the soliloquies of her plays, Baillie's theoretical discourse likewise is prophetic. Her plays are designed for actors capable of performing in a style that would come to be called "romantic," making use of "muttered, imperfect articulation, which grows by degrees into words"; "that heavy, suppressed voice, as of one speaking through sleep"; "that rapid burst of sounds which often succeeds the slow languid tones of distress"; "those sudden, untuned exclamations . . . with all the corresponding variety of countenance that belongs to it" (232–33).

Before looking more closely at *De Monfort*, the play that received the most stage productions during Baillie's lifetime (Aloma Noble documents fourteen different mountings), I will briefly trace its dramaturgical contours. Set in Germany in an unspecified era (in keeping with the tendency of English plays in the 1790s to draw on German culture for translations, technique, and stage devices), the play concerns De Monfort's ungovernable disdain for Rezenvelt, a man whose talent for performing the cultural code of polite behavior arouses De Monfort's fury. The play starts with

De Monfort's arrival at the Frebergs' estate; he has found it necessary to flee his home and beloved sister, Jane, because Rezenvelt has made De Monfort beholden to him by sparing his life in a duel (an event that will occur again during the drama). Jane De Monfort, described from play's start as the consummate social performer, soon follows De Monfort to the Frebergs and urges him to make peace with Rezenvelt, who has also arrived on the scene. But although De Monfort tries to please Jane De Monfort by going through a public ritual in which he expresses his intent to behave according to the cultural code, his performed reconciliation with Rezenvelt is short-lived. Conrad, "an artful knave," repeats to De Monfort rumors about an attraction between Jane De Monfort and Rezenvelt. From this moment, De Monfort no longer tries to closet his overwhelming passion: he murders Rezenvelt in a wild wood. Apprehended and taken to a convent, De Monfort's greatest trial occurs when he must confront his sister, who persists in trying to persuade him to behave according to her vision of the manly man and noble brother. After nursing him for a short interval until he dies, supposedly from remorse, Jane De Monfort eulogizes De Monfort as someone who should be remembered, although the play does not make it clear on what basis her brother merits such adulation. The final scene, which Baillie later suggested might be unnecessary in a future staging[18], seems indispensable in light of the play's preoccupation with both closeted and public performances. It shows Jane De Monfort performing a eulogy of De Monfort in which she lauds him as "noble" (a synonym in the play for the admirable social actor) in spite of his having committed an inexcusable crime.

That the play is titled *De Monfort* should not, as Cox has suggested, compel readers to focus solely on the way in which the dramaturgy moves the male member of the De Monfort family through the culture of the play. Why Jane De Monfort has so much at stake in De Monfort's performance of the politely aristocratic and emotionally repressed man is one of the play's more interesting questions. One can certainly sympathize with Jane De Monfort's compulsion to act as guardian of a particular code of behavior even while observing that her commitment to a particular performance of gender oppresses both her and her brother. For Jane De Monfort seems so bent on assuring herself that De Monfort has indeed performed according to her ideal that she spends time telling others how to interpret his public scenes. When, for instance, Freberg calls De Monfort "suspicious grown" at the start of the play, Jane De Monfort counters with language suggesting that De Monfort is only masking his true identity, urging the count toward an alternative interpretation:

Not so, Count Freberg; Monfort is too noble.
Say rather, that he is a man in grief,
Wearing at times a strange and scowling eye;
And thou, less generous than beseems a friend,
Hast thought too hardly of him.
(2.1, 82, my emphasis)

Jane De Monfort also rescues from De Monfort's murder of Rezenvelt an interpretation that maintains the illusion of his heroic stature. Knowing that he has killed a man because he hates him so intensely, still Jane De Monfort distinguishes De Monfort from more common criminals: "He died that death which best becomes a man, / Who is with keenest sense of conscious ill / And deep remorse assail'd, a wounded spirit. / A death that kills the *noble* and the brave, / And only them" (5.6, 103, my emphasis). Straining on, she ends the play with an epitaph that rings hollowly: De Monfort's "nameless tomb" will be consecrated to one "[w]ho, but for one dark passion, *one dire deed*, / Had claim'd a record of as noble worth, / As e'er enrich'd the sculptur'd pedestal" (5.6, 104, my emphasis). Of course, this "one dire deed" is one too many. Jane De Monfort may try to minimize De Monfort's murderous action in the interest of proclaiming his "dignity," but her words do not convince. Instead of speaking "what we feel, not what we ought to say" as Edgar urges at the end of *King Lear* (5.3.322)—the play to which Baillie alludes several times and that, perhaps more than any other Shakespearean drama, argues against the use of "pomp" and empty rhetoric—Jane De Monfort seems driven to control public opinion about her brother's identity, to cast De Monfort in the mold of an idealized hero whom the play never shows us. This is because the play's focus is elsewhere: on the charting of discrepancies between the noble, manly figure whom Jane De Monfort desires and De Monfort's oscillation between identities both sanctioned and devalued by the play's culture and clearly allied with closeted and public spaces as well as with the performance of gender.

From the beginning of the play, De Monfort is described in ways that forecast the typical Romantic hero, also prefiguring, as Joseph Donohue has noted, Byron's antisocial and melancholy protagonist in *Manfred* (1817) (*Dramatic Character*, 81), and, one could add, Emily Brontë's Heathcliff. De Monfort's "violent conflict of mind" (5.6, 103), his sporadic desire for oblivion—"I now am nothing," he says toward play's end, "I am . . . / Out of the pale of social kindred cast" (5.4, 99)—as well as his characterization of himself as "a sullen wanderer on the earth" (2.2, 85), comprise, from Donohue's perspective, an innovation in the English theater's development of dramatic character for which Baillie is responsible. She redefines the "Fletcherian disjunction of character and event" as "an ethical disjunction of human virtue from human acts," internalizing the Gothic tradition of allowing "an event that took place years before . . . to exert its effects thereafter" (*Dramatic Character*, 81).

Reminiscent also of the Gothic villain-hero that Ann Radcliffe popularized in *The Mysteries of Udolpho* (1794) and *The Italian* (1797),[19] De Monfort is presented as a personality whose agony is self-inflicted and whose sense of identity is confused. In contrast to Jane De Monfort's seemingly unreflective enactment of her social role of noble womanhood, De Monfort arrives on the scene a self-consciously troubled person, and others recognize the change: from "comely gentleman" his hatred for Rezenvelt has transformed him into one who now possesses "that gloomy sternness in his eye / Which powerfully repels all sympathy" (1.1, 77). De Monfort's oscillation between hidden and uncloseted pensiveness is also contrasted with the consistently cheerful actions of the revel-loving Frebergs, who seem to live from one "midnight mask" to another. Theirs is a world of flattery, of false, feigned and indiscriminate friendships, of hyperbolic and superficial discourse. "[A]ll men are thy friends" (1.2, 80), De Monfort complains to Freberg, whose grand gestures are evocative of the "exaggerated" and "false" acting style indigenous to the large, licensed London theaters that Baillie criticized in her preface to the third volume of *Plays on the Passions* (1812).

De Monfort protests against the kind of cheerful social theater that his acquaintances perform, and he often tries to read bodies for the discrepancies between what they reveal and conceal. In De Monfort's view, Rezenvelt *must* mask a soul corrupt in proportion to the zealous consistency with which he enacts the fluttering, chivalric courtier. That others do not seem to mind Rezenvelt's exaggerated gesture causes De Monfort no end of agony. The ecumenical Freberg, for instance, wants the two men to reconcile, exulting that Rezenvelt is "so full of pleasant anecdote, / So rich, so gay, so poignant in his wit, / Time vanishes before him as he speaks, / And ruddy morning through the lattice peeps / Ere night seems well begun" (1.2, 78).

Nor can Jane De Monfort appreciate De Monfort's desire to wear openly his hatred for Rezenvelt, even though she begs him to confess to her his feelings. At the start of the drama De Monfort has left Jane De Monfort precisely because he knows that, in her presence, he may not experiment with performing as the spoiler of social play because she directs his social behavior with an eye to audience approval. Once at the Frebergs', however, he does experiment with a number of performance modes that confound his social audience, and by act 4, when he duels with Rezenvelt, he dares to shout, "now all forms are over" (4.2, 94). These "forms" refer to what Freberg has earlier called the "culture of kind intercourse" (3.2, 90), a system requiring an upbeat cheerfulness to mask "open villainy" (4.2, 94) or any expression not in the social repertoire. While De Monfort's rebellion against the "forms" finds its most extreme expression in his murder of Rezenvelt, this rebellion may also be read as either a conscious or unconscious resistance to imitating the performance style embodied by Jane De Monfort, a style grand and classical, indeed antithetical to the performance mode that Baillie discusses in her prefaces as conducive to bodying forth the subtleties of a character's most intimate passions.

Jane De Monfort's enactment of what Mary Poovey has at length described as the early-nineteenth-century "proper lady"—self-censoring, self-effacing, and self-sacrificial—is symbolized by her "homely" dress (2.1, 82) that arouses the envy of Countess Freberg; other characters (especially the count) respond to Jane De Monfort's plain clothes with enthusiasm: "Such artless and majestic elegance, / So exquisitely just, so nobly simple, / Will make the gorgeous blush" (2.1, 82), Freberg says, pointing directly to Jane De Monfort's clothing. The play's preoccupation with women's dress is significant from a feminist perspective, for throughout Western history, costume (both on and off the stage) has been used to gender the wearer and thus create and transmit messages about a person's political position. While Anne Hollander has urged scholars to study costumes "not primarily as cultural by-products or personal expressions but as connected links in a creative tradition of image-making,"[20] she reminds us of the cultural connotations of middle-eighteenth-century theater stage dress: classical drapery, for example, signaled that the wearer possessed an affinity for "simple truth" (p. 276). Because Jane De Monfort wears simpler lines, the dramaturgy suggests that she is to be read not only as more tasteful but also as more trustworthy, as the voice of rectitude and unshakable virtue. On the one hand, female costume and makeup are described in the play as producing "grafted charms, / Blending in one the sweets of many plants" (2.1, 83), but on the other, women who use theatrical techniques to embellish and disguise themselves are targeted as masking their actual loss of youth, physical attractiveness, naturalness, and "couth." Their theatrical impulse evokes the fear that female identity is unstable; the prude and the coquette might, through artifice, transform their physicalities into social bodies that appear interchangeable. At the Frebergs' party in act 2, for example, Rezenvelt describes the process by which theatrical devices can obscure the "true" identity of the female performer:

> Aged youth,
> With borrowed locks, in rosy chaplets bound,
> Clothes her dim eye, parch'd lips, and skinny cheek
> In most unlovely softness:
> And youthful age, with fat round trackless face,
> The downcast look of contemplation deep
> Most pensively assumes.
> Is it not even so? The native prude,
> With forced laugh, and merriment uncouth,
> Plays off the wild coquette's successful charms
> With most unskilful pains; and the coquette,
> In temporary crust of cold reserve,
> Fixes her studied looks upon the ground,
> Forbiddingly demure. (2.1, 83)

The count's reaction to his wife's "gaudy" party costume and the dressing room scene that follows in act 3 serve to set the countess against Jane De Monfort for the purpose, it would seem, of underscoring the "desirable" traits of noble womanhood and for suggesting that, in the world of *De Monfort*, a woman's true character can be known through the semiotics of costume.[21]

When Jane De Monfort exits to prepare for the Frebergs' party (ironically, to dress herself in the countess's clothes in order to have access to her brother's unguarded confessions), the count expresses his dissatisfaction with his wife by berating her dress code: "How hang those trappings on thy motley gown?" he asks. "They seem like garlands on a May-day queen, / Which hinds have dress'd in sport" (2.1, 83). This is but one of several instances when Freberg portrays the countess as an unsuccessful performer of femininity, whose fashion blunders are emblematic of her failure to approach Jane De Monfort's moral rectitude and propriety. The play even suggests that the countess's gaudy taste signals a deceptive "nature," since she may be regarded as ultimately responsible for inflaming De Monfort to commit murder. The lie that she spreads about Jane De Monfort and Rezenvelt kindles De Monfort's rage, which results in his killing Rezenvelt and then dying himself. Yet the misogyny that lies just beneath the surface of characters' chuckles about the "art" of "female cultivation" (2.1, 83), an art in which the much-maligned Countess Freberg is well practiced, might caution us against condemning the countess too readily. While Jane De Monfort's comparatively "simple" and natural style of speech and dress is valorized, the play also troubles her adherence to a code of behavior in which passionate outburst, improvisational acting—even gaudy costumes—are looked askance at in social performance.

The dramaturgical ambivalence toward the play's dominant performance styles emerges more clearly in act 2, when De Monfort and Rezenvelt nearly come to blows over the issue of who may touch Jane De Monfort's "thick black veil" (2.1, 84). At this moment Jane De Monfort's significance recedes in the face of the men's intense responses to each other as they move toward Jane De Monfort's stark hymenal costume. De Monfort may be dedicated to the idea of Jane De Monfort's chaste devotion to him and, with pride, describe how she has become "the virgin mother of an orphan'd race" (2.1, 84), but he is even more committed to the idea that Rezenvelt "woos" his hate. Certainly, De Monfort seems most confused about his sexuality and gendered identity when he is in his enemy's presence, casting him as a kind of Satan to his Eve—calling Rezenvelt "fiend," "devil," "villain," and "serpent"—and locating Rezenvelt's power in his potential not only to seduce his sister but also to cause De Monfort to lose control of the tenor of his social acting.

Indeed, Rezenvelt raises the possibility that De Monfort is fighting his physical charms at the Frebergs' party. Smiling "archly" (according to the stage directions) because De Monfort refuses to be sociable, Rezenvelt says that, were De Monfort to "swerve" from his "native self" and "grace my folly with a smile of his," one might call him a "woman turn'd" (2.1, 83). While De Monfort tries to distinguish himself from those who are "besotted" and "bewitched" by Rezenvelt, his obsession with the marquis signals a complicated, closeted longing for the knowledge of a (perhaps sexual) experience outside his own, a desire that instead takes the form of a frenzied murder and, shortly to follow, De Monfort's expulsion from the "culture of kind intercourse."

After the murder, Jane De Monfort again tries to inspire De Monfort to perform according to the culture's standard for the socially valuable man. The stage directions tell us that De Monfort "endeavour[s] to look cheerful" (5.4, 101) as he leads Jane De Monfort from the convent to the prison. Perhaps because he has earlier failed to perform to her satisfaction in the reconciliation scene with Rezenvelt, De Monfort tries harder now. In act 3, De Monfort had resisted Rezenvelt's proffered bear hug ("I'll have thee [De Monfort] to my breast," Rezenvelt exults), having said throughout the play that he cannot act what he does not feel: "I will not offer you an hand of concord, / And poorly hide the motives which constrain me" (3.2, 90). The public aspect of this third act scene—the fact that spectators assemble to watch De Monfort perform his apologies—pleases Jane De Monfort but is exactly what De Monfort rejects: "Must all the world upon our meeting stare?" he asks her before the Frebergs troop onto the stage (3.2, 89).

While at play's end De Monfort is so grateful for Jane De Monfort's presence that he assumes a posture that she can describe as "noble"— restraining his outbursts and behaving with enough classical stoicism to earn her posthumous praise—his countenance and language throughout the drama indicate his recognition that social intercourse frequently requires the performance of identities that cannot be anticipated, cataloged, or consistently defined. One of the reasons that De Monfort keeps butting up against the play's valuation of an ostensibly cheerful restraint that manifests itself in a stiff and carefully controlled gestus is that his spontaneous overflow of powerful feelings works against the cultivation of a single, unified identity with which to perform in social settings. De Monfort's general refusal to act in a familiar and consistent way challenges other characters' seeming desire to hold onto a society in which class and gender performances are carefully rehearsed, where the improvisational mode is contrasted unfavorably with the French neoclassical style. De Monfort's is an interestingly uncomfortable character primarily because he will not let others forget that they have adopted performance modes that allow them to glide by each other without the trauma of confronting their closeted selves, their secret longings, their hidden responses to a power structure at odds with unmediated expression. De Monfort's repression of his hatred, his attempt to meet the public with a "tamed countenance" (3.2, 88), has only ensured that he will, whenever he is alone, give vent "to all the fury of gesture" of which he is capable (2.1, 80). His resistance to performing a single identity in a socially sanctioned performance style ultimately results in the violent consummation he so fears: murdering Rezenvelt, he knits their fates together; in the last scene the bodies of both men, swaddled in black, lie close to each other on a low table. It is this aspect of the play that suggests it is a "closet drama" in the contemporary sense: the story of sexual suppression and of the horrific consequences that follow.

In recent years, discussions about canon formation have revealed that, when a writer like Baillie is dropped from anthologies of English Romantic literature and collections of plays, we should suspect the canonizers' motives rather than automatically doubt the author's historical, intellectual, or cultural worth. Terry Eagleton, for example, has intensively analyzed the ways in which aesthetic judgments mask ideology.[22] Theater historians and literary critics have also begun to examine how ideology informs the traditional dismissal of closet drama and Romantic theater, focusing on closet playwrights in order to reconsider such categories as "theatricality," "the dramatic," and "performability." Are closet dramas less theatrical because, as is the case with Baillie's canon, they did not often receive the stage productions that the author desired? What does it mean to describe a work of dramatic literature as unperformable? Might a play labeled "literary" rather than "theatrical" teach us about shifting concepts of the dramatic as we ask in whose terms, in what settings, and for what kinds of audiences certain plays have been removed to the library? As we turn to Baillie's work in the future, specifically *De Monfort*, it is important to keep in mind that distinctions used in the past to shelve closet drama from view—distinctions between stage and page, mind and body, text and performance—are coming under such scrutiny that Julie Carlson's suggestion that we now have the opportunity to experience a "new stage for romantic drama" (p. 419) seems a real possibility.[23]

A contemporary production of *De Monfort* that stresses the play's various performance modes as an index to the conflicting acting methods on the London stage, which were, in turn, allied with cultural attitudes toward gender, is ultimately about the similarities and differences between one historical moment and another. The issue of closeting and uncloseting identity that *De Monfort* dramatizes so beautifully and that is an important feature of Baillie's canon (from the early comedy, *The Trial* [1798], to *Rayner* [1804] and later works such as *Orra* [1812] and *The Bride* [1826]) links Baillie's work to the project of contemporary theater artists, some of whom are trying to establish a tradition of women who have theorized the stage. It is my hope that when readers become more familiar with Baillie's canon of plays, as well as with her theory of theater and dramatic criticism, they will discover that Baillie's importance to the Romantic period and to our own era lies less in her identity as a female playwright than in her concept of the closet as a showcase for the subtle mechanisms that women theater artists in the Romantic era developed for questioning the ideological restraints that governed—and still govern—gendered experience. If the (re)discovery of Baillie's significance continues apace, then Mary Russell Mitford will have been prophetic when she wrote, shortly after Baillie's death: "of Mrs. Joanna Baillie, the praised of Scott and of all whose praise is best worth having for half a century, what can I say, but that many an age will echo back their applause!"[24]

Susan Levin

The Gipsy Is a Jewess
Harriett Abrams and Theatrical Romanticism

"It is said the Little Gipsy is a Jewess, and her name is Handler. The number of Jews at the Theatres is incredible." So concludes a review on the front page of the 28 October 1775 *London Chronicle* of Harriett Abrams's debut performance. In a similarly pitched review, *Town and Country Magazine* of November 1775 observes of fifteen-year-old Abrams's appearance in "May-Day or the Little Gipsy," a musical farce written especially for her by David Garrick: "A young lady, named Abrahams, and said to be a Jewess, made her first appearance in the Gipsy, and met with great applause, her voice being very melodious and her taste for music very correct."

"Handler," "Abrahams," and also "Hendler," "Abraham," and "Adams"—whom exactly did reviewers wish to praise? A pretty Jewess, evidently. These variations on Abrams's name point to one prejudice that characterized the chaotic, repressive world of late eighteenth- and early nineteenth-century London theater: an invented idea of Jewishness to which Harriett Abrams is imagined to conform. To counteract rumors of her Jewishness among the anti-Semitic public, Maria Bland, the great singing actress whom Charles Lamb waspishly described as a "pudding" that "smoked upon the board," sewed at her window on Saturday and bought a live pig, which she often said she intended to have for dinner.[1] That world was also one of imperious male management, so much so that Signora Catalini, another soprano, attempted to purchase a theater, "thereby becoming sole proprietor, sole manager, and sole actress."[2]

Managing to avoid these strategies to which so many talented women were driven, Harriett Abrams both exhibited and shaped the music of her era. By making herself adaptable to different and popular entertainment venues, she defined and managed her professional talents and feminine, Jewish identity in ways that benefited both. Moreover, the shape her career took illustrates key aspects of music and performance art during the early Romantic period. As a Jewish woman artist, Abrams was placed squarely in the theatrical arena of London; as a Jewish woman artist she was nonetheless an alien presence in that essentially bigoted scene. Even as her career depended on the social community, her life and work resisted the forms of conventional and social organization. A consideration of her biography, the music she composed, and her position in the world of early Romantic London theater all demonstrate her shrewd management of a career that included performance, production, and composition, a career during which she became celebrated for the musical taste and awareness that distinguished her first performance.

Hers is a life, however, obscured since the nineteenth century, one that must be understood by way of a scant public record and no known private records. Abrams's contemporary, W. T. Parke, perhaps the leading oboist of the time, provides one context for her work in his memoirs, whose full title suggests its descriptive scope: *Musical Memoirs Comprising an Account of the General State of Music in England from the First Commemoration of Handel in 1794, to the Year 1830*. Charles Burney and Lord Mount-Edgucumbe, musical men of letters; actors such as David Garrick, Thomas Dibdin, and J. DeCastro; and William Hopkins, the Drury Lane prompter and theater amanuensis, also provide accounts of Abrams's development from being the protégé of prominent men to being herself an impresario. Using the comprehensive *London Stage, 1660–1800*, in which the Hopkins diary is frequently cited, and newspapers and periodicals of the period, we can reconstruct the events of Abrams's performing career to see the ways in which she established herself as an important presence in the London theater. The recovery work of this essay is necessarily grounded in such information. Abrams's compositions and the public commentaries on her career form the basis of this study in the absence of private records such as letters and diaries that may exist but have not yet come to light.[3]

I

Abrams's large, somewhat unruly family, including siblings by her father's various wives and mistresses, was immersed in music and theater;

as the daughter of such a family, Abrams was born into the possibility of having a profession. Young women who were given any education at all were provided with musical training, but what they could do with that proficiency was strictly controlled. An exchange in de Staël's *Corinne* delineates the issue. Oswald, Lord Nevil, attempts to get Lady Edgermond, her stepmother, to appreciate Corinne's theatrical genius. The noblewoman sniffs: "There are actresses, musicians, artists if you will, to entertain society, but the only suitable life for women of our station is to be devoted wives and to raise their children properly."[4] On a similar note, Erasmus Darwin, in his 1797 *Plan for the Conduct of Female Education in Boarding Schools*, warns about what can happen when young women develop their talents too fully. Such accomplishment might "be attended with vanity, and extinguish the blush of youthful timidity, which is in young ladies the most powerful of their exterior charms."[5]

Abrams's parents had an entirely different perspective. At least three of her sisters and half sisters performed with her. She was probably the half sister of John Braham, one of England's most famous male singers, whose forty-year career received constant publicity. As house servant at Drury Lane, Harriett's father, John Abraham, used his contacts to arrange the best training for her. Her voice teacher was the composer Thomas Arne, whose operas, masques, and settings of Shakespeare's songs made him a leading composer of his own day and whose "Rule, Brittania," which Parke dubs "our national song" (*Musical Memoirs*, 1:190), ensures his continued representation in ours.

With David Garrick, Arne composed the debut piece "Mayday" for his talented student. Fascinated with Abrams, Garrick wrote of his protégé in a letter of October 1775: "I am somewhat puzzled about introducing my little jew Girl—she is surprizing! I want to introduce her as the little Gipsy with 3 or 4 exquisite Songs" (*Letters* no. 948, 3:1042). So enthusiastic did Garrick become during the frenzied rehearsal period that he jumped up on the stage and kissed a surprised Thomas Arne, with whom he then began dancing.

"Mayday," however, was not an unqualified success. The tale of William, a young rustic who defies his father to marry the little Gipsy, a creature of wisdom and virtue, was praised for its music and enactment but not for its story line, which *Town and Country* characterized in November 1775 as being "simple and not very interesting." In his "Advertisement" to the published edition of the play, Garrick tries to shift responsibility for his weak book to Abrams's lack of professional experience:

The author of this Musical Farce, begs leave to inform the readers, if there should be any, that it was merely intended to introduce *The Little Gipsy* to the public, whose youth and total inexperience of the stage, made it necessary to give as little dialogue to her character as possible, her success depending wholly upon her singing—This reason added to another, which is, that the piece was produced at an early part of the season, when better writers are not willing to come forth, is the best apology the Author can make for its defects. (*London Stage*, pt. 4, 3:1923)

Abrams, however, seems to have taken advantage of the way the plot was structured to point up her entrance and ensure a personal success for herself. When she finally came onstage and sang her first song, the October 1775 *Ladies Magazine* reports, "the house was in a roar of applause." William Hopkins trots out the usual observations about her taste and Jewishness: "This musical farce of one act was wrote by Mr. G. on purpose to introduce Miss Abrams (a Jew) about 17 years old. She is very small, a swarthy complexion, has a very sweet voice and a fine shake, but not quite power enough yet—both the Piece and Young Lady were received with great applause" (*London Stage* pt. 4, 3:1923). The Little Gipsy became a signature role for Abrams. When she appeared in December 1775 as Leonore in *The Padlock*—a performance Hopkins judges "so, so"—she was listed as "The Young Lady who performed the Little Gipsy."

On the roster of Drury Lane from 1775 to 1780, she was hired sometimes as a singer, sometimes as an actress. The steadiness with which she worked and the variety of things she did are impressive. Performing in some twenty-five different plays, she appears never to have canceled because of illness and to have been consistently well prepared. After she left Drury Lane at the end of the 1780 season, she focused on straight singing. Her appearances at Astley's Amphitheatre and in the Handel Memorial Concerts demonstrate her negotiation of various poles of the London performing scene.

An advertisement for one of Philip Astley's nineteen theaters indicates the setting for Abrams's work there. The program was to feature "the famous Monkey, General Jackoo, the Dancing Dogs, the Learned Pig, Horsemanship, Tumbling, Rope-Dancing, Musical pieces, a Dance and a Pantomime, called the Vauxhall Jubilee, with the Temple and Temple Walks superbly illuminated."[6] For William Wordsworth, such entities, "amid the uproar of the rabblement," contribute to a scene of "blank confusion" in book 7 of *The Prelude* (1805; ll. 295, 696). Indeed, the performances at Astley's were of a kind of organized chaos that differentiated them from those at the houses licensed for legitimate theater and opera—Drury Lane, Covent Garden, Haymarket, and the King's Opera House.

Also setting Astley's apart from these establishments was the number of Jews who performed there—so many, in fact, that the troupe became both affectionately and derisively called "Astley's Jews."[7] When he returned from exile in 1660, Charles II took two steps pertinent to Abrams: allowing women to perform on the stage and continuing Cromwell's policy of permitting Jews to settle in England. In her essay on Mrs. Siddons, Ellen Donkin shows how women actresses of the period who occupied space and public imagination released anxieties about the accepted limits of feminine behavior and about woman as active subject rather than observed object.[8] The same observation applies to Jewish performers of this period. The power of Jews both as performers and as audience seems to have set off extensive and often hostile discussions of their presence. For example, Dibdin's *Reminiscences* relates how his play "Family Quarrels" had to be rewritten after Jewish audiences demonstrated to protest a song in it that portrayed Jewish women as prostitutes; the *Oracle* expressed outrage at Jewish behavior and at management capitulation to it (Dibdin, 1:336–352). As a strong, popular, theatrical presence, Abrams's brother, John Braham, was frequently stereotyped. Even the usually genial Parke tells an anecdote about Braham, demonstrating "that ruling passion, gain, which so particularly sways persons of his persuasion, is so strongly implanted in their natures, that it may sometimes be discovered in their children, even while infants" (*Musical Memoirs*, 2:50).[9] And when Charles Lamb praises Braham in a letter of 2 January 1810 as "a rare composition of the Jew, the gentleman, and the angel," the inclusion of "Jew" suggests an anomaly: it is remarkable that a Jew could also be a gentleman and an angel.

As a Jew at Astley's, then, Abrams was one of that "persuasion." On the other hand, the place she created for herself in the Handel Memorial Concerts positioned her at the center of the WASP establishment in Westminster Abbey. Those concerts were associated with confusion of a different sort from that characteristic of Astley's. Burney's contemporary account warrants inclusion here for its incisive description of what were perhaps the most successful concerts of the 1780s and for the information it provides about a popular venue in which Abrams performed among ladies and gentlemen. Burney tells how people quitted their carriages early in the morning because the doors of the Abbey were to open at nine o'clock. They didn't, however, and chaos ensued:

Such a crowd of ladies and gentlemen were assembled together as became very formidable and terrific to each other, particularly the female part of the expectants; for some of them being in full dress, and every instant more and more incommoded and alarmed by the violence of those who pressed forward, in order to get near the door, screamed; others fainted; all were dismayed and apprehensive of fatal consequences: as many of the most violent among the gentlemen, threatened to break open the doors; a measure, which if adopted, would probably, have cost many of the most feeble and helpless their lives; as they must, infallibly, have been thrown down, and trampled on, by the robust and impatient part of the crowd. (*An Account*, 40)

When a small side door opened, the crowd surged through and "except hair, and torn garments, no real mischief seems to have happened" (26). In less than an hour, the Abbey was so full that only "their Majesties and their suite" could be squeezed in.

The second round of performances proved equally successful: "by seven, though the performance was not to begin till Eight, the whole building was so full, that not another place could be obtained on any terms" (Burney, 45). Abrams sang "Dite che fà," an air from *Ptolemy* composed in 1728. Burney emphasizes once again her ability to bring her particular strengths to the presentation: "This air, which is pleasing, and modern in melody, for one that has fifty-six years on its head, is called the *Echo Song*. . . . So few passages, however, are repeated, and those chiefly in the second part, that it had a very good effect, as a solo song, from the taste and expression with which it was sung by Miss Abrams" (58).

As Burney's description suggests, Abrams's voice was particularly suited to concert and oratorio formats because it was light, clear, and small. Commenting on its sweetness and quality, Burney observes that Abrams's voice was "not regarded as 'Theatrical,' but such as the Italians denominate *voce di camera*" (81). She found a number of ways to use her particular vocal talents in an effective manner. Given the information available, we can only speculate about how much of Abrams's success was owing to her being in the right place at the right time and how much was owing to her own agency. As in all careers, however, some combination of both timeliness and self-assertion must have been at work. Subscription concert series presented in an intimate setting provide one example of a venue that developed in Abrams's time that was particularly suited to her small, tastefully produced instrument and that she utilized to her advantage.

The oldest and perhaps most prestigious of these was the Concert of Antient Music series established in 1776 and continued until 1848. Parke describes it as "a select subscription concert, under the management of directors, generally noblemen, who alternately preside for the evening." Music presented had to be at least twenty-five years old because the directors, Parke explains, "wish their music, like their wine, to be of a certain age" (*Musical Memoirs*, 2:142). By 1785, George III was a regular subscriber and Abrams a regular performer, whose taste and musicianship are emphasized by the reviewers. The London Times of 1 December 1787, for example, states that "Miss Abrams' solo 'Laudamus Te' was very much approved and indeed deserved it." Concert series were also organized by J. P. Salomon, who contracted Haydn to produce twenty new compositions for his 1792 concerts, and by men such as Venanzio Rauzzini and Muzio Clementi.

In 1792, Harriett Abrams became a concert impresario. Parke writes: "This Winter (1792) I was engaged by Miss Abrams for a series of concerts denominated the ladies' concerts conducted by that lady at Lord Vernon's, in which I performed a concerto on the oboe, and some of Handel's music, which were greatly applauded by the elegant auditors. Mr. Harrison sang the favourite song composed by S. Webbe, 'The Rose;' and Miss Abrams Paesiello's beautiful air 'Madamina,' with great taste" (*Musical Memoir*, 1:148). Abrams again shows herself as a savvy performer, finding a situation in which she can excel. Parke observes, "The physical powers of Miss Abrams were not great, but she sang with much sweetness and delicacy" (1:149). Such qualities are more suited to the rooms of the subscription concert than to large theaters or opera houses.

As an independent entrepreneur, Abrams brought the qualities of "the little Gipsy" to high society. While they may have been called "Ladies' Concerts," her productions were far more than yet another female amusement to be patronized by men. Abrams repeated the series in 1794 and 1795. On more than one occasion, she persuaded Josef Haydn to participate as her accompanist. Pohl's chronicle of Haydn's time in London describes the "exquisite high society" that gathered to listen to music under Abrams's "supervision."[10]

2

"Ladies' concerts" enabled Abrams to display her own talents and to help shape a culture of women's music. The pieces she composed for her concerts and the programs she put together allowed her to make the most of her performance skills. She molded musical forms both for herself and her sisters, writing two- and three-part catches and glees as well as solo songs. According to Lord Mount-Edgucumbe, Abrams's compositions, her concerts, and her work with her sisters must be taken into account to understand the London musical scene: "There is but one name more that

I shall mention, and that very slightly; but when excellence in music is the subject, it cannot be omitted. It is that of the Misses Abrams, who were unrivaled in their line, and whose united voices formed the very perfection of harmony. . . . [T]heir merits of every kind are too widely known to need my panegyric, and too universally acknowledged to admit of the possibility of contradiction" (*Musical reminiscences*, 142).

Mount-Edgucumbe suggests that Abrams's compositions typify the style of music in which the English of this period excelled—church music, Handel's oratorios, and glees (136). Twentieth-century musicologists, who do not mention Abrams, echo Mount-Edgucumbe's assessment. *The New Harvard Dictionary of Music*, for instance, finds the eighteenth and nineteenth centuries "in general a low point in the vitality of native English music, unless Handel is considered to have become an English composer." The musical life of London, however, is considered strong and active, although "dominated by foreigners." What "native tradition" there was "survived in church music, and in local genres such as the catch, the glee, and the ballad opera."[11]

In the first of sixty compositions she produced, Abrams made sustained use of the vocal idiom of early English Romantic culture. British Museum holdings include sixteen of her solo pieces. She produced a collection of Scottish songs harmonized for three voices. Her music was performed frequently enough to warrant reprinting twelve of her songs in book form in 1803. Her music was also published in America and can still be found in libraries from Boston to California.

Perhaps because she was a singer herself, her music is extremely well written for the voice. Aware of potential vocal problems, she provides alternative notes to match individual ranges. She provides places to show off vocal agility, often writing out ornamentations around a fermata.[12] Her very singable songs were picked up by many prominent artists of her time. Her music is meant for women's voices, and the lyrics she works with can best be projected by a female performer.

A frequent collaborator was Maria Susanna Hunter, a well-known actress who, as Maria Susanna Cooper, published *The History of Fanny Meadows, In a Series of Letters*, a 1775 imitation of *Pamela*. Of course, Abrams also set pieces by men, and indeed her favorite lyricist seems to have been M. G. Lewis, better known as "Monk" Lewis. He wrote the lyrics of "Crazy Jane," perhaps Abrams's most popular piece, as well as the words of numerous other songs. (In fact, Highfill gives him sole credit for "Crazy Jane" [2:165].) Many other prominent writers of the period provided her with texts.

In considerations of songs by women composers, certain questions about lyrics become relevant. Do the lyrics that attract women differ in some way from those male composers set? Do songs by women composers reflect through their lyrics women's special concerns? While any sustained discussion of these issues lies beyond the bounds of this essay, it is worth noting how the texts Abrams chose to work with often involve issues of particular concern to women.

Many pertain to women victimized by the sexual codes and female powerlessness of the late eighteenth and early nineteenth centuries. In "The Gaoler," for example, an upper-class young woman is separated from her child and thrown into an asylum through the machinations of her tyrant husband. She tries to convince the jailer of her rationality, insisting at the end of each verse, "I am not mad." She tells of her husband's plot, of what she is sure will be her father's frantic search for her, and contrasts her privileged upbringing with her current deplorable condition. Finally, she speaks to her child, describing her maternal anxiety about how they were pried apart and of her fear of being forgotten. As a madman breaks his chain and lunges at the bars of her cell, she realizes in a chilling quarter-note statement: "I am not mad, but soon shall be." The forms of male power used to destroy this woman's mind and body are epitomized in the figure of the jailer, a brute to whom she is forced to kneel and beg for help but who has the wherewithal to ignore and thereby crush her.

Exhibiting a certain resistance to social convention, Abrams set pieces that portray the horror or frivolity or boredom of marriage, a condition she chose to avoid. In "The Gamester," Julia sits to "count the lonely hours." At the end of each stanza, the clock strikes, and at four in the morning the husband stumbles home from the gambling table to blow his brains out. This narrative is an interesting revision of Edward Moore's popular play *The Gamester*. Abrams's Julia seems almost well rid of her "drooping husband," in contrast to Moore's Mrs. Beverly, whose devotion to her wastrel husband makes the focus of the play a study in female self-abasement.

The music and lyrics of "The Soldier's Grave" and those of "William and Susan" give cynical twists to clichéd romance plots. The scene of "The Soldier's Grave" is Guilford Churchyard, where a man happens upon a woman sobbing at the grave of her beloved. He asks if he can help her, and they agree to meet the next day when he will dig her a grave. He courts her instead, however, so that she soon forgets her dead soldier. The sardonic version of male-female relationships is provided in "The Soldier's Grave" in part by a theme and variation technique through which the piano accompaniment grows progressively more lively. As the man and woman talk, the bass chords maintain her despair and purported desire to follow her lover to the grave. The dotted sixteenth/thirty-second-note treble rhythms, however, point to the possibility of the piece's happy resolution.

In "William and Susan," the hero must leave to seek his fortune, and the lovers do not know how they will survive the separation. William prospers, returns, and marries Susan, but " 'ere the Honey Moon was flown, They cursed the Married Life." Each thinks the other is being unfaithful, and they wish "we ne'er had met."

Many of Abrams's songs are very long, proceeding through verse after verse to narrate their tales, a song form typical of the late eighteenth-century sentimental ballad. Her tendency to set out narrative in both the melody and accompaniment is favored by many early nineteenth-century ballad composers as well as by Schubert in his early work. Abrams often keeps listener interest through the accompaniment. While the singer's melody often remains the same throughout many verses, the accompanying instrument, usually the "pianoforte" and occasionally the harp, provides extensive variation.

Maria Bland, commonly considered the best ballad singer of her generation and a performer who, according to Parke and Hopkins, had her pick of any material she wished, programmed Abrams's music frequently. "Crazy Jane," which seems to evoke some of the tragic events of Bland's own chaotic life, was one of her favorite pieces. In this song, a woman driven insane by abandonment tries to approach a young woman, who shrinks from her in terror. Although her speech makes people regard her as crazy, Jane must tell other women her story in order to warn them. In 1799, the song became a hit in London after Bland sang it four times in two weeks as an entr'acte piece at Drury Lane (*London Stage*, pt. 5, 2:2197–99).

Wandering through the countryside of her betrayal, Crazy Jane might well have been part of the landscape of *Lyrical Ballads*. While Abrams's songs are grounded in eighteenth-century musical structures rather than in the lush melodies of composers like Clara Schumann or Alma Mahler, and while their topics often appear in eighteenth-century ballads, their subjects are also those of the great Romantic poets. One song, "The Aeolian Harp," evokes the instrument that M. H. Abrams characterizes as "a persistent romantic analogue of the poetic mind."[13] Figures like Blake's beggars and Wordsworth's vagrants fill the texts of her songs.

Common folk and outcasts like the Felon, the Orphan Girl, and the Emigrant narrate their own sad stories, sounding sometimes like Wordsworth's forsaken Indian woman or his mad mother.

3

As a composer and as a performer, Harriett Abrams profited from certain theatrical trends that developed in the early Romantic period. After 1775, songs were often inserted between the acts of a play, and Abrams frequently wrote and performed this material. She was also able to capitalize on other theatrical conventions, among them the practice of giving certain actresses benefits and the movement of theater into private houses.

Typically, an evening at the theater consisted of a full-length play and then a shorter piece, often a two-act farce. These performances were often very long, and one theatergoer, Mr. Wendeborn, observed how much people yawned. He suggests that "good humour is to be kept up between the acts, by means of songs, dances, processions and things of that kind." Until the 1770s, most audiences preferred dance to keep them awake, although Hogan mentions the many discussions involving the inappropriateness of performing "A Hornpipe in Wooden Shoes" between the acts in *Hamlet*. Taste changed, however, and singing replaced dancing between acts. It seems as if everyone began singing, as participants in private clubs and societies and also as a demonstration of patriotism. Fearing a possible French invasion, audiences and actors frequently broke into choruses of "God Save the King" during performances (*London Stage*, pt. 5, 1:lxxxi).

Abrams appeared as the soloist who sang between acts of a play or as the singer of numbers inserted into the play itself. In act 2 of many productions of *A Winter's Tale*, for instance, she came on stage to sing "A Sheep Shearing Song." "The Soldier's Grave" and "Crazy Jane" were especially popular entr'acte pieces.

Abrams also provided material for a number of benefits and was herself given the honor of several such performances. The whole procedure of the benefit was artistically, financially, and above all politically complex, as Garrick's letters and Hopkins's notes suggest. Theater managers and performers often negotiated contracts that provided for a salary plus a benefit. For their benefits, performers would sell as many tickets as they could to friends and patrons at more than the usual price. After reimbursing the theater for various expenses, the performers kept the proceeds from all tickets sold. Of course, certain times were more popular than others, and performers cajoled and threatened to get the night of choice. Although perpetually at odds with Garrick, Frances Abington, one of London's star performers, seems to have reached new heights of rancor when it came to her benefits. An actress "taking a benefit" could cast herself as she chose and invite others to appear with her.[14]

A prominent enough member of the company to be given at least five benefits, Abrams seems to have had the artistic and managerial skills to run her performances a bit more smoothly. She cast herself in leading roles that suited her well. On her nights, she played, for the first time, Ariel in *The Tempest*, Gillian in *The Quaker*, and Sylvia in *Cymon*. This last role particularly was an important one for her; having proved herself, she was engaged often for the part. Hopkins indicates that she profited both artistically and financially from her benefits (*London Stage*, pt. 4, 3:1970; pt. 5, 1:73, 170, 255, 340).

Abrams's vocal and personal qualities rendered her an ideal candidate for participation in the private theatricals that became the fashion during the last part of the eighteenth century and the early nineteenth century. Garrick's retirement affected theatrical London in a number of ways. An article in the *London Packet* of 4 November 1776 explains that audiences deserted public London theaters, where they could no longer see him, and turned to private productions: "Since the theatrical resignation of Roscius, the rage for dramatic entertainments in private families has increased astonishingly; scarce a man of rank either has, or intends to have his petite theatre, in the decoration of which the utmost taste and expense are lavished." Abrams's voice was ideally suited to this more intimate format. She sang and acted in these private entertainments, especially in the theater at Hinchingbrook, the home of the earl of Sandwich.

A well-known caricature entitled "A Sandwich" shows the earl standing between two women, the one on his right presumably Harriett Abrams; the one on his left, Miss West the actress (Highfill et al., *Biographical Dictionary*, 1:24). This etching of an older man dangling a long cane and flanked by two pretty women implies a sexual connection among the three. Sandwich was notoriously involved with at least one singer, Martha Ray, the woman he molded to be his mistress and hostess, the woman who presided at his theatricals before she was shot dead by a rejected lover. Many rich men took actresses as their mistresses. Before he became King George IV, the Prince Regent was involved with Mary "Perdita" Robinson, and William IV, before ascending the throne, lived

A Sandwich. ("Pub. Jany. 1, 1788, by S. W. Fores, Satirist, No. 3 Piccadilly."
Miss Abrams   Lord Sandwich   Miss West
Alfred Rubens, *Anglo-Jewish Portraits*, London: The Jewish Museum, 1935, plate 3 (Copyright British Museum).

with Dorothy Jordan, who had ten children by her royal lover. Robert Walpole promised to marry Hannah Norsa as soon as his wife died, but she outlived him. The nature of Abrams's relationship with patrons like Sandwich is not known, but the caricature probably seeks to implicate her in the sexual notoriety identified with him. As Donkin points out, the eighteenth- and nineteenth-century assumption that actresses were prostitutes understood the female on stage as on display and thus sexually available. For this reason, Donkin argues, the reputation of an actress "had little to do with her private conduct offstage and everything to do with the projected desires of the viewing audience" ("Mrs. Siddons," 276–77).

"A Sandwich" conveys a version of those "projected desires" by sexual innuendo. Its visual argument asserts that the theatrical proximity of actors, singers, and the aristocracy is inherently transgressive of class barriers and, for this reason, likely to be transgressive in other ways as well. Performing and making music together can be an intimate experience. In private theatricals and concerts the classes mixed, as nobles and other amateur actors mixed with professionals in lavishly staged productions, which were both seriously reviewed and ridiculed by the newspapers, where columns called "Ton Theatrical" or "Theatrical of Ton" described them. The frenetic, almost deranged activity of this world is captured in a Gillray print inscribed "DILETTANTI — THEATRICALS; — or — A Peep at the Green Room—vide Pic Nic Orgies." The title of the caricature establishes it as satirizing both the Society of Dilettanti and the Pic Nic Society, so called because each person involved contributed something to the performance.[15] An extended description of this caricature, written by one of Gillray's contemporaries, warrants repeating here because of the way in which it describes the social, political, and theatrical scene and Abrams's position in it as both an alien and facilitating presence.

The great Lord Cholmondley with his quiver girdle inscribed "Amor Vincit Omnia" implies his boasted powers in the field of Venus. Under him is the "great Alexander," little Lord Valletort, who lost his life in a pair of too tight stays! Lady Salisbury is drawing on boots and about to assume the breeches necessary for the part of the "Squire's Groom"; her noble Lord, the Lord Carlisle, is filling the bassoon and the Lord Spooner is tingling the triangle. The singers are the celebrated professionals, the Misses Abraham. Lady Albina Buckinghamshire is touching up her charms at the toilette. Behind, the Heir Apparent is tripping it with Lady Jersey and Mrs. Fitzherbert. The quintessence of foppery, Sir Lumley Skeffington, is harlequin and that annoyance of milliners' apprentices, Lord Kirkcudbright, is a sort of human monkey. Behind the screen, Old Queensberry, the Piccadilly Duke is saluting Lady——and George Hanger is touching the lips

DILETTANTI-THEATRICALS;—or—A Peep at the Green Room—vide Pic Nic Orgies.
Jewish Historical Society of England, Transactions, vol. 24, Miscellaneous, 9, 1974, plate VIII (Copyright British Museum).

of her pretty sister. Lord Derby, as usual, is entertaining the fashionables with a flourish on the horn.[16]

Abrams's position in this composite of everybody who was anybody in the circle of George, the heir apparent, indicates her and her sister's stature in the Romantic world of private, aristocratic theatricals and musical entertainments. Of all of the many performers connected with the royal family, Gillray chose to depict the Abrams sisters and identify them as "celebrated professionals." Lewdness, vanity, and foppery characterize everyone else. The crown prince, for instance, is with both Lady Jersey and Maria Fitzherbert—not one but two mistresses. While Abrams becomes a part of this most fashionable society, she is still the professional woman. She may be visually satirized, and she is the lady with the Jewish name that is persistently misspelled, but she remains at the center of the portrait as the working woman who maintains a certain dignified self-assurance.

The prince's cohort shown in this 1803 sketch formed a court that set itself against that of George III and his wife, Queen Charlotte. Negotiations involving the Regency Bill of 1789 had intensified the battling of George and the Whigs against Charlotte and Pitt. Abrams's 1803 song collection, however, was published dedicated "To the Queen." The frontispiece, with an etching by Gillray, includes the words: "with Her Majesty's most Gracious Permission this Work is respectfully inscribed by Her Majesty's most faithful, obedient and humble servant Harriett Abrams." Abrams here anticipates the actions of the prince himself, who by 1814 had become completely reconciled with his mother.[17] The company she kept and her dedication to the Queen suggest Abrams capably negotiated social and political intricacies by, in this case, maintaining relations with both sides. For Abrams, femininity and Jewishness became marketable qualities. Her career demonstrates how and what a woman could accomplish as part of the early Romantic performance scene.

Judith Pascoe

Mary Robinson and
the Literary Marketplace

A contemporary poem characterizes the *Morning Post* of the early 1800s as a hodgepodge of gossip and political intrigue, providing a list of news items a reader of that journal might encounter:

> Bonaparte, Paris fashions,
> Chapels, Cyprian assignations:
> Captain Sash, the sea-side shark—
> Slander's arrow shot i' th' dark.
> Villa of Rochampton Jew,
> Horrid murder done at Kew;
> Queries, critical corrections,
> Galvinistic resurrections.
> Treatise on the Moon's eclipse
> Paint for cheeks, and salve for lips.[1]

The poem exposes a journalistic eclecticism that offered accounts of hideous crime and fashion whimsy in adjoining columns. What constituted news was anything that lured the eye to the printed page; more spectacular events—a murder at Kew Gardens, for instance—assumed priority. The paper's merging of high tragedy and cultural frivolity was paralleled by an increasing affinity between political and theatrical realms. Political events were appropriated for the London stage: elaborate productions of the fall of the Bastille or, later, a ninety-minute facsimile production of George IV's coronation. Journalists provided material for the stage, and a substantial portion of the "news" printed in papers like the *Post* was provided by actors and playwrights.[2]

The theatrical imperative governing newspaper production carried over into the literary columns of these papers, placing particular demands on the poets who published there and winning them, for better or worse, a kind of celebrity status. While Daniel Stuart, the editor of the *Morning Post*, published the poems of a distinguished coterie of poets that included Wordsworth, Coleridge, Southey, and Mary Robinson, the peculiar aggregate of newsmaking and personality worship that characterized the paper accommodated (and was accommodated by) these poets to varying degrees. I will focus on the *Morning Post*'s poetry column in order to suggest the ways in which the poetry venue provided by a daily newspaper in the 1790s was particularly suited to performative modes of self-representation and, as a result, was especially hospitable to Mary Robinson.[3] The record of Robinson's tenure with the *Post* also demonstrates the connection between poetry consumption and newspaper profits in the last years of the decade. Robinson's theatrical self-fashioning was the result of both artistic and financial imperatives, forces whose intermingling was a source of considerable anxiety for more reluctant members of Stuart's poetic stable.

In writing for a newspaper, a poet was more acutely aware of audience than he or she would be in publishing collections of verse. A newspaper's readership, much like a theater audience, was confronted on a regular, even daily, basis and without the distancing effects built into publication in a more expensive format. A published book took longer to produce and was received by a small and relatively homogeneous audience, one that could be conceptualized by the poet as a select group, in the way that Wordsworth constructs an ideal audience for his poetry in his "Preface" to the *Lyrical Ballads*. Although Daniel Stuart similarly attempted to shape his reading audience—or at least to shape an image of his reading audience—his task was compounded by the range and heterogeneity of his readership.

Jon Klancher's ground-breaking analysis of reading audiences in the period from 1790 to 1832 suggests the ways in which readers were created by the periodicals that sought to define and solidify a particular kind of audience. Klancher writes, "By special acts of circulating—repeated acts of certain kinds of writing and reading—a public is shaped to read discourses in deliberate, directed ways."[4] Klancher goes on to credit the periodical press with playing a formative role in the evolution of a middle-class identity, one that, in his analysis, realizes its cultural power through dismantling and reconstituting signs, that is, by reading (73). Klancher's study focuses primarily on the monthly rather than the diurnal press, but his observations retain a critical currency when applied to the latter, quite different print milieu. The fact that, in the England of the 1790s, one could characterize an individual's political leaning by his or her choice of newspaper provides support for the notion that periodicals create and shape a particular readership.[5] Lucyle Werkmeister neatly divides English newspapers published between 1792 and 1793 in terms of their stance toward the party in power (*Newspaper History*, 22, 31). Wordsworth's status as a loyal reader of the *Morning Post*—it was the only periodical he admitted to reading on a regular basis—would presumably indicate that he sympathized with Daniel Stuart's opposition to the ruling government.[6]

If the *Morning Post* sought to gather and shape a readership united by particular political views, a similar controlling interest displayed itself in one of its less overtly polemical features: the literary column. The headnotes to the poems printed in these columns bespeak a desire to fashion an audience sophisticated enough to appreciate the poetry's particular virtues. The poems submitted by Coleridge, especially, are often preceded by headnotes that provide readers with a lesson in poetry appreciation. Coleridge's "The Recantation, An Ode" (better known as "France: An Ode") is preceded by the following testimony: "The Poem . . . is written with great energy. The second, third, and fourth stanzas, contain some of the most vigorous lines we have ever read. The lines in the fourth stanza . . . are particularly expressive and beautiful."[7] A similar note announcing another Coleridge submission, "Lewti; or, The Circassian's Love Chant," includes this knowing comment: "The fifth and last stanzas are, we think, the best" (*MP*, 13 April 1798, p. 3).

These asides to the reader suggest the existence of an exclusive club of discerning critics, one the reader might be permitted to join if he or she managed to acquire the necessary critical acumen. That Stuart was quite consciously working to construct at least the semblance of a select and discerning readership is evidenced by announcements like this one, directed at "the *Literati*": "The Poetry of the Morning Post will in future be critically select. None but first rate compositions will be admitted to our columns; and we are promised the aid of several of the most distinguished writers of the present day" (*MP*, 17 April 1798, p. 3). In attempting to establish his paper as a repository of literary art, Stuart directly mimics the audience-shaping efforts of the monthly journals that Klancher takes as his focus. The inaugural number of the *Monthly Magazine*, published two years before Stuart's announcement, stakes a similar claim to critical distinction, contrasting the poetry it plans to publish with the "trivial and imperfect attempts at writing verse" characteristic of prior magazine verse: "It has been their [the editors'] earnest wish to establish a very different character of the pages devoted to this pleasing object in the Monthly Magazine, and if they can lay any claim to judgment in poetical merit, they may venture to refer to many of their correspondents' favours as proofs, that true genius and correct taste have not disdained to present their productions to the public through the medium of a periodical Miscellany."[8] While Stuart's efforts to emulate the audience-cultivating strategies of the monthlies may have had a number of desirable effects—his depiction of *Lyrical Ballads* as required reading for people of taste surely helped that volume's sales[9]—his readers shaped the poetry contributions of the paper at least as much as they were shaped by them. The readership of a daily newspaper was too large and unruly to accommodate the paper's efforts to construct a company of suitable readers for its poets. And in the demands of such a diverse audience lay the special challenge to those writers who joined Stuart's literary stable.

The relatively small price of a daily newspaper ensured it a far larger readership than one could count on for a published collection of poems, even one with the impressive subscription lists that Mary Robinson gathered in advance of publication. The already large circulation resulting from the comparatively small (six-penny) price of a paper like the *Post* was greatly amplified through the sharing of issues among readers, by either formal or informal arrangement. A correspondent to the editor of the *Monthly Magazine* notes: "[T]here . . . exist in every parish and hamlet of the empire, *Newspaper Societies*, in which seven, eight, or nine persons club their sixpence a week to take in and circulate from one to the other, a London, and one, two, or three provincial papers."[10] The fact that newspapers commonly reprinted poetry selections from other newspapers—for example, a tribute poem that Coleridge penned for Robinson was reprinted in *The Express and Evening Chronicle* a few days after appearing in the *Post*—assured a newspaper poet a huge audience for his or her work.[11]

The size of the readership, however, also ensured that it was the most heterogeneous audience a poet could confront, precisely of the sort that Wordsworth castigated in the "Preface" for its fondness for "frantic novels, sickly and stupid German Tragedies, and deluges of idle and extravagant stories in verse."[12] If the selection and presentation of poems published in the *Morning Post* managed in a small way to define the poetic taste of this audience, it is also true that to an even greater extent the maverick desires of the audience determined this selection and presentation.

While these readers were, of course, important as purchasers, they also represented a commodity that could be used to entice advertisers, another source of newspaper revenue. Stuart's pronouncement on the literary status of his paper served not just as an enticement to readers but as a signal to potential advertisers that cultivated readers, of the type that might buy books, read his paper in substantial numbers. Stuart underscores the connection between literary quality and readership, announcing in 1800: "The MORNING POST under its present Conductors has, within the last four years, more than *trebled* in Circulation, while every other Paper has either been stationary or declining. . . . With what attention we have procured intelligence, and with what solicitude we have endeavoured to make our Paper respectable in respect of literary merit, the public are best able to judge, and from the past will decide our future merits" (*MP*, 27 Jan. 1800, p. 2). Such an announcement encouraged the advertising business of publishers, who liked taking large front-page ads to impress the reading public with the size of their catalogs.[13]

The poetry columns of the *Morning Post*, then, aimed both to satisfy a large, heterogeneous reading audience and to fabricate of this undifferentiated group of readers a select coterie of the book-buying public, whose allegiance to the *Post* would sell advertising space. One can read this double agenda in terms of both low-cultural and high-cultural production, a need for poems in quantity to satisfy the demands of a large audience versus a requirement for poems of quality to create the appearance of high-minded readers in order to satisfy book publishers and, possibly, poets like Coleridge and Robinson, who took a role in writing the headnotes that attempted to teach readers how to read. Klancher describes how such a hierarchization invites the language of "reception" and "consumption," the bestowing of texts on sensitive readers versus an impersonal supply and demand (*Making*, 13). The most successful *Post* poets, however, did not operate within a rigidly bifurcated view of the poem as either aesthetic object or commodity—a hierarchization that owes its critical currency to Romantic habits of thought—but rather found these two views of the poem compatible.

Robert Southey, who was Stuart's most prolific poet between 1798 and 1799, and who was, with Mary Robinson, quite comfortable with the "habit of versifying" that writing for the *Post* required, made explicit the connection between newspaper verse and a commercial marketplace.[14] When, in 1807, he rejected an offer to resume his former role as feature poet, producing a stipulated number of poems per week for a regular wage, Southey suggested another alternative: "Though I cannot work by time, I can by piece. When I can get a sheet full it shall be sent;

and the verses may be rated, like oysters, by the hundred, or like bricks, by the thousand" (Stuart, 393). This massing together of poems for the market may have served to liberate Southey's poetic career; within the pages of the *Post* he published poems as disparate as "Elegy on a Quid of Tobacco" and "July Thirteenth. Charlotte Cordé Executed for Putting Marat to Death."

For Coleridge, the close association of poems with other commodities proved a more unsettling reality, possibly because he was incapable of producing the steady outpouring of poems that Stuart needed, but also for less practical reasons. Writing to Stuart in a similar vein to that of Southey, Coleridge strikes a more somber note: "A newspaper is a market for flowers and vegetables, rather than a granary or conservatory; and the drawer of its Editor, a common burial ground, not a catacomb for embalmed mummies, in which the defunct are preserved to serve in after times as medicines for the living."[15] The newspaper drawer reminds Coleridge that the newspaper poem is not only a product but a perishable one; in this reservoir, the timeless creation of the Romantic poet inevitably and frighteningly succumbs to rot. The date of this letter to Stuart— 1811—is significant because it comes many years after Coleridge's most active association with the *Post*. The commonness that Coleridge here associates with newspaper poetry is a retroactive attribute, one that Coleridge may not have associated with the paper when he published "France. An Ode" there. Coleridge's letter signifies a cultural narrowing, a belated discomfort with the role of newspaper poet.

A poem by Isabella Lickbarrow takes as its subject a source of Coleridge's anxiety—the ephemeral nature of a poem published on cheap newsprint. In "The Fate of Newspapers," she points to the mercurial nature of the audience for newspaper verse as well as to the undignified ends to which it eventually must succumb:

> The "*Advertiser*," you must know,
> Fresh from the Mint not long ago,
> We welcomed with abundant pleasure,
> Impatient for the mighty treasure,
> In what an alter'd state forlorn,
> 'Tis now in scatter'd fragments torn,
> Part wrapped around the kettle's handle,
> Part twisted up to light the candle . . . [16]

Mary Robinson similarly calls attention to the material constraints of newspaper publication in a poetic metanarrative, "To the New Type of the Morning Post," published in the *Post* on 27 January 1800. The poem begins:

YE SABLE LEGIONS, here you stand,
A thousand *Subjects* to command!
All dimly clad in *leaden* mail,
To triumph o'er your *Victim pale!*
To blur the white and spotless scene,
And sport your Columns dark between! (3)

This poem indicates Robinson's willingness to write occasional and whimsical poetry aimed at entertaining a general audience. Although we should not overread a poem that so obviously delights in its own figurative cleverness, it is worth pausing over the violent trope Robinson uses to portray the printing process, the subjugation of a feminized page to the brute pressure of the printer's lead. The poem provides a veiled commentary on the appropriation of the poet in the pages of the *Post*.

If the poem's status as commodity was underscored by a poetic venue that valued sheer productivity over singular and seminal innovation, it is also true that the newspaper poet too could become transformed into a product for sale, a "personality" with an additive celebrity status. A comparison to the position of the actress is appropriate—the figure of an actress like Sarah Siddons could draw people to the theater as much, or more than, the actual play in which she was performing. Writing to Coleridge in 1798, Stuart describes his unwilling participation in a cult of personality that helped to sell papers: "[Y]ou must know that personalities among fashionable People, are the very best ingredient in a Morning Newspaper. I disapprove of personalities as much as any one but I must administer to the Public taste. The fault is in the public, not in me."[17] The personalities most often featured by the *Post* were those of actresses such as Dorothy Jordan, but a poet could be made to serve as well. It was to Stuart's advantage to feed public interest in his poets through puffs and frequent mention. By constantly providing the reading public with information about his poets, he helped to position these individuals as "fashionable people," thus creating a demand for more details about their life and work. Of Stuart's chief poets, the one who participated most fully and willingly in this publicity venture was Mary Robinson.

Robinson was enmeshed in the fabric of the newspaper in a way that even Southey, who preceded her as poetry editor, was not; her bold-print last name stood out from the page in numerous contexts. As well as being responsible for the contents of the columns devoted to ORIGINAL POETRY, as the *Post* heralded its literary selections, she was also the subject of frequent flattering comments and news briefs. The *Morning Post* of 20 January 1798 reports: "The Publisher of 'The Lives of Living Authors,' has confirmed to Mrs. ROBINSON the dignified title of *the English Sappho*: a title which was long since bestowed on her by the *literary tribunal* of the country"(2), and, in one of an endless series of observations on Robinson's health, sounds this alarm on 11 June of the same year: "Mrs. ROBINSON's nervous fever has again attacked her, and her health suffers hourly by its influence" (2). In the regular feature "To Correspondents," which notified writers of contributions received and pending publication dates, Robinson's work (under a variety of signatures) is constantly promoted: "LAURA MARIA — To-morrow" (*MP*, 6 February 1800, p. 2) or "OBERON's beautiful lines to Mrs. JORDAN shall appear to-morrow" (*MP*, 4 March 1800, p. 2) or "The pretty Poetical Tale, by TABITHA BRAMBLE, is omitted till to-morrow, for want of room" (*MP*, 19 March 1800, p. 2), the last coming on a day that Bramble acolytes had been led to anticipate her "pretty Ode" (*MP*, 18 March 1800, p. 2). Over the course of two or three days, a *Post* reader and Robinson fan might come across a front-page advertisement for a subscription to a new Robinson volume, a poem, a puff, a promotion for a soon-to-be-published poem, and a medical prognosis. The reader might also come across a poem written by an idolatrous fan in response to a poem previously published by Robinson.

Other poets associated with Stuart receive similar promotional mention but not with the frequency and intensity of the coverage devoted to Robinson. And even the relatively slight attention of this kind that Wordsworth received was not appreciated by his sister: Dorothy Wordsworth called Stuart's coverage of her brother's wedding "the most ridiculous paragraph that ever was penned."[18] Robinson's personal history made her, more than Stuart's male poets, perfectly suited for the role of celebrity poet. Her past career as an actress and her scandalous liaison with the Prince of Wales had, nearly twenty years before, earned her a special place in the public interest.

But if Robinson had in the past been the pawn of scandal sheets, she now took an active and decisive role in the celebrity coverage Stuart used to help sell papers. There is evidence of this in the way the paper's allusions to those she knew fluctuated according to their place in her affections. As her relationship with Banastre Tarleton (the military hero with whom she had a protracted relationship) soured, the references to Tarleton in the *Post* became more derisive. Similarly, as her friendship with William Godwin grew, he became the recipient of a number of compliments.[19] The *Telegraph* of 11 February 1797 counts Robinson among a list of forty-two persons who regularly paid to have themselves puffed in newspapers.[20] Given Stuart's stake in Robinson's public persona and her position as his poetry editor, it is unlikely that she had to pay for flattering coverage in the *Post*. The two evolved a symbiotic relationship that served the ambitions of each.

Robinson used her prominence within the pages of the *Post* to reinvent herself, to substitute for her old notoriety a new, distinguished status as a serious literary figure. And just as she played a role she fashioned for herself in the gossip items of the *Post*, she resorted to a performative mode of self-representation in the paper's poetry offerings. The most striking aspect of Robinson's tenure with the *Morning Post* is her strategic employment of pseudonyms. All of Stuart's poets seem to have written under pen names at least occasionally; Coleridge used them with some frequency, publishing poems as "Albert" or "Francini" or "Laberius." But Robinson's pseudonyms—at least eight in all—represent a sustained and sustaining experiment in self-representation (an experiment that possibly motivated Coleridge's own—his pseudonym usage dropped off fairly dramatically after Robinson's death). Stuart's poets met the public in a number of different guises, ranging from the obfuscation of pen names through the veil of anonymity (the guise Southey most often employed) to the stable signature of their proper names (all three published at least occasionally in this way). These three strategies range from "theatrical" to "natural" modes of self-representation, from a misrepresented self to an authentic one. A closer examination of pseudonym usage in the *Post*, however, complicates this polarizing of theatricality and sincerity.

Robinson employed at least eight different pseudonyms during her association with the *Post*, writing as "Laura Maria," "Oberon," "Sappho," "Julia," "Lesbia," "Portia," "Bridget," and "Tabitha Bramble." She used these pseudonyms to proliferate herself; the numerous guises facilitated poetic experimentation. Although the poems Robinson published under each pseudonym are not uniform in style, the separate pen names do, to a large extent, represent distinctive voices. "Oberon," for example, most often pens graceful tributes like "Lines on Seeing the Duchess of Devonshire in Her New and Splendid Carriage" or "On Seeing the Countess of Yarmouth at Her Window in Piccadilly, On Sunday Last." Oberon, an identity employed primarily to lavish praise on women, is interestingly the only nonfemale pseudonym in Robinson's repertoire. And his historical place in fairy literature grants him a liminal rather than a clearly masculine status. Robinson's alternate identities are not, then, an effort to seize a masculine authority but rather an effort to explore the possibilities of a multiply constituted female one.

In contrast with Oberon, Tabitha Bramble, who served as the author of thirty-nine poems published in the *Post* between December 1797 and October 1800, brought to mind a character more concretely delineated than any of Robinson's earlier embodiments and in direct contrast to the mellifluous Laura Maria of her Della Cruscan days. Thomas Rowlandson's depictions of Bramble for the 1793 edition of *Humphry Clinker* portray an old, ugly, witchlike crone. The figure of this brusque, sexually undesirable female—the polar opposite of the glamorous construction of Robinson favored by newspapers of the period—enabled Robinson to write sharply critical poetry utterly unlike the softer effusions of Laura Maria or Oberon.

Robinson as Bramble directly flouted the tradition of newspaper verse that was primarily occasional and devoted to lauding those in power. She positions herself in opposition to the commemorative poets of her time, most notably Henry James Pye, poet laureate, who was also featured in the *Morning Post*. It does not take a large sampling of Pye's self-congratulatory, patriotic verse to understand what fueled Bramble's response. Pye's "Ode for the New Year—1798" ends with this representative stanza:

> From hoary Greenland's frozen lands
> To burning Libya's golden sands,
>   Aloft the British ensign flies
> In folds triumphant to the skies;
> While to the notes that hail'd the isle
>   Emerging from its parent main,
> The Sacred Muse with raptur'd smile
>   Responsive pours the exulting strain,
>   "Rule Britannia, rule the waves,
>   "Britons never will be slaves." (*MP*, 18 January 1798, p. 2)

Robinson (in the guise of Bramble) begins her own poem for the new year, "Ode Fourth / For New Year's Day," by mimicking exactly the kind of poem with which Pye ushered forth every national occasion. She proceeds to sketch out an alternative conception of the national poet, in which the poet casts a critical rather than caressing eye on the votaries of the court. Addressing these denizens of the fashionable world, she asks:

> Why does the Laureat pen forbear to shew
> Your well-plac'd features—simpering in a row?
> Waiting the nod familiar, or the joke
> Which, to be *laugh'd at*—only needs be *spoke*? (*MP*, 1 January 1798, p. 3)

Robinson's donning and shedding of authorial identities might be ascribed to a theatrical impulse held over from her early years as an actress. Given her checkered past, Robinson may simply have been enjoying a respite from the burden of her own name, an appellation charged with old scandals so publicly historicized that it could never achieve the serene stability of a name like Wordsworth. Marjorie Levinson has written that for Keats, the one canonical Romantic poet whose social status in any way resembled that of Robinson, " 'self' is 'not-self,' a fetishized, random collection of canonical figures."[21] By contrast, for Robinson, the "self" that claims authorship of the poems is a curious array of free-floating and nontotalized personae. If, as Foucault suggests, "[a] text has an inaugurative value precisely because it is the work of a particular author, and our returns are conditioned by this knowledge,"[22] then Robinson's resolute refusal to fix her poems under a single name might be conceived as disrupting reader expectations and, in turn, liberating the figure of the poet from any single poetic stance. In place of the simple gesture of a single name reliably situated at the top or bottom of a poem, Robinson substitutes an act of legerdemain, a decentering multiplication of pseudonymous entities.

In addition, Robinson's deliberate creation of multiple selves can be read as an attempt to rescue some stable and constitutive self from public display and commodity status. A discomfort with the too-close association of poems and money contributed to Wordsworth's defensiveness about his early and fairly modest involvement with newspaper production. "[C]ertain I am," he wrote in 1838, "that the last thing that could have found its way into my thoughts would have been to enter into an agreement to write for any newspaper—and that I never did so."[23] Wordsworth wanted it clearly known that when he did write for the paper, he did so without financial remuneration, insisting that the record be set straight when one of Stuart's publications suggested otherwise. Wordsworth writes: "The Sonnets and the Pamphlets were written by me without the slightest view to any emolument whatever; nor have I, nor my Wife or Sister, any recollection of any money being received for them either directly from yourself (As E. and P. of those Papers), or mediately through C.; and I wish to know from you, if you have any remembrance or evidence to the contrary."[24] But Robinson, and to lesser extents Coleridge and Southey, could not afford to be so squeamish about establishing pecuniary ties to Stuart's paper. While no evidence exists of the exact remuneration Robinson received from the *Post*, she was almost certainly as grateful for Stuart's patronage as Southey, who recalled his poetry tenure fondly: "I never think of that Laureateship without satisfaction. The guinea a week while I held it came every quarter very seasonably in aid of slender means" (Stuart, *Letters*, 434).

Rather than read Robinson's use of pseudonyms as an escape from either her own tarnished reputation or from the commodity status of the poem and poet, however, I wish to consider the double aspect of theatrical forms of self-presentation, their ability to heighten as well as to disguise. Jean-Christophe Agnew, in his brilliant analysis of the symbiotic relationship of the market and the theater in Anglo-American thought, underscores the importance of display in the establishment of the medieval marketplace. He writes: "The legitimacy of the marketplace as a social institution was inseparable from its theatricality, for the medieval criteria of authority and authenticity required that both attributes be bodied forth: deliberately displayed, performed, and witnessed."[25] According to Agnew's argument, the evolution of a theatrical metaphor that equated theatricality with subterfuge was inextricably linked to a growing uneasiness with the defamiliarizing effects of commodity exchange. But even in times of great "antitheatrical prejudice," theatrical strategies are often employed to assert a singular authority.[26] The annual spectacular celebrations of royal birthdays, to which I will return later, serve as an example of this kind of conservative display.

That Robinson's theatrical donning and shedding of personae did not serve primarily as a form of subterfuge is evidenced by the way she invariably came out from behind the cover of each *nom de plume,* sometimes almost immediately, at other times upon publication of a volume of poems that had previously appeared in the periodical press. The *Morning Post* reported on 27 January 1800 that "Mrs. JORDAN has composed a beautiful air to the elegant lines of SAPPHO which appeared in the paper a few days ago" (3). This is followed on 8 February by "The Poem of *Sappho,* set to music by Mrs. JORDAN, is from the pen of Mrs. ROBINSON" (3). The dedication to her 1791 *Poems,* in which Robinson confirms her identity as the Della Cruscan Laura Maria, explains pseudonym usage as a strategy to ensure an honest response: "Mrs. ROBINSON has the particular gratification of knowing that the efforts of her pen were warmly and honourably patronized under FEIGNED Signatures: had she avowed them at an earlier period the pleasure she now feels would have been considerably diminished, in the idea that the partiality of friends had procured the sanction her POEMS have been favoured with from the candid and enlightened."[27]

While a desire to attain an honest assessment of her work might explain Robinson's use of a pseudonym, it does not go far enough to explain her pseudonymous excess. I would suggest that Robinson's "disguises" actually contribute to a presentation of self that is no less "authentic" than Wordsworth's opposite mode of presentation, the institution of an authorial voice so stable that the poet is conflated with the narrator of the poem. Robinson's pseudonyms, which overlap each other rather than issuing forth in consecutive order, project a self constructed from a mélange of antithetical cultural forces rather than a self developing over time in the sequential style of Wordsworth's *Prelude*, which by its very title suggests temporal progression. Wordsworth, no less than Robinson, struck a pose, but his was that of the sincere rural dweller, the natural talent. Robinson's theatrical personae depict a fragmented consciousness that is, paradoxically, precisely what Wordsworth's anti-theatrical sincerity works to conceal.

If Robinson's multiple poetic voices represent a form of truth concerning a fragmented self, her pseudonyms also seem to have allowed her to speak a truth that could not be conveyed by "Mary Robinson," the fallen woman. Publishing as Tabitha Bramble, she provides a succinct commentary on the festivities attending the queen's birthday celebration, an event the *Post* reported with fetishistic zeal. The largest part of this coverage was devoted to minutely particular descriptions of what people wore to the celebration, such as the following account of the queen's birthday costume:

HER MAJESTY, as usual on her own birth-day was plainly, though tastefully attired in a salmon coloured satin petticoat, ornamented with a patent lace trimming, in perpendicular folds, and two draperies of the same, drawn up on each side in festoons with goats beard, headed with wreaths of puce coloured frivolity, and a deep flounce of the same round the bottom of the coat. Body and train of puce coloured velvet, trimmed with goats beard and frivolity. (*MP*, 19 January 1798, p. 2)

A similar concern for sartorial exactitude extended to the coverage of figures far less exalted than the royal family.

In sharp contrast to this absorption with the queen's petticoat, Robinson writes "Birth-Day Poem" from the removed perspective of one who is neither of the royal cortège nor of the street but ironically poised in between. Published in the *Post* just after the birthday celebration, over the signature of Tabitha Bramble, the poem begins:

> HERE bounds the gaudy gilded chair,
>   Bedeck'd with fringe, and tassels gay;
> The melancholy mourner there
>   Pursues her sad and painful way.
> Here, guarded by a motley train,
>   The pamper'd countess glares along;
> There wrung by poverty and pain
>   Pale Misery mingles with the throng.[28]

The poem continues in this vein, bifurcating a scene visually dominated by the royal party so that the onlookers gathered by the roadside are fixed in every other frame. The poem ultimately renders the decorated ladies of the court obscene in their indifference. Robinson writes:

> Here, amidst jewels, feathers, flowers,
> The senseless dutchess sits demure;
> Heedless of all the anguish'd hours
> The sons of modest worth endure.

> All silver'd and embroider'd o'er,
> She neither knows nor pities pain;
> The beggar freezing at her door
> She overlooks with nice disdain. (*PW*, 321–22)

The poem is careful in its critique—there is no direct reference to the royal family per se, only to the countesses, duchesses, and dames who make up its entourage. But one can substitute a throne for the bounding, gaudy, gilded chair of the first line of the poem. The poem provides a scathing editorial comment on the excesses of the royals. In a nice irony, Robinson, while playing the role of Tabitha Bramble, critiques the obfuscating theatricality of the birthday celebration.

While Robinson is thoroughly imbricated in the conspicuous display that assumes so large a place in the news reports of the *Post*, she manages, in the guise of Bramble, to underscore the triviality of such display, mimicking the paper's regular fashion feature to comic effect. The companion poems "Female Fashions for 1799" and "Male Fashions for 1799" are diminished by removal from their newspaper context, since their titles exactly mirror a newspaper headline. In "FEMALE FASHIONS FOR JULY 1798," the *Post* issues the following edicts: "The prevailing *colours* for the month are *white* and *lilac*. The *hair* is worn *à la Grecque*, after the Parisian mode. The *waists* are much longer. The *chemise* tied close around the neck, with a double ruff, and confined with a cord is a morning dress of increasing fashion" (4 July 1798, p. 3). The lists Robinson provides in her fashion poems underline the arbitrariness of such dictates and bring to light the market imperative driving this fashion whimsy. She writes:

> Long petticoats to hide the feet,
> Silk hose with clocks of scarlet;
> A load of perfume, sickening sweet,
> Bought of Parisian varlet.
>   . . . .
> A bowl of straw to deck the head,
> Like porringer unmeaning;
> A bunch of poppies flaming red,
> With motley ribands streaming.[29]

Finding within the pages of the *Post* a rich source of poetic inspiration, Robinson uses the already sensational "news" reports printed in the paper as material for her poems. Just months before her death, when newspapers were fascinating readers with reports of the discovery of a savage child, Robinson was writing a poem on the same topic, transforming the newspaper narrative of this event into a poetic meditation on the boy's life and state of mind. The *Post* reported: "He lived on potatoes, chesnuts, and acorns. . . . His features are regular, but without expression; every part of his body is covered with scars; these scars attest the cruelty of the persons by whom, it is presumed, he has been abandoned; or, perhaps, they are attributable only to the dangers of a solitary existence, at a tender age, and in a rude tract of country" (*MP*, 3 October 1800, p. 3). In Robinson's poem (which was obviously influenced by Coleridge's "Kubla Khan," a poem she saw in manuscript)[30] these details become part of an intricately rhymed poetic fantasy:

> On chesnuts wild he fed beside.
>   Steep'd in the foamy flood.
> Chequer'd with scars his breast was seen.
> Wounds streaming fresh with anguish keen,
> And marks where other wounds had been
>   Torn by the brambles rude.
> Such was the boy of Aveyron,
>   The tenant of that solitude,
>   Where still, by misery unsubdued,
> He wander'd nine long winters, all alone. (*PW*, 145)

The range of poems Robinson publishes in the *Post*, along with the range of poetic guises under which the poems are presented, represent a poetic strategy calculated to dazzle a reading audience with the variety and virtuosity of the literary performance. While Wordsworth sought the wide audience provided by a newspaper primarily for didactic purposes, allowing "a very, very, few sonnets upon Political Subjects" along with a part of his pamphlet on the Convention of Cintra to appear in the *Post*, Robinson strove to entertain as well as to edify her audience.[31] A series of comic poems that includes "Mistress Gurton's Cat," "Old Barnard—a Monkish Tale," "The Tell Tale. Deborah's Parrot," "The Confessor. A Tale," and "The Granny Grey. A Tale"—all written in the guise of Tabitha Bramble and evincing a folksy, often antifeminist sensibility—can be read as bits of comic business meant primarily, if not solely, to amuse.[32]

Robinson's sense of herself as a poet was inextricably connected with her capacity to perform. Her stint with the *Post* bears some resemblance to an actress's tenure with a popular and long-running play; she was proud of her ability to come up with a fresh performance day after day. "I continue my daily labours in the Post," she wrote to Samuel Pratt in August 1800, the last year of her life and one marked by declining health. "[A]ll the Oberons Tabithas MR's and indeed most of the Poetry, you see there is mine."[33] Once, in response to an offer from William Blackwood, Coleridge quoted "words which Mr. Wordsworth once used to Longman: 'You pay others, sir, for what they write; but you must pay me for what I do not write, for it is in this (i.e. the omissions, erasures, &c.) that costs me both time and toil.'"[34] Robinson could not afford unproductive labor; an incomplete "List of Poetical Pieces, written between December 1799 and December 1800," appended to the second volume of her *Memoirs*, credits her with seventy-four poems. This is not "emotion recollected in tranquility" but rather, performance on demand.

A poetic strategy, as Levinson has demonstrated for Keats, is rooted in a poet's material and social circumstances, in Robinson's case, a need for steady income—in the last year of her life she was arrested for debt—a fact reflected also in her tendency to print and reprint poems.[35] Individual poems appear again and again, not, it seems, because she was altering them substantially but rather because she could increase their earning power in this way. The fragments of what eventually became the long poem *The Progress of Liberty* were printed first in a number of different venues, including the *Morning Post*, the *Monthly Magazine*, and Robinson's *Lyrical Tales*.

Robinson's poetic productivity, gratifying as it may have been for the popular audience represented by the readership of the *Morning Post*, drew critical fire. Commenting on the second volume of her *Poems*, published in 1793, a reviewer for the *Critical Review* writes:

We could wish that a fancy naturally brilliant, and numbers so flowing might, by careful cultivation, be improved into poetry, able to stand the test of criticism, but our voice will not be listened to, where there are so many who write from calls more pressing than the impulse of genius or the desire of fame. Many authors know they might write better, but then they could not write so much, and in that state of society in which the labour of the brain becomes an article of merchandise, its texture, like that of every other manufacture from strong and substantial, becomes slight and shewy.[36]

The alignment of articles of merchandise and that which is "slight and shewy" in this review lends further credence to Agnew's well-documented association of market and theater. When the poem's status as a marketable product stands revealed—as it does when a value is placed upon volume of production—the reviewer adopts an antitheatrical rhetoric, linking the poem with the insubstantiality and glitter of a stage performance. As recently as 1978, Robinson was described as having "overworked a slim literary talent," an assessment that recapitulates an old concern that market forces impinge upon the Muse, motivating an all too earthbound productivity.[37]

Wordsworth's unwillingness to have his reputation sullied by the taint of newspaper ink has earned him critical accolades. Woof approvingly notes, "There was no question of Wordsworth's being the journalist that Coleridge had become, nor of his prostituting his poetry for a newspaper as Coleridge and Southey had done" ("Wordsworth's Poetry," 150). And Mary Jacobus accuses Southey of returning poems from *Lyrical Ballads* "to the level of the magazine poetry from which they had been raised, stripped of their new thematic depth and narrative sophistication."[38] More recently, Kathryn Shevelow notes the critical propensity for seeing the periodical's significance as residing "in its position as one rung on the ladder of literary evolution to the novel."[39]

If Robinson's performative mode of poetic self-representation did not serve her well in terms of critical reception, it did provide a remarkably fluid self with which she could wrest herself from the stultifying subject position of the publicly fallen woman and the potentially limiting position of the Della Cruscan Laura Maria, the persona in which she early presented herself to the literary world. Robinson the performing poet was well served by the theatrical poetic medium provided by the *Post*, which provided her a stage, an eclectic audience, and a steady supply of dramatic material.

Notes

Introduction (pp. 1–10)

1. See Butler, "Repossessing the Past: The Case for an Open Literary History," in *Rethinking Historicism: Critical Readings in Romantic History*, ed. Marjorie Levinson (Oxford: Blackwell, 1989), 73–74; and Curran, "The 'I' Altered," in *Romanticism and Feminism*, ed. Anne K. Mellor (Bloomington: Indiana University Press, 1988), 185–86.

2. She is certainly not, however, the only example. The early twentieth century saw reprintings of works by Jane Taylor, Agnes Strickland, Anna Letitia Barbauld, Mary Shelley, Maria Edgeworth, Carolina Oliphant (Baroness Nairne), Caroline Norton, Joanna Baillie, Mary Tighe, and others.

3. Jane Austen was said to be of the age of Johnson, Pope, and Swift, never mind her publication dates. Ann Radcliffe was designated a "pre-Romantic," and the Brontës were neatly labeled Victorians. The absence of women Romantics is reflected in books such as William Marshall's *The Major English Romantic Poets: An Anthology* (New York: Washington Square Press, 1966, 1972). It includes only the "five giants of English Romanticism": Byron, Shelley, Keats, Wordsworth, and Coleridge. Similarly, the MLA's fourth edition of *English Romantic Poets: A Review of Research and Criticism*, ed. Frank Jordan (New York: Modern Language Association of America, 1985), features only secondary material concerning the six canonical male poets. Alfred Noyes's *English Romantic Poetry and Prose* (New York: Oxford University Press, 1956), another popular textbook, included only Mary Wollstonecraft and Dorothy Wordsworth; their combined entries constituted only 22 pages of a total of 1,324. David Perkins's monumental 1,255-page anthology *English Romantic Writers* (New York: Harcourt, Brace and World, 1967, rev. ed. 1970), the most successful and influential anthology of the 1970s and 1980s, includes one woman writer, Dorothy Wordsworth, among 30 authors (including Edward John Trelawny, John Clare, and Thomas Hood). Dorothy Wordsworth's headnote and excerpts from her journal take up 6 pages, or about 0.5% of the volume; the excerpts themselves tend to concern the work of her brother and S. T. Coleridge. For an instructive discussion of the changes to the Romantic canon over time, see Harriet Linkin's article, "The Current Canon in British Romantics Studies," *College English* 53 (September 1991): 548–70.

4. Ellen Moers, *Literary Women* (Garden City, N.Y.: Doubleday, 1976). Other significant early works include Sandra Gilbert and Susan Gubar's *Madwoman in the Attic* (New Haven, Conn.: Yale University Press, 1979) and Margaret Homans's *Women Writers and Poetic Identity* (Princeton, N.J.: Princeton Univ. Press, 1980).

5. Other valuable books in these genres have followed. See, for example, J. R. de J. Jackson, *Romantic Poetry by Women* (Oxford: Oxford University Press, 1993); Florence Boos, *Bibliography of Women and Literature*, 2 vols. (New York and London: Holmes & Meier, 1989); Gwenn Davis and Beverly A. Joyce, *Poetry by Women to 1900: A Bibliography of American and British Writers* (Toronto and Buffalo: University of Toronto Press, 1991); R. C. Alston, *A Checklist of Women Writers, 1801–1900: Fiction, Verse, Drama* (Boston: G. K. Hall, 1991); Paul and June Schlueter, *An Encyclopedia of British Women Writers* (New York: Garland, 1988); and Peter Bell, *Regency Women: An Index to Biographies and Memoirs* (Edinburgh: Peter Bell, 1991). Another useful reference work is Anne Crawford et al., eds., *The Europa Biographical Dictionary of British Women: Over 1000 Notable Women from Britain's Past* (Detroit: Gale Research, 1983).

6. Curran's essay appeared in *Romanticism and Feminism* (1988), ed. Anne Mellor (Bloomington: Indiana University Press, 1988), a collection that included other valuable articles. Mellor's *Romanticism and Gender* (New York: Routledge, 1993) contains a provocative discussion of the implications of gender for our understanding of the literature of the period.

7. Some libraries are showcasing their collections in catalogs and on computer disks. For example, see the three-part catalog, Bernard Kreissman, *Minor British Poets: Part One: The Romantic Period, 1789–1839* (Davis: The Library, Univ. of California, Davis, 1983). The Harry Ransom Research Center at the University of Texas at Austin has been distributing on disk a descriptive bibliography, "Manuscript Holdings of Selected Nineteenth-Century Women Writers."

8. See Levinson, "The New Historicism: Back to the Future," in *Rethinking Historicism*, 51–55.

9 The review was of Hemans's *Records of Woman* and *The Forest Sanctuary* in *The Edinburgh Review* L (October 1829): 47. We thank Susan Wolfson for bringing this passage to our attention.

10. Butler, "Repossessing the Past," 82.

11. Robertson's analysis of the usefulness of contorting, ironizing figures in feminist literary history appears in "Deconstructive 'Contortion' and Women's Historical Practice," *Poetics Today* 7 (1986): 712–17. See as well de Certeau, *The Practice of Everyday Life* (Berkeley: University of California Press, 1984), xv–xxiv. Bourdieu construes "habitus" as a powerfully determinist frame that controls what we call cultural innovation. Figural contortion as a mark of agency neither free nor wholly determined is elucidated by Anthony Giddens's critique of Bourdieu, which takes the form of a theory of structuration—a process whereby individuals within a culture may participate in making its structures. See Bourdieu, *Outline of a Theory of Practice*, trans. Richard Nice (Cambridge: Cambridge University Press, 1977), 78; Giddens, "Structuration Theory: Past, Present and Future," in Giddens, *Theory of Structuration*, ed. Christopher G. A. Bryant and David Jary (New York: Routledge, 1991), 207–21. Frederick C. Hoerner brought the Bourdieu-Giddens debate about agency to our attention.

12. A. O. Lovejoy, "On the Discrimination of Romanticisms," in *Romanticism: Points of View*, ed. Robert F. Gleckner and Gerard E. Enscoe (1924; reprint, Englewood Cliffs, N.J.: Prentice-Hall, 1970), 66–81.

The Gush of the Feminine (pp. 13–32)

1. Monica Ellis, *Ice and Icehouses through the Ages* (Southampton, U.K.: Southampton Industrial Archaeology Group, 1982), 2–7, 23–34. Icehouses were mainly the prerogative of the rich. In his *Rural Residences* (London: R. Ackerman, 1818), John Papworth designed a monumental icehouse "calculated for an embellishment to the grounds of a nobleman" (7). Ice was exported not only from Norway to England but as a major industry from America to Europe and even (1805) to Calcutta (23). See also Sylvia P. Beamon and Susan Roajof, *The Ice-Houses of Britain* (London: Routledge, 1990).

2. William Michael Rossetti, ed., *The Poetical Works of Mrs Hemans* (London: Ward, Lock and Co., 1873), xvii.

3. Mary Wollstonecraft, *Vindication of the Rights of Woman* (1792), ed. Miriam Kramnick (Harmondsworth, U.K.: Pengruin Books, 1975), 143.

4. Anna Letitia Barbauld's *Eighteen Hundred and Eleven: A Poem* (London: J. Johnson, 1812) was reviewed in *Quarterly Review* (June 1812): 309–13. The *Dictionary of National Biography* lists Robert Southey as author, but John Wilson Croker is named in the checklist in *The Quarterly Review Under Gifford, 1809–24*, ed. Hill Chadwick and Here Shins (Chapel Hill: University of North Carolina Press, 1949), 31.

5. Edmund Burke, *A Philosophical Enquiry into the Origin of Our Ideas of the Sublime and Beautiful* (1757), ed. J. T. Boulton (Notre Dame: University of Notre Dame Press, 1958), pt. 3, sec. 9, p. 110 (on "weakness and imperfection" as the cause of beauty); see also pt. 3, sec. 16, "Delicacy," p. 116.

6. Ibid., pt. 1, sec. 17, p. 50.

7. *The Poems of James Thomson*, Oxford Standard Authors, ed. J. Logie Robertson (London and New York, 1908), 239–44. See Robert Inglesfield, "James Thomson, Aaron Hill and the Poetic 'Sublime,'" *British Journal for Eighteenth-Century Studies* 8 (autumn 1990): 217–21.

8. Thomas Malthus, *An Essay on the Principle of Population* (1798), ed. Antony Flew (Harmondsworth, U.K.: Penguin Books, 1970). No "human ingenuity" (101) could relieve the distress of the poor, but Malthus made it clear that the poor *were* oppressed: "The parish persecution of men whose families are likely to become chargeable, and of poor women who are near lying-in" (100) was disgraceful but an inevitable consequence of the poor laws, which encouraged the increase of population without allowing for support. Malthus's triple purpose, to argue that inequality consequent on population increase was inevitable, to attack the poor law in favor of the market, and to satirize the rational belief in equality put forward by William Godwin in *Political Justice* (1793), continually exposed not only the plight of women but the fundamental drives of sexuality. "But towards the extinction of the passion between the sexes, no observable progress whatever has hitherto been made" (148), he wrote ironically.

His views were predicated on the inevitability of women's overproduction of children and on the recognition that while men could evade paternity, women never could disclaim the birth of a child issuing from their own bodies. "The offence is besides more obvious and conspicuous in the woman, and less liable to any mistake" (142).

9. "Dialogue in the Shades," in Anna Letitia Barbauld, *Works*, 2 vols. (London: Longman, Hurst, Rees, Orme, Brown and Green, 1825), 1:339–49.

10. Adam Smith, *An Enquiry into the Nature and Causes of the Wealth of Nations*, 3 vols. (London: J. Strahan and T. Cadell, 1784), bk. 2, ch. 1, 2:1–7. For a discussion of women's education and that of operatives, see bk. 5, ch. 1, 3:180–87.

11. See Smith's notorious analysis of the making of a pin as an example of the division of labor: "and the important business of the making of a pin is, in this manner, divided into about eighteen distinct operations." *Wealth*, bk. 1, ch. 1, 1:16–19. Smith also tackled the problem of the dullness of the mechanized consciousness, suggesting that minimal education such as that given to women be extended to workmen to assuage the atrophy created by repetitive labour, bk. 5, ch. 1, 3:181–185.

12. W. F. Bynum, "The Nervous Patient in 18th and 19th-Century Britain: The Psychiatric Origins of British Neurology," in *The Anatomy of Madness*, 2 vols., ed. W. F. Bynum et al. (London and New York: Tavistock Publications, 1985), 1:90, 95. Nervous diseases tended to be seen functionally rather than structurally, and thus any malfunction involving spasm became classified as a nervous disease, a classification shaped by social and ideological assumptions.

13. Letitia Landon, *Poetical Works*, ed. William B. Scott (London: George Routledge and Sons, n.d.), 378–80.

14. John Cooke, *A Treatise on Nervous Diseases*, 2 vols. (London: Longman, Hurst, Rees, Orme and Brown, 1820), 1:104. For the theory of vibration, see 1:115: "sensation and motion are referred to vibrations in the brain and nerves, either directly or by means of an elastic aether." J. C. Prichard, *A Treatise on Diseases of the Nervous System* (London: Underwood, 1822) speculated that the body/mind relation was so close that the effect of forms of life on the senses, such as hard labor, is the cause of revolution (pp. 337–40).

15. William Wordsworth, "Lines Composed a Few Miles Above Tintern Abbey," in *Poetical Works*, ed. Thomas Hutchinson, rev. ed. Ernest de Selincourt (London and New York: Oxford University Press, 1936), 165.

16. David Hume, *A Treatise of Human Nature*, (1739), ed. L. A. Selby-Bigge, 2d ed. rev. (Oxford: Clarendon Press, 1951).

17. David Hume, *An Enquiry Concerning Human Understanding* ed. L. A. Selby-Bigge, 3rd ed. rev. P. H. Nidditch (Oxford: Clarendon Press, 1975), 152, 153. For cause and effect, see Hume, *Treatise*, bk. 1, pt. 3, sec. i–xvi.

Gendering the Soul (pp. 33–68)

1. My epigraphs are from *The Tatler* 172 (16 May 1710), in *The Tatler; or Lucubrations of Isaac Bickerstaff, Esq.*, 4 vols. (London: J. and R. Tonson et al., 1764), 3:247; *Biographium Fæmineum. The Female Worthies: or, Memoirs of the*

Most Illustrious Ladies of all Ages and Nations . . . who have shone with a particular Lustre, and given the noblest Proofs of the most exalted Genius, 2 vols. (London: S. Crowder et al., 1766), 1:vii; Mary Wollstonecraft, *A Vindication of the Rights of Woman,* ed. Carol H. Poston, 2nd ed. (New York: Norton, 1988), 35, 60 (cited hereafter parenthetically); *The Notebooks of Samuel Taylor Coleridge,* ed. Kathleen Coburn, 3 vols. (Princeton, N.J.: Princeton/Bollingen, 1973), 3:3531, cited hereafter parenthetically; Samuel Taylor Coleridge, *Satyrane's Letters: Letter II (To a Lady), The Friend,* no. 16 (7 December 1809), in *The Friend,* ed. Barbara E. Rooke, 2 vols. (Princeton, N.J.: Princeton University Press, 1969), 2:209.

2. For a good survey of Coleridge's idealizing poetics of androgyny, see Jean Watson's essay, "Coleridge's Androgynous Ideal," *Prose Studies* 6 (1983): 36–56. His speculation about androgyny is in *Table Talk,* 1 September and 17 March 1832, in *Table Talk* (recorded by Henry Nelson Coleridge and John Taylor Coleridge), ed. Carl Woodring, 2 vols. (Princeton, N.J.: Princeton University Press, 1990), 2:190, 2:158. Sketching her own "plan of the soul," Woolf recalls Coleridge's speculation, aware that he did not mean that the androgynous mind was one "that has any special sympathy with women" or "takes up their cause or devotes itself to their interpretation." Even so, she follows Coleridge in asking "whether there are two sexes in the mind corresponding to the two sexes in the body, and whether they also require to be united in order to get complete satisfaction and happiness . . . in harmony, spiritually cooperating. If one is a man, still the woman part of the brain must have effect; and a woman must also have intercourse with the man in her" (*A Room of One's Own* [1929; reprint, New York: Harcourt, Brace, 1957], 102). For an example of Coleridge's antipathy to actual female encroachments on male preserves, see his dismay at a contemporary instance of female political power: "I never dared figure the Russian Sovereign to my imagination under the dear and venerable Character of WOMAN — WOMAN, that complex term for Mother, Sister, Wife!" Against this grid of archetypal, domestic relations, a woman of political authority appears only as an "evil Principle impersonated" (manuscript note to "Ode to the Departing Year" in *The Poems of Samuel Taylor Coleridge,* ed. Ernest Hartley Coleridge [1912; reprint, London: Oxford University Press, 1960], 162).

3. See, for example, the first chapter of Margaret Homans's *Women Writers and Poetic Identity* (Princeton, N.J.: Princeton University Press, 1980); Irene Taylor and Gina Luria, "Gender and Genre: Women in British Romantic Literature," in *What Manner of Woman: Essays on English and American Life and Literature,* ed. Marlene Springer (New York: New York University Press, 1977), esp. 113–15; Alan Richardson, "Romanticism and the Colonization of the Feminine," in *Romanticism and Feminism,* ed. Anne K. Mellor (Bloomington: Indiana University Press, 1988), 13–25; the first chapter of Marlon Ross's *The Contours of Masculine Desire: Romanticism and the Rise of Women's Poetry* (New York and Oxford: Oxford University Press, 1989); and Anne K. Mellor, *Romanticism and Gender* (New York and London: Routledge, 1993).

4. 12 March 1811; *Collected Letters of Samuel Taylor Coleridge,* ed. Earl Leslie Griggs, 6 vols. (Oxford: Clarendon Press, 1956–71), 3:305; cited hereafter parenthetically.

5. It is Coleridge, moreover, who helped develop a vocabulary for this effect, proposing, for example, that there is "something feminine—not *effeminate,*

mind—discoverable in the countenances of all men of genius" (*Table Talk*, 17 March 1832 [2:158]). Recollections of Keats make extended use of Coleridge's distinction. See Benjamin Bailey, *The Keats Circle*, ed. Hyder E. Rollins, 2 vols. (Cambridge, Mass.: Harvard University Press, 1948), 2:268; Mrs. Procter (ibid., 2:158, and in Richard Monckton Milnes's *Life, Letters, and Literary Remains, of John Keats*, 2 vols. [London: Edward Moxon, 1848], 1:103–4); and Frances Mary Owen, *John Keats: A Study* (London: C. Kegan Paul, 1880), 8. See also my "Feminizing Keats," in *Critical Essays on John Keats*, ed. Hermione de Almeida (Boston: G. K. Hall, 1990), 317–56.

6. Coleridge, *Biographia Literaria, or Biographical Sketches of My Literary Life and Opinions* (1817), ed. James Engell and W. Jackson Bate, 2 vols. (Princeton, N.J.: Princeton University Press, 1983), 2:16–17; cited hereafter parenthetically.

7. Bate and Engell identify these lines from Sir John Davies's *Nosce Teipsum: Of the Soule of Man and the Immortalitie Thereof* (1599), 4, sts. 11–13, and provide the correct text.

8. Thus, Homans argues that only women's poetry is pressured by a sensation of the "apparent otherness of [the] mind's powers," the "alien centers of imaginative power," a dislocation in which "the sources of poetic power are not to be felt within the self" (*Women Writers*, 104).

9. Quotations follow *William Wordsworth: The Poems*, ed. John O. Hayden, 2 vols. (Middlesex, U.K.: Penguin, 1977).

10. Quotations of *The Prelude*, here and hereafter, follow *The Thirteen-Book "Prelude,"* ed. Mark L. Reed, 2 vols. (Ithaca, N.Y.: Cornell University Press, 1991): unless otherwise indicated, all references are to the collation of the 1805 manuscripts, "A-B Stage Reading Text" (1:107–324) and are cited parenthetically by book and line numbers.

11. Quotations of the 14-book *Prelude* follow *The Fourteen-Book "Prelude,"* ed. W. J. B. Owen (Ithaca, N.Y.: Cornell University Press, 1985); Owen uses manuscript D instead of the 1850 publication as the base text.

12. Quotations follow *Paradise Lost*, ed. Merritt Y. Hughes (1962; reprint, New York: Macmillan, 1985) and are cited parenthetically by book and line number.

13. Although *Paradise Lost* articulates the paradigm of masculine "Reason" that foregrounds Wordsworthian instabilities, it also complicates this paradigm with ambivalences that forecast Wordsworthian dilemmas. Wordsworth's notice of one such site appears in the summary argument of *The Prelude* ("hence . . . endless occupation for the soul, / Whether discursive or intuitive: [13:111–13]) by its echo of Raphael's instruction of Adam in terms that idealize a feminine, or perhaps androgynous, presence within: "the Soul / Reason receives, and reason is her being, / Discursive, or Intuitive" (5:486–88).

14. Lawrence Kramer discerns some of the same elements but in a different perspective: he sees the potential creative power of "the Wordsworthian mother, including maternal nature," as ultimately isolated from "the gendered sexuality" of Wordsworth's adulthood, whose language "reserves—or alienates—such creative agency to the male, both in his cultural and his sexual roles" ("Gender and Sexuality in *The Prelude*: The Question of Book Seven," *ELH* 54 [1987]: 635).

15. See Jonathan Culler's influential essay, "Apostrophe," in his book *The Pursuit of Signs: Semiotics, Literature, Deconstruction* (Ithaca, N.Y.: Cornell

University Press, 1981), 135–54. Mellor's *Romanticism and Gender* takes moments such as this as the ones most truly representative of the poem's politics of gender, claiming for Wordsworth a "surpassing confidence [in] the construction of an autonomous poetic self that can stand alone" (148) precisely because it has dominated or effaced the feminine (18, 144–53).

16. Unless otherwise indicated, quotations of Percy Bysshe Shelley follow *Shelley's Poetry and Prose*, ed. Donald H. Reiman and Sharon B. Powers (New York: Norton, 1977), cited hereafter by line number and as *SPP* when page numbers are given.

17. The fullest study of the ambiguous place of the feminine in these homosocial dynamics is Eve Kosofsky Sedgwick's *Between Men: English Literature and Male Homosocial Desire* (New York: Columbia University Press, 1985); see especially the chapter on Shakespeare's sonnets (28–48).

18. Quotations follow vol. 2 of *The Poetical Works of William Wordsworth*, ed. E. de Selincourt and Helen Darbishire (Oxford: Clarendon Press, 1947). The epigraph appears for the first time in the text of *Poems* of 1815, the year Shelley was composing *Alastor*. For a sharp reading of these attenuations in the language of the epigraph and their consequences for the "Ode," see Frances Ferguson, *Wordsworth: Language as Counter-Spirit* (New Haven, Conn.: Yale University Press, 1977), 98–101. For an incisive account of the involvement of *Alastor* with the "Ode," see William Keach, "Obstinate Questionings: *The Immortality Ode* and *Alastor*," *The Wordsworth Circle* 12 (1981): 36–44.

19. In the 1950s, Roland Barthes described the gendering of the gaze (*Mythologies* [1957], trans. Annette Lavers [1972; reprint, New York: Hill and Wang, 1986], 51); Laura Mulvey's influential essays have elaborated this dynamic in film (*Visual and Other Pleasures* [London: Macmillan, 1989] and "Visual Pleasure and Narrative Cinema," *Screen* 16.3 [1975]: 6–18).

20. Quotation follows *The Complete Works of Percy Bysshe Shelley*, ed. Neville Rogers, 4 vols. (Oxford: Clarendon Press, 1975). Mary Shelley's note in her edition describes this poem as "a good deal modelled on *Alastor*"—with the stark difference that its story makes explicit the betrayal of the poet's soul by female agency (Mrs. Shelley [Mary Wollstonecraft Shelley], ed., *The Poetical Works of Percy Bysshe Shelley* [London, 1840; reprint, *The Complete Poems of Keats and Shelley with Mrs. Shelley's Notes* [New York: Modern Library, n.d.], 176). Earl K. Wasserman applies these lines as well as the essay "On Love" to the "Visionary's dream lady" in *Alastor* (*Shelley: A Critical Reading* [Baltimore: Johns Hopkins University Press, 1971], 22–23); his discussion is not concerned with sexual difference or the politics of gender, but his terms reflect the issue: "The lady . . . is not to be understood as a spirit distinct from the Visionary . . . but as the union of all that he yearns for in his intellect, his imagination. . . . she is created out of the desire of his total nature." For him, the chief problem has to do with the way a "visionary fulfillment" of the soul guarantees a "pervasive vacancy" in the aftermath of its worldly existence (25).

21. For various interpretations of the root, prefix, and suffix of Shelley's title, see Wasserman, *Shelley*, 418–19.

22 The eagle-poet is further feminized, William Veeder proposes, by the penetrating snake, "the now phallic beloved" (*Mary Shelley and "Frankenstein": The Fate of Androgyny* [Chicago: University of Chicago Press, 1986], 94–95).

23. See Wasserman's discussion of how implicit tensions in the tenuous ideal-

ism of "Necessity" within which Shelley develops *Queen Mab* yield a set of poems in the *Alastor* volume of 1816 that are obsessed with "the theme of man's transience and nature's inconstancy" (*Shelley*, 5).

24. I owe the description of this dyad to Tilottama Rajan, although she is not concerned with gender (*Dark Interpreter: The Discourse of Romanticism* [Ithaca, N.Y.: Cornell University Press, 1980], 76).

25. Quotations here and hereafter follow *The Poems of John Keats*, ed. Jack Stillinger (Cambridge, Mass.: Harvard University Press, 1978).

26. *Keats and His Poetry: A Study in Development* (Chicago: University of Chicago Press, 1971), 199.

27. *Keats's Life of Allegory: The Origins of a Style* (London: Basil Blackwell, 1988), 27.

28. *The Letters of John Keats, 1814–1821*, ed. Hyder E. Rollins, 2 vols. (Cambridge, Mass.: Harvard University Press, 1958), 1:281; cited hereafter parenthetically as *LJK*.

29. Theresa M. Kelley focuses on how the factitiousness of figures like Keats's La Belle Dame signals an allegorical otherness ("Poetics and the Politics of Reception: Keats's 'La Belle Dame sans Merci,'" *ELH* 54 [1987], 333); my sense is that the female gendering is another, perhaps primary sign of otherness.

30. Thus, I think Marlon Ross's discussion only half right in its thesis that Keats, in his "'mature' poetry . . . is forced to contain or crystallize the feminine as a sign of his manhood, as evidence of his self-control" (*Contours*, 73).

31. This is John Wilson, after 1820 professor of philosophy at Edinburgh University and as "Christopher North," a regular contributor to *Blackwood's Edinburgh Magazine*. Quotations of Jewsbury's "History" follow "The History of an Enthusiast" in *The Three Histories. The History of an Enthusiast. The History of a Nonchalant. The History of a Realist.* (1830; Boston: Perkins & Marvin, 1831).

32. As Marlon Ross remarks, she has no function in the poem separate from Prometheus's fate: "Asia acts in his behalf since he is bound. . . . She serves as an extension of him" (*Contours*, 144).

33. These lines do not appear in the 1816 publication, *The Restoration of the Works of Art to Italy: A Poem. By a Lady* (Oxford: W. Baxter, 1816); they are part of some dozen stanzas added to a second edition of 1816, published by John Murray. I follow *The Poetical Works of Mrs. F[elicia]. Hemans* (London and Edinburgh: Gall and Inglis, 1876).

34. This severing (and implicit concession to the cultural contraction) of domestic romance from female spiritual quest at the conclusion of Jewsbury's *History* is one of the ideologically fraught narrative patterns of nineteenth-century women's fiction, according to Rachel Blau DuPlessis (*Writing beyond the Ending: Narrative Strategies of Twentieth-Century Women Writers* [Bloomington: Indiana University Press, 1985], 1–19). The removal of Julia to Europe predicts the "critical dissent from the dominant narrative" that DuPlessis sees as an emergent strategy of twentieth-century women's writing (5).

35. Jewsbury would have known the anecdote of the apple tree from Hemans herself. It became a staple in memoirs. See Henry F. Chorley, *Memorials of Mrs. Hemans, with Illustrations of Her Literary Character from Her Private Correspondence*, 2 vols. (London: Saunders and Otley, 1836), 1:17–18 (cited hereafter as "Chorley"); and Harriett Mary [Browne] Hughes (later Owen), *Memoir of the*

Life and Writings of Felicia Hemans: By Her Sister; with an Essay on Her Genius: By Mrs. Sigourney (New York: C. S. Francis/Boston: J. H. Francis, 1845), 34; this memoir was first published as vol. 1 of *The Works of Mrs. Hemans*, 6 vols. (London: Thomas Cadell; Edinburgh: William Blackwood & Sons, 1839).

36. *Edinburgh Review* 50 (October 1829): 37.

37. *The Letters of Elizabeth Barrett Browning to Mary Russell Mitford 1836–1854*, ed. Meredith B. Raymond and Mary Rose Sullivan, 3 vols. (Winfield, Kans.: Wedgestone Press, 1983), 2:88.

38. *Poetical Works* (Gall and Inglis), 574. For other examples, see *The Poetical Works of Mrs. Hemans* (London: Frederick Warne, n.d. [c. 1889]): "A Thought of the Sea" ("my soul's dream, which through all nature sought . . . some bower of *steadfast* bliss, . . . Now turns from earth's green valleys . . . to that sole changeless world" [p. 651, her italics]); "Distant Sound of the Sea" ("the soul hears [in its] distant voice profound" a tone that "[s]peaks to our being of the Eternal One" [651]); "The Return to Poetry" (hearing "eternal melodies from far," "Thither my soul, fresh-winged by love, is turning" [655]); "Intellectual Powers" ("Subdue the soul to lowliness profound, / Guiding its chastened vision to discern / How by meek Faith heaven's portals must be passed" [658]); and "Sickness Like Night," in which the poet welcomes sickness in the extreme imagination of its spiritual agency, as the rod of a prophet "[b]efore whose touch my soul unfolds itself to God" (658). Almost all of these poems express a strong elegiac affection for the life that Hemans feels slipping away. In a late sonnet, "On Retzsch's Design of the Angel of Death," she confesses this affection to the Angel of Death itself: "the chords of strong affection twine / So fast around my soul, it *cannot* spring to thee!" (658).

39. Felicia Dorothea Browne, *The Domestic Affections and Other Poems* (London: T. Cadell and W. Davies, 1812); cited by *DA* and page number.

40. Quotations follow *Poetical Works* (Gall and Inglis), 478–79.

41. Hemans, *Records of Women: With Other Poems* (Edinburgh: William Blackwood, London: T. Cadell, 1828), 83–96; references are to page numbers.

42. Jewsbury, *Phantasmagoria; Or, Sketches of Life and Literature*, 2 vols. (London: Hurst, Robinson/Edinburgh: Archibald Constable, 1825), 1:122–24.

43. Burke, *Reflections on the Revolution in France, 1790*; in *Two Classics of the French Revolution* (New York: Anchor/Doubleday, 1973/1989), 88–89.

44. For an interesting survey of Romantic alignments of "gender and genius," see Christine Battersby, *Gender and Genius: Towards a Feminist Aesthetics* (Bloomington: Indiana University Press, 1989), 13, 35–38, 46–47, also chaps. 8 and 10.

45. My text follows Warne's *Poetical Works* (656–57).

46. This is Angela Leighton's evaluation (*Victorian Women Poets: Writing against the Heart* [New York and London: Harvester/Wheatsheaf, 1922]), though our views are more congruent in her sense that Hemans's "verse achieves another kind of originality in the persistent and ostentatious gendering" of these recognizable voices (21).

47. *The Letters of Mary Wollstonecraft Shelley*, ed. Betty T. Bennett, 3 vols. (Baltimore: Johns Hopkins University Press, 1980–88), 2:246. Thanks to Theresa Kelley and Stephen Behrendt for calling this letter to my attention.

48. *Lélia* was published in 1833 and reviewed in *The Athenæum* 309 (28 September 1833): 646–47; its last sentence is worth quoting in full: "We shall not

again dip our pen in this mire of blood and dirt, over which, by a strange perversity of feeling, the talent of the writer, and that writer a woman! has contrived to throw a lurid, fearful and unhallowed light" (647). I am indebted to Leighton (*Victorian Women Poets*, 81) for alerting me to this review.

49. *The Brownings' Correspondence*, ed. Phillip Kelley and Ronald Hudson, 10 vols. (Winfield, Kans.: Wedgestone Press, 1984–92), 1:361; the editors of this untitled essay date its composition in the early 1840s and discern Elizabeth Barrett in the portrait of Beth.

50. For their valuable attention to this essay, my thanks to Ronald Levao, Theresa Kelley, Esther Schor, and Peter Manning.

Mary Shelley (pp. 69–87)

1. See Mary Jacobus, *Reading Woman: Essays in Feminist Criticism* (New York: Columbia University Press, 1986), 28.

2. Ellen Moers, *Literary Women: The Great Writers* (1963; reprint, New York: Oxford University Press, 1985), 126.

3. 5 January 1828, *The Letters of Mary Wollstonecraft Shelley*, ed. Betty T. Bennett, 3 vols. (Baltimore and London: Johns Hopkins University Press, 1983), 2:22.

4. Barbara Johnson, "My Monster / My Self," *Diacritics* 12 (1982): 2–10; Anne K. Mellor, *Mary Shelley: Her Life, Her Fiction, Her Monsters* (New York and London: Methuen, 1988).

5. Moers, *Literary Women*, 163; Virginia Woolf, "Dorothy Osborne's 'Letters,'" in *The Second Common Reader*, ed. Andrew McNeillie (San Diego, Calif.: Harcourt Brace Jovanovich, 1986), 59–70.

6. Deborah Cameron, *Feminism and Linguistic Theory* (New York: St. Martin's, 1985), 161. Mellor writes that "that unique phenomenon envisioned by Mary Wollstonecraft, the wife as the lifelong intellectual equal and companion of her husband, does not exist in the world of nineteenth-century Europe experienced by Mary Shelley" ("Possessing Nature: The Female in *Frankenstein*," in *Romanticism and Feminism*, ed. Anne K. Mellor [Bloomington: Indiana University Press, 1988], 223).

7. Shelley to Frances Wright [Darusmont], 12 September 1827, and to Maria Gisborne, 11 June 1835, *Letters* 2:4, 246.

8. *The Letters of William and Dorothy Wordsworth*, ed. Ernest de Selincourt et al., 2nd ed., 6 vols. (Oxford: Clarendon Press, 1967–93), vol. 1, no. 239.

9. John Stuart Mill, *The Subjection of Women*, ed. Sue Mansfield (Arlington Heights, Ill.: AHM Publishing, 1980), 15. Mill's essay was written in 1861 and published in 1869.

10. See Mary Poovey, *The Proper Lady and the Woman Writer: Ideology as Style in the Works of Mary Wollstonecraft, Mary Shelley, and Jane Austen* (Chicago: University of Chicago Press, 1984); and Mellor, *Mary Shelley*, 56.

11. Percy Bysshe Shelley's review may have been intended for Leigh Hunt's *Examiner*. It did not appear until Thomas Medwin published it in *The Atheneum* in 1832.

12. See Mellor, *Mary Shelley*, 22–23, and Emily W. Sunstein, *Mary Shelley:*

Romance and Reality (Boston, Toronto and London: Little, Brown, 1989), 85–86.

13. Stuart Curran, Gaye Tuchman, and Marlon Ross have most notably reminded us of women's significant presence in the literary milieu. See Stuart Curran, *Poetic Form and British Romanticism* (New York: Oxford University Press, 1986); Gaye Tuchman, with Nina E. Fortin, *Edging Women Out: Victorian Novelists, Publishers, and Social Change* (New Haven, Conn.: Yale University Press, 1989); Marlon Ross, *The Contours of Masculine Desire: Romanticism and the Rise of Women's Poetry* (New York: Oxford University Press, 1989). See too Cheryl Turner, *Living by the Pen: Women Writers in the Eighteenth Century* (London: Routledge, 1992).

14. Quoted in Rupert Christiansen, *Romantic Affinities: Portraits from an Age, 1780–1830* (London: Cardinal, 1988), 102.

15. This volume, which is readily available in a facsimile edited by Marilyn Williamson (Detroit: Wayne State University Press, 1981), typifies the woman writer's treatment by the (male) Victorian anthologizer. Parenthetical page citations in this portion of my discussion refer to this facsimile.

16. Mrs. Henry [Mary] Tighe, *Psyche, with Other Poems*, 5th ed. (London: Longman, 1816), iii–iv.

17. Margaret Visser, *The Rituals of Dinner: The Origins, Evolution, Eccentricities, and Meaning of Table Manners* (New York: Grove Weidenfeld, 1991), 273.

18 Shelley to John Murray III, 8 September 1830, *Letters*, 2:115.

19. *Women Romantic Poets, 1785–1832: An Anthology*, ed. Jennifer Breen (London: J. M. Dent, 1992), xix.

20. This is, in fact, the picture often painted of Mary Shelley: "Mary was never a woman of action. Her pursuits were intellectual, her pleasure domestic" (Jane Dunn, *Moon in Eclipse: A Life of Mary Shelley* [London: Weidenfeld and Nicolson, 1978], 278).

21. Stuart Curran, "Romantic Poetry: The 'I' Altered," in *Romanticism and Feminism*, ed. Anne K. Mellor (Bloomington: Indiana University Press, 1988), 189.

22. As Betty T. Bennett's three volumes of Shelley's letters amply demonstrate, she was an avid letter writer, and the style of those letters is richly interactive, inviting a variety of kinds of response from her correspondents. Even in letters from the years immediately following Percy Bysshe Shelley's death, letters in which postured self-pity mingles with spontaneous expressions of genuine misery, the correspondent is never shut off from *communication* or from what Shelley clearly structures as an ongoing dialogue.

23. [Mary Tighe], *Psyche, or the Legend of Love* (London, privately printed, 1805), ii.

24. "Preface," in *The Poetical Works of the Late Mrs. Mary Robinson*, 3 vols. (London: Jones and Company, 1824), 1:4.

25. Susan J. Wolfson, "Individual in Community: Dorothy Wordsworth in Conversation with William," in Mellor, *Romanticism and Feminism*, 162.

26. The painful ambivalences about ambition, ability, and gender-related expectations that surface so frequently in what Dorothy Wordsworth's writings tell us about herself, her situation, and the life she led have at last been addressed in a number of sympathetic revisionist studies. See esp. Wolfson, "Individual in

Community," Margaret Homans, *Women Writers and Poetic Identity: Dorothy Wordsworth, Emily Bronte, and Emily Dickinson* (Princeton, N.J.: Princeton University Press, 1980); and Susan M. Levin, *Dorothy Wordsworth and Romanticism* (New Brunswick, N.J.: Rutgers University Press, 1987).

27. Shelley to Edward J. Trelawny, 1 April 1829, *Letters*, 2:72.

28. Shelley to John Murray III, 10 February 1835, *Letters*, 2:223.

29. Sandra M. Gilbert and Susan Gubar, *The Madwoman in the Attic: The Woman Writer and the Nineteenth-Century Literary Imagination* (New Haven, Conn., and London: Yale University Press, 1979), 49–50.

30. Sonia Hofkosh, "The Writer's Ravishment: Women and the Romantic Author—the Example of Byron," in Mellor, *Romanticism and Feminism* 94.

31. Mellor, "Possessing Nature," 129, and *Mary Shelley*, 169, 215.

32. Mary Shelley [with James Montgomery], *Lives of the Most Eminent Literary and Scientific Men of Italy, Spain, and Portugal*, 3 vols. (London: Longman, 1835), 2:351.

33. Shelley, December 1834, *The Journals of Mary Shelley: 1814–1844*, ed. Paula R. Feldman and Diana Scott-Kilvert, 2 vols. (Oxford: Clarendon Press, 1987), 2:543.

34. Annette Kolodny, "Dancing through the Minefield: Some Observations on the Theory, Practice, and Politics of a Feminist Literary Criticism," in *The New Feminist Criticism: Essays on Women, Literature, and Theory*, ed. Elaine Showalter (New York: Pantheon Books, 1985), 162.

35. Shelley to E. J. Trelawny, 27 July 1829, *Letters*, 2:82.

36. Shelley, 30 January 1825, *Journals*, 2:489.

De-Romanticizing the Subject (pp. 88–110)

I wish to thank the American Philosophical Society, the American Council of Learned Societies, and the John Simon Guggenheim Memorial Foundation for their generous support of my research.

1. The remarkable recent upsurge of critical interest in storying takes a variety of cross-disciplinary forms, but most theorists agree that people make narratives to make sense of the world—and themselves. My thinking about what people, especially children, are doing when they write self-referentially is informed by *Narratives from the Crib*, ed. Katherine Nelson (Cambridge, Mass.: Harvard University Press, 1989), and by Jerome Bruner's many studies, in particular, *Actual Minds, Possible Worlds* (Cambridge, Mass.: Harvard University Press, 1986). For a psycholanalytical study of female desire that uses some stories for girls, see Jean Wyatt's *Reconstructing Desire: The Role of the Unconscious in Women's Reading and Writing* (Chapel Hill: University of North Carolina Press, 1990). The postmodern interest in narrative's function and possibilities as a basic form of organizing subjectivity is elucidated in Donald E. Polkinghorne's *Narrative Knowing and the Human Sciences* (Albany: State University of New York Press, 1988) and *Narrative in Culture: The Uses of Storytelling in the Sciences, Philosophy, and Literature*, ed. Cristopher Nash (London and New York: Routledge, 1990).

2. Edgeworth herself was touched by Scott's tribute to her in *Waverley*; he

was the big literary hero of her later life. Her letters are tart about Wordworth's egotism and preachiness; neither she nor other contemporary readers mythologized him as the founder of childhood as later literary historians came to do. Freud's paper on "Family Romances" (in *Collected Papers*, ed. James Strachey [London: Hogarth P and the Institute of Psycho-Analysis, 1950], 5:74–78) doesn't concern incestuous family relations (as some casual references seem to suppose); it is instead an attempt to explain how the child's feelings of not being loved enough generate hero myths. Replacing the real father by a fantasized superior parent whose affection need not be shared with the brothers and sisters of everyday life, the slighted "orphan" corrects and idealizes actual life. One doesn't need to be a Freudian to find the formulation provocative for juvenile storying (as in the interpretation that follows) or adult canon creation (as in the literary institutionalization of Wordsworth as Romantic hero).

3. See especially chapters 8, 16, and 17 of *Memoirs of Richard Lovell Edgeworth, Esq.: Begun by Himself and Concluded by His Daughter, Maria Edgeworth*, 2 vols. (London: R. Hunter and Baldwin, Cradock, and Joy, 1820), in which Edgeworth converts the very grown-up young lady of her letters in the 1780s, fresh from seven years of boarding school and fourteen when she returned to Ireland, into the pupil, "almost a child," who had always lived with her father.

4. Jane Austen's aesthetic stock rose to its current height long after her death; like the canonical construction of Romanticism itself, her reputation is largely a modern phenomenon. Madame de Staël, Edgeworth's real rival, is just now beginning to receive the critical attention she deserves. For the twentieth-century emergence of "Romanticism," see David Perkins, "The Construction of 'The Romantic Movement' as a Literary Classification," *Nineteenth-Century Literature* 45.2 (1990): 129–43.

5. See U. C. Knoepflmacher's many essays on nineteenth-century child-adult relationships, especially "The Balancing of Child and Adult: An Approach to Victorian Fantasies," *Nineteenth-Century Fiction* 37.4 (1983): 497–530; "Little Girls without Their Curls: Female Aggression in Victorian Children's Literature," in *Children's Literature*, ed. Francelia Butler (New Haven, Conn., and London: Yale University Press, 1983), 11:14–31; "Mutations of the Wordsworthian Child of Nature," in *Nature and the Victorian Imagination*, ed. U. C. Knoepflmacher and G. B. Tennyson (Berkeley: University of California Press, 1977): 391–425; and "Thoughts on the Aggression of Daughters," in *The Endurance of Frankenstein: Essays on Mary Shelley's Novel*, ed. George Levine and U. C. Knoepflmacher (Berkeley: University of California Press, 1979): 88–119. Most rehabilitation of women's juvenile writing so far focuses on Victorian fantasies, rather than the earlier "realistic" modes I consider, though both traditions abound in strong, resolute little girls and are more narratively sophisticated than they're usually given credit for; Nina Auerbach and U. C. Knoepflmacher's anthology, *Forbidden Journeys: Fairy Tales and Fantasies by Victorian Writers* (Chicago: University of Chicago Press, 1992) situates a sampling of subversive fantasies within a revisionist framework. Recent work demonstrating the complexities of historical juvenile literature includes Sarah Gilead's "Magic Abjured: Closure in Children's Fantasy Fiction," *PMLA*, 106.2 (1991): 277–93, and some essays in *Romanticism and Children's Literature in Nineteenth-Century England*, ed. James Holt McGavran, Jr. (Athens: University of Georgia Press, 1991). Literary histories of children's literature too numerous to cite follow the orthodox Romantic line; for intelligent

recent restatements, see Judith Plotz, "The Perpetual Messiah: Romanticism, Childhood, and the Paradoxes of Human Development," in *Regulated Children/Liberated Children: Education in Psychohistorical Perspective*, ed. Barbara Finkelstein (New York: Psychohistory Press, 1979): 63–95; and Alan Richardson's "Childhood and Romanticism," in *Teaching Children's Literature: Issues, Pedagogy, Resources*, ed. Glenn Edward Sadler (New York: Modern Language Association, 1992): 121–30. For a response to Richardson's emphasis on masculine childhood, see my essay in the same volume, "Little Girls Lost: Rewriting Romantic Childhood, Righting Gender and Genre."

6. Dorothy Wordsworth is perhaps also a contender. Not a public literary figure in her own day, she is enjoying a vogue in ours. It's not surprising that women affiliated with major male writers grab attention first.

7. Alan Richardson's work exemplifies this pattern. In "Romanticism and the Colonization of the Feminine," in *Romanticism and Feminism*, ed. Anne K. Mellor (Bloomington: Indiana University Press, 1988): 13–25, he speaks as a feminist critic against the appropriation of the feminine in masculine Romantic texts, but "The Politics of Childhood: Wordsworth, Blake, and Catechistic Method," *ELH* 56.4 (1989): 853–68, exemplifies the critic's own reenactment of the colonizing move he critiques; women writers for children here figure as the deficient backdrop for a discussion of major male poets.

8. *Romanticism and Feminism*, ed. Anne K. Mellor (Bloomington and Indianapolis: Indiana University Press, 1988), a pioneering and much-cited anthology that attempts to count women in, is usefully reviewed by Patricia Yaeger, who celebrates the collection's strengths but also points out that the "and" works to tack women onto a Romantic canon already in place, rather than reinventing Romanticism itself (*Studies in Romanticism* 30.3 [Fall 1991]: 499–503). Mellor's "Why Women Didn't Like Romanticism: The Views of Jane Austen and Mary Shelley," in *The Romantics and Us: Essays on Literature and Culture*, ed. Gene Ruoff (New Brunswick, N.J.: Rutgers University Press, 1990), implies that women won't fit into conventional definitions; Stuart Curran's "Romantic Poetry: The 'I' Altered," in Mellor's anthology makes a case for a different Romanticism, but revisionist work continues to concentrate on the six major male Romantic poets; women's genres and women's alternative Romanticisms remain peripheral. See, for example, the recent anthologies edited by Philip W. Martin and Robin Jarvis, Stephen Copley and John Whale, and Kenneth R. Johnston and Gene W. Ruoff.

9. No critic writing now would feel comfortable generalizing about invariant Woman and her experience, but the Child still looms large in most discussion of the juvenile. Usually, the Child turns out to be the Romantic boy.

10. Besides having gestated the modern child and the Romantic self, Wordsworth—so it's recently been announced—turns out to be the grandfather of the innovative approaches to the teaching of reading and writing that are currently transforming classrooms. Important pedagogic thinking, anxious for an impressive genealogy, again invokes the canonical fathers instead of the actual parents of the past, like the Edgeworths, who pioneered family literacy. See, for example, *The Educational Legacy of Romanticism*, ed. John Willinsky (Waterloo, Canada: Wilfrid Laurier University Press for Calgary Institute for the Humanities, 1990), Kieran Egan, *Romantic Understanding: The Development of Rationality and Imagination, Ages 8–15* (New York and London: Routledge, 1990), and Don H. Bialostosky, *Wordsworth, Dialogics, and the Practice of Criticism* (Cambridge:

Cambridge University Press, 1992). Bialostosky's Wordsworthian metonymic chain equates the poet first with Romanticism and then with the reformation of academic teaching practices, so the poet whose claim is disparaging lettered society becomes its patron saint; Victorian educators were more attuned to the ironies of endorsing Wordsworth: see J. P. Ward, "'Came from Yon Fountain': Wordsworth's Influence on Victorian Educators," *Victorian Studies* 29.3 (1986): 405–36. It's appropriate to describe Wordsworth as both father and mother because that's how he represents himself, as Mary Jacobus's "'Behold the Parent Hen': Romantic Pedagogy and Sexual Difference," in *Romanticism, Writing, and Sexual Difference: Essays on* The Prelude (Oxford: Clarendon Press, 1989), demonstrates.

11. Women's educational writing and vernacular pedagogy suffer the same occlusion: male theorists get credit for what mother-teachers had long since practiced. I use "pro-woman" instead of "feminist" because the latter is not a term the writers themselves could have known and because its meaning in contemporary criticism has become so variable and complex. The quoted phrase comes from Marlon B. Ross's *The Contours of Masculine Desire: Romanticism and the Rise of Women's Poetry* (New York: Oxford University Press, 1989), one of the first studies to deal with the period's female poetry. Ross's "Romanticism" remains essentially masculinist, however, with women's contribution relegated to an affective space: women come across as failed Romantics who cannot, as Wordsworth wants to do in *The Prelude*, constitute themselves without the intervention of others.

12. Edgeworth habitually jokes about her stories' smallness and their minutely detailed "Dutch" art, as in this phrase from an 1825 letter to Scott (*Private Letter-Books of Sir Walter Scott*, ed. Wilfred Partington [New York: Frederick A. Stokes, 1930], 269). Edgeworth recurrently refers to the "romance of real life," as in *Patronage*, 4 vols. 2nd ed. (London: J. Johnson, 1814), 2:316, and several women wrote works with that title, among them Charlotte Smith in 1787. For an overview of gender and the status of the detail in representation, see Naomi Schor's *Reading in Detail* (Methuen: New York and London, 1987).

13. Page references subsequently incorporated in the text refer to the Garland edition (New York and London, 1976) of the revised and enlarged *Parent's Assistant* of 1800, which reprints six volumes in two. Each volume is separately paged. "The Bracelets" was originally published in the 1796 first edition of this juvenile anthology with two other stories about girls. In the revised edition, it makes up a volume with "The Little Merchants" so that a society of girls is contrasted with one of boys. Edgeworth wrote a number of stories about boys' school life, including two in *Parent's Assistant*—"The Barring Out; or, Party Spirit" and "Eton Montem"—but she did not draw on her boarding school experience again. Like those of her sister authors for children, her school stories miniaturize larger cultural issues; as Elizabeth Sandham remarks in her girls' school tale: "A school may be styled the world in miniature. There the passions, which actuate the man, may be seen on a smaller scale" (*The School-Fellows: A Moral Tale for Young Ladies*, new ed. [London: J. Souter, 1822], preface, iv).

14. "Anxiety of authorship" refers to Sandra M. Gilbert and Susan Gubar's argument in their now classic 1979 study, *The Madwoman in the Attic* (New Haven, Conn., and London: Yale University Press, 1979).

15. I'm thinking of Ursula K. Le Guin's provocative contribution, "It Was a

Dark and Stormy Night; or, Why Are We Huddling about the Campfire?" *Critical Inquiry: On Narrative* 7.1 (1980): 191–99, because her "why" emphasizes the "we" of storying. That volume, *On Narrative*, might be said to have initiated the critical interest in what people get out of telling stories. For a postmodernist overview of this interest, see Martin Kreiswirth's "Trusting the Tale: The Narrativist Turn in the Human Sciences," *New Literary History: History, Politics, and Culture* 23.3 (1992): 629–57. So far, academic narratologists haven't much melded their insights with similar research from workers in child development and literacy, as this chapter seeks to do.

16. See especially Barrie Thorne's "Re-Visioning Women and Social Change: Where Are the Children?" *Gender and Society* 1.1 (1987): 85–109, and "Children and Gender: Constructions of Difference," in *Theoretical Perspectives on Sexual Difference*, ed. Deborah L. Rhode (New Haven, Conn., and London: Yale University Press, 1990), 100–13.

17. See Jessica Benjamin, *The Bonds of Love: Psychoanalysis, Feminism, and the Problem of Domination* (New York: Pantheon, 1988), and Seyla Benhabib, "The Generalized and the Concrete Other," in *Feminism as Critique*, ed. Seyla Benhabib and Drucilla Cornell (Minneapolis: University of Minnesota Press, 1987), 77–95.

18. As Jay Clayton's "Narrative and Theories of Desire," *Critical Inquiry*, 16.1 (1989): 33–53, points out, much narrative theory presupposes an ahistorical and implicitly masculinist desire. Teresa de Lauretis proposes that the work of narrative is to reproduce sexual differentiation, yet if female stories like "The Bracelets" do so, that's not all the generative work they do. We need not accept De Lauretis's oedipal conceptual model to welcome her generous approach to what theorists like to call the "problem of the subject" (*Alice Doesn't: Feminism, Semiotics, Cinema* [Bloomington: Indiana University Press, 1984]).

19. Those who consider the Edgeworths the arch-foes of fantasy may be interested to learn that Richard Lovell had such a passion for the Arabian Nights stories that his friends teased him, and Maria's always allusive writing is full of such references to these tales. (He also read fairy tales to his children; he just didn't think that should be their sole diet.) This assignment might also have derived from the pseudo-Oriental tale popularized by Samuel Johnson and others.

20. Hyde discusses the gift exchange as an " 'erotic' commerce, opposing *eros* (the principle of attraction, union, involvement which binds together)" to the market economy, which is an emanation of *logos* (reason, logic, differentiation rather than incorporation), an opposition relevant to the themes of "The Bracelets," as well as to Maria Edgeworth's general practice. See Hyde's *The Gift: Imagination and the Erotic Life of Property* (New York: Vintage/Random House, 1983), xiv; Marcel Mauss's *The Gift*, 1950, trans. W. D. Halls, (New York and London: W. W. Norton, 1990); and Ronald A. Sharp's chapter, "Friendship as Gift Exchange," in his *Friendship and Literature: Spirit and Form* (Durham, N.C.: Duke University Press, 1986). In her later years, Edgeworth refers to herself as a "New Year's gift" to her father because she was born on the first of January; she likes to set up a metonymic chain in which the writing, the gift, and the self become one (S. C. Hall and Mrs. S. C. Hall, "Memories," *Art-Journal* 28 [1866]: 345–49). The same economy of desire, reciprocity, and return characterizes Edgeworth's notorious penchant for lengthy letters. Embodying and enacting

relationship, the letter as gift becomes a metaphor for friendship; like her stories, her letters were read and reread communally.

21. Words like *amiable, prudent, useful, temper,* and so on, which play so big a part in the emotional vocabularies of eighteenth-century letters and fiction, aren't the innocuous or negative counters modern readers sometimes take them for. Amiable, for example, implies a whole register of values associated with good nature and warmth of heart; for details, see Myra Stokes, *The Language of Jane Austen* (New York: St. Martin's Press, 1991), 162–65. Johnson's *Dictionary*, which the Edgeworths used extensively, is another good source. When Maria Edgeworth talks about *use*, she typically has in mind social and personal happiness, although a simplistic utilitarian calculus is usually projected back on her structures of feeling. For her reading of utilitarianism as a discourse of pleasure and happiness, see her review of Dumont's version of Bentham's *Théorie des Peines et des Récompenses*, in *The Philanthropist: or Repository for Hints and Suggestions Calculated to Promote the Comfort and Happiness of Man*, vol. 7 (London: R. Taylor and Co., 1819), 149–71. Her father identifies the piece as entirely Maria's work in the *Romilly-Edgeworth Letters,* ed. Samuel Henry Romilly (London: John Murray, 1936). *The Philanthropist* was reprinted in the Greenwood reprint series, Radical Periodicals of Great Britain, *Period 1: Protest Literature of the Industrial Revolution,* in 1968.

22. The problem, as Edgeworth remarks in an unpublished letter, wasn't with her vision but with her ciliary glands; her face also swelled terribly, perhaps from a blockage of tears. Although no one makes the connection, her illness dated from her father's third marriage and persisted well after the return to Ireland. As she began to define herself as a writer and her father's literary partner, the problem resolved. It's tempting to read her eye troubles as a less overt somatic analogy of her naughtiness at Richard Lovell's second marriage. She also suffered eye troubles, shortly after her father's death, from crying so much and overuse in bad light.

23. The Huntington letter (HM28587) is tentatively dated 1783, but it must belong to December 1782, since both this letter and one printed in Maria's continuation of the *Memoirs of Richard Lovell Edgeworth* (2:71–72) refer to his trip to Dublin to get her Genlis translation published.

24. Although the Edgeworths still get described as slavish followers of Rousseau, their innovative educational system is quite different. Richard's career demonstrated Rousseau's weaknesses; the boy was hardy, ingenious, and charming, but he lacked self-command. Richard had emigrated to America and died there of an illness contracted during his last visit home. See Edgar E. Macdonald's *The American Edgeworths: A Biographical Study of Richard Edgeworth (1764–1796)* (Richmond, Va.: n.p., 1970).

25. Maria Edgeworth's teenage letters to Fanny Robinson, a classmate at Mrs. Devis's, are an invaluable source for her early writings and the attitudes of need that shape "The Bracelets." The surviving manuscripts at the Huntington Library, which aren't the whole of the correspondence, were written from 1782, when Maria was fourteen and freshly returned to Ireland, to December 1784, shortly before her seventeenth birthday on 1 January, as she herself mentions. (Although 1767 is still being recorded as Edgeworth's birthdate, considerable evidence, including letters like this, exists for the amended date of 1768.) When she wrote about her return in her father's memoirs, she reduced her age to twelve

to emphasize her extreme youth, perhaps unconsciously, for she had no personal vanity whatever about her looks or her age. The two quotations come from HM28591 6 December [1783].

26. The phrase, one Edgeworth uses throughout her life, is not, as we've been taught to expect, a locus for anxiety. A late example of Edgeworth's playfulness and her personal equation of writing and friendship comes from an 1838 letter to George Ticknor, a distinguished American academic who had visited her and whom she urges to come to Ireland again: "like or . . . love us as much as [you did] when you only knew the authorship part" (George Ticknor, *Life, Letters, and Journals of George Ticknor* (Boston: James R. Osgood & Co., 1877], 2:174).

27. In a letter to another friend, Thomas Day, once his unsuccessful rival for her mother Honora's affections, Richard Lovell again expresses his pride and deep attachment: "My daughter Honora—at fifteen, this tall, beautiful, graceful form, begins to fade." Noting "her resemblance to her mother," he knows Day would like her for her "cultivated, clear, judicious understanding" and "kind heart full of every good affection appear[ing] in every thing she says and does" (quoted in Desmond Clarke, *The Ingenious Mr. Edgeworth* [London: Oldbourne, 1965], 121–22).

28. The father remarks that "an early acquaintance with the accuracy of mathematical demonstration does not, within our experience, contract the powers of the imagination. On the contrary, we think that a young lady of twelve years old, who is now no more, and who had an uncommon propensity to mathematical reasoning, had an imagination remarkably vivid and inventive," with a note to see "'Rivuletta,' a little story written *entirely* by her in 1786" (*Practical Education*, 2 vols. [London: J. Johnson, 1798], 448). The story was reprinted in the later editions of the educational manual.

29. The Bodleian manuscript of Honora's untitled story (MS Eng. misc. c. 898) was copied by her stepmother and dated 1787, when she would have been about thirteen. Since my argument isn't about influence, what story came first matters less than their mutual implication in family politics.

30. Marilyn M. Cooper's "The Ecology of Writing" surveys the emergent paradigm of writing as a social action within a web of relationships (in *Writing as Social Action*, eds. Marilyn M. Cooper and Michael Holzman [Portsmouth, N.H.: Boynton/Cook, Heinemann, 1989]).

31. "The Bracelets" is textually interesting too, since as far as I can discover, it's the only story she wrote for children extant in two manuscript versions. There are very few surviving Edgeworth manuscripts, and the existence of two for a single story is most unusual. One manuscript in four unidentified handwritings has been described by Christina Edgeworth Colvin in "Maria Edgeworth's Literary Manuscripts in the Bodleian Library," *Bodleian Library Record* 8.4 (April 1970), 196–201; the other is a holograph manuscript copied by Edgeworth (along with two other very early stories) for her young cousin Margaret Ruxton, which is owned by UCLA. The two copies probably testify to Edgeworth's investment in this early story. The two other stories, which are part of UCLA's holograph, were evidently written for Henry, the little half brother who was her special pupil; they too work as rewards or gifts, for many of their details connect with his small educational triumphs.

32. In 1803, Edgeworth wrote her cousin, "I shall work hard with the hopes of having something to read to my father—This has always been one of my

greatest delights and strongest motives for writing"; she names "The Bracelets" among several stories "written whilst my father was out somewhere or other, on purpose to be read to him on his return" (Marilyn Butler, *Maria Edgeworth: A Literary Biography* [Oxford: Clarendon Press, 1972], 288). She regularly wrote stories to solicit nurturing from other family members too.

33. Robert Donald Mayo, *The English Novel in the Magazines, 1740–1815* (Evanston: Northwestern University Press, 1962). Since Mayo's concern is what young authors wrote for adult periodicals, juvenile works with formal or informal educational settings don't come within his purview, but women's stories about children's everyday life and learning are legion.

34. *Fraser's* 1852 "Nursery Literature" (London: J. Fraser) remarks that despite the new Romantic emphasis on fairy tales, "Miss Edgeworth's early tales still keep the foremost place as depicting the characters of children without blinking or exaggeration" (571). The early nineteenth-century Enlightened child was eventually displaced by the Romantic innocent. Like modern stories such as Robert Cormier's *The Chocolate War*, Louise Fitzhugh's *Harriet the Spy*, and Judy Blume's *Blubber*, Edgeworth's "The Bracelets" shocks some modern critics who don't like to see schoolchildren hurt one another in juvenile fiction. Bette P. Goldstone deplores Edgeworth's "power plays, and mean, petty behaviors. . . . These boarding school stories are so realistic, so true to life, the child is left in one of the nastier places of childhood" (*Lessons to Be Learned: A Study of Eighteenth Century English Didactic Children's Literature* [New York: Peter Lang, 1984], 182–83).

35. The standard overview of Oriental tales is still Martha Pike Conant's 1908 study (1908; New York: Octagon Books, reprinted 1966), but she includes no works for children. The very popular *Fairy Spectator* by "Mrs. Teachwell" (Ellenor Fenn) has a handful of scopic and monitory devices shape up the young heroines. For a wonderful example of the dumbing down of the eighteenth-century concept in contemporary books for girls, see Elizabeth Koda-Callan's *The Magic Locket* (New York: Workman, 1991); $12.95 buys a few lines of text and a trinket in which a little girl who once couldn't do anything right sees her own reflection: "*I'm* the magic in the locket." The book is so popular that it's spawned a whole series. The Edgeworth library included such tales of magical measurement as "The Mussulman's Mirror" from *The Mirror* and John Hawkesworth's story of Amurath and his warning ring from *The Adventurer*, as well as Johnson's *Seged*, and Edgeworth often refers to them. She puts a modern scientific twist on such gadgets in an 1821 Rosamond story, "The Bracelet of Memory."

36. Although the "Address" that introduces *Continuation of Early Lessons* (London: J. Johnson & Co., 1814) speaks from the father's place, it was actually written by the daughter.

37. Historians of children's literature who see fantasy as childhood's natural fare like to point out that *The Governess* also includes a few moralized fairy tales. But when Sarah Fielding's pioneering school story has been noticed in recent analyses of women's writing, it's usually been read as just another conservative conduct book for girls, with messages like love your brother and rely on him to protect you. (See, for example, Elizabeth Bergen Brophy, *Women's Lives and the Eighteenth-Century English Novel* [Tampa: University of South Florida Press, 1991], 55–56, and Julia Briggs, "Women Writers and Writing for Children: From Sarah Fielding to E. Nesbit," in *Children and Their Books*, ed. Gillian Avery and Julia Briggs [Oxford: Clarendon Press, 1989].)

38. For 1 May in the calendar of childhood and school customs like sending to Coventry, see Iona and Peter Opie, *The Lore and Language of Schoolchildren* (Oxford: Oxford University Press, 1987), 199, 255–62.

39. See the Huntington letters HM28587 [December 1782]; HM28592 18 December 1784; and HM28590 15 September 1783—on one occasion Mrs. Devis herself evidently thought Maria was laughing at her and punished her: "If I live a thousand years I shall never forget [a classmate's] coming up to me when I was perched up in the middle of the Room upon a high Stool, when it was *Sin* to approach and *Death* to pity me she came up & whispered *ne pleurez pas ma chère Edgeworth*."

40. Edgeworth's gradual and realistically depicted psychological changes are a far cry from the instantaneous conversions in many of the period's moral tales. They are also thoroughly secular; nobody just *has* a "bad heart," though one can of course gradually become wicked by continually giving way to one's own passions and cutting oneself off from communal sympathy. Not surprisingly, believers in original sin found Edgeworth's morality wanting.

41. Butler thinks the Edgeworthian heroine too unspecific to suggest a real-life original but feels the Leonora figure may owe something to Edgeworth's schoolgirl correspondent, Fanny Robinson. Since Fanny is characterized throughout the letters as sprightly and lively, even a bit giddy, she certainly doesn't seem anything like Leonora. Butler is probably thinking of Fanny's defending Maria and being her friend at school when no one else would, but this isn't exactly what's going on in "The Bracelets" either.

42. Edgeworth, *Letters from England*, ed. Christina Colvin (Oxford: Clarendon Press, 1971), 44.

43. Edgeworth much prefers quirky characters to ideal exemplars; she remarks to her Aunt Ruxton that a minor lead in *Patronage* (1814) "is very stupid & so was every good young man I ever attempted to draw. I am afraid I have no taste for good young men" (28 January 1814).

44. To Lady Moira, 1 April 1805. Edgeworth's letters to friends as well as to family continually testify to her need for love and her expertise in making people love her. Thanking the mother of her friend and sister writer, Joanna Baillie, for a gift, she writes of "how very much I enjoy the thought of being *loved* in any degree by those whose love is to my taste" (January 1831, UCLA Collection 100, Box 82).

45 Edgeworth's letters and self-representational tales exuberantly celebrate her volatility: "I was born impatient & spite of discipline fear I must continue so as long as I am Maria Edgeworth," she writes in 1826 (H. W. Haüsermann, *The Genevese Background* [London: Routledge & Kegan Paul, 1952], 131).

46. "To be amiable and to be meritorious; that is, to deserve love and to deserve reward, are the great characters of virtue. . . . What so great happiness as to be beloved, and to know that we deserve to be beloved?" (Adam Smith, *Theory of Moral Sentiments*, ed. D. D. Raphael and A. L. Macfie [Indianapolis: Liberty Classics, 1982], 113). Edgeworth's own desire for love made her feel the author a congenial soul, and she recommends Smith to Fanny Robinson in an early letter (HM28590–15 September 1783).

47. See J. L. Austin's "A Plea for Excuses" and "Performative Utterances," in *Philosophical Papers*, ed. J. O. Urmson and G. J. Warnock, 3rd ed. (Oxford: Clarendon Press, 1979). Also see Judy Dunn's *The Beginnings of Social Under-*

standing (Cambridge, Mass.: Harvard University Press, 1988), and Jerome Bruner's *Acts of Meaning* (Cambridge, Mass.: Harvard University Press, 1990), esp. chap. 3.

48. Since Edgeworth's writing for children can't be bracketed off from her writing for adults, "The Bracelets" needs to be linked with her adult feminocentric fiction as well as her life. The self-representational impatience at not being loved enough also informs Edgeworth's last novel, *Helen*, written almost a half-century later.

49. Edgeworth records her father's words for their friend Etienne Dumont, the translator of Bentham (Rowland Grey, "Maria Edgeworth and Etienne Dumont," *Dublin Review* 145 (1909): 239–65).

50. Wordsworth's line from "The Rainbow" became part of the epigraph to "Ode: Intimations of Immortality from Recollections of Early Childhood" in the 1815 edition of his poems (*Poetical Works*, ed. Thomas Hutchinson, 1904; rev. ed. Ernest de Selincourt [London: Oxford University Press, 1960], 62, 460). As J. P. Ward points out in his study of Wordsworth's impact on Victorian educational thinking, everyone embraced that line, but the poet's nineteenth-century influence was far from pervasive: Wordsworth's monopoly of the child image belongs to later academic histories.

"We Hoped the *Woman* Was Going to Appear"
(pp. 113–137)

1. William Woodfall, *Monthly Review* 48 (1773): 54–59, 133–37. Anna Letitia Barbauld, *Poems* (London: printed for Joseph Johnson, 1773). Although I am treating the poems Aikin wrote before she became Mrs. Barbauld (1774), I use her married name because it is the name by which she is known to posterity.

2. Mary Wollstonecraft, *Vindication of the Rights of Woman*, ed. Miriam Kramnick (1792; reprint, New York: Penguin, 1975), 143. Wollstonecraft prints the entire poem in a footnote, asking indignantly, "how could Mrs. Barbauld write the following ignoble comparison?"

3. *Works of Anna Letitia Barbauld. With a Memoir* (London: Longman, 1825), 1:xvii–xxiv. "Some distinguished persons [writes Lucy Aikin], amongst whom was Mrs. Montague, . . . were induced to propose to [Barbauld] to establish under their auspices what might almost have been called a College for young ladies." In the letter that her niece prints, Barbauld argues at length against the project. "Young ladies . . . ought only to have such a general tincture of knowledge as to make them agreeable companions to a man of sense. . . . The best way for women to acquire knowledge is from conversation with a father, a brother or friend . . . and by such a course of reading as they may recommend. . . . I am . . . convinced that to have a too great fondness for books is little favourable to the happiness of a woman." Barbauld gives other reasons also, including personal ones; she feels unfit to teach young women (see n. 44 below). Lucy Aikin lets it appear that this letter was written to Elizabeth Montague, but it was not. The occasion and thrust of the letter are subtly distorted in Aikin's "Memoir," more by omission than by commission; but a footnote is not the place to sort them out, and I do not yet know their full details.

4. Marilyn Williamson, "Who's Afraid of Mrs. Barbauld? The Blue Stockings and Feminism," *International Journal of Women's Studies* 3 (1980): 90–91; Marlon Ross, *The Contours of Masculine Desire: Romanticism and the Rise of Women's Poetry* (New York: Oxford University Press, 1989), 216–17. More sympathetic but making fundamentally the same case is Miriam Leranbaum, "'Mistresses of Orthodoxy': Education in the Lives and Writings of Late Eighteenth-Century Women Writers," *Proceedings of the American Philosophical Society* 121.4 (August 1977): 281–300.

5. "Mira," "To Miss AIKIN, on reading her Poems," *Gentleman's Magazine*, 44 (July 1774): 327; Mary Scott, *The Female Advocate* (London: Johnson, 1774), 35; Mary Robinson, *Memoirs of the late Mrs. Robinson, written by herself* (London: Phillips, 1801), 1:102; Hannah Cowley, *The Scottish Village* (London: Robinson, 1786), 17–20 passim.

6. *Poems* comprises only a selection of the poems Barbauld had written. Because they are the poems known to her public and to us, this essay will emphasize them; but because I aim to understand Barbauld's motives and the nature of her feminism, I take account also of poems written before 1773 but not published until later or not at all. Texts of the poems are those in *The Poems of Anna Letitia Barbauld*, ed. William McCarthy and Elizabeth Kraft (Athens: University of Georgia Press, 1994). In our edition the poems are numbered; I cite them hereafter by poem and line number.

7. In materialist-feminist commentary, the subject whom I seek would, of course, be only a "subject." The most thorough exercise in that commentary known to me is Felicity Nussbaum, *The Autobiographical Subject: Gender and Ideology in Eighteenth-Century England* (Baltimore: The Johns Hopkins University Press, 1989). That I am constructing from the poems a text that I call a subjectivity and attribute to Barbauld is obvious and inevitable; I agree with Nussbaum that the persons inferred from texts are verbal constructs, subject to all of the influences that act on and in verbal culture. I do not share her (seeming) belief that the persons who wrote the texts are therefore unknowable or even (as she sometimes seems to imply) nonexistent.

8. Mary Poovey, *The Proper Lady and the Woman Writer: Ideology and Style in the Works of Mary Wollstonecraft, Mary Shelley, and Jane Austen* (Chicago: University of Chicago Press, 1984), x; William St. Clair, *The Godwins and the Shelleys: The Biography of a Family* (Baltimore: The Johns Hopkins University Press, 1991), 504–6; G. J. Barker-Benfield, *The Culture of Sensibility* (Chicago: University of Chicago Press, 1992).

9. For example, "Mrs. P——" (poem 3), "Miss B＊＊＊＊＊" (poem 4), "Miss R——" and her mother (poem 8), "Mrs. Jennings" (poem 17), "Mrs. Rowe" (poem 57), "Lissy" (poem 39), "Chloris" (poem 25), "Araminta" (poem 26), "Delia" (poems 4 and 53), "a Lady" (poems 51 and 55).

10. The lines to which Woodfall objected read, in the first edition: "Where chearless Saturn 'midst her wat'ry moons / . . . majestic sits / . . . like an exil'd queen / Amongst her weeping handmaids." In the third edition, "her" becomes "his," "queen" becomes "monarch," and the handmaids are banished. The changes, presumably Barbauld's, do not necessarily amount to admission of error.

11. A model of this reading is Ann Messenger, *His and Hers: Essays in Restoration and Eighteenth-Century Literature* (Lexington: University Press of Kentucky, 1986), 175–84.

12.   Was it for this you took such constant Care
                        The *Bodkin, Comb,* and *Essence* to prepare;
                        For this your Locks in Paper-Durance bound,
                        For this with tort'ring Irons wreath'd around?
                        For this with Fillets strain'd your tender Head,
                        And bravely bore the double Loads of Lead?

(Pope, *The Rape of the Lock* 4:97–102 [*Poems,* ed. John Butt (New Haven, Conn.: Yale University Press, 1963), 235]).

13. David Mallett, *Works* (London, 1759), 1:3.

14. As if to confirm this reading, the first edition contains a "Freudian" typographical error in line 2 of the poem: "the wond'rous theme a reverend *ear* require[s]" (emphasis mine). An errata slip changes it to "reverent." Perhaps Barbauld's manuscript contained the "error." The occasion of the poem, as reported by William Turner in 1825, is suggestive as well: "a large old family-tankard used to stand on her father's sideboard, filled with water, his only beverage. A gentleman dining with the Dr. observed on the degradation to which this noble vessel was subjected, after having been accustomed to pass round the festal board as the vehicle of so much more generous liquors. The hint was taken [by Barbauld] and happily improved" (quoted in McCarthy and Kraft, *Poems of . . . Barbauld,* 257). The tankard, that is, *belongs* to Dr. Aikin, and *his* use of it is the subject of complaint.

15. Barker-Benfield, *The Culture of Sensibility,* 290, quoting John Gregory's popular *A Father's Legacy to his Daughters* (1774): "in your sex [overeating] is beyond expression indelicate and disgusting."

16. That Barbauld in fact experienced her mother as an agent of repression is suggested by Lucy Aikin; see n. 44, below.

17. "Somebody was bold enough to talk of getting up private theatricals. This was a dreadful business! All the wise and grave, the whole tutorhood, cried out, it must not be! The students . . . and . . . my aunt, took the prohibition very sulkily; and my aunt's Ode to Wisdom was the result" (Aikin to Henry Bright, quoted by Bright, *A Historical Sketch of Warrington Academy* [Liverpool: Brakell, 1859], 14).

18. Joseph Priestley to Theophilus Lindsey, 30 July 1770 (Priestley, *Theological and Miscellaneous Works,* ed. J. T. Rutt [New York: Kraus Reprints, 1972], 1:i, 117. According to his son, John Aikin was also "too diffident" to become an author despite his knowledge and ability (Lucy Aikin, *Memoir of John Aikin, M.D.* [London: Baldwin, Cradock and Joy, 1823], 1:13).

19. Bright, *Historical Sketch,* comments, "Mr. Edwards, the lively West Indian, had to slip away from his creditors and leave Warrington for ever" (12).

20. In fairness to the Rev. John Aikin, we need to distinguish "psychic" from historical reality. Aikin did not in fact withhold higher learning from his daughter; however, Lucy Aikin implies that he granted it only reluctantly, after long importunity (*Works of . . . Barbauld,* 1:vii). And of course, medical education would have been unthinkable.

21. Mary Astell, *A Serious Proposal to the Ladies: Part II* (1967; reprint, New York: Source Book Press, 1970), 159.

22. On Barbauld's sending poems to Belsham, see "History of the Poems" in McCarthy and Kraft, *Poems of . . . Barbauld* (xxix).

23. I allude to the title of Sandra Gilbert's 1980 essay, "What Do Feminist Critics Want? A Postcard from the Volcano," reprinted in *The New Feminist*

Criticism, ed. Elaine Showalter (New York: Pantheon, 1985), 29–45. The phrase is really Wallace Stevens's, but Gilbert appropriates it with reference to volcano poems by Emily Dickinson.

24. Barker-Benfield argues in *The Culture of Sensibility* that in fact the range of expression permitted to women widened during the century. Certainly it did, albeit against opposition. Its expansion must be regarded as a feminist tendency, and Barbauld should be seen as having contributed to the expansion.

25. Marilyn French, *Beyond Power: On Women, Men, and Morals* (London: Cape, 1985), 487.

26 Barbauld's need for stronger feeling and a more fervent experience of religion, as well as her resentment of Warrington rationality, emerged (to the discomfiture of her co-religionists) in an essay, "Thoughts on the Devotional Taste," published with her selection of psalms in 1775.

27. Barbauld's model for the songs was probably Elizabeth Rowe, to whose muse she dedicates herself in "Verses on Mrs. Rowe" (poem 57); for examples of Rowe, see *Eighteenth-Century Women Poets,* ed. Roger Lonsdale (Oxford: Oxford University Press, 1989). In Barbauld's "Ode to Spring" (poem 56), where female desire for a male object is admitted without displacement, it is admitted only in a "whisper'd sigh" (18–20). A poem of unknown date, published posthumously (poem 157), is an allegory of the passage of the year in the figure of a highly erotic courtship of the earth by the sun. Earth (female, of course) is the speaker.

28. See Polwhele's description of modern girls who "with bliss botanic as their bosoms heave, / Still pluck forbidden fruit, with mother Eve, / For puberty in sighing florets pant, / Or point the prostitution of a plant" (*The Unsex'd Females: A Poem* [London: Cadell & Davies, 1798], 8–9). Polwhele's principal targets are Wollstonecraft and Erasmus Darwin's *Botanic Garden.* He speaks kindly (if nervously) of Barbauld and does not quote this poem.

29. "Some [women warriors] laugh out loud and manifest their aggressiveness by thrusting their bare breasts forward brutally" (Wittig, *Les Guérillères,* trans. David Le Vay [Boston: Beacon Press, 1985], 100).

30. Lucy Aikin tells anecdotes of Barbauld's own agility in her youth, agility she would have been expected to inhibit. "In her youth, great bodily activity, and a lively spirit struggled hard against the tight [parental] rein which held her. London cousins wondered sometimes at the gymnastic feats of the country lass" (Aikin's "Family History," in Anna LeBreton, *Memoir of Mrs. Barbauld* [London: Bell, 1874], 25). At age 15, to escape an importunate suitor, Barbauld "ran nimbly up a tree which grew by the garden wall, and let herself down into the lane beyond." (ibid.). See also n. 44, below.

31. Elizabeth Benger, *The Female Geniad* (London: Hookham, 1791), 5 (emphasis mine).

32. The year after *Poems* was published, Hester Mulso Chapone's *Letters on the Improvement of the Mind* (3rd ed. [London, 1774]) would claim astronomy for women. Chapone describes her own rapture at being taught to consider the stars as "worlds formed like ours for a variety of inhabitants," and she urges young women to study the stars in order to "enlarge [the] mind and excite in it the most profound adoration" (2:140–41).

33. Henry Crabb Robinson to Dorothy Wordsworth, 6 January 1826 (MS HCR Letters 6:141, Dr. Williams's Library).

34. Wollstonecraft, *Vindication*, 143.

35. Barbauld to Elizabeth Belsham, February 1771, (*Works . . . of Barbauld*, 2:59). Fordyce wrote that "so far as he has been able to observe, young men have appeared more frequently susceptible of a generous and steady friendship for each other, than females as yet unconnected; especially if the latter have had, or been supposed to have, pretensions to beauty not yet adjusted by the public voice" (*Sermons to Young Women* [reprinted, Boston, 1767], 1:114).

36. Pope, *The Rape of the Lock*, 2:10 (*Poems*, 223).

37. Nussbaum, *Autobiographical Subject*, xxii. Nussbaum does not, in fact, revalue Pope in this way; yet such a revalorization would be deducible from a Foucaultian project like hers.

38. Pope, "Of the Characters of Women," line 3 (*Poems*, 560). Cf. *The British Apollo* (1708): women "are cast in too soft a mould, are made of too fine, too delicate [a] composure to endure the severity of study" (quoted in Barker-Benfield, *Culture of Sensibility*, 23). In her study of seventeenth- and eighteenth-century misogynist satire, *The Brink of All We Hate* (Louisville: University Press of Kentucky, 1984), Felicity Nussbaum contends that "Of the Characters of Women" is not "finally misogynist" (140) but acknowledges that it was "long seen" as antifeminist (138). As late as 1804, Pope was accused of misogyny by one "Camilla" in the *Monthly Magazine*, 17 (1804): 109–10. "Camilla" is particularly offended by his claims that women have "no character" and that their characters are inconsistent.

39. Nussbaum, *The Brink*, chaps. 7 and 8.

40. The name Flavia may come from William Law's *A Serious Call to a Devout and Holy Life* (London: printed for William Innys, 1729); Law's Flavia is fashionable and dissipated, a cautionary example to women.

41. The general shift in the direction of feminizing culture throughout the eighteenth century is treated in Barker-Benfield's *Culture of Sensibility*.

42. One reading of that line is to see it as bitterly ironic: "Given the low esteem in which women are held, the most you can hope to do is please." I would not summarily reject this reading, given the degree of conflict that Barbauld's texts exhibit; but I would argue that it is not consistent with the general trend in these poems of associating the female with pleasure.

43. In the published poem "To Miss R[igby] . . ." (poem 8), however, Sarah is praised not for frivolity but for self-effacing caregiving. That the Rigby sisters were regarded as troublesome by the Academy authorities is evident from a 1769 incident (details unknown) concerning one of them and a "Mr. G"; the Trustees ordered Mr. Rigby to remove his daughters from Warrington (Warrington Academy "Minutes," 26 January 1769 [MS, Manchester College, Oxford]). A practical joke attributed to them is reported by Bright, *A Historical Sketch*, 23.

44. One reason she declined to manage a college for young women was that she felt incompetent to teach the skills expected in young women of her class: "I know myself remarkably deficient in gracefulness of person, in my air and manner, and in the easy graces of conversation" (*Works . . . of Barbauld*, 1:xxiii). Lucy Aikin's account of Barbauld's education by her mother is guarded but sufficiently informative: To avoid the danger of contamination by the manners of the boys who attended her father's school, "maternal vigilance" instilled into Barbauld "a double portion of bashfulness and maidenly reserve; and she was accustomed to ascribe an uneasy sense of constraint in mixed society . . . to the

strictness" of her education (ibid., 1:viii). See also n. 30: the "rein" was her mother's.

45. The "classic" account is by Helene Deutsch; I depend on the summary given by Nancy Chodorow in *The Reproduction of Mothering* (Berkeley: University of California Press, 1978), chap. 8 (esp. 137).

46. Alan Richardson, "Romanticism and the Colonization of the Feminine," in *Romanticism and Feminism*, ed. Anne K. Mellor (Bloomington: Indiana University Press, 1988), 21. Richardson cites Mary Jacobus.

47. Wittig, *Guérillères*, 48.

48. A manuscript text of the poem (Liverpool Record Office 920 NIC 22/5/3) associates it with Sarah Scott's *Millenium Hall* (1762) and testifies that Barbauld had probably read that story of a fictional gynetopia.

49. See Dianne Dugaw, *Warrior Women and Popular Balladry 1650–1850* (Cambridge: Cambridge University Press, 1989). The middle-class intellectual *Monthly Magazine* published "An Account of Frances Scanagatti, . . . who served . . . as an Ensign and Lieutenant . . . during the last War" (22 [1806]: 465–68). The youthful Amelia Opie met a sailor named "William Henry Renny," who turned out to be a woman; Opie was both fascinated and repelled by her (Cecilia Brightwell, *Memorials of the Life of Amelia Opie* [Norwich and London, 1854], 18–20). A striking instance of "amazonizing" is Henry Fuseli's illustration, *Lady Macbeth Presenting the Daggers*, in which conventional gender postures are reversed: she strides powerfully toward her husband, and he shrinks back in fear. Ideas about amazons are discussed in Barker-Benfield, *Culture of Sensibility*, 351–59.

50. For advice and criticism I am grateful to Brenda Daly, Paula Feldman, Mitzi Myers, and Rosanne Potter.

Felicia Hemans and the Effacement of Woman
(pp. 138–149)

I owe much to the students in successive years of English 831.6, 830.3, 431.6, and 231.6 at the University of Saskatchewan, whose interest in women writers of the Romantic period has helped to sustain and extend my own, particularly Susan Dawson, Joanne Epp, Catherine Gutwin, Leah Jones, Lisa Martin, Anne McDonald, Marge Stabler, and Asha Varadharajan. This essay was first delivered as a conference paper at a special session of the December 1990 convention of the Modern Language Association in Chicago. I would like to thank Paula Feldman, who organized the session, and Nan Sweet, who invited me to contribute to a special session on Felicia Hemans the following year, for their help and encouragement.

1. Percy Bysshe Shelley, "On Frankenstein," in *Complete Works*, ed. R. Ingpen and W. Peck, 10 vols. (London and New York: Julian Editions, 1926–30), 6 (1929): 263–64.

2. The works of Hemans cited herein are *The Poetical Works*, ed. William Michael Rossetti (London: Ward, Lock and Co., n.d.); *The Forest Sanctuary; and Other Poems* (1825; reprint, with *The Vespers of Palermo*, New York: Garland, 1978); *Records of Woman: With Other Poems* (1828; reprint, New York: Gar-

land, 1978); and *Songs of the Affections, With Other Poems* (1830; reprint, New York: Garland, 1978).

3. Kurt Heinzelman, "The Cult of Domesticity: Dorothy and William Wordsworth at Grasmere," in *Romanticism and Feminism*, ed. Anne K. Mellor (Bloomington: Indiana University Press, 1988), 53.

4. Gail Griffin, "Alma Mater," in *Profession 90* (New York: Modern Language Association, 1990).

5. Dorothy Mermin, "Women Becoming Poets: Katherine Philips, Aphra Behn, Anne Finch," *ELH* 57 (1990): 349.

6. See August Mau, *Pompeii: Its Life and Art*, trans. Francis W. Kelsey (1902; reprint, New Rochelle, N.Y.: Caratzas, 1982), 26; and Michael Grant, *Cities of Vesuvius: Pompeii and Herculaneum* (London: Weidenfeld and Nicolson, 1971), 31–32. Reports appeared frequently in the *Times* (London) between 1821 (when the discovery at Pompeii of tradesmen's shops, barracks, a Temple of Justice, and an amphitheater was reported) and 1827 (the visit of the king and queen of Naples to Pompeii; see the *Times* [London], 5 February 1821, p. 3, and 4 July 1827, p. 2). Even though modern excavation in the Pompeii area began at Herculaneum in 1709, little was found there initially, and in the 1740s interest turned to Pompeii, which seemed to offer more to interest the archaeologist. The medium in which the woman's form was preserved must have been warm volcanic mud, rather than lava, strictly speaking (see Grant, *Cities*, 31). Neither Mau nor Grant mentions a woman with an infant being discovered at Herculaneum in the 1820s, however, and I have been unable to identify the precise source of Hemans's information.

7. I have in mind here a remark of David Punter's: "in the eighteenth century . . . it became a crime against the social code for any woman to admit her real feelings or to confess to passion, and the main purpose of the education of 'ladies of condition' becomes this suppression of feeling and passion. Under these circumstances, one could say that male and female discourse developed increasingly into separate languages, insulated from each other by the different interests of the sexes in relation to the maintenance of the social order" (*The Literature of Terror: A History of Gothic Fictions from 1765 to the Present Day* [London: Longman, 1980], 95).

8. I am grateful to Harriet Linkin for suggesting that I explore this alternative approach to Hemans and for pointing out the possible relevance of Cixous to the question of identity and its limitations as the site of feminist value.

9. Nancy Chodorow, *The Reproduction of Mothering: Psychoanalysis and the Sociology of Gender* (Berkeley: University of California Press, 1978), 168–169.

10. This poem, Anne K. Mellor points out, "endorses Burke's conservative political model of good government as the preservation of 'our little platoon,' of a nuclear English family controlled by the authority of 'canonized forefathers'" (*Romanticism and Gender* [New York: Routledge, 1993], 126).

11. Judith Lowder Newton, *Women, Power, and Subversion: Social Strategies in British Fiction, 1778–1860* (Athens: University of Georgia Press, 1981), 19.

12. *Westminster Review* 52 (1849–1850) no. 103 (January 1850): 354–55.

13. Jan Mukařovský, *Aesthetic Function, Norm and Value as Social Facts*, trans. with notes by Mark E. Suino (Ann Arbor: University of Michigan, 1970), 60–61.

Resurrection of the Fetish (pp. 150–168)

1. Christian Metz, "Photography and Fetish," *October* 34 (1985): 81.

2. The focus on the inanimate quality of the fetish is not, of course, limited to modern or contemporary thought but rather refers to its original Western African cultural context, where the privileging of inanimate objects, invested with a supernatural "charm," gave rise to the cult of fetishism. Charles de Brosses, an eighteenth-century anthropologist, was one of the early Westerners whose research on the fetish brought the term into currency for the West. See Charles de Brosses's *Le culte des dieux fétiches* (1760; reprint Famborough, England: Gregg International, 1972).

3. Parveen Adams, "Of Female Bondage," in *Between Feminism and Psychoanalysis*, ed. Teresa Brennan (London: Routledge, 1988), 252.

4. Mary Shelley, *Frankenstein* (New York: Signet, 1963), 92. All subsequent parenthetical references are to page numbers in this edition.

5. Sigmund Freud, *The Standard Edition of the Complete Psychological Works of Sigmund Freud*, trans. and ed. James Strachey et al., 24 vols. (London: Hogarth Press, 1953–74), 9:23. All subsequent references are to this edition and will be given parenthetically in the text.

6. Hanold's vehement response also relates to his repugnance to houseflies, described earlier in the text, when he came to equate these insects with all the honeymooning couples infesting Italian cities.

7. I would also suggest that if we read Freud's analysis of Jensen's text *nachträglich*, through his later texts "Fetishism" and *Group Psychology and the Analysis of the Ego* (1921), we would discover that it is not so much, as Freud argues, that the patient is cured but rather that the fetish is "cured" of its pathological status and legitimized by romantic love. Hanold could still relish his plaster replica of Gradiva, only now it would be interpreted as a tribute to romantic love rather than as a signifier of a particular pathology.

8. I use the term *exquisite corpse* to describe the idealization of the dead body as it appears in both literature and art, especially during the eighteenth century and nineteenth century as part of the cult of mourning. For a historical overview of the cult of mourning, see Philippe Ariès's *The Hour of Our Death*, trans. Helen Weaver (New York: Alfred A. Knopf, 1981), 508–13, and Ann Douglas's *The Feminization of American Culture* (New York: Avon, 1977), 240–72.

9. Here, I am using *sublime* in a dual sense to portray two very different aspects of this figure of the dead body. In its first sense, *sublime* is used more conventionally to denote the aesthetic category as outlined by Burke and Kant. Second, I am referring to the Lacanian concept of the sublime body, which is a secondary or "surplus" body existing beyond the natural one; it is an imaginary and indestructible body, perpetually capable of resurrection. See Slavoj Žižek, *The Sublime Object of Ideology* (London: Verso, 1989), 131–49.

10. Edmund Burke, *A Philosophical Enquiry into the Origin of Our Ideas of the Sublime and Beautiful*, ed. Adams Phillips (Oxford: Oxford University Press, 1990), 36.

11. Burke draws a distinction between "delight," which is the painful pleasure aroused by the sublime experience, and "positive pleasure," which the beautiful inspires. "I say, *delight*, because as I have often remarked, it is very

evidently different in its cause, and its own nature, from actual and positive pleasure" (ibid., 122).

12. Although the monster is not an intact corpse but rather a fragmented body composed of many corpses, it functions on an imaginary level as an exquisite corpse.

13. Evelyn Fox Keller, *Reflections on Gender and Science* (New Haven, Conn.: Yale University Press, 1985), 48.

14. See Phil Berger, *The State-of-the-Art Robot Catalog* (New York: Dodd, Mead & Company, 1984), 20. For a concise study of the early history of automata, see John Cohen's *Human Robots in Myth and Science* (New York: A. S. Barnes, 1967). See also Jean-Claude Beaune's "The Classical Age of Automata: An Impressionistic Survey from the Sixteenth to the Nineteenth Century" in *Fragments for a History of the Human Body,* ed. Michel Feher (New York: Urzone, 1989), 430–80.

15. Jacques Lacan, *The Four Fundamental Concepts,* trans. Alan Sheridan (New York: W. W. Norton, 1978), 53–54.

16. See Douglas, *Feminization,* chap. 6.

17. Although the cult of mourning was instrumental in the expansion and development of the popularity of garden cemeteries, the rural cemetery movement was actually prompted by the deterioration and overcrowding of urban cemeteries, which led to severe sanitation problems that were affecting public hygiene.

18. For a thorough discussion and historical account of the rise of the rural cemetery movement, see Richard A. Etlin's *The Architecture of Death: The Transformation of the Cemetery in Eighteenth-Century Paris* (Cambridge, Mass.: MIT Press, 1984). For a general survey on the ideological shift in cultural representations of death from the early eighteenth century to Romanticism, see Philippe Ariès, *Western Attitudes Towards Death: From the Middle Ages to the Present,* trans. Patricia M. Ranum (Baltimore: Johns Hopkins University Press, 1974).

19. Jean-Pierre Petit, *Emily Brontë* (Harmondsworth, U.K.: Penguin, 1973), 31.

20. J. Hillis Miller, *Fiction and Repetition* (Cambridge, Mass.: Harvard University Press, 1982), 70.

21 Emily Brontë, *Wuthering Heights* (Harmondsworth, U.K.: Penguin, 1985), 46. All subsequent references are to this edition.

22. Carol Jacobs, *Uncontainable Romanticism* (Baltimore: Johns Hopkins University Press, 1989), 61–62.

23. James H. Kavanagh, *Emily Brontë* (Oxford: Basil Blackwell, 1985), 21.

24. Wade Thompson, "Infanticide and Sadism in *Wuthering Heights,*" in *Emily Brontë: A Critical Anthology,* ed. Jean-Pierre Petit (Harmondsworth, U.K.: Penguin, 1973), 193.

25. The correlation between horror and caprice is perhaps best illustrated by Goya's powerful series of etchings Los Caprichos (The Caprices) published in 1799. *The Sleep of Reason Produces Monsters,* the best-known print in this series, became one of the most provocative icons of Romantic art, exposing the darker side of the human psyche and sensibility.

26. Sandra Gilbert and Susan Gubar, *The Madwoman in the Attic: The*

Woman Writer and the Nineteenth-Century Literary Imagination (New Haven, Conn.: Yale University Press, 1979), 291.

27. In both Goethe's *Elective Affinities* and Dumas *fils'* *The Lady of the Camellias*, the maid is responsible for preparing the female body and not only renders it decent for viewing but ultimately transforms the female dead body into an exquisite corpse.

28. Here, I am referring to the Lacanian notion of the sublime body as that surplus body that is indestructible.

Gender, Nationality, and Textual Authority (pp. 171–193)

1. Morgan, quoted in Mary Campbell, *Lady Morgan: The Life and Times of Sydney Owenson* (London: Pandora Press, 1988), xi. The major source for Morgan's life is Morgan's *Memoirs: Autobiography, Diaries, and Correspondence*, 2 vols., ed. W. Hepworth Dixon, 2nd ed. (London: William H. Allen & Co., 1863), hereafter cited parenthetically as *Memoirs*. The reader may also consult: W. J. Fitzpatrick, *Lady Morgan: Her Career, Literary and Personal, with a Glimpse of Her Friends, and a Word to her Calumniators* (London, 1860); Lionel Stevenson, *The Wild Irish Girl: The Life of Sydney Owenson, Lady Morgan (1776–1859)* (London: Chapman and Hall, 1936); Elizabeth Suddaby and P. J. Yarrow, eds., *Lady Morgan in France* (Newcastle upon Tyne: Oriel Press, 1971); and James Newcomer, *Lady Morgan the Novelist* (Cranbury, N.J.: Associated University Presses, 1990).

On the Grand Tour, see Jeremy Black, *The British and The Grand Tour* (Dover, U.K.: Croom Helm, 1985); Heinz-Joachim Müllenbrock, "The Political Implications of the Grand Tour: Aspects of a Specifically English Contribution to the European Travel Literature of the Age of Enlightenment," *Trema* 9 (1984): 7–21; J. Stoye, *English Travellers Abroad, 1604–1667: Their Influence in English Society and Politics* (1952; rev. ed., New Haven, Conn.: Yale University Press, 1989); Constantia Maxwell, *The English Traveller in France, 1698–1815* (London: George Routledge and Sons, 1932); and W. E. Mead, *The Grand Tour in the Eighteenth Century* (Boston and New York: Houghton Mifflin, 1914).

2. Jean Baker Miller, "The Construction of Anger in Women and Men," in *Women's Growth in Connection*, ed. Judith V. Jordan et al. (New York: Guilford Press, 1991), 184.

3. See Elizabeth Kowaleski-Wallace, *Their Fathers' Daughters: Hannah More, Maria Edgeworth, and Patriarchal Complicity* (New York: Oxford University Press, 1991).

4. Newcomer, *Lady Morgan the Novelist*, 22, 46; Campbell, *Lady Morgan*, 132.

5. George Gordon, Lord Byron, Letter to Thomas Moore, 24 August 1821, in *Byron's Letters and Journals*, ed. Leslie A. Marchand, 12 vols. (Cambridge, Mass.: Belknap Press of Harvard University Press, 1973–1982), 8:189; Mary Wollstonecraft Shelley, *Rambles in Germany and Italy in 1840, 1842, and 1843* (London: E. Moxon, 1844; reprint, Folcroft, Penna.: Folcroft Library Editions, 1975), 2 vols., 1:x. The *Quarterly Review* called *France* "her latest and most important work" (17 [1817]: 262).

6. Campbell, *Lady Morgan*, 149. I have been unable to trace an exact statement to this effect, but Lafayette's esteem for Morgan's *France* is clear from his letter: "It will be purchased more than it will be praised in England because it upsets intolerant patriotism by demonstrating the results of the Revolution in France and the errors of your [British] opposition to this national movement which has become today a continental movement" (Lafayette to Morgan, 12 February 1818 [Lafayette Mss., Lilly Library at Indiana University in Bloomington], translated by Lloyd S. Kramer and quoted in his *Lafayette in Two Worlds*, forthcoming.) My thanks to Professor Kramer for allowing me to read his work in manuscript.

7. Margery E. Elkington, *Les Relations de Société entre L'Angleterre et la France sous la Restauration (1814–1830)* (Paris: Librarie Ancienne Honoré Champion, 1929), 106.

8. *Quarterly Review* 17 (1817): 260–86; Byron, Letter to John Murray, 20 February 1818, *Letters and Journals*, 6:13.

9. Stendhal is quoted in Patrick Raifroidi, *Irish Literature in English: The Romantic Period (1789–1850)*, 2 vols. (Gerrards Cross, U.K.: Colin Smythe, 1980), 1:245. Originally published as *L'Irlande et le Romantisme* (1972). For the literary controversy, see Morgan's *France in 1829–30*, 2 vols. (London: Saunders and Otley, 1830), 1:51–89; and Elkington, *Les Relations*, 101–42.

10. Sandra M. Gilbert and Susan Gubar, *The Madwoman in the Attic: The Woman Writer and the Nineteenth-Century Literary Imagination* (1979; reprint, New Haven, Conn.: Yale University Press, 1984); Mary Poovey, *The Proper Lady and the Woman Writer: Ideology as Style in the Works of Mary Wollstonecraft, Mary Shelley, and Jane Austen* (Chicago: University of Chicago Press, 1984); Margaret Homans, *Woman Writers and Poetic Identity* (Princeton, N.J.: Princeton University Press, 1980). See also Jerome J. McGann, *The Romantic Ideology* (Chicago: University of Chicago Press, 1983).

11. Quoted by Eric J. Leed, *The Mind of the Traveler: From Gilgamesh to Global Tourism* (New York: Harper Collins, 1991), 114.

12. Mary Wollstonecraft, *Letters from Norway*, in *The Works of Mary Wollstonecraft*, ed. Janet Todd and Marilyn Butler, 7 vols. (New York: New York University Press, 1989), 6:248. See Jeanne Moskal, "The Picturesque and the Affectionate in Wollstonecraft's *Letters from Norway*," *Modern Language Quarterly* 52 (1991): 263–94.

13. Genette, "Introduction to the Paratext," *New Literary History* 22 (1991): 261–72; Morgan, *Book of the Boudoir*, 2 vols. (London: Henry Colburn, 1829), 1:99.

14. See Alan Richardson, "Romanticism and the Colonization of the Feminine," in *Romanticism and Feminism*, ed. Anne K. Mellor (Bloomington: Indiana University Press, 1988), 13–25.

15. Joseph Th. Leerssen, "How *The Wild Irish Girl* Made Ireland Romantic," *Dutch Quarterly Review* 18 (1988): 221–22.

16. In addition to Newcomer and Campbell, cited above, see on Morgan's novels: Anne K. Mellor, *Romanticism and Gender* (New York: Routledge, 1993), 97–103; Joseph Th. Leerssen, "Fiction Poetics and Cultural Stereotype: Local Colour in Scott, Morgan and Maturin," *Modern Language Review* 86 (1991): 273–84; Joseph W. Lew, "Sidney [sic] Owenson and the Fate of Empire," *Keats-Shelley Journal* 39 (1990): 39–65; Leerssen, "How *The Wild Irish Girl*, 209–27;

Elmer Andrews, "Aesthetics, Politics, and Identity: Lady Morgan's *The Wild Irish Girl,*" *Canadian Journal of Irish Studies,* 12, no. 2 (1987): 7–19; Tom Dunne, "Fiction as 'the Best History of Nations': Lady Morgan's Irish Novels," in *The Writer as Witness: Literature as Historical Evidence,* ed. Tom Dunne (Cork: Cork University Press, 1987), 133–59; Robert Tracy, "Maria Edgeworth and Lady Morgan: Legality versus Legitimacy," *Nineteenth-Century Fiction* 40 (1985): 1–22; Colin B. Atkinson and Jo Atkinson, "Sydney Owenson, Lady Morgan: Irish Patriot and First Professional Woman Writer," *Eire-Ireland* 15.2 (1980): 60–90; and Thomas Flanagan, *The Irish Novelists 1800–1850* (New York: Columbia University Press, 1959), 107–64.

17. Julia M. Wright has pointed out to me that the footnotes are uneven in supporting Irish nationalist sentiment as well as in explicit attribution (personal correspondence).

18. Morgan's Horatio also compares Ireland to the West Indies and new British colonies in the East. Lew argues that in "creat[ing] a narrator who . . . is incapable of seeing anything in its own terms," Morgan critiques the paternal ideology of colonial power ("Sidney Owenson," 41).

19. References to *The Wild Irish Girl* (*WIG*) follow the facsimile of the three-volume 1806 edition, with an introduction by Robert Lee Wolff (New York: Garland, 1979), unless otherwise noted. There is also a modern reprint with an introduction by Brigid Brophy (New York: Pandora Press, 1986).

20. For Irish antiquarians, see Joseph Th. Leerssen, "Antiquarian Research: Patriotism to Nationalism," *Canadian Journal of Irish Studies* 12.2 (1986): 71–83.

21. Shari Benstock, "At the Margins of Discourse: Footnotes in the Fictional Text," *PMLA* 98 (1983): 204–25.

22. Anthony D. Smith, "Introduction," *Nationalist Movements,* ed. Anthony D. Smith (London: Macmillan, 1976), 8.

23. Lynda E. Boose, "The Father's House and the Daughters in It," in *Daughters and Fathers,* ed. Lynda E. Boose and Betty S. Flowers (Baltimore: Johns Hopkins University Press, 1988), 38.

24. *Dictionary of National Biography,* s.v. "Thomas Charles Morgan."

25. *Quarterly Review* 17 (1817): 267, 286; William Playfair, *France as it is, not Lady Morgan's France,* 2 vols. (London: W. M'Dowell, 1819), l:xli.

26. Maxwell, *English Traveller,* 125, 138, 58.

27. Lady Morgan, quoted in William Fitzpatrick, *The Friends, Foes, and Adventures of Lady Morgan* (Dublin: W. B. Kelly, 1959), 49; Ina Ferris, "Writing on the Border: The National Tale, Female Writing, and the Public Sphere," paper delivered at the conference of the North American Society for the Study of Romanticism, August 1993. My thanks to Professor Ferris for allowing me to read her work in manuscript.

28. Wolfe Tone, a leader of the aborted 1798 rebellion, negotiated at various times with the French in hopes of instigating a French invasion of Ireland to throw off English rule, an invasion the English regarded as a clear and present danger for much of the war. To counteract an alliance between France and Ireland, England passed the Relief Act of 1793, extending the franchise to Roman Catholics. See T. W. Moody and F. X. Martin, eds., *The Course of Irish History,* rev. ed. (Cork: The Mercier Press, 1984), 241–45. Still, the Napoleonic wars tended to strengthen Irish antipathy to England, since the wartime inflation hit

Ireland harder than England, creating more beggars because of the lack of a Poor Law in Ireland and over 30,000 troops that were quartered in Ireland to stave off French invasion. See Gearoid O'Tuathauigh, *Ireland before the Famine, 1798–1848*, vol. 9 of the Gill History of Ireland (Dublin: Gill and Macmillan, 1972), 108–109, 188, 140; Moody and Martin, esp. chap. 15, "The Protestant Nation (1775–1800)," by R. B. McDowell; and chap.16, "The Age of Daniel O'Connell (1800–47)," by J. H. Whyte.

29. Raifroidi 1:221–59. The review of *The Wild Irish Girl* that he quotes (on p. 227) is from *Revue de Deux Mondes* of 3 July 1813.

30. *Journal de Paris*, 25 July 1813, quoted by Elkington, 105.

31. *Quarterly Review* 17 (1817): 265.

32. Gerald Newman, *The Rise of English Nationalism: A Cultural History, 1740–1830* (New York: St. Martin's, 1987), 50.

33. Kramer, *Lafayette in Two Worlds*, 52–62.

34. For generic conventions of travel writing, see Mary Louise Pratt, *Imperial Eyes: Travel Writing and Transculturation* (New York: Routledge, 1992); Leed, cited above; Charles L. Batten, Jr., *Pleasureable Instruction: Form and Convention in Eighteenth-Century Travel Literature* (Berkeley: University of California Press, 1978); Percy G. Adams, *Travelers and Travel Liars, 1660–1800* (1962; 2nd ed. New York: Dover, 1980).

35. *Quarterly Review* 17 (1817): 266.

36. *Encyclopedia Britannica*, 1967, s.v. "Denon"; see Edward W. Said, *Orientalism* (New York: Random House, 1979), 73–92.

37. Marilyn Gaull, *English Romanticism: The Human Context* (New York: Norton, 1988), 191–92. Felicia Hemans contributed *The Restoration of the Works of Art to Italy* (1816) to the controversy about Napoleon and Italian art.

38. Marguerite Power, Lady Blessington, *Lady Blessington's Conversations of Lord Byron*, ed. Ernest J. Lovell, Jr. (Princeton, N.J.: Princeton University Press, 1969), 82. Cf. Stendhal's observation: "Amusingly, it was not at all the despotic and odious part of Napoleon's character which displeased the English peer" (quoted in *His Very Self and Voice: Collected Conversations of Lord Byron*, ed. Ernest J. Lovell, Jr. [New York: Macmillan, 1954], 198).

39. Byron, note to *Childe Harold's Pilgrimage*, 3:369, in Jerome J. McGann, ed., *Byron* (New York: Oxford University Press,1986), 140. On Byron and Napoleon, see Christina M. Root, "History as Character: Byron and the Myth of Napoleon," in *History and Myth: Essays on English Romantic Literature*, ed. Stephen C. Behrendt (Detroit: Wayne State University Press, 1990), 149–65; Bernhard Reitz, "'To die as honour dies': Politics of the Day and Romantic Understanding of History in Southey's, Shelley's, and Byron's Poems on Napoleon," in *Hannover Byron Symposium* (Salzburg, 1979): 117–40; and Carl Woodring, *Politics in English Romantic Poetry* (Cambridge, Mass.: Harvard University Press, 1970). On Wordsworth's reaction to Napoleon, see Alan Liu, *Wordsworth: The Sense of History* (Stanford, Calif.: Stanford University Press, 1989), 24–31, 437–40.

40. Marlon B. Ross, *The Contours of Masculine Desire: Romanticism and the Rise of Women's Poetry* (Oxford: Oxford University Press, 1989), 44.

41. Quoted in O'Tuathauigh, 66–68, 233.

42. Morgan, *Italy*, 2nd ed., 3 vols. (London: Colburn, 1824). Hereafter cited parenthetically.

43. Her construction of Napoleon as superior pontiff continues in a note about one of his bridges in Turin, containing a Napoleonic medallion in its foundation. After Napoleon's defeat, the king wanted to erase all traces of Napoleon and replace Napoleon's likeness with his own, only to discover that the bridge would fall if the original medallion were removed (*Italy*, 1:63n).

44. Some research for this essay was conducted at the Library of Congress. The author particularly thanks Victoria C. Hill and Bruce Martin of the library's staff. A grant from the Institute for the Arts and Humanities at the University of North Carolina at Chapel Hill allowed me time to write the essay. The author also thanks Marilyn Butler, Paula R. Feldman, Theresa M. Kelley, Lloyd S. Kramer, Karen R. Lawrence, Mark L. Reed, Virginia Sickbert, James Thompson, Weldon Thorton, and Julia M. Wright for their comments on previous drafts, and Andrea Moore Kerr, Tim Logue, and Christine Sneed for their research assistance.

Expanding the Limits of Feminine Writing (pp. 194–206)

For helpful commentary on versions of this essay, I thank Theresa Kelley and Anne Wallace.

1. I borrow the phrase "ideological work" from Mary Poovey because it suggests both "the work of ideology" and "the work of making ideology." See her *Uneven Developments: The Ideological Work of Gender in Mid-Victorian England* (Chicago: University of Chicago Press, 1988), 2–4. See Maria and Richard Edgeworth, *Practical Education*, 3 vols. (London: J. Johnson, 1801), 3:6.

2. On the subject of sensibility, see Janet Todd, *Sensibility: An Introduction* (New York: Methuen, 1986), and Stephen Cox, "Sensibility as Argument," in *Sensibility in Transformation: Creative Resistance to Sentiment from the Augustans to the Romantics*, ed. Syndy McMillen Conger (Rutherford, N.J.: Fairleigh Dickinson, 1990), 63–84. Cox's attention to the increasing dissatisfaction of the rhetorical formulations for sensibility in the late eighteenth century has informed my argument.

3. It is unclear whether or not manual labor of women did actually decline. See, for example, Judith Lowder Newton's argument that married women's work became less visible as work in the nineteenth century (*Women, Power, and Subversions: Social Strategies in British Fiction, 1778–1860* [Athens: University of Georgia Press, 1981], 17–19). On the subject of the rise of domestic servants in middle-class households, see Theresa M. McBride, *The Domestic Revolution* (New York: Holmes and Meier, 1976), esp. chap. 1.

4. *The Polite Lady, Or a Course in Female Education* (London: Newberry and Carnan, 1769), 19. Any discussion of the gendering of the sketch must first acknowledge an apparent confusion of terms: *sketching* and *drawing* were and often are used interchangeably. However, from the Royal Academy's perspective, drawing was the more exact and technical term, often assuming knowledge of perspective, of proportion, and of anatomy. Sketching was the feminized version of drawing because it presumed little technical knowledge.

5. Catharine Macaulay, *Letters of Education with Observations on Religious and Metaphysical Subjects* (New York: Garland Reprints, 1974), 62.

6. Erasmus Darwin, *Plan for the Conduct of Female Education* (Derby, U.K.: J. Drewney, 1797), 27; Maria Edgeworth, *Practical Education*, 3 vols. (London: J. Johnson & Co., 1801), 3:6.

7. Dr. Gregory likewise advised: "One of the chief beauties in the female character, is that modest reserve, that retiring delicacy, which avoids the public eye, and is disconcerted even at the gaze of admiration" (*A Father's Legacy to his Daughters* [London: W. Strahan and T. Cadell, 1775], 26).

8. Octavia Stopford, *Sketches in Verse, and Other Poems* (Hull, U.K.: Author, 1826), v.

9. Hannah More, *Strictures on the Modern System of Female Education*, 2 vols. (London: T. Cadell, 1799), 3:12.

10. Helen Maria Williams, *Letters Containing a Sketch of the Politics of France and of the Scenes Which Have Passed in the Prisons of Paris*, in *Letters from France*, vol. 2 [4 vols. in 1], ed. Janet M. Todd (Delmar, N.Y.: Scholars' Facsimiles and Reprints, 1975). All subsequent references are to this second volume and will be cited parenthetically in the text by (local) volume and page number. Mary Poovey, *The Proper Lady and the Woman Writer* (Chicago: University of Chicago Press, 1984), 56–57.

11. Shari Benstock, "From Letters to Literature: *La Carte Postale* in the Epistolary Genre," *Genre* 18.3 (1985): 257–96.

12. Helen Maria Williams, *Sketches of the State of Manners and Opinions in the French Republic Towards the Close of the Eighteenth Century in a Series of Letters* (London: G. and J. Robinson, 1801), 6.

13. The reviewer for *Gentleman's Magazine* first took issue with the fact that such a publication was written by a woman and then proceeded to claim that "the work is well denominated a sketch; and so hasty a sketch is it, that the materials are huddled together in the most confused and indistinct manner, so to perplex and confound, rather than to afford the information sought for" (65.2 [1795]: 672–73).

14. In "Helen Maria Williams and Radical Sensibility," *Prose Studies: History, Theory, Criticism* 12.1 (May 1989): 1–23, Chris Jones defines "radical sensibility" as a belief in the primacy of the passions, but these passions can be regulated by man's universal innate benevolence (3–4). Although Jones traces the role of radical sensibility throughout Williams's work, he does not argue that for Williams female sensibility becomes an antidote to the Terror.

15. Ibid., 12–13.

16. Janet Todd demonstrates how suspect "sensibility" was by the mid-1790s (*Sensibility*, 3–9).

17. For further background on Lady Morgan, see Dale Spender, *Mothers of the Novel* (London: Pandora, 1986), 305. For a useful analysis of how Morgan uses oriental allusions and metaphors in her novels, see Joseph W. Lew's "Sydney Owenson and the Fate of Empire," *Keats-Shelley Journal* 39 (1990): 39–65. Lew, however, overstates his case when he claims that romance allowed Morgan access to political issues. Even Morgan's two-volume biography, *The Life and Times of Salvator Rosa* (London: Henry Coburn, 1823), centers on politics: what makes Rosa worthy of biography is his "moral independence and political principle of the patriot" (vi). The Rosa biography also perhaps indicates how she would have liked her own sketches to be received. She argues that even Rosa's "most petulant sketches and careless designs" evinced his "powerful intellect and deep feeling, no less than his wild and gloomy imagination" (iv). Whereas the sketches of men

were signs of genius, those by women were nevertheless praiseworthy if they were correct.

18. Mary Campbell, *Lady Morgan: The Life and Times of Sydney Owenson* (London: Pandora, 1988), 52.

19. For a useful survey of Irish writers on colonialism, see Tom Dunne, "Haunted by History: Irish Romantic Writing 1800–50," in *Romanticism in National Context*, ed. Roy Porter and Mikulas Teich (Cambridge: Cambridge University Press, 1988), esp. 68–78.

20. Mary Russell Mitford, *Our Village: Sketches of Rural Character and Scenery*, 3rd ed., 5 vols. (London: George B. Whitaker, 1825), preface.

21. Jean Hagstrum, *The Sister Arts: The Tradition of Literary Pictorialism and English Poetry from Dryden to Gray* (Chicago: University of Chicago Press, 1958), 240–41. See also Wendy Steiner on Bishop Sprat and logical argument in *The Colors of Rhetoric* (Chicago: University of Chicago Press, 1982), 97–99. For Sprat, the seventeenth-century historian of the Royal Society, plain style and scientific discourse had to eschew rhetorical coloring and ornament.

Janet Little and Robert Burns (pp. 207–219)

1. James Paterson, *The Contemporaries of Burns and The More Recent Poets of Ayrshire* (Edinburgh: Adam Hugh Paton, 1840). Janet Little, *The Poetical Works of Janet Little: The Scotch Milkmaid* (Ayr: Printed by John & Peter Wilson, 1792). All parenthetical references will be to this edition. Please note that this edition is mispaginated. For information about Ayrshire and dairy farming at this time, see John Strawhorn, *Ayrshire in the Time of Burns*, (Ayr, Scotland: Archaeological Natural History Society, 1959); James Handley, *The Agricultural Revolution in Scotland* (London: Faber & Faber, 1953); William Fullerton, *General View of the Agriculture of the County of Ayr, with Observations on the Means of Its Improvement* (Edinburgh: Printed by John Patterson, 1793). For the countess of Loudoun, see *The Scots Peerage Founded on Wood's Edition of Sir Robert Douglas's Peerage of Scotland*, ed. Sir James Balfour Paul (Edinburgh: D. Douglas, 1904–14). For details of the Loudoun family, see also Strawhorn, 39–40 and passim; Frank Brady, *James Boswell: The Later Years 1769–1795* (New York: McGraw-Hill, 1984), 464.

2. Robert T. Fitzhugh, *Robert Burns: The Man and the Poet: A Round, Unvarnished Account* (Boston: Houghton Mifflin Company, 1970), 202. For public support for national leaders, see *Ancient Laws and Customs of the Burghs of Scotland*, Burgh Records Society, preface, xlix. For Burns's pro—working-class sentiments, see also Thomas Johnston, *The History of the Working Class in Scotland* (Yorkshire: EP Publishing, Rowman & Littlefield, 1974), 61. David Craig, *Scottish Literature and the Scottish People, 1630–1830* (London: Chatto and Windus, 1961), 90. For Burns's views on the French Revolution and reaction to them, see Johnston, 222.

3. Frances Dunlop comments on Janet Little to Burns on several occasions, with a view, it seems, to securing Burns's good opinion of Janet Little. See, for example, Dunlop to Burns, 23 September 1790, in *Robert Burns and Mrs. Dunlop: Correspondence Now Published for the First Time*, ed. William Wallace,

2 vols. (New York: Dodd, Mead and Company, 1898), 1:102–103. DeLancey Ferguson concludes that Mrs. Dunlop saw "no *essential* difference between [Robert Burns] and Janet Little" (*Pride and Passion* [1939; reprint, New York: Russell and Russell, 1964], 159).

   4. Paterson, *Contemporaries of Burns*, 80.

   5. Craig, *Scottish Literature*, 110. For a background to Janet Little's class and conditions of female laborers, see T. C. Smout, *A History of the Scottish People, 1560–1650* (London: Collins, 1969), 302–308.

   6. The vernacular writing of Allan Ramsay, a patron of the arts who introduced theater to Edinburgh and the only Scottish publisher of "Cadenus and Vanessa," did not preclude friendship with Englishmen. Both John Gay and Richard Steele subscribed to Ramsay's poems and visited him in Edinburgh.

   7. Burns to Dunlop, 6 September 1789, in J. DeLancey Ferguson, *The Letters of Robert Burns*, ed. G. Ross Roy, 2 vols. (Oxford: Clarendon Press, 1985), 1:438.

   8. Robert Fergusson was one among many Scottish detractors of Samuel Johnson for his mockery in the *Tour*. See his "To Dr. Samuel Johnson: Food for a New Edition of his Dictionary" in *The Works of Robert Fergusson* (Edinburgh: The Mercat Press, 1970), 203–206.

   9. Given the popularity and wide circulation of Johnson's *Lives of the Poets* and the controversy over John Bell's multiple volumes of *The Poets of Great Britain*, printed in Edinburgh, Janet Little had easy access to Johnson's *Lives*, if only through Mrs. Dunlop's collection. See Thomas F. Bonnell, "John Bell's *Poets of Great Britain*: The "Little Trifling Edition Revisited," *Modern Philology* 85.2 (November 1987): 128–52.

   10. Craig, *Scottish Liberature*, 57; 62–63.

   11. David Daiches, *Robert Burns* (New York: Macmillan, 1966), 104.

   12. Dunlop to Burns, 16 March 1793, *Correspondence*, 2:242.

   13. James E. Handley, *Scottish Farming in the Eighteenth Century* (London: Faber and Faber, 1953), 71; Paterson, *Contemporaries*, 88.

   14. Daiches, *Robert Burns*, 75. John Ramsay records that Burns referred to himself as a "Jacobite, an Arminian, and a Socinian" (*Scotland and Scotsmen in the Eighteenth Century* [Edinburgh and London: William Blackwood and Sons, 1888], 554). See also John C. Weston, "Robert Burns's Satire," in *The Art of Robert Burns*, ed R. D. S. Jack and Andrew Noble (New York: Vision & Barnes and Noble, 1982), 53.

   15. Craig, *Scottish Literature*, 125. In a letter to Mrs. Dunlop, Burns spoke about his "sentiments respecting the present two great Parties that divide our Scots Ecclesiastics.—I do not care three farthings for Commentators and authorities" (J. DeLancey Ferguson, *The Letters of Robert Burns*, 2nd ed. 2vols. [Oxford: Clarendon Press, 1985], 1:422). Note also that Janet Little was a Burgher. For information, see J. H. S. Burleigh, *A Church History of Scotland* (London: Oxford University Press, 1960), 323.

   16. Fitzhugh, *Robert Burns*, 68. Previously the Kirk Session had denounced Gavin Hamilton, Burns's friend and landlord, for "breaking the Sabbath" and for "contumacy." Little mentions Hamilton somewhat ambiguously in her poem about the Scottish literary tradition, "Given to a Lady." In "Holy Willie's Prayer," Burns ridiculed this censure, which Gavin Hamilton subsequently and successfully appealed. This title appears only in the Alloway manuscript. The other

title is "A Poet's Welcome to his love-begotten Daughter" (Glenriddle MS); "Address to an Illegitimate Child" (Stewart, 1801). For Burns's response in verse to religious controversies in Mauchline parish, see Thomas Crawford, *Burns: A Study of the Poems and Songs* (Stanford, Calif.: Stanford University Press, 1960), 67–69. Note also that negative narratives to Burns's public behavior are manufactured after his political opinions became controversial. See Donald Low, ed., *Robert Burns: The Critical Heritage* (London: Routledge & Kegan Paul, 1974).

17. I am indebted here and elsewhere to David Morris's study of Burns's poems from a Bakhtinian point of view. See Morris, "Burns and Heteroglossia," *The Eighteenth Century: Theory and Interpretation* (winter 1987): 3–27.

18. See Morris, "Burns and Heteroglossia"; Alexander Warrack, *Scots Dictionary Serving as a Glossary for Ramsay, Fergusson, Burns, Galt, Minor Poets, Kailyard Novelists, and a Host of Other Writers of the Scottish Tongue* (1911; reprint, University, Ala.: University of Alabama Press, 1965), 427; and William Graham, *The Scots Word Book* (Edinburgh: The Ramsay Head Press, 1977), 165. Burns's relationship to women has frequently been distorted because of inaccuracies in an earlier biography by James Currie. For a reevaluation, see Fitzhugh, *Robert Burns*, esp. 91–111, and 75. See also Hilton Brown, *There Was a Lad* (London: Hamish Hamilton, 1949), esp. 103–65.

19. John Strawhorn, *Ayrshire*, 142.

20. *Correspondence*, 1:xiv—xv.

21. Dunlop to Burns, 18 August 1790, *Correspondence* 2:96.

22. In critiquing her poems, Robert Burns may well have been trying to help her. He operated similarly toward male poet-friends, virtually rewriting John Lapraik's poems. It is also possible that Robert Burns's relationship to Janet Little was part of his complex relationship with Mrs. Dunlop. Janet Little may have been caught unwittingly in the middle.

23. Dunlop to Burns, 30 March 1791, *Correspondence*, 2:137.

24. See Bridget Hill, *Women, Work, and Sexual Politics in Eighteenth-Century England* (Oxford: Basil Blackwell, 1989).

25. Ibid., 146; Fitzhugh, *Robert Burns*, 70.

26. Donna Landry, *The Muses of Resistance: Laboring-Class Women's Poetry in Britain, 1739–1796* (Cambridge: Cambridge University Press, 1990), 220–37.

27. See Little's "Janet" and "To the Public." If she were Janet Nichol, she would have no such dilemma. In her poem to Janet Nichol, rather ambiguously entitled "A Poem on Contentment. Inscribed to Janet Nichol, a Poor Old Wandering Woman, Who Lives by the Wall at Loudoun and Used Sometimes to Be Visited by the Countess" (173), Little addresses her namesake Janet Nichol and imbricates her dilemma as a woman and a poet. Little informs Nichol how lucky she is to avoid snares set for females. In particular, she congratulates her for never feeling the pain "we heedless scribbling fools sustain."

28. In 1737, Janet Little's parish kirk in Galston, south of the River Irvine, became part of a Scottish-style secession from the Church of Scotland, led by the Reverend Ebenezer Erskine. For historical and geographical details about Galston and Erskine, see Robert Chambers, *A Biographical Dictionary of Eminent Scotsmen*, new ed., ed. Thomas Thomson (1855; reprint, New York: George Olms Verlag, 1971).

29. Unlike Ann Yearsley, however, she appears to cultivate her patrons, and this in turn enables her to challenge critics less acrimoniously.

"Out of the Pale of Social Kindred Cast" (pp. 223–235)

I would like to thank the editors of this volume, Paula Feldman and Theresa Kelley, for their interest in my work and for their helpful commentary during the process of composition.

1. Virgina Woolf, *A Room of One's Own* (1929; reprint, New York and London: Harcourt Brace Jovanovich, 1989), 45.

2. For reevaluations of Baillie's work, see Stuart Curran, "Romantic Poetry: The 'I' Altered," in *Romanticism and Feminism*, ed. Anne K. Mellor (Bloomington: Indiana University Press, 1988), 185–207, and Marlon B. Ross, *The Contours of Masculine Desire: Romanticism and the Rise of Women's Poetry* (New York and Oxford: Oxford University Press, 1989). For Baillie's influence on Mary Brunton's novel *Self Control* (1810), see Mary McKerrow, "Joanna Baillie and Mary Brunton: Women of the Manse," in *Living by the Pen: Early British Women Writers*, ed. Dale Spender (New York: Teachers College Press, 1992): 160–74, and Daniel P. Watkins's materialist analysis of *De Monfort* in "Class, Gender, and Social Motion in Joanna Baillie's *De Monfort*," *The Wordsworth Circle* 23.2 (1992): 109–117. Other reassessments of Baillie may be found in P. M. Zall, "The Cool World of Samuel Taylor Coleridge: The Question of Joanna Baillie, *Wordsworth Circle* 23.1 (1982): 17–20; Barbara Schnorrenberg, "Joanna Baillie," *A Dictionary of British and American Women Writers, 1660–1800*, ed. Janet Todd (London: Methuen, 1987), 35–36; Priscilla Dorr, "Joanna Baillie," in *An Encyclopedia of British Women Writers*, ed. Paul Schlueter and June Schlueter (New York: Garland Press, 1988) 15–16; Catherine B. Burroughs, "Joanna Baillie," *Encyclopedia of Romanticism: Culture in Britain from the 1780s to 1830s*, ed. Laura Dabundo (New York: Garland Press, 1992): 21–23. See also my "English Romantic Women Writers and Theatre Theory: Joanna Baillie's Prefaces to the *Plays on the Passions*," in *Re-Visioning Romanticism: British Women Writers, 1776–1837*, ed. Carol Shiner Wilson and Joel Haefner (Philadelphia: University of Pennsylvania Press, forthcoming). For Baillie's centrality to the Gothic tradition, see the introduction to *Seven Gothic Dramas, 1789–1825*, ed. Jeffrey Cox (Athens: Ohio University Press, 1992).

For earlier criticism of Baillie's work, see Joseph Donohue, *Dramatic Character in the English Romantic Age* (Princeton, N.J.: Princeton University Press, 1970) and *Theatre in the Age of Kean* (Totowa, N.J.: Rowman and Littlefield, 1975); A. G. Lasch, "Joanna Baillie's *De Monfort* in Relation to Her Theory of Tragedy," *Durham University Journal* 23 (1961): 114–20; Bertrand Evans, *Gothic Drama from Walpole to Shelley* (Berkeley: University of California Press, 1947); M. Norton, "The Plays of Joanna Baillie," *Review of English Studies* 23 (1947): 131–43; and Margaret Carhart, *The Life and Work of Joanna Baillie*, vol. 64 of *Yale Studies in English*, ed. Albert S. Cook (New Haven, Conn.: Yale University Press, 1923).

3. Carhart (*Life and Work*, 109) lists seven of Baillie's plays as having been professionally staged, but, as Noble notes, she provides no account of the production(s) of *Basil*. Noble has compiled a helpful record of the productions of Baillie's plays that occurred between 1800 and 1836 in England, Scotland, Ireland, and the United States. She lists productions of six, rather than seven, plays (Aloma Noble, "Joanna Baillie as a Dramatic Artist," [Ph.D. diss., University of Iowa, 1983]: 188–93).

4. Mary McKerrow, "Joanna Baillie and Mary Brunton," has called attention to the following passage in Walter Scott's introduction to the third canto of *Marmion* (1808), in which the footnote identifies "the bold Enchantress" as Joanna Baillie and refers to two of the three plays in her first volume of *Plays on the Passions* (1798):

> Restore the ancient tragic line,
> And emulate the notes that rung
> From the wild harp which silent hung
> By silver Avon's holy shore
> Till twice an hundred years rolled o'er;
> When she, *the bold Enchantress*, came
> With fearless hand and heart on flame,
> From the pale willow snatched the treasure,
> And swept it with a kindred measure,
> Till Avon's swans, while rung the grove
> With Monfort's hate and Basil's love,
> Awakening at the inspired strain,
> Deemed *their own Shakespeare* lived again.
> (pp. 90–91, my emphases)

In her introduction to *De Monfort* in the *British Theatre* series, Elizabeth Inchbald sought to distinguish between Baillie and Shakespeare, even though she called Baillie a "genius" in the same preface (*Remarks for the British Theatre (1806–09)* [Delmar, N.Y.: Scholars Facsimiles and Reprints, 1990]).

5. Mary Berry, *Extracts of the Journals and Correspondence of Miss Berry*, ed. Lady Theresa Lewis, 3 vols. (London: Longman, Greens, and Company, 1865), 2:88.

6. Inchbald, *Remarks for the British Theatre*, n.p.

7. For a fuller discussion of the Romantic debate about acting style, see the following: Lily Campbell, "The Rise of a Theory of Stage Presentation in England during the Eighteenth Century," *PMLA* 32.2 (1917): 163–200; Alan S. Downer, "Nature to Advantage Dressed: Eighteenth-Century Acting," *PMLA* 58.4 (1943): 1002–37, and "Players and Painted Stage: Nineteenth-Century Acting," *PMLA* 61.2 (1946): 522–76; William Angus, "Actors and Audiences in Eighteenth-Century London," *Studies in Speech and Drama in Honor of Alexander M. Drummond* (Ithaca, N.Y.: Cornell University Press, 1944): 123–38; Earl Wasserman, "The Sympathetic Imagination in Eighteenth-Century Acting," *Journal of English and German Philology* 46 (1947): 264–72; Carol J. Carlisle's "Edmund Kean on the Art of Acting," *Theatre Notebook* 12.3 (1968): 119–20; Gloria Flaherty, "Empathy and Distance: Romantic Theories of Acting Reconsidered," *Theatre Research International* 15.2 (1990): 125–41; Bryan Forbes, *That Despicable Race: A History of the British Acting Tradition* (London: Elm Tree Books, 1980); Joseph R. Roach, *The Player's Passion: Studies in the Science of Acting* (London and Toronto: Associated University Presses, 1985); Monica Murray, "English Theater Costume and the Zeitgeist of the Eighteenth Century," *Studies in Voltaire and the Eighteenth Century* 265 (1989): 1340–43.

8. See Cox, *Seven Gothic Dramas*, for an excellent discussion of how Baillie sought to "draw upon the power of Siddons' performances in *De Monfort*" (53) in order to encourage audiences to "think about Siddons and her conventional roles" (55). His thesis, that "Baillie uses Gothic techniques to reflect upon the Gothic itself and its underlying ideology, particularly its construction of the

feminine" (57), can be extended to include her investigation of masculinity as socially constructed.

9. For discussions of Romanticism and gender see especially Anne K. Mellor, *Romanticism and Feminism*; "Why Women Didn't Like Romanticism: The Views of Jane Austen and Mary Shelley," in *The Romantics and Us*, ed. Gene Ruoff (New Brunswick, N.J.: Rutgers University Press, 1990): 274–87; and *Romanticism and Gender* (New York and London: Routledge, 1993).

10. Joanna Baillie, "Introductory Discourse" to the first volume of *Plays on the Passions* (1798), in *Dramatic and Poetical Works* (1851; reprint, Hildesheim and New York: Georg Olms Verlag, 1976), 15. All quotations throughout my text refer to this edition; in the case of the plays, I have included act, scene, and *page* numbers because no line numbers appear. Jeffrey Cox's edition of *De Monfort* has just become available to give readers a better sense of the play in performance (*Seven Gothic Dramas*, 83).

11. See my "English Romantic Women Writers and Theatre Theory."

12. For further discussions of closet drama, see especially Michael Evendon, "Inter-mediate Stages: The Body in 'Closet Drama,'" in *Reading the Social Body*, ed. Catherine B. Burroughs and Jeffrey David Ehrenreich (Iowa City: Univ. of Iowa Press, 1993) 244–69; Om Prakash Mathur's chapter, "The Theatre and the Closet," in *The Closet Drama of the Romantic Revival* (Salzburg: Salzburg University, 1978); Murray Biggs, ed., "Byron's *Sardanapulus*," *Studies in Romanticism* 31.3 (special issue, 1992); David Wagenknecht, ed., "*The Borderers*: A Forum," *Studies in Romanticism* 27.3 (special issue, 1988); Richard Allen Cave, "Romantic Drama in Performance: Goethe and Schiller," *Keats-Shelley Review* (1988): 108–20; and Terence A. Hoagwood and Daniel P. Watkins, ed., "Romantic Drama: Historical and Critical Essays," *The Wordsworth Circle* 23.2 (special issue, 1992).

13. Baillie to William Sotheby, 12 December 1804, "The Letters of Joanna Baillie (1801–1832)," ed. Chester Lee Lamberton (Ph.D. diss., Harvard University, 1956). In his unpublished dissertation, Lamberton compiled a complete edition of the letters by Baillie that have survived into the twentieth century.

14. Harry Berger, Jr., *Imaginary Audition: Shakespeare on Stage and Page* (Berkeley, Los Angeles, and Oxford: University of California Press, 1989), xii.

15. Class and gender conflicts in *De Monfort* are discussed from a materialist perspective in Daniel P. Watkins, "Class, Gender, and Social Motion in Joanna Baillie's *De Monfort*," *The Wordsworth Circle* 23.2 (1992): 109–17.

16. Judith Butler, "Performative Acts and Gender Constitution: An Essay in Phenomenology and Feminist Theory," *Theatre Journal* 40.4 (1988): 519–31.

17. Butler's essay (see n. 16) evokes the work of feminist theater theorists like Sue-Ellen Case, Jill Dolan, and Elin Diamond, who suggest that fundamental changes in theatrical staging can effect transformations in the way that women are treated in social arenas. See Sue-Ellen Case, *Feminism and Theatre* (New York: Methuen, 1988); neither Dolan nor Diamond are in the Works Cited list. Butler's postmodernist theory and the feminist materialist arguments of Case, Dolan, and Diamond constitute the most recent phase of feminist theater scholarship, which has, as Susan Steadman notes in her overview (*Dramatic Re-Visions: An Annotated Bibliography of Feminism and Theatre, 1972–1988* [Chicago and London: American Library Association, 1991], 29), paralleled the contributions of feminist literary critics between 1972 and 1988.

18. In a footnote attached to the 1851 edition of her collected works, Baillie

wrote: "Should this play [*De Monfort*] ever again be acted, perhaps it would be better that the curtain should drop here [5.4]; since here the story may be considered as completed, and what comes after, prolongs the piece too much when our interest for the fate is at an end" (101).

19. See Donohue (*Dramatic Character*) and Cox (*Seven Gothic Dramas*) for discussions of Baillie and the Gothic tradition.

20. Mary Poovey, *The Proper Lady* (Chicago: Univ. of Chicago Press, 1984); Anne Hollander, *Seeing Through Clothes* (New York: Viking Press, 1978), xvi.

21. Another paper is required to investigate the extent to which women in Romantic theater protested the culture's tendency to read character through costume (and, in the case of female actors, to confuse the adorned body of the performer with the behavior of the wearer, especially since women actors often wore their own clothes and jewelry on London stages). Baillie's dueling dress codes in *De Monfort* set the stage for such an inquiry. For a helpful article, which includes a discussion of Siddons's interest in drapery costume, see Lily Campbell, "A History of Costuming on the English Stage Between 1660–1823," *Collected Papers of Lily B. Campbell* (1918; reprint, New York: Russell and Russell, 1968), 103–39.

22. See Terry Eagleton, *The Ideology of the Aesthetic* (London: Basil Blackwell, 1990).

23. Julie Carlson, "A New Stage for Romantic Drama," *Studies in Romanticism* 27.3 (1988).

24. Mary Russell Mitford, *Recollections of a Literary Life: or, Books, Places, and People*, 3 vols. (London: Richard Bentley, 1852), I, 242.

The Gipsy Is a Jewess (pp. 236–251)

1. Philip Highfill, Kalman Burnim, and Edward Langhans, 16 vols., *A Biographical Dictionary of Actors, Actresses, Musicians, Dancers, Managers and Other Stage Personnel in London, 1660–1800* (Carbondale: Southern Illinois University Press, 1973), 2:168.

2. Lord Richard Mount-Edgucumbe, *Musical reminiscences of an old amateur chiefly respecting the Italian opera in England for fifty years, from 1773–1823* (London: W. Clarke, 1824), 107.

3. See William Thomas Parke, *Musical Memoirs* (London: H. Colburn and R. Bentley, 1838); Charles Burney, *An Account of the Musical Performances in Westminster Abbey and The Pantheon* (London: Payne & Son, 1785); Lord Richard Mount-Edgucumbe, *Musical reminiscences*; David Garrick, *Letters*, ed. David M. Little and George M. Kahrl, 3 vols. (Cambridge, Mass.: Harvard University Press, 1963); Garrick, *Private Correspondence of David Garrick with the Most Celebrated Persons of his Time*, ed. James Boaden (London: Colburn & Bentley, 1831–32); Thomas Dibdin, *Reminiscences* (London: Henry Colburn, 1834); J. DeCastro, *Memoirs of J. DeCastro*, ed. R. Humphreys (London: Sherwood, Jones & Co., 1824); and *The London Stage, 1660–1800*, vol. 4, ed. George W. Stone; vol. 5, ed. Charles B. Hogan. (Carbondale: Southern Illinois University Press, 1962 and 1968).

4. Germaine De Staël, *Corinne, or Italy*, trans. Avriel Goldberger (New Brunswick, N.J.: Rutgers University Press, 1987), 323.

5. Erasmus Darwin, *A Plan for the Conduct of Female Education in Boarding Schools* (Derby, U.K.: J. Drewry, 1797), 12. For a discussion of the relationship between amateur and professional musicians, see Howard Irving, "Music as a Pursuit for Men: Accompanied Keyboard Music as Domestic Recreation in England," *College Music Symposium* 30.2 (1990): 126–37.

6. Edward W. Brayley, *Historical and Descriptive Accounts of the Theatres of London* (London: J. Taylor, 1826), 61n.

7. Philip Astley was a maverick who managed to circumvent the licensing acts that governed London's theaters. J. DeCastro, the son of the rabbi of London's Portuguese Jewish synagogue, worked with Astley for thirty-eight years and was undoubtedly responsible for introducing so many Jewish performers to the impresario. For discussion of the position of Jews at Astley's and in the theatergoing public in general, see DeCastro, *Memoirs*; Dibdin, *Reminiscences*; Alfred Rubens, "Jews and the English Stage, 1667–1850," *The Jewish Historical Society of England, Transactions* 24 (1974): 151–70; and Lucien Wolf, "Astley's Jews," *Jewish Chronicle*, 26 May 1893.

8. See Ellen Donkin, "Mrs. Siddons Looks Back in Anger: Feminist Historiography for Eighteenth-Century British Theatre," in *Critical Theory and Performance*, ed. J. G. Reinelt and J. R. Roach (Ann Arbor: University of Michigan Press, 1992), 276–77.

9. The story Parke tells involves a friend who visits Braham and asks his five-year-old son to sing him a song. The child agrees but only if he is paid sixpence. The friend asks if he would sing one for less. "No," the child replies, "but I'll sing three for a shilling" (Parke, *Musical Memoirs*, 2:50).

10. In a lengthy passage, Pohl discusses in Harriett and her sisters and gives a full account of Harriett's debut performance on a Friday evening as the little Gipsy. (Karl F. Pohl, *Haydn in London* [Vienna: Carl Gerold's Son, 1867], 54). The choice of Friday evening, "freitag-abenden," invites speculation. Before describing these concerts, Pohl describes the controversy surrounding Sunday afternoon concerts. One newspaper enthuses over the nobility's enjoyment of them; another finds it disgraceful to have such entertainment on Sunday, presumably a time for religious observance. Would the scheduling of concerts on Friday evening, the Jewish Sabbath, have the effect of disassociating them from Jewish religious practices?

11. *The New Harvard Dictionary* (Cambridge, Mass.: Harvard University Press, 1986), 287. The entry also states that because they influenced Gilbert and Sullivan's work, the ballad operas are really the only British work of Abrams's period to survive. Edward Elgar, the entry concludes, was the first prominent English composer since Purcell. In his more detailed history, Percy Young writes of "various directions" in British music as outlined by Charles Burney and John Hawkins. While Hawkins "was adamant in regarding Handel as the end of musical excellence," Burney saw him as heralding a new beginning for English music (Percy Young, *A History of British Music* [London: Benn, 1967], 375). Young also writes of the popularity of "indigenous musical forms"—catches and glees—and of music as a mass cultural phenomenon, widely practiced by amateurs and professionals of the upper and middle classes.

12. The practice of writing out ornaments varied at this time. Sometimes composers indicated exactly what they wanted; sometimes they left ornamentation up to the performer. Parke suggests that singers frequently provided their own ornamentation. Writing from the accompanist's perspective of a concert he

gave with Mara, Parke points out: "The singer, has the advantage of studying the embellishments she intends to introduce while the instrumental performer who had nothing but what is written by the composer before him, must, if his talent will carry him so far, follow the singer spontaneously through all the mazes of a luxuriant fantasy" (*Musical Memoirs*, 1:291).

13. M. H. Abrams, "The Correspondent Breeze: A Romantic Metaphor," in *English Romantic Poets*, ed. M. H. Abrams (New York: Oxford University Press, 1960), 38.

14. After quarreling violently with Garrick about her benefit night, Abington, well aware of his popularity, demanded that he play opposite her. He finally complied but not before writing of her in exasperation: "The above is a true copy of the letter, examined word by word, of that worst of bad women Mrs. Abington, to ask my playing for her benefit, and why?" (Garrick, *Private Correspondence*, 2:140).

15. Originally, the word *picnic* described a fashionable social entertainment to which each person brought something. "Picnic" as a meal eaten out of doors is a later meaning.

16. Alfred Rubens, *Anglo-Jewish Portraits* (London: The Jewish Museum, 1935), 2.

17. For accounts of the tumultuous relationship that existed between George and his parents, see the following biographies: Dormer Creston, *The Regent and His Daughter* (London: Eyre and Spottiswoode, 1947), and Roger Fulford, *George the Fourth* (London: Duckworth, 1935). Beginning as a doting mother who had a full-length wax effigy made of her baby son, Queen Charlotte quarreled violently with George, partly to protect her husband, partly to protect her own power. George sought his mother as an ally against Caroline, the wife he despised, especially in the raising of Princess Charlotte. After about 1814 they were devoted to one another. The queen gave a lavish birthday party each year for her son and spent summers with him at Brighton. When Charlotte came to Carlton House, George would not let servants wait on her; he himself brought his mother tea and refreshments.

Mary Robinson and the Literary Marketplace
(pp. 252–268)

1. "The Printer's Cauldron," in *The Poetical Register, and Repository of Fugitive Poetry, for 1806–1807* (London: F. and C. Rivington, 1811), 291.

2. Marilyn Gaull, "Romantic Theater," *The Wordsworth Circle* 14 (1983): 255–63, esp. 257. For the relationship between newspapers and the theater, see Lucyle Werkmeister, *A Newspaper History of England, 1792–1793* (Lincoln: University of Nebraska Press, 1967), 42. Werkmeister's history is an invaluable guide to English newspapers in the 1790s.

3. David Erdman, R. S. Woof, and Kenneth Curry have compiled enormously helpful indices of the contributions of Coleridge, Wordsworth, and Southey to the *Post*. See David Erdman, Appendix D to *Essays on His Times*, by Samuel Taylor Coleridge, vol. 3 of *The Collected Works of Samuel Taylor Coleridge*, gen. ed. Kathleen Coburn (London: Routledge and Kegan Paul, 1978), 3.3: 285–99; R. S. Woof, "Wordsworth's Poetry and Stuart's Newspapers: 1793–1803," *Studies in*

Bibliography 15 (1962): 149–89; Kenneth Curry, *The Contributions of Robert Southey to the* Morning Post (University, Alabama: University of Alabama Press, 1984).

4. Jon P. Klancher, *The Making of English Reading Audiences, 1790–1832* (Madison: University of Wisconsin Press, 1987), 33.

5. That this is true as well in the United States of our day is suggested by a recent advertising campaign launched by the Philadelphia *Daily News*. The campaign uses television commercials to disrupt the conventional association of this tabloid with a working-class reader more interested in box scores than in international affairs.

6. William Wordsworth, "To John Thelwall," mid-January 1804, letter 200A of *The Letters of William and Dorothy Wordsworth*, ed. Ernest de Selincourt, *The Early Years, 1787–1805*, rev. by Chester L. Shaver (Oxford: Clarendon Press, 1967), 433. Referring to Jeffrey's notorious review of Southey's *Thalaba*, he wrote in January 1804: "As to the School about which so much noise (I am told) has been made, (I say I am told, because I neither read reviews, magazines nor any periodical whatsoever except the Morning [Post]), I do not know what is meant by it nor of whom it consists."

7. *Morning Post*, 16 April 1798, p. 2 (hereafter cited in text as *MP*).

8. *Monthly Magazine and British Register* 1 (1796): iii.

9. See, for example, this notice from the 21 June 1800 *Morning Post:* "TO CORRESPONDENTS—It has been repeatedly asked why we have published no further extracts from the Lyrical Ballads, from which we some time ago took the Beautiful Poem of The Mad Mother. We would continue those extracts, if it were not the rule of this Paper to give none but Original Poetry, and if the volume of Lyrical Ballads were not already in the hands of every one who has a taste for Poetry. It is to be had the corner of Lombard and Gracechurch-streets" (2).

The extensive reprinting of *Lyrical Ballads*, first in Stuart's newspaper and then in the *Lady's Magazine*, helped to make Wordsworth's reputation. See Woof, "Wordsworth's Poetry," and Robert Mayo, "The Contemporaneity of the *Lyrical Ballads*," *PMLA* 69 (1954): 486–522. Mayo claims, "It seems likely that Wordsworth's reputation in these first two years [1798–1800] owes far more to the semi-piratical printers of reviews and magazines than to his legitimate publishers" (520).

10. "Facts relative to the State of Reading Societies and Literary Institutions in the United Kingdon," *Monthly Magazine or, British Register* 55.1 (1821): 398. Werkmeister estimates that in 1792–93 every newspaper sold had thirty readers, some of whom rented it for a penny or even half a penny (*Newspaper History*, 31). An account of the circulation figures of the *Morning Post* is provided by Stuart in the paper's 3 December 1802 edition. He claims that between 1796 and 1802 the circulation increased from 400 to 3,500 per day. See Erdman, "Introduction," 3.1:lxx.

11. Werkmeister (*Newspaper History*) discovered the reprinting of Coleridge's "The APOTHEOSIS, of the Snow-Drop" in the 6–9 January 1798 edition of the *Express and Evening Chronicle*. The Morning Post for 3 January 1798, in which it first appeared, is not extant, but the *Post* for the day following contains this announcement: "Mrs. ROBINSON'S WALSINGHAM has never received a more gratifying tribute of praise than the *beautiful poem*, by FRANCINI, in our paper of yesterday: such commendation is honourable, a flowing from the pen of classical

elegance, and true poetic inspiration" (4 January 1798, p. 4). David V. Erdman, "Lost Poem Found," *Bulletin of the New York Public Library* 65 (1961): 249–68.

12. William Wordsworth, "Preface" to *Lyrical Ballads* (1800), in *The Prose Works of William Wordsworth*, eds. W. J. B. Owen and Jane Worthington Smyser, 3 vols. (Oxford: Clarendon Press, 1974), 1:128.

13. According to Stuart, "The booksellers and others crowded to the Morning Post when its circulation and character raised it above all its competitors. Each desirous of having his cloud of advertisements inserted at once on the front page" ("Anecdotes of Coleridge and of London Newspapers," *Gentleman's Magazine* n.s. 10 [1838]: 26). Werkmeister claims that it was not uncommon for advertisements to be copied or even invented because the number of advertisements was seen as a gauge of a newspaper's prosperity (*Newspaper History*, 19).

14. Quoted in Daniel Stuart, *Letters from the Lake Poets* (London: West, Newman and Co., 1889), 392.

15. S. T. Coleridge, "To Daniel Stuart," 4 June 1811, letter 828 of *Collected Letters of Samuel Taylor Coleridge*, ed. Earl Leslie Griggs, 6 vols. (Oxford: Clarendon Press, 1956), 3:332.

16. Isabella Lickbarrow, "The Fate of Newspapers," in *Poetical Effusions* (London: J. Richardson, 1814), 73.

17. Manuscript letter from Daniel Stuart to Samuel Taylor Coleridge, 20 January 1798, British Library Division of Western Manuscripts, Add. 35, 344. f.196.

18. Dorothy Wordsworth, "To Lady Beaumont," 7 Aug. 1805, letter 277 of *The Letters of William and Dorothy Wordsworth*, 615.

19. Of Tarleton, the *Post* noted: "It is strange that, in these *warlike times*, General Tarleton should be consigned to a *mountain obscurity*: popularity is a mere vapour—which dazzles, but evaporates" (13 August 1800, p. 2). On the same day and page, the *Post* stated: "Mr. GODWIN is so popular in Ireland, that he is courted and caressed in all the most distinguished societies, both of *genius* and of *political* importance."

20. *Telegraph*, 11 February 1797, p. 2. For a discussion of this practice, see Werkmeister, *Newspaper History*, 20.

21. Marjorie Levinson, *Keats's Life of Allegory* (Oxford: Basil Blackwell, 1988), 15.

22. Michel Foucault, "What Is an Author?" in *Language, Counter-Memory, Practice*, ed. Donald F. Bouchard (Oxford: Basil Blackwell, 1977), 136.

23. William Wordsworth, "To Daniel Stuart," 17 May 1838, letter 1247 of *The Letters of William and Dorothy Wordsworth*, ed. Ernest de Selincourt, *The Later Years 1835–1839*, rev. Alan G. Hill (Oxford: Clarendon Press, 1982), 590.

24. Ibid.

25. Jean-Christophe Agnew, *Worlds Apart: The Market and the Theater in Anglo-American Thought, 1550–1750* (New York: Cambridge University Press, 1986), 40.

26. The phrase was coined by Jonas Barish, whose study is essential reading for students of the theater (*The Antitheatrical Prejudice* [Berkeley: University of California Press, 1981]).

27. *Poems* (London: J. Bell, 1791), iii. In writing this defense, Robinson provides a rebuttal to the rebuke she would get from one sector of the reviewing

press. The *Gentleman's Magazine* wrote of Robinson's *Poems*: "[W]ithout at all detracting from the merits of her publication, we are inclined to apprehend that, had she been less distinguished by her personal graces and accomplishments, by the impression which her beauty and captivating manners have generally made, her poetical taste might have been confined in its influence, and might have excited the complacent approbation of her friends, with little attention, and with less reward, from the public" (*Gentleman's Magazine* 61 [1791]: 560).

28. *The Poetical Works of Mary Robinson* (Providence, R.I.: Brown/NEH Women Writers Project, 1990), 321. This text is based primarily on the edition published in 1824 by Jones & Co., London, titled *The Poetical Works of the Late Mary Robinson*. All subsequent references to the Women Writers Project edition will be cited as *PW*. Robinson's "Birth-day Poem" was published more than one time in the *Morning Post*, the first time under the title "St. Jame's Street, on the Eighteenth of January, 1795" (*MP* 21 January 1795, p. 3). This earlier version was attributed to "Portia." Possibly alluding to Shakespeare's clever heroine, Robinson published only a handful of poems under this name. The poem was republished in the *Morning Post* as the work of "T. B." on 19 January 1798.

29. "Female Fashions for 1799," *PW*, 516–17. The poem first appeared as "Modern Female Fashions" (*MP* 28 December 1799, p. 2).

30. For evidence of Robinson's familiarity with "Kubla Khan," as well as for an overview of her relationship with Coleridge, see Martin J. Levy, "Coleridge, Mary Robinson, and 'Kubla Kahn,'" *Charles Lamb Bulletin*, n.s. 77 (January 1992): 156–66.

31. William Wordsworth, "To Daniel Stuart," 590.

32. These poems were all reprinted in Robinson's *Lyrical Tales*, the last volume of poems she published before her death, giving the lie to a dismissive assessment of the poems penned by the unidentified "friend" (possibly her daughter) who completed the *Memoirs*. The writer refers to the poems as "lighter compositions, considered by the author as unworthy of a place with her collected poems" (*Memoirs of the Late Mrs. Robinson, Written by Herself*, 4 vols. [London: R. Phillips, 1801], 2:148–49).

33. Robinson to S. J. Pratt, 31 August 1800, in *Shelley and His Circle*, ed. Kenneth Neill Cameron, 2 vols. (Cambridge, Mass.: Harvard University Press, 1961), 1:232.

34. Coleridge to William Blackwood, 2 April 1819, *Collected Letters*, 4:931.

35. She writes to William Godwin on 30 May of being in custody for £63. This letter is quoted at length in Robert D. Bass's *The Green Dragoon* (New York: Henry Holt, 1957). Vital material evidence of Robinson's meager book publication earnings is provided by Jan Fergus and Janice Farrar Thaddeus in their exploration of the Hookham and Longman archives, "Women Publishers, and Money, 1790–1820," in *Studies in Eighteenth-Century Culture*, vol. 17 (East Lansing, Mich.: Colleagues Press, 1987), 191–207.

36. Review of *Poems*, by Mrs. Robinson, *Critical Review* (April 1794): 382.

37. John Ingamells, *Mrs. Robinson and Her Portraits* (London: Wallace Collection Monograph, 1978), 30.

38. Mary Jacobus, "Southey's Debt to *Lyrical Ballads* (1798)," *Review of English Studies*, n.s. 22 (1971): 24.

39. Kathryn Shevelov, *Women and Print Culture* (London: Routledge, 1989), 18.

Index